LORD BROGHILL
AND THE CROMWELLIAN UNION
WITH IRELAND AND SCOTLAND

Broghill's years of political influence included a distinctive initiative in Ireland in the early 1650s calling for limits on army power and religious radicalism, and urging closer ties with England; domestic reforms and keen promotion of the Cromwellian regime in Scotland, of which he was president during 1655–6; and in 1656–7 the introduction of the Humble Petition and Advice, which sought to re-establish a civilian state with Oliver Cromwell as king. Cromwell's refusal of the crown marked the beginning of the end of Broghill's political aspirations, and here these years of influence are seen in the context of the rest of his life, especially his early years as understudy of his father, the 1st earl of Cork, and his later life, as earl of Orrery. A thematic section deals with Broghill's private motives: the importance of his extended family, his financial situation, and, above all, his deep religious beliefs.

Patrick Little is Senior Research Fellow, History of Parliament Trust.

Irish Historical Monographs

ISSN 1740–1097

Series editors:
Marie Therese Flanagan, Queen's University, Belfast
Eunan O'Halpin, Trinity College, Dublin
David Hayton, Queen's University, Belfast

Roger Boyle, first earl of Orerry, by unknown artist
(by courtesy of the National Portrait Gallery, London)

LORD BROGHILL
AND THE CROMWELLIAN
UNION WITH IRELAND
AND SCOTLAND

Patrick Little

THE BOYDELL PRESS

First published 2004
The Boydell Press, Woodbridge

ISBN 1 84383 099 X

The Boydell Press is an imprint of Boydell & Brewer Ltd
PO Box 9, Woodbridge, Suffolk IP12 3DF, UK
and of Boydell & Brewer Inc.
668 Mount Hope Avenue, Rochester, NY 14620, USA
website: www.boydellandbrewer.com

A CIP catalogue record for this book is available
from the British Library

Library of Congress Cataloging-in-Publication Data
Little, Patrick, 1969–
Lord Broghill and the Cromwellian union with Ireland and Scotland / Patrick Little.
p. cm. – (Irish historical monographs series)
Includes bibliographical references and index.
ISBN 1-84383-099-X (hardback : alk. paper)
1. Orrery, Roger Boyle, Earl of, 1621–1679. 2. Cromwell, Oliver,
1599–1658–Relations with Irish. 3. Ireland–Politics and government–17th century.
4. Ireland–History–1649–1660–Biography. 5. Politicians–Ireland–Biography.
6. Scotland–History–1649–1660. I. Title. II. Series.
DA940.5.O8L58 2004
941.506′092–dc22
2004012756

This publication is printed on acid-free paper
Typeset by Keystroke, Jacaranda Lodge, Wolverhampton
Printed in Great Britain by
Cromwell Press, Trowbridge, Wiltshire

Contents

Acknowledgements   ix
Abbreviations   xi
Family trees   xv

Introduction   1

PART I: A POLITICAL APPRENTICESHIP, 1621–49

1 Cork and Broghill, 1621–43   11
2 The rise of the Irish Independents, 1644–9   33

PART II: THE RISE AND FALL OF THE CROMWELLIAN UNION

3 Ireland and England, 1649–55   59
4 Scotland and 'Britain', 1655–6   91
5 The Union Parliament and the kingship debates, 1656–7   124
6 From King Oliver to King Charles, 1657–79   161

PART III: BROGHILL IN CONTEXT

7 Family   193
8 Finance   209
9 Faith   221

Conclusion   236

Bibliography   243
Index   259

For Susanne, Peter and Michael,
and in memory of Elizabeth

Acknowledgements

Many thanks are due to the staff of the History of Parliament Trust, where I have worked in the 1640–60 section since 1994. I am especially grateful to the successive editors of the section, Dr John Adamson and Dr Stephen Roberts, and to my colleagues, Dr Andrew Barclay, Dr Jason Peacey and Dr David Scott, for friendly and informative discussion of various matters arising from this book. Other historians have also given me enormous help during this project, in many different ways: Dr Toby Barnard, Dr David Smith, Professor Allan Macinnes, Professor Jane Ohlmeyer, Dr Robert Armstrong, Dr David Farr, Dr Raymond Gillespie, Dr Carol Egloff, Dr Paul Hunneyball, Dr Lloyd Bowen, Dr David Edwards, Dr Beverly Adams, Dr Sean Kelsey and Dr Chris Kyle. Last, but certainly not least, I would like to express my gratitude to the supervisors of the Birkbeck thesis which led to this book, Professor Barry Coward and Professor Michael Hunter; to its examiners, Professor John Morrill and Dr Nicholas Tyacke; and to one of the commissioning editors of this series, Professor David Hayton. Professor Hayton, and the 'anonymous' reader of the first draft of the book have saved me from many errors, and infinitely improved the end result. My thanks also to Peter Sowden and the staff at Boydell and Brewer for making the publication process a happy experience.

For assistance in my research, I would like to thank the staff of the British Library, the Public Record Office, the Bodleian Library, Cambridge University Library, the Institute of Historical Research, the National Libraries of Ireland and Scotland, the Public Record Office of Northern Ireland, the National Archives of Ireland and Scotland, the City Archives of Edinburgh and Coventry, and the county record offices at Dorchester, Chichester, Huntingdon and Woking. I am indebted to the duke of Devonshire and the trustees of the Chatsworth settlement for allowing me to consult the Lismore papers in their collection, and to Lord Egremont for giving me access to the manuscripts at Petworth. The portrait of Lord Broghill is included by courtesy of the National Portrait Gallery, London.

I have benefited greatly from the support and encouragement of my friends and family in England, Ireland and Germany, and my parents, in particular, have been (as ever) an inspiration. My greatest debt is acknowledged in the dedication.

Abbreviations

A & O	C. H. Firth and R. S. Rait (eds), *Acts and ordinances of the interregnum, 1642–1660* (3 vols, 1911)
Abbott, *Writings and speeches*	W. C. Abbott (ed.), *The writings and speeches of Oliver Cromwell* (4 vols, Cambridge Mass., 1937–47)
Add.	Additional MS (B.L.)
Baillie letters	David Laing (ed.), *The letters and journals of Robert Baillie* (3 vols, Edinburgh, 1841–2)
Barnard, 'Cork'	Toby Barnard, 'Land and the limits of loyalty: the second earl of Cork and first earl of Burlington (1612–98)' in Tony Barnard and Jane Clark (eds), *Lord Burlington: architecture, art and life* (1996), pp 167–99
Barnard, 'Protestant interest'	Toby Barnard, 'The Protestant interest, 1641–1660' in Jane Ohlmeyer (ed.), *Ireland from independence to occupation, 1641–1660* (Cambridge, 1995), pp 218–40
B.L.	British Library, London
Bodl.	Bodleian Library, Oxford
Boyle's correspondence	Michael Hunter, Antonio Clericuzio and Lawrence Principe (eds), *The correspondence of Robert Boyle* (6 vols, 2001)
Boyle's works	Thomas Birch (ed.), *Works of the Honourable Robert Boyle* (new ed., 6 vols, 1772)
Burton diary	*The diary of Thomas Burton, Esq.*, ed. J. T. Rutt (4 vols, 1828)
Cal. Clar. S.P.	Octavius Ogle, W. H. Bliss, W. D. Macray and F. J. Routledge (eds), *Calendar of the Clarendon state papers preserved in the Bodleian Library* (5 vols, Oxford, 1869–1932)

Cal. Com. Comp.	M. A. E. Green (ed.), *Calendar of the proceedings of the committee for compounding, 1643–60* (5 vols, 1889–92)
Cal. S.P. Dom.	*Calendar of State Papers, domestic*
Cal. S.P. Ire.	*Calendar of State Papers, Ireland*
Cal. S.P. Ven.	*Calendar of State Papers, Venetian*
Canny, *Upstart earl*	Nicholas Canny, *The upstart earl: a study of the social and mental world of Richard Boyle, first earl of Cork, 1566–1643* (Cambridge, 1982)
C.J.	*Journals of the House of Commons* (1803–13).
Complete Peerage	G. E. Cokayne, *The Complete Peerage* (new ed., 12 vols, 1910–59)
C.U.L.	Cambridge University Library
D.N.B.	*Dictionary of National Biography*
Dunlop, *Ireland*	Robert Dunlop (ed.), *Ireland under the commonwealth* (2 vols, Manchester, 1913)
Eg.	Egerton MS (B.L.)
E.H.R.	*English Historical Review*
Grosart, *Lismore papers*	A. B. Grosart (ed.), *The Lismore papers* (1st and 2nd series, 10 vols, 1886–8)
H.J.	*Historical Journal*
H.M.C.	*Historical Manuscripts Commission*
I.H.S.	*Irish Historical Studies*
J.C.H.A.S.	*Journal of the Cork Historical and Archaeological Society*
Ludlow memoirs	*The memoirs of Edmund Ludlow*, ed. C. H. Firth (2 vols, Oxford, 1894)
Lynch, *Orrery*	Kathleen Lynch, *Roger Boyle, 1st earl of Orrery* (University of Tennessee, Knoxville, 1965)
Morrice, *Memoirs*	Thomas Morrice, *Memoirs of the . . . the life and death of the right honourable Roger, earl of Orrery* (first part of *A collection of the state letters of the Rt. Hon. Roger Boyle, the first earl of Orrery* (1742))
N.A.I.	National Archives of Ireland (formerly Public Record Office of Ireland), Dublin
N.A.S.	National Archives of Scotland (formerly Scottish Record Office), Edinburgh

N.L.I.	National Library of Ireland, Dublin
N.L.S.	National Library of Scotland, Edinburgh
P.R.O.	Public Record Office, London
P.R.O.N.I.	Public Record Office of Northern Ireland
S.C.L.	Sheffield Central Library
S.H.R.	*Scottish Historical Review*
Stephen, *Register*	William Stephen (ed.), *Register of consultations and minutes of the ministers of Edinburgh* . . . (2 vols, Edinburgh, 1921 and 1930)
S.U.L.	Sheffield University Library
Thurloe S.P.	*A collection of the state papers of John Thurloe, Esq.*, ed. Thomas Birch (7 vols, 1742)
Wariston diary	*Diary of Sir Archibald Johnston of Wariston, vol. iii, 1655–60*, ed. J. D. Ogilvie (Edinburgh, 1940)
W.C.O.	Worcester College, Oxford
Whitelocke diary	*The diary of Bulstrode Whitelocke, 1605–75*, ed. Ruth Spalding (Oxford, 1990)

Note

The place of publication of all works cited is London, unless otherwise stated. All quotations have been kept in their original form, but 'thorns' have been rendered as 'th', to aid clarity. Similarly, all dates are in Old Style (unless stipulated), but with the year beginning on 1 January, rather than 25 March.

Family trees

Boyle Family Tree

Richard Boyle
first earl of Cork
m.
Catherine Fenton

- Richard, Visc. Dungarvan (second earl of Cork 1643)
  m. (1634) Elizabeth, da. & h. of Henry Ld. Clifford

- Lewis, Visc. Kinalmeaky
  m. (1639) Elizabeth Feilding, da. of earl of Denbigh

- Roger, Lord Broghill
  m. (1641) Margaret Howard, da. of second earl of Suffolk

- Francis
  m. (1639) Elizabeth Killigrew

- Robert
  d. unm.

- Sarah
  m. (1) (1621) Sir Thomas Moore of Mellifont
       (2) (1626) Robert Lord Digby of Geashill

- Alice
  m. (1621) David, earl of Barrymore

- Lettice
  m. (1629) George Goring, s. & h. of Lord Goring

- Joan
  m. (1630) George Fitzgerald, sixteenth earl of Kildare

- Katherine
  m. (1630) Arthur Jones, s. & h. of Visc. Ranelagh

- Dorothy
  m. (1632) Arthur, s. & h. of Sir Adam Loftus of
  Rathfarnham

- Mary
  m. (1641) Charles Rich, third s. of earl of Warwick

Howard Family Tree

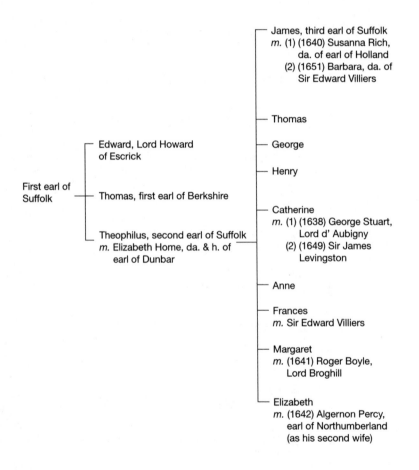

First earl of Suffolk

— Edward, Lord Howard of Escrick

— Thomas, first earl of Berkshire

— Theophilus, second earl of Suffolk
  m. Elizabeth Home, da. & h. of earl of Dunbar

— James, third earl of Suffolk
  m. (1) (1640) Susanna Rich, da. of earl of Holland
    (2) (1651) Barbara, da. of Sir Edward Villiers

— Thomas

— George

— Henry

— Catherine
  m. (1) (1638) George Stuart, Lord d' Aubigny
    (2) (1649) Sir James Levingston

— Anne

— Frances
  m. Sir Edward Villiers

— Margaret
  m. (1641) Roger Boyle, Lord Broghill

— Elizabeth
  m. (1642) Algernon Percy, earl of Northumberland (as his second wife)

Introduction

Roger Boyle, Lord Broghill (1621–79), was a man of great political influence in all three British nations. The third surviving son of the wealthiest New English planter, the first earl of Cork, he was born and raised in Ireland, and spent the first decade of his adult life fighting for the Protestant community in Munster against the Catholic insurgents during the Irish rebellion. In 1649 he joined Oliver Cromwell, encouraging the Munster towns to defect to parliament, and acting as the commander of the local forces against the remaining pockets of Catholic resistance. In the 1650s he became an influential figure in the Irish administration, and supported the moderate reforms introduced by the protector's son, Henry Cromwell. In 1655–6 he was in Scotland, as president of the protector's council there, and was instrumental in re-establishing civilian rule in the country. In the 1656 Westminster parliament, Broghill became the driving force behind the Humble Petition and Advice, which sought to bring permanent 'settlement' to all three nations, and offered the crown to Oliver Cromwell. With the fall of the protectorate in 1659, Broghill retired to Ireland, where he helped to establish the General Convention in Dublin in 1660, and his co-operation ensured the smooth transition from interregnum to restoration later in the same year. As a result, he retained his lands and influence in Ireland, was appointed president of Munster, and, in September 1660, was created earl of Orrery. He governed Munster until the presidency was abolished in 1672, and continued as an influential critic of the crown until his death in 1679. The bare outline of Broghill's career is not in dispute, but there are many facets which have not been explored, and many myths which need to be re-examined. Above all, Broghill's part in the upheavals of the period between 1649 and 1660, when he appears to have changed sides at least twice, became important as a proponent of union between the three nations, and acted as the would-be 'kingmaker' in the offer of the crown to Oliver Cromwell, demands revaluation. This difficult period will be the central focus of this book.

Broghill has always been the victim of misrepresentation. Contemporaries saw him in black-and-white terms. As a young and successful statesman in the 1650s, he was praised by his friend, Bulstrode Whitelocke, as 'a gentleman of great witt[,] learning & civillity', while his enemy, Edmund Ludlow, thought of him as proud, ambitious and quick to take offence.[1] In the years after his

---

[1] *Whitelocke diary*, p. 250; *Ludlow memoirs*, i, 263–4.

elevation as earl of Orrery in 1660, he made influential enemies: he was attacked by the earl of Arlington as 'a deceitful and vain man'; by the duke of Ormond, who thought his 'vanity, ostentation and itch to popularity' intolerable; and by Bishop Burnet as one who 'pretended to knowledge, but was very ignorant; to wit, but it was very luscious; to eloquence, but had the worst style in the world; to religion, but was thought a very fickle and false man, and was vain to the pitch of the earl of Shaftesbury'.[2] It was partly to counter this broadside, that Orrery's chaplain, Thomas Morrice, wrote his *Memoirs of the most remarkable passages in the life and death of the right honourable Roger, Earl of Orrery*, which was eventually printed in the 1742 edition of Orrery's state papers. In order to vindicate Broghill/Orrery, Morrice set about rewriting the history of the 1640s and 1650s, changing crucial details and even making up incidents which proved his master's secret loyalty to the crown.

According to Morrice, Broghill reacted to 'the horrid murther [that] was committed upon the king's sacred person' by rejecting the parliamentarian cause,[3] and in the summer of 1649 he went to London to secure a pass to cross to the continent and join the court in exile. As he was preparing to leave, however, he was suddenly summoned by Cromwell, with whom 'he had never had any acquaintance . . . nor ever exchanged one word with him'.[4] Cromwell confronted Broghill, revealing that he had full knowledge of his plan to join the king, and warning him that the council of state would arrest him unless 'he would serve in the wars against the Irish'. Cromwell went on to promise him 'a general officer's command', and to accommodate his conscience by allowing that he 'should have no oaths nor engagements laid upon him, nor should be obliged to fight against any but the Irish'. Broghill, so Morrice asserts, saw that he had no choice: 'Seeing no subterfuges could any longer be made use of, and finding his liberty and life were in danger, whereby he might be rendered utterly incapable of serving his majesty, and not knowing but, by accepting this offer, he might afterwards be serviceable to the royal party, he resolved to accept of it'.[5] This terrible dilemma, and the reluctance with which Broghill resolved it – agreeing to serve the hated usurper until he could reveal his true loyalty to the Stuarts once again – is undeniably an attractive story. As such it has been incorporated, apparently uncritically, into twentieth-century accounts of Broghill's career: especially those of W. C. Abbott (whose true focus was, of course, Cromwell) and Kathleen Lynch. As Lynch concluded, 'Broghill genuinely desired to serve the King and managed to convince himself that it was "a very great Providence" that he could be preserved for this ultimate end'.[6] Yet Morrice's account is deeply flawed. Although Broghill

---

[2] Cited in B. D. Henning (ed.), *The history of parliament: the House of Commons 1660–90*, (3 vols, 1983), i, 702.
[3] Morrice, *Memoirs*, p. 9.
[4] Ibid., p. 10.
[5] Ibid., p. 11.
[6] Lynch, *Orrery*, p. 71; Abbott, *Writings and speeches*, ii, 83–4.

was indeed in correspondence with the royalists in exile during 1648–9, all contact ceased in April 1649 – shortly after Oliver Cromwell's appointment as lord lieutenant of Ireland became public knowledge.[7] Broghill did not leave his retirement in Somerset before August 1649, by which time he could no longer rely (as Morrice claims) on a pass from the earl of Warwick, who had been sacked as parliamentarian admiral in the previous February.[8] In any case, by early August Broghill was already on the Cromwellian payroll.[9] These factual inconsistencies reinforce the more general concerns that Morrice's story cannot be corroborated from other evidence, and that it runs counter to much that can be gleaned of Broghill's attitudes in the 1640s, culled from less biased sources.[10]

A similar incident, also from 1649, presents similar problems. In November or December, as the Cromwellian army entered winter quarters in Munster, Michael Jones approached Broghill with news 'that Cromwell designed to ruin both his lordship and himself', and proposing that 'if he would join him, they would set up for themselves, and beat Cromwell out of Ireland'. Broghill agreed with Jones's sentiments, but 'he thought it was not at that time seasonable, to free themselves from their yoke' because the Irish were undefeated. Jones died soon afterwards, and Broghill was left to wait for the right season for his plans.[11] This story would seem to be entirely fictitious. There is no evidence of either Broghill or Jones supporting Charles Stuart at this time. Indeed, the peace deal between the royalists and Confederates had confirmed their worst fears about royal duplicity. Nor is there any indication that Cromwell was suspicious of either man, and in the winter of 1649–50 he expressed great sorrow at Jones's death, and celebrated Broghill's achievements by joining him in a triumphal progress around the Munster towns.[12]

The manuscript version of Morrice's work is full of deletions, some of which are significant. In his draft account of Broghill's role in offering the crown to Cromwell in 1657, Morrice was forced to employ some tortured logic:

His Lordship being one of Cromwel's Council and observing him to be very ambitious, he advis'd the Protector to take upon himself the stile and Dignity of king . . . [for] If Cromwel had taken upon himself the name of king, as he did the Power, his party wou'd certainly have fallen from him, and his Majesty had been sooner Restor'd. Which was the thing My L[or]d designed in giving that advice.[13]

---

[7] See below, ch. 2.
[8] *Boyle's correspondence*, i, 80; *Cal. S.P. Dom., 1649–50*, p. 9.
[9] *Cal. S.P. Dom., 1649–50*, p. 584.
[10] See below, chs 1, 2.
[11] Morrice, *Memoirs*, pp 16–17.
[12] James Scott Wheeler, *Cromwell in Ireland* (Dublin, 1999), pp 117–18.
[13] B.L., Sloane MS 4227, f. 57r–v.

Realising the danger of raising the question at all, Morrice (or his later editor) crossed out this passage in his manuscript, and the printed *Memoirs* omit all mention of the offer of the crown to Cromwell, concentrating instead on Broghill's attempts to remove the decimation tax on cavaliers in the same parliament,[14] and his general importance in the months before the restoration in 1660. The latter makes Morrice's bias all too plain. A passive supporter of the crown throughout the 1650s, early in 1660 Broghill was at last able to act, writing to Charles II 'inviting his majesty to come into his kingdom of Ireland' and assuring him that the Irish army was now ready 'to declare for his majesty'. Only a better offer from General George Monck, who took charge of London in the same period, foiled Broghill's plan to be the chief architect of the restoration.[15] As Aidan Clarke has pointed out, Morrice's account of the months leading up to the restoration in 1660, 'is unsupported by the evidence'.[16] And, as we shall see, there is good reason for seeing Broghill as resisting the Stuarts right up until the last moment.[17] Even his later career, as earl of Orrery, has been embellished by Morrice, whose story of the earl's nomination to succeed Clarendon as lord chancellor of England in 1667 (on the interest, bizarrely, of the duke of York) is pure fantasy.[18] Stranger still is Morrice's story that Charles II approved of Orrery in 1669 because (as he told the French ambassador) the earl 'was a catholic in his heart' – a claim which subverts all other evidence of Orrery's trenchant, even aggressive, Protestant beliefs.[19] Even a brief survey shows that the inconsistencies and fabrications of Morrice's biography are legion. Whether considering 1649, 1657, 1660, 1667 or 1669, Morrice's work must be used only with extreme caution.

Morrice intended his *Memoirs* to set Broghill in a favourable light, and in this he was more than successful – in the past century almost every account of the lord's life has been based upon it. The old *Dictionary of National Biography* of the 1890s portrayed Broghill as 'a zealous royalist' during the 1640s; it retells Morrice's account of his 'extraordinary bargain' with Cromwell in 1649, and sees his career in the 1650s as running contrary to his true desires: 'realising that the royal cause was for the time hopeless, [he] devoted all his energies to make the rule of Cromwell a success'.[20] Alongside Morrice, the D.N.B. was the primary influence on later interpretations of Broghill's career.[21]

---

[14] Morrice, *Memoirs*, pp 25–6.

[15] Ibid., pp 30–2.

[16] Aidan Clarke, *Prelude to restoration in Ireland: the end of the commonwealth, 1659–60* (Cambridge, 1999), p. 161.

[17] See below, ch. 5.

[18] Henning (ed.), *House of Commons, 1660–90*, i, 702.

[19] James McGuire, 'Why was Ormond dismissed in 1669?' in *I.H.S.*, xviii (1972–3), pp 309–10.

[20] *D.N.B.*, ii, 1031–4.

[21] See, for example, Abbott, *Writings and speeches*, ii, 83–4; Antonia Fraser, *Cromwell, our chief of men* (1994 ed.), pp 321–2; Henning (ed.), *House of Commons, 1660–90*, i, 701–3.

The one exception was that of Sir Charles Firth, who repeatedly questioned both Morrice (as containing 'a number of fictions' about Broghill in the 1650s) and the *D.N.B.* (which 'gives a very inadequate account of his military and political activities').[22] Yet Firth's warnings were ignored by Broghill's most recent biographer, Kathleen Lynch. In her 1965 book, *Roger Boyle, first earl of Orrery*, Lynch devotes three chapters to Broghill's career before 1660. The first, taking the story to 1641, gives a valuable account of his early life, and his position within the Boyle family. The second chapter improves on the *D.N.B.*, but is less than sophisticated in its view of the complexities of Irish politics in the 1640s. The third, dealing with the 1650s, is heavily reliant on Morrice, repeating his account of the interview with Cromwell, accepting the view that Broghill was a closet royalist throughout the decade, and skirting around difficult topics such as Broghill's term as president of Scotland in 1655–6.[23]

Since Lynch's book was published, an increasing amount of work has been undertaken on Irish Protestantism: the social, political and mental world of the New English settlers; the strategies for survival developed by the 'Old Protestants' in the 1640s and 1650s; and the growth of a separate identity before and after 1660. The work of Toby Barnard, in particular, has done much to elucidate the position of the Protestant community in this period, and to highlight the subtleties and ambiguities which other historians have glossed over in the pursuit of tidiness.[24] In his various articles and books on the subject, Barnard makes frequent reference to Broghill. His study of the second earl of Cork, has much to say about his subject's 'supple brother', who is characterised as 'an adept of intrigue and cajolery' and 'the superlative political fixer', especially in the years after 1660.[25] In his article on 'The Protestant Interest, 1641–60', published in the same year, Barnard touched on the earlier career of Broghill, whom he describes as 'Protestant Ireland's most subtle politician'. Though 'excoriated for a pliancy tantamount to apostasy', Broghill 'exhibited great courage – political as well as physical – in expressing robust opinions'. His pet scheme, for setting up a Protestant militia in Ireland, which was to become his hobby-horse even in his years of declining influence after 1660, revealed something of his 'obsessive' character, as well as reflecting his concern for Irish self-reliance.[26] Yet, despite frequent hints in this and other articles, even Toby Barnard has not examined Broghill's pre-1660 career in detail, and the majority of historians are still happy to toe Morrice's line.[27] James Scott Wheeler, in his study of the Cromwellian conquest of Ireland, repeats Morrice's

---

[22] *Ludlow memoirs*, i, 263n; C. H. Firth and G. Davies (eds), *The regimental history of Cromwell's army* (2 vols, Oxford, 1940), ii, 589.
[23] Lynch, *Orrery*, pp 1–105.
[24] See especially Barnard's magisterial overview: *A new anatomy of Ireland: the Irish Protestants, 1649–1770* (New Haven, 2003).
[25] Barnard, 'Cork', pp 174–8.
[26] Barnard, 'Protestant interest', pp 218, 232–6.
[27] Aidan Clarke being a notable exception: *Prelude*, p. 161.

account of Cromwell's ultimatum to Broghill in 1649, when the latter was 'en route through London to the continent to offer his services to Charles II', although he gives short shrift to the story that Broghill and Michael Jones were plotting against Cromwell by the end of the year.[28] Colin Davis, in his recent biography of Cromwell, includes the 1649 incident, saying that Broghill 'was intercepted on his way to join the Stuart court in exile and persuaded to work for Cromwell in Ireland'.[29] Others preface their comments on Broghill by emphasising that he was a 'former royalist' – a view also derived, if only at second hand, from Morrice's myths.[30]

It is perhaps fitting that this re-examination of Broghill's early career should be focused on the one aspect omitted altogether from Morrice's published biography – his role in the kingship debates of 1657, which was the *acme* of his attempts to create a workable, stable settlement across the three nations. Without guidance from Morrice and his acolytes, historians have initiated a lively debate on the nature of Broghill's involvement in the new constitution (the Humble Petition and Advice) which reduced the power of the army and increased civilian control over the political process by returning England to its ancient form of king, lords and commons, and at the same time continued the parliamentary union established in 1653, which had brought Ireland and Scotland into partnership with their larger neighbour. Sir Charles Firth first identified the 'Anglo-Irish' basis of the kingship party, but the greatest claims for Broghill's part in the events of 1656–7 have been made by Hugh Trevor-Roper.[31] For Trevor-Roper, Broghill was central to the new attempt at settlement, acting as 'a great parliamentary manager, like the earls of Warwick and Bedford in 1640', and providing the protector with 'an organized party in Parliament', for the first and last time. Broghill's efficiency contrasted with that of Cromwell, who 'again and again . . . by his own refusal to organize . . . created in Parliament a vacuum of leadership'.[32] Trevor-Roper's view of Broghill was supported by Toby Barnard's early work on the 1650s,[33] but has now been challenged by other historians, notably Peter Gaunt, who has

[28] Wheeler, *Cromwell in Ireland*, pp 72, 117–8.

[29] J. C. Davis, *Oliver Cromwell* (2001), p. 103.

[30] Christopher Hill, *God's Englishman: Oliver Cromwell and the English revolution* (1971), p. 112; Frances Dow, *Cromwellian Scotland, 1651–1660* (Edinburgh, 1979), p. 165; Hugh Trevor-Roper, 'Oliver Cromwell and his parliaments' in his *Religion, the reformation and social change* (3rd ed., 1984), p. 381; Ronald Hutton, *The restoration: a political and religious history of England and Wales, 1658–1667* (Oxford, 1986), pp 15, 36.

[31] C. H. Firth, 'Cromwell and the crown' in *E.H.R.*, xvii (1902), pp 429–42; ibid., xviii (1903), pp 52–80.

[32] Trevor-Roper, 'Oliver Cromwell and his parliaments', pp 376, 380–3; see also Trevor-Roper, 'The union of Britain in the seventeenth century' in his *Religion, the reformation and social change*, pp 445–67.

[33] T. C. Barnard, 'Planters and policies in Cromwellian Ireland' in *Past and Present*, lxi (1973), pp 57–9.

condemned Trevor-Roper's 'portrayal of the 1656–7 session as dominated by Broghill's "kingship party"' as 'particularly sweeping'. While admitting that Broghill 'actively favoured the offer of the crown', Gaunt concludes that the surviving sources 'do not suggest that he led the House, either during the kingship debates or at other times during the session'.[34] Instead, Gaunt suggests that the protector's councillors were more important in managing the commons, even though he admits that 'on many occasions and over many issues, there existed no courtier grouping and no clear Protectoral intentions'.[35] In place of distinct parties (or even looser coalitions) we are offered a chaotic vision which does not fit with the clear progression from, for example, the militia bill to the kingship debates; nor is it suggested who drafted the new constitution and why. While the Trevor-Roper thesis has been cast into doubt (or at least, proved to need revision), and his view of Cromwell's inactivity is not sustainable, its opponents have little to put in its place.[36]

This present study hopes to change the terms of the debate, by approaching Broghill's role in the new constitution from an Irish angle. In essence, its argument is that Broghill's place in the Cromwellian government can only be understood as part of a radical tradition within Irish Protestantism, which saw union with England as the ultimate solution to the political and religious problems of Ireland. This tradition originated from the New English community itself, rather than being derived from any *Ur-text* imported from the mainland, and can be traced from the 1620s and 1630s through the Irish wars and into the Cromwellian era.[37] Broghill, through his experience in Scotland and his reaction to events in England, was encouraged to widen this unionist approach, seeking settlement for all three nations through formal acts of union, and, in due course, proposing a return to a monarchical structure. This allowed the construction of a broad-based coalition within the 1656 parliament, made up of Irish and Scots, English Presbyterians and Cromwellian 'courtiers', which nearly succeeded in securing a new-modelled monarchy early in 1657. For Broghill, as ringleader of this group, kingship had religious as well as political and constitutional elements, based on a providential understanding of the role of Oliver Cromwell, both nationally and internationally. This mixture of

---

[34] Peter Gaunt, 'Oliver Cromwell and his protectorate parliaments: co-operation, conflict and control' in Ivan Roots (ed.), *Into another mould: aspects of the interregnum* (2nd ed., Exeter, 1998), pp 91–2; see also Carol Egloff, 'Settlement and kingship: the army, the gentry and the offer of the crown to Oliver Cromwell' (unpublished Ph.D. thesis, Yale University, 1990), passim; for a more balanced approach, which leaves the 'kingship party' intact, see Roger Howell, jr, 'Cromwell and his parliaments: the Trevor-Roper thesis revisited' in R. C. Richardson (ed.), *Images of Oliver Cromwell* (Manchester, 1993), pp 124–35.

[35] Gaunt, 'Protectorate parliaments', p. 89.

[36] For a recent attempt to address this problem see Barry Coward, *The Cromwellian protectorate* (Manchester, 2002), pp 80–93, 233–6.

[37] See below, especially ch. 1; cf. Nicholas Canny, *Making Ireland British, 1580–1650* (Oxford, 2001), passim.

political principle and religious belief explains not only Broghill's desire to crown Cromwell, but also his lukewarm reaction to the return of Charles II in 1660, and his continuing discontent with the Stuarts and their policies in the following decades.

This book is not intended to be a biography of Lord Broghill, still less one of the earl of Orrery. His career after 1660 is touched on only briefly, and no attempt has been made to explore his literary output in detail. Such matters must be left to others. Instead, the focus is on the 1650s, when Broghill was an important political figure in all three 'British' nations. This narrow focus explains the structure of the book, which falls into three parts. Parts one and two are chronological: the first looks at Broghill's early career, up to 1649, which is essential to understanding his activities in the ensuing decade; the second deals with his years of influence, between 1649 and 1660, and glances ahead at the impact that this period would have on his later career. Part three is thematic, taking a wider view of the most important personal factors underlying Broghill's political activities during the 1650s, in the hope of providing an account not only of his public policies, but also of the private motivations which lay behind them.

Part I

A Political Apprenticeship, 1621–49

1

Cork and Broghill, 1621–43

Lord Broghill's career during the Cromwellian period has rarely been set in its proper context. Historians have tended to gloss over Broghill's early years, basing their accounts on such unreliable sources as Thomas Morrice's biography or the entry in the old *D.N.B.* The result is very misleading, as Broghill is portrayed as a staunch royalist, who was then forced to act as an opportunist; a man whose support for Cromwell was either the choice of the lesser of two evils or a mark of inconsistency, rather than the positive decision of a committed parliamentarian. In this and the next chapter I shall attempt to strip away the gloss, and examine the reality of Broghill's political position, especially during the crucial decade of the 1640s. It is only then that Broghill's activities under Cromwellian rule can be considered in their true light. As a preliminary it is necessary to revaluate the influence on Broghill of his greatest mentor – his father, Richard Boyle, first earl of Cork. Recent accounts have distorted the earl's career, and made his political, religious and social views appear inconsistent and hypocritical – as bad, in fact, as those usually attributed to his inconstant son. The two certainly had much in common, but in a very different way than the traditional line suggests. In the 1620s and 1630s, Cork was remarkably clear in his aims and direct in the ways he tried to achieve them; and his agenda for Ireland was the basis for the equally coherent policy followed by Broghill during the 1640s, which in turn became the foundation of his attempt to refashion the Cromwellian regime in England and Scotland as well as Ireland in the 1650s.

The first two decades of Broghill's life were profoundly influenced by his father; and this influence would continue long after the old man's death in 1643. In his religious and political views, in his attachment to Ireland, and in his driving ambition, Broghill was very much his father's son – much more so than his surviving brothers, the diffident second earl of Cork, the dissolute Viscount Shannon, or the donnish Robert Boyle. The first earl of Cork's career encountered as many twists and turns as that of Broghill. 'The second son of a younger brother', Cork was born in Canterbury in 1566, and came from a family of yeoman status, which claimed descent from a minor gentry family from Herefordshire. After studying at Bene't College, Cambridge, he went to Ireland in 1588 and soon became involved in the administration, gaining lands in Munster through his office as deputy-escheator. With the rebellion of the earl of Tyrone, and the Nine Years War that followed, Cork lost all his newly acquired estates, and was imprisoned by the government for his irregular dealings while in office. On his release (at the behest of the president of Munster, Sir George Carew) he married Catherine Fenton, daughter of the Irish secretary of state, and, with official support, began to amass a vast estate in the south-west, the income of which reached perhaps £20,000 per annum in the 1630s. Social advancement came with increasing wealth: he was knighted in 1603, created Baron Boyle in 1616 and earl of Cork in 1620; served as lord justice (in effect acting governor) of Ireland in 1629–33 and lord high treasurer from 1631. His initial good relationship with the new lord deputy, Viscount Wentworth (appointed in 1632), soon soured, with Cork falling victim to investigations into impropriated church property, but by the end of the decade the two men had settled their differences and Cork was free to pursue a successful career at the English court, culminating in his appoint-ment to the English privy council in 1640. The fall of Wentworth (now earl of Strafford) in 1641, and the Irish rebellion later in that year threw into doubt the political certainties of the previous decades, and by the time of his death in 1643 Cork's estates were in ruins and the prospects for Ireland bleak.[1]

Cork's dramatic rise from obscurity has attracted the attention of historians interested in the nature of planter society and the mindset of individual settlers. Nicholas Canny's study of 'the social and mental world' of the 'upstart earl' (published in 1982) has become the most influential pen-portrait of Cork. According to Canny, the earl's ruthless ambition was matched by a sense of social inferiority, which led him to crave titles and dignities for himself and to secure marriages for his numerous children with established families in both England and Ireland. Never comfortable with his peers, Cork tried, but ultimately failed, to buy himself the respect he desired. Yet Canny's emphasis on Cork as 'the most remarkable parvenu in Stuart England' misses the point on two counts.[2] First, religious conviction, not social insecurity, was the hallmark of Cork's character; and second, his primary focus for most of his life was not on his private, social elevation in England, but on the prosperity of the Protestant interest in Ireland.

Cork's success was founded not on craven self-doubt, but on Calvinist confidence. His 'spiritual reading' was Calvinist in tone, including William Perkins, George Downham and Archbishop Ussher.[3] His private chaplain in the 1620s was the violently anti-Catholic Stephen Jerome, whose hatred of Spain, in particular, was something he shared with his master. During the mid-1620s Cork was vigilant lest the Munster Catholics made common cause with the Spanish crown,[4] and in 1630 he warned the English government of

---

[1] Canny, *Upstart earl*, pp. 4–7; Patrick Little, 'The earl of Cork and the fall of the earl of Strafford, 1638–41' in *H.J.*, xxxix (1996), pp 619–35.
[2] Canny, *Upstart earl*, p. 76.
[3] Ibid., pp 27–8.
[4] Grosart, *Lismore papers*, ser. 1, ii, 142, 169.

the continuing threat from 'the Contagion of Popery', which encouraged the Irish to look to 'that never sleeping Adversary of Spaine'.[5] Cork's awareness of the international situation encouraged him to send his sons on grand tours of Europe, but with strict intineraries, which included visits to Geneva and the Huguenot academy at Saumur. He sought out Protestant spouses for his children and other relatives, and went to great lengths to encourage private devotion in his sons and daughters.[6] Cork drew up strict rules of religious observance for his children, and insisted that the whole household met 'every morning before dinner and every evening after supper at prayers'.[7] Twice daily prayers, Sunday sermons, and long periods of religious reading and reflection formed the routine of the Boyle household in the 1630s,[8] and this cycle of daily observance and religious contemplation was continued by his children in later decades. In the early 1640s the earl and countess of Barrymore heard 'sermons . . . twice a day, Sundays, Wednesdays, and ffrydays' at their house at Castlelyons in County Cork.[9] In the 1650s Viscount Dungarvan (by then second earl of Cork) attended two sermons each Sunday, and took his 'private devotions' and the 'publique service of God' very seriously.[10] The writings and correspondence of his younger brother, Robert Boyle, and his sisters, Katherine Jones (who became Lady Ranelagh in 1643) and Mary Rich, also show a depth of personal piety.[11] This was something that Broghill shared, and attempted to extend to those under his influence. His own household was run on very similar lines, and, as commander of the County Cork town of Youghal in 1640s, he introduced a regime of church attendance, sermons and fast-days, for the officers and soldiers of the garrison.[12] Under Cork's influence, the Boyle family became steeped in religion.

This religious imperative was not, as Canny has suggested, at odds with Cork's 'secular' career. Indeed, the distinction is a false one. For Cork, worldly success was an indication of divine favour, and an encouragement to strive for still greater things. His obsession with the workings of providence has been noted by Canny, but its pervasiveness in his public life has not been acknowledged.[13] Cork saw the Boyle family as an instrument of divine providence,

---

[5] Cork to Dorchester, 8 Dec. 1630 (P.R.O., S.P. 63/251, f. 248r).

[6] For a parallel case see Patrick Little, 'Providence and posterity: a letter from Lord Mountnorris to his daughter, 1642' in *I.H.S.*, xxxii (2001), pp 556–66.

[7] B.L., Add. MS 19832, f. 22r.

[8] Raymond Gillespie, *Devoted people: belief and religion in early modern Ireland* (Manchester, 1997), p. 12.

[9] This fact was noted with approval by Broghill's chaplain, Urban Vigors: see Thomas Fitzpatrick, *Waterford during the Civil War (1641–53)* (Waterford, 1912), p. 129.

[10] Second earl of Cork's diary (Chatsworth, Lismore MS 29, unfol.), esp. entries for 24 Sept. 1654 and 4 Apr. 1656.

[11] See *Boyle's works*, i. p. xxvii; Michael Hunter (ed.), *Robert Boyle by himself and his friends* (1994), p. 25.

[12] Broghill's order of 8 Nov. 1644 (B.L., Add. MS 25287, f. 20r).

[13] Canny, *Upstart earl*, pp 23–9.

and his 'autobiography' of 1632 was designed 'to show how God's providence had cared for him'.[14] Providential success was also something he claimed for his children. In the same year, Cork told his new son-in-law, the earl of Kildare, that 'to make him passage to this Earldome God hath removed and taken to himselfe sundrie brave Earles without heires males, to make waie for this Earle to ascend to this high tytle of honnour'.[15] This was a theme to which Cork returned in 1642, when he drew up his will, 'It being the Pleasure of Almighty God, for the settling of such Worldly Estate which it hath pleased God in His Mercy plentifully to bless me withall'.[16] In his injunctions to his son and heir, Viscount Dungarvan, sacred and secular duties were entwined. Dungarvan was warned that the fulfilment of Cork's bequests was vital 'as he intends the Salvation of his own Soul and his Honour, Reputation and Conscience, both with God and Man in this world and the world to come'.[17] The earl's trustees, as well as his son and heir, were warned that 'they will answer the Neglect or Breach of this my Great Trust, Will and Testament before God at the Dreadfull day of Judgment'.[18] For Cork, as for other Calvinists among the New English, providence and posterity were merely different sides of the same coin. His choice of family motto, 'God's providence is mine inheritance', put this in a nutshell.[19]

Cork's intentions for the Boyle dynasty were inextricably linked with his commitment to Ireland. Until the mid-1630s, when rough treatment at Wentworth's hands encouraged him to look to England, Cork's private ambitions were focused on Ireland. This can be seen in his choice of marriage partners for his children. Until 1634, with one exception, Cork arranged marriages only with Irish families, whether New English, like the Moores, Joneses or Loftuses, or Old English, like the Barrys and Fitzgeralds, or both – as in the case of the Digbys. Even in 1634, when Cork married Viscount Dungarvan to the daughter of Lord Clifford, an English peer, his true focus was on Ireland. Clifford was the brother-in-law of Wentworth, the new lord deputy of Ireland, and Cork soon used the family connexion to head off government investigations into his illegal landholdings. It was only in a brief period, from 1639 until 1641, that Cork sought spouses for his children in England. Before then, the marriage policy reflected the earl's desire to embed himself and his family into Irish soil. He invested heavily in Irish lands, maintained Irish tenants on his estates, encouraged his children to learn Gaelic, and employed native bards and musicians.[20] Cork's decision to pursue

---

[14] Gillespie, *Devoted people*, p. 42.
[15] Fitzgerald pedigree, presented to Kildare by Cork, c.1632 (Dorset R.O., KG 1474).
[16] Dorothea Townshend, *Life and letters of the great earl of Cork* (1904), p. 470.
[17] Ibid., p. 491.
[18] Ibid., p. 487.
[19] Little, 'Providence and posterity', pp 562–4; Canny, *Upstart earl*, p. 19.
[20] Canny, *Upstart earl*, pp 126–8.

marriages with the prominent Fitzgerald clan (especially the earl of Barrymore, Lord Digby of Geashill and the earl of Kildare) in the 1620s was based on extensive research into histories and pedigrees, assisted by Sir James Ware and other antiquarians. Canny is surely wrong to see this merely as social climbing. While Cork undoubtedly valued the association of the Boyles with ancient families, there was much more to it than that. Cork saw his role as the saviour of these families, not only resurrecting their estates, but also converting them (or, in the case of the Digbys, confirming their attachment) to his particular brand of Protestantism. Thus, the young earl of Kildare was not just given money to redeem mortgages: he was also provided with suitably godly chaplains; Cork did not just fund the rebuilding of Kildare's ancestral seat of Maynooth Castle: he rebuilt the local parish church as well.[21]

Cork's private initiatives went hand-in-hand with his public agenda. His chance to make a direct impact on Irish affairs came only in the late 1620s, when he took charge of the political grouping formerly centred on Lord Deputy Falkland, eventually becoming joint lord justice of Ireland in 1629–33. His allies from this period and throughout the 1630s included Sir William Parsons, Roger Jones, Viscount Ranelagh, and Sir Adam Loftus. These were relatives as well as political associates: Parsons was Cork's cousin, and the earl's daughters married the sons of Ranelagh and Loftus in 1630. At the countess of Cork's funeral in the same year, Parsons, Ranelagh and Loftus were among the pall-bearers. In 1632 their political opponent, Sir Francis Annesley, Lord Mountnorris, ruefully acknowledged that these men were 'all birds of a feather and of the earl of Cork's party'.[22] The coincidence of this political and genealogical grouping is in itself evidence of the fusion of the public and private worlds among the New English of the period. More important, however, is their common attitude towards Ireland and the Irish. In 1625 Sir William Parsons wrote to the secretary of state, Viscount Conway, with advice on the future government of Ireland. He called for the re-education of Irish lords under the existing wardship arrangements, the extension of English plantations into Irish areas, and for the Irish to be brought into obedience to 'the Lawes & Empier of England'.[23] Parsons' views were echoed by Cork's policies as lord justice, as outlined to Secretary Dorchester in 1630. The final destruction of the old Catholic lordships had opened the way for a new political and social order, 'ffree from other dependency then on the king and his Ministers', and reinforced by further plantation. There was even scope for a new kind of militia, based on English settlers and the loyal Irish – the 'Irish British . . . reformed in manners and religion' – who would be able to resist

---

[21] Grosart, *Lismore papers*, ser. 1, iii, 135; see Patrick Little, 'The Geraldine ambitions of the first earl of Cork' in *I.H.S.*, xxxiii (2002), p. 163.

[22] Patrick Little, 'The Irish "Independents" and Viscount Lisle's lieutenancy of Ireland' in *H.J.*, xliv (2001), pp 941–61.

[23] P.R.O., S.P. 63/241, ff 338v–9r [*Cal. S.P. Ire.*, 1625–32, pp 56–8].

foreign invasion and domestic unrest alike.[24] Cork's public policies during this period followed this programme: he promoted plantations in the Ormond baronies of Tipperary; he enforced the recusancy laws, persecuting Catholic priests and destroying St Patrick's Purgatory; and he also tried to put the burden of maintaining a Protestant standing army onto the Catholic gentry.[25] As we have seen, at the same time Cork sought to unite, revitalise, and convert the various branches of the Fitzgerald clan, investing much effort, and large sums of money, into a private scheme which entirely agreed with his plans to reform Ireland as a whole. And Cork's intentions for the Fitzgeralds were underpinned with the belief that he was doing not only what was best for his family and for the state, but also what God demanded.

The extent to which Cork's private ambitions and public policies were fully integrated can be seen in his relations with the traditional rivals of the Fitzgeralds, the Butler earls of Ormond. Cork's own landed power base rested on that of the Fitzgerald earls of Desmond, and with the lands he acquired many of the rights and privileges associated with the Desmond lordship. He soon found himself involved in the same territorial disputes which had caused tensions between the Desmonds and the Ormonds in previous centuries. The first of these concerned areas of Tipperary and Waterford which had formed the borders of the Butler and Fitzgerald lordships since the Middle Ages. The regional influence of the Butlers had been in decline since the beginning of the century, and James I undermined the Catholic eleventh earl of Ormond by promoting the interests of the Butler heiress-general, who had married his favourite, Richard Preston.[26] With Preston's death in 1628 Cork tried to force through the plantation of the baronies of Upper and Lower Ormond in Tipperary, against the interests of the Butlers, and he used his influence as lord justice to promote the scheme.[27] Similarly, in 1631 Cork snatched the wardship of the heir of the Fitzgeralds of the Decies in Waterford from under the earl of Ormond's nose, and married him to a Protestant relative.[28] Worse tensions were created by Cork's insistence on claiming the right to be paid duty on wine imports – the prizage – in the County Waterford port of Dungarvan, which had been enjoyed by the Butlers since the reign of Edward III. In the sixteenth century the earls of Desmond had challenged the Butlers' right to the prizage in this and other ports, causing violent feuding.[29] Cork inherited this dispute from the Desmonds, and collected prizage payments from

[24] P.R.O., S.P. 63/251, ff 248r–50r [*Cal. S.P. Ire.*, 1625–32, pp 589–90].

[25] Little, 'Irish Independents', pp 943–4; Canny, *Upstart earl*, p. 29.

[26] *Cal. S.P. Ire.*, 1625–32, pp 325–6, 686; for the fortunes of the Butlers see David Edwards, *The Ormond lordship in County Kilkenny, 1515–1642: the rise and fall of Butler feudal power* (Dublin, 2003).

[27] *Cal. S.P. Ire.*, 1625–32, p. 536; Cork to Lord Weston, 9 Aug. 1630 (Chatsworth, Cork Letterbook I, p. 167).

[28] Little, 'Geraldine ambitions', p.155.

[29] David Edwards, 'The Butler revolt of 1569' in *I.H.S.*, xxviii (1993), pp 228–55.

the Dungarvan merchants throughout the 1620s and 1630s.[30] This caused friction first with the Prestons, and then, in the late 1630s, with the twelfth earl of Ormond, who resented Cork's interference in this as in other areas of the Butler inheritance.[31] Cork's awareness of his place as territorial successor to the Desmonds may have increased his enthusiasm for marriages with those traditionally associated with the Fitzgerald interest in Munster; and it is interesting that the deal to secure the marriage of his daughter to the head of the clan, the earl of Kildare, was concluded in August 1629 – the same month that the future twelfth earl of Ormond contracted to marry his cousin, the Butler heiress, Elizabeth Preston.[32] Cork's relations with the Butlers offer an insight into his attitudes in general. His territorial ambitions in Munster took place within a historical context, and were informed by a deep understanding of local politics, both past and present; and his own private ends coincided with his wider programme for Ireland, reducing the power of native lordships and converting old families to Protestantism.

One final aspect of Cork's social and mental world needs to be considered: his attitude to authority, and more specifically, to the crown. When Cork's ambitions were thwarted by an unsympathetic Wentworth in the mid-1630s, he turned his attentions towards England, and curried favour with the English court. Between 1638 and 1641, in particular, he made great efforts to break into English court circles, even to the extent of marrying two younger sons into families closely associated with the Catholic queen, Henrietta Maria. This period has always caused problems for historians of Cork's career, as it suggests that his earlier, Irish, career, was something he could readily abandon, and with it his Protestant zeal. But the changes are less marked than they first appear, the choices less stark. For, although Cork's identity was founded on his faith and on his commitment to Ireland, both were linked to his sense of duty towards the crown. This was not a new phenomenon. In 1625, when Charles I was proclaimed king at Lismore, in an extravagant gesture Cork and his friends 'all dranck King Charles his health on our knees'.[33] While lord justice in 1630, Cork pronounced his eagerness to serve the interests of 'our great Master the King of England'.[34] Dungarvan's reception at court in 1633 gave the earl immense pleasure, as did the prominence of the king and

[30] Despite pressure from Preston, supported by Buckingham, Cork continued to collect the prizage: see Lord Esmond to Cork, 3 Aug. 1624 (Chatsworth, Lismore MS 15, no. 62); Cork to Preston, 9 Apr. 1625 (N.L.I., MS 11,056(1)); Cork receipts, 1626–32 (N.L.I., MS 6897, unfol.), entry for 13 Mar. 1628. I owe the second reference to the kindness of Dr David Edwards.

[31] Joshua Boyle to Cork, 28 Sept. 1639 (N.L.I., MS 13, 237(13), unfol.); Cork to Ormond, 16 Mar. 1640, Ormond to Cork, 23 Apr. 1640 (B.L. Add. MS 19,832, ff 47r–v, 49r–v); John Walley to Cork, 30 May 1640 (Chatsworth, Lismore MS 21, no. 20).

[32] Cal. S.P. Dom., 1629–30, p. 38; Grosart, Lismore papers, ser. 1, ii, 336.

[33] Gosart, Lismore papers, ser. 1, ii, p. 153.

[34] Cork to Visc. Dorchester, 8 Dec. 1630 (P.R.O., S.P. 63/251, f. 248v).

queen in the marriage ceremonies of two other sons in 1639.[35] The departure of the king to fight against the Scots in the spring of the same year caused Cork to write in his diary that he was gone 'to reduce his Rebellows subiects of Scotland; wherin I beseech god to bless him, and his army'.[36] Dungarvan, Kinalmeaky and Broghill all served with the royal army in 1639; and in 1640, when Broghill presented a gift of £1,000 to the king on his father's behalf, Cork described it as 'my free guifte and Tribute of my duety'.[37] Cork's appointment as privy councillor in June 1640 evoked a similar response: 'ffor which addicon of honnor, god make me everlastingly thanckfull to my god and to my Kinge'.[38] The last quotation is particularly revealing. For Cork, duty to the crown was connected with his duty to God. Again, this was not double-thinking. In the providential world, the secular and the sacred became counterparts, and this was as true for Cork in England in 1640 as it had been for him in Ireland in 1632.

The Irish rebellion in October 1641 came as a terrible shock to Cork and his sons, who had just returned to Munster from England. Cork's response was, however, entirely predictable. He saw the rising as the culmination of a long-standing Catholic conspiracy. As he told his youngest sons' tutor, the Catholics 'had vowed or receaved the Sacrament to roote us all out of Ireland, both roote and branch, which hitherto they have pursued, in the most bloudy and merciles manner'.[39] He added that all that stood between the rebels and victory in Munster were the Protestant forces commanded by the Boyles. The rebellion hardened Cork's attitudes. The Irish Catholics were now proved to be enemies of the king as well as enemies of God; the Boyles were confirmed in their providential role as champions against the papal Anti-Christ. Once again, the keystone of Cork's policies, whether public or private, was his faith in God. In more peaceful times, Protestantism, and specifically Calvinism, was to be Ireland's panacea. The forces opposed to this – Catholicism and the tendency of the 'mere Irish' to degeneracy – must be rooted out. This belief gave Cork's activities an internal logic. The Boyles were the agents of this change, whether through their territorial power in Munster, their marriages with ancient families, or their involvement in the national government. After 1641, the course of the Catholic rebellion, resisted by the Boyles, merely confirmed Cork's prejudices. Whether in peace or war, Cork cannot credibly be accused of 'inconsistency and double-thinking'.[40] As we shall see, Cork's consistent, integrated thinking was to have a significant impact on the career of his third surviving son, Lord Broghill.

---

[35] Cork to Dungarvan, c.1633 (B.L., Add. MS 19832, f. 33); Grosart, *Lismore papers*, ser. 1, v, 63, 112.

[36] Grosart, *Lismore papers*, ser. 1, v, 82.

[37] Ibid., pp 89, 159.

[38] Ibid., p. 144.

[39] Cork to Marcombes, 9 Mar. 1642 (Chatsworth, Lismore MS 22, no. 165).

[40] Canny, *Upstart earl*, p. 32.

I

Lord Broghill's upbringing was entirely guided by his father's beliefs. Born on 25 April 1621 at Lismore Castle in County Waterford, Broghill was baptised soon afterwards, and his three godparents were all from ancient Irish families: David Barry, Viscount Buttevant (and soon to be earl of Barrymore) was related to the Fitzgeralds, and would become the infant's brother-in-law later in the year; Donnell O'Sullivan of Berehaven was a Gaelic nobleman from West Cork; and Thomasine Bourke, baroness of Castleconnell, was from another local anglo-norman (or 'Old English') family.[41] Even before his marriage policy got under way, Cork was intent on associating his family with the traditional lords of Munster, and through his godparents Broghill was being drawn into a specific historical and geographical context within days of his birth. Little is known of Broghill's life until February 1628, when, at the age of six, he was created Baron of Broghill; he was knighted by Lord Deputy Falkland in April of the same year.[42] Broghill's education was religious as well as social. In May 1630 he went to Dublin with his brother, Viscount Kinalmeaky, and was admitted to Trinity College Dublin, an institution which had already acquired a reputation for Calvinism.[43] Cork also provided a suitably godly chaplain for Broghill in the early 1630s: Richard Jermyn M.A., whose recommendation in the earl's eyes was his reputation as 'a good preacher'.[44] In 1635 Cork sought a tutor to accompany Broghill and Kinalmeaky on a grand tour of Europe. The earl took great care in making this appointment. First, he contacted the godly earl of Bedford to ask him to 'procure' Lord Russell's former tutor, Monsieur Rosamunde, to accompany the boys. On failing to secure this, he turned to the provost of Eton, the Calvinist Sir Henry Wotton, asking him for an introduction to a Swiss Protestant, James Battiere – again, to no avail. Finally, on the recommendation of Wotton, Sir Thomas Stafford, Philip Burlamachi and the tailor and financier, William Perkins, Cork engaged the services of a French Huguenot, Isaac Marcombes.[45] Cork only accepted Marcombes after a personal interview in Dublin in January 1636,[46] which convinced him that the new tutor truly was 'very sound in religion, and well conversant with religious men'.[47]

---

[41] Grosart, *Lismore papers*, ser. 1, ii, 14, 111.

[42] Ibid., p. 111.

[43] Ibid., iii, 30, 36, 50.

[44] Ibid., iv, 170; ibid., v, 116.

[45] Ibid., iv, 109, 125, 149; Battiere was naturalised by the Irish Parliament in 1634–5: see W. A. Shaw, *Letters of denization and acts of naturalization, 1603–1700* (Lymington, 1911), pp 51–2.

[46] Grosart, *Lismore papers*, ser. 1, iv, 149.

[47] Logan Pearsall Smith (ed.), *The life and letters of Sir Henry Wotton* (2 vols, Oxford, 1907), ii, 356.

On 13 February 1636 Broghill and Kinalmeaky left Ringsend near Dublin, arriving in London on 2 March.[48] There they met Marcombes, and were given the latest advice on the political situation on the continent by Wotton's friend, M. Battiere.[49] Gaining licences to travel, the Boyle brothers left Rye on 19 March, arriving safely in Dieppe on the following day.[50] The tour was carefully managed from afar by the earl of Cork. The earl had stipulated that they would go to study in Geneva.[51] One reason for Marcombes's appointment was his position as nephew by marriage of the Genevan theologian, John Diodati; and when the brothers reached Switzerland (after a brief visit to Paris), they would stay there for the remainder of 1636 and much of 1637, as guests in Diodati's house.[52] By May 1638 the Boyles had taken up residence at the French Huguenot academy at Saumur,[53] where they stayed with the Scottish professor, Mark Duncan, and had access to the library of the great Huguenot divine, Philippe du Plessis Mornay.[54] The more relaxed Calvinism of Saumur, as well as the orthodoxy of Geneva, would prove an important religious influence for Broghill in later years.

Residence at Saumur also brought opportunities for Broghill and Kinalmeaky to widen their circle of social and political contacts. The academy, with its reputation for riding and language masters as well as theologians, was a popular watering-hole on the English grand tour itinerary. Broghill, who was described by Marcombes as 'a gentl[eman] of a very good fashion',[55] later said that in France he 'assotiated my selfe with Persons of my owne Age', who had encouraged his interest in romances and other modish pastimes.[56] Broghill's sojourn at Saumur coincided with the stay of Viscount Lisle, the earl of Leicester's son and heir, who had been resident at the academy since August 1636. The Boyles' host at Saumur, Mark Duncan, had corresponded with Leicester about the studies of Lisle and his brother, Algernon Sidney (the future republican), and this mutual contact may have brought the two families together in 1638.[57] On Cork's insistence,[58] Broghill and his brother returned to

---

[48] Grosart, *Lismore papers*, ser. 1, iv, 157.
[49] Broghill to Cork, 20 Mar. 1636 (Chatsworth, Lismore MS 18, no. 125).
[50] *Cal. S.P. Dom., 1635–6*, pp 298, 354; Broghill to Cork, 20 Mar. 1636 (Chatsworth, Lismore MS 18, no. 125).
[51] Grosart, *Lismore papers*, ser. 1, iv, 157.
[52] Lynch, *Orrery*, p. 14; Cork's accounts record payments to his sons in Geneva throughout 1637: see N.L.I., MS 6899, unfol.: entries for 5 Jan., 26 May, 8 Nov. 1637.
[53] N.L.I., MS 6899, pp 15–16.
[54] Kinalmeaky to Cork, 28 May 1638 (B.L., Add. MS 19832, f. 45r).
[55] Marcombes to Cork, 28 May 1638 (ibid., f. 44v).
[56] Roger Boyle, *Parthenissa, a romance* (5 vols., 1655–6), i, Sig Av; these associates may have included Thomas Windebanke (son of the secretary of state): see Windebanke to his cousin in England, 6 Jan. 1639 [n.s.] (P.R.O., S.P. 78/106, f. 402r).
[57] H.M.C. *de Lisle*, vi, 47; Jonathan Scott, *Algernon Sidney and the English republic, 1623–77* (Cambridge, 1988), p. 53.
[58] Broghill to Cork, 17 Dec. 1638 (Chatsworth, Lismore MS 19, no. 75).

Paris in November 1638, and soon afterwards Lisle also left for the French capital, to attend his father, who was the English ambassador extraordinary.[59] The Boyles came into frequent contact with the Sidneys during the winter festivities.[60] Cork was proud of his sons' social achievements, but constantly interfered with their other arrangements. In the last weeks of 1638 he criticised Broghill's 'neglect of not writinge' and told him to stop wasting his time reading French romances, 'Pamphelets Playbooks Commical and Tragediall'.[61] The earl's complaints against Kinalmeaky, who was already proving unruly and acquiring a taste for drink, were perhaps more justifiable.[62] These, and numerous other trivial examples, and also the frequency of Cork's correspondence with his sons and their tutor (and his complaints when letters did not arrive), confirm the impression that the earl was stage-managing the whole tour.

Broghill and Kinalmeaky left Paris in the early weeks of 1639, and arrived in London on 4 March. Ten days later they reached Cork's country mansion at Stalbridge in Dorset.[63] On his return to England, Broghill found that the political situation had changed greatly. Incensed by a ham-fisted attempt to impose English religious forms north of the border, the Scots had risen against Charles I in 1637, signed the national covenant in 1638, and in early 1639 were preparing an army to march into England. This crisis had stiffened the resolve of the loyalist earl of Cork to reach a compromise with Lord Deputy Wentworth over the disputed church properties at Youghal and elsewhere in Ireland; and the earl had also started to strengthen his existing contacts with the court of Queen Henrietta Maria.[64] Cork's efforts to curry favour with Wentworth and the English court had an immediate impact on his sons. In the spring of 1639 his eldest son, Viscount Dungarvan, and his son-in-law, the earl of Barrymore, both offered to raise Irish forces to serve in the royal army against the Scots. Cork was less than thrilled with Dungarvan's offer to raise a troop of horse at his own expense, which he claimed had been made 'rashly without my privitie',[65] and he continued to grumble, despite Barrymore's assurances that, at the court, 'your lordship has the thancks'.[66] The troop mustered at Stalbridge, and left for the north on 9 May, with Dungarvan accompanied by Kinalmeaky and Broghill.[67] No sooner had Dungarvan's troop joined its regiment on the Scottish borders, than the royal army was disbanded, as the king made an undignified peace with the still-unbeaten Scots at Berwick in June 1639. Broghill, riding post from the camp, returned to

[59] Grosart, *Lismore papers*, ser. 1, v, 63; H.M.C. *de Lisle*, vi, 154.
[60] Broghill to Cork, 17 Dec. 1638 (Chatsworth, Lismore MS 19, no. 75).
[61] Ibid.
[62] Lynch, *Orrery*, pp 18–19.
[63] Grosart, *Lismore papers*, ser. 1, v, 78, 80.
[64] Little, 'Cork & Strafford', pp 622–3.
[65] Grosart, *Lismore papers*, ser. 1, v, 78–9.
[66] Ibid., ser. 2, iv, 14–15.
[67] Ibid., ser. 2,. v, 89.

his father at Stalbridge on 24 June, 'and brought hether the firste happie news that his Ma[jes]ty had concluded an honorable peace with the Scotts'.[68] Cork's optimistic view of the pacification of Berwick would not last long. By August 1639 the earl was in contact with such critics of the crown as the earls of Essex, Hertford and Bristol: all were present at a dinner-party held by Bristol at Sherborne Castle in Dorset, which Cork attended with Broghill and other members of the Boyle family resident at nearby Stalbridge.[69]

Despite his links with men who were becoming increasingly hostile to the Caroline regime, during 1639–40 Cork's interests still lay in appeasing the court, and in courting Wentworth. The Boyle household moved from Dorset to London on 1 October 1639, and took lodgings in the Savoy.[70] The immediate cause of the move to the capital was the imminent marriage between Francis Boyle and Elizabeth Killigrew, which was celebrated on 24 October; this was followed by Kinalmeaky's marriage to Elizabeth Feilding on 26 December.[71] Through his new sisters-in-law – both of whom were members of the queen's court – Broghill developed a passionate interest in Frances Harrison, daughter of Sir Richard Harrison, and 'one of the Queenes maydes of honor'.[72] By mid-January he was reported to have 'grown so settled in his love now that he will suffer nobody to be in company of his mistress but himself'.[73] This possessive attitude riled his rival suitors, who included Charles Rich, a Mr Neville, and Thomas Howard.[74] It was the last of these who challenged Broghill to a duel in the third week of January. According to Cork's (not entirely disapproving) account, Broghill 'was secretly called away by a messadge from Charles Riche, son to thearle of Warwick, to answer a challendge he brought him from Mr Tho. Howard, son of thearle of Barckshier'. Broghill quickly found a second, and met Howard in 'the ffeilds', where a bloodless fight took place, and 'their seconds parted them, and made them ffrends; and soe they came home, supped together; and all this for Mrs Harrison'.[75] This duel – which evidently took place between close associates, if not firm friends – reveals the aristocratic circles within which Broghill was now moving. Moreover, Charles Rich would soon become his brother-in-law (marrying Mary Boyle in July 1641), and Thomas Howard, the second son of the earl of Berkshire, was first cousin of Margaret Howard, the future

[68] Ibid., p. 96.

[69] Ibid., pp 104–5.

[70] Ibid., p. 111.

[71] Ibid., pp 112, 119.

[72] Cork to Isaac Marcombes, 18 Jan. 1640 (Chatsworth, Cork Letterbook II, f. 406).

[73] Cal. S.P. Dom., 1639–40, p. 365.

[74] E. A. Parry (ed.), Letters from Dorothy Osborne to Sir William Temple, 1652–4 (1903), pp 124–5.

[75] Grosart, Lismore papers, ser. 1, v, 121; see also Chatsworth, Cork Letterbook II, f. 406; and Cal. S.P. Dom., 1639–40, p. 365. The sources disagree as to the date of this incident, which may have taken place on 17 or 20 January.

Lady Broghill.[76] The Rich and Howard connexion, which clearly predated the 1641 marriages, would prove to be a recurring aspect of Broghill's later political career.

While Broghill was fretting – and fighting – over Mrs Harrison, his father was carefully putting into place the last stages of his reconciliation with Wentworth, who in January 1640 had at last received full, and public, support from the king, in the form of the earldom of Strafford and the lord lieutenancy of Ireland. Cork's dual ambitions – to appease Strafford and to please the king and queen – encouraged him to support the government in the unpopular second Bishops' War, through financial and political support in England and Ireland.[77] This situation promised to bring Broghill his first independent military command, through the patronage of his father's new friends, the earls of Strafford and Northumberland, who held high commands in the new army, and had strong ties with the queen at this time.[78] By 6 April, therefore, Broghill had been given command of a troop of 100 horse in the royal army.[79] Yet when the army mustered in the following summer, Broghill's troop was not on the payroll;[80] and its commander was still at Stalbridge, only moving to London with his father in July.[81] The probable explanation is that Cork had refused to pay for Broghill's troop. Mindful of the potential cost of such a venture (which had cost Dungarvan several thousand pounds in the previous year), the earl decided on a more economical way of supporting the king, and on 17 September 1640 – long after the end of the fighting – he noted that 'I have this day sent my son Broghill from Stalbridge towards Yorck, with one Thowsand pownds in gowld, to be by him presented to his Maty'.[82]

By the autumn of 1640 the earl of Cork's enthusiasm for the Caroline regime had started to cool, and he quickly re-established links with his old friends in Ireland, and the oppositionist peers in England, notably the earls of Bristol and Bedford. Broghill's marriage to Margaret Howard, solemnized on 27 January 1641, can be seen as the first public sign of the earl's shift of political allegiance. The match was not a financial venture: at his death in 1640, Margaret's father, the second earl of Suffolk, was close to bankruptcy,

---

[76] M. F. Keeler, *The Long Parliament, 1640–1641: a biographical study of its members* (Philadelphia, 1954), pp 223–4; this circle of young courtiers overlapped with those whom Broghill had known in France: see letters of Thomas Windebanke, 6 Jan. 1639 [n.s.] and 17 Feb. 1639 [n.s.] (P.R.O., S.P. 78/106, f. 402r, and S.P. 78/107, f. 60r) which suggest that the marriage of Mrs Harrison was also of great interest in Paris.

[77] Little, 'Cork & Strafford', pp 624–7.

[78] Morrice, *Memoirs*, p. 6; although Morrice mistakenly says this happened immediately after Broghill's return to England, there is no reason to question the other details.

[79] Grosart, *Lismore papers*, ser. 1, v, 133–4.

[80] Accounts of Sir William Uvedale, treasurer at wars, 1640 (P.R.O., E 351/293).

[81] Lynch, *Orrery*, p. 31.

[82] Grosart, *Lismore papers*, 1st ser. v, 159.

and his heir would have to sell estates to pay the marriage portion of £5,000.[83] Yet the financial instability of the Howards was more than matched by the value of their family connexions, which included such prominent opponents of the crown as Lord Howard of Escrick, the earl of Holland and (after the marriage of another Howard sister in 1642) the earl of Northumberland. Broghill and his wife were welcomed by their respective in-laws. Lady Broghill acted as godmother to the son of her new sister-in-law, Katherine Jones, in February 1641;[84] Suffolk sent Broghill a warrant to take a buck from his park at Audley End in May;[85] and Lady Broghill would accompany her husband and father-in-law when they returned to Ireland in September 1641.[86]

Like almost all other aspects of his early life, Broghill's marriage was arranged by his father, the earl of Cork. It reflected Cork's desire for political alliances with the opposition elements in the peerage, and his desire for matches for his children which were socially prestigious. As usual, Broghill had little option but to follow his father's lead – and that lead was very short. His childhood, foreign tour, courtly adventures and finally his marriage, were all dominated by his father. Others in the Boyle family had been prompted to rebel: Kinalmeaky became a drunken rake; the earl of Kildare lied and cheated to gain funds which he spent on parties in London; Mary Boyle had the temerity to marry for love, apparently without her father's consent. Even the compliant Dungarvan ran beyond his father's wishes by raising a horse troop without 'privitie'. Yet Broghill had never stepped out of line. His duel, like his love-affair, was not a serious matter, and he did not resist Cork's authority when it came to selecting a bride. Unlike his older (or bolder) siblings, he was willing to go along with his father's wishes, apparently to the letter. This may have been owing to lack of choice; but it may also reflect his basic agreement with Cork's approach to life. And the experience of rebellion and war in Ireland would soon draw father and son even closer together.

II

The Irish rebellion of 1641 came as a complete surprise to the Irish Protestants. The attempt on Dublin Castle, planned for the night of 22 October, was only foiled by an informer, and the simultaneous rising in Ulster caught many local settlers unprepared. Angered by the high-handed policies of Lord Deputy Wentworth, and fearful of the radical agenda of the lords justices who succeeded him, the Gaelic rebels at first intended to force the king to make

---

[83] Account of debts of second earl of Suffolk since June 1640 (C.U.L., Add. MS 7094, ff 7v, 11v); account of sale of Suffolk estates, 1641–6 (ibid., MS Ee.iii.25, ff 8v–9r).
[84] Grosart, *Lismore papers*, ser. 1, v, 169.
[85] Ibid., p. 175.
[86] Ibid., p. 195.

concessions; but the rising soon ran out of control.[87] The rapid spread of the rebellion laid bare the true instability of the country, which had long been disguised beneath the confidence of the Dublin administration and the complacency of the Irish Protestants. The Ulster rebels had moved south to threaten Drogheda by early November, but in the same month disturbances were reported further south, and Wicklow rose in rebellion. Connacht was only contained by the activities of the lord president of the province, Viscount Ranelagh, and the most influential Catholic landowner, the royalist earl of Clanricarde. In a move that shocked the government in Dublin, the Old English of the Pale defected in December, and rebellion broke out in the Old English strongholds of Tipperary and Limerick soon afterwards. Southern Munster remained quiet until the new year of 1642, but thereafter the Protestant settlers were forced back into the fortified towns of Cork, Bandon, Kinsale and Youghal.[88] The southern ports, along with Dublin, Drogheda, and a few areas in Connacht and Ulster, became the last refuges for Protestant families forced to flee from the violence of the Irish rebels.

The rising had a devastating affect on Broghill and his family. The earl of Cork and his entourage had arrived in Munster only a few days before rebellion broke out. In later years Broghill remembered this 'sudden storm of lightning and thunder', with its atrocities and savagery, and concluded that 'the con-tention between the two Parties in Ireland will never have an end', as a result of 'this implacable enmity of the Irish to the English'.[89] As Broghill hinted, the impact of war was mental as well as material. Cork's cherished policy of winning over the great aristocratic houses of Ireland, through conversion and intermarriage, and his confidence that Ireland might thereby be 'civilised', was shaken to its very foundations. The earl's wealth was based on his massive land holdings in Munster, mostly farmed by Old English and Gaelic tenants. Within a few months of its outbreak, the Irish rebellion had destroyed the wealth of the Boyles. The family's Munster estates had yielded an average of £1,937 in the first quarter of each year in the late 1630s, but in the first quarter of 1642 the rent collectors could only raise £16, less than one per cent of the peacetime income.[90] A similar problem affected other Munster landowners, and the ability of individuals to defend their own houses and castles, to put men into the field, and to service their existing debts, became dependent on irregular sources of income (for example, contracts for provisioning troops)

[87] For the early stages of the Irish rebellion see the essays in Brian Mac Cuarta (ed.), *Ulster 1641: aspects of the rising* (Belfast, 1993), and Michael Perceval-Maxwell, *The outbreak of the Irish rebellion of 1641* (Belfast, 1994).

[88] Aidan Clarke, *The Old English in Ireland* (Cornell, 1966), pp 160–5, 169–70, 180–6, 195, 197–9; Perceval-Maxwell, *Outbreak*, pp 257–9.

[89] Roger Boyle, *The Irish colours displayed* (1662), pp 2, 6.

[90] Raymond Gillespie, 'The Irish economy at war, 1641–52', in J. H. Ohlmeyer (ed.), *Ireland from independence to occupation, 1641–60* (Cambridge, 1995), p. 165; in this article Gillespie gives other examples of Protestant destitution in Munster.

and, more importantly, on military commissions which provided regular salaries (whether real or promised), which could then be borrowed against. The crisis thus put immense power into the hands of those authorised to grant military positions, especially the newly-appointed lord lieutenant, the earl of Leicester, the lieutenant-general, the earl of Ormond, and the lord president of Munster.[91]

The fact that the presidency was held by Sir William St Leger, a rival of the Boyles, proved extremely dangerous for Cork's family financially as well as politically. It was small wonder that the government of Munster became the focus for a bitter faction-fight, which dominated Boyle politics in England and Ireland throughout the 1640s. At first, the target for Boyle resentment was St Leger himself, whose influence in pre-1641 Munster had rivalled that of the Boyles. St Leger's allies included Sir Philip Percivalle and William Jephson (both neighbours of St Leger in north County Cork), Sir Hardress Waller of Castletown, County Limerick, and St Leger's son-in-law, the Gaelic but Protestant nobleman, Murrough O'Brien, Lord Inchiquin. St Leger had crossed swords with the earl of Cork on a number of minor issues during the 1630s, and the sense of ill-feeling between the two men continued in 1641.[92] At the start of the Irish rebellion St Leger had offered to settle his differences with Cork, so that a united front might be set against the Catholic Irish,[93] but it was not long before the two parties fell out once more, with military commissions and financial resources provoking much ill-feeling on both sides. In June 1642, at the height of this quarrel, Lord President St Leger fell ill and suddenly died. This did nothing to abate the feuding, however, for the presidency of Munster was now up for grabs. The ambitions of the Boyles in this regard had been anticipated by St Leger, who, on 14 June 1642, passed orders to 'intrust the management of the affairs of this province' to his son-in-law, Lord Inchiquin, and the existing council of war. The latter consisted of a mixture of established settlers and newly-arrived military men, all of whom were hostile (or at best lukewarm) to the Boyles.[94] This gave Inchiquin effective control of Munster affairs, and he set about pruning Boyle influence within the army in Munster.[95] The lords justices in Dublin, however, recognising the danger of alienating the earl of Cork, soon ordered a compromise, whereby

---

[91] For Ormond's activities before September 1643 see W. P. Kelly, 'The early career of James Butler, twelfth earl and first duke of Ormonde (1610–43), 1610–88' (unpublished Ph.D. thesis, Cambridge University, 1995); see also Edwards, *Ormond lordship*, pp 290–332.

[92] Canny, *Upstart earl*, p. 134; Perceval-Maxwell, *Outbreak*, pp 69, 156; Sir William Parsons to Cork, 14 Sept. 1641 (Chatsworth, Lismore MS 22, no. 63).

[93] St Leger to Cork, 7 Nov. 1641 (ibid., Lismore MS 22, no. 84).

[94] Inchiquin and others to William Lenthall, 14 June 1642 (Bodl., MS Carte 3, f. 259r); printed in James Hogan (ed.) *Letters and papers relating to the Irish rebellion* (Dublin, 1936), p. 42.

[95] Barrymore to Inchiquin and Vavasour, 24 June 1642 (Chatsworth, Lismore MS 23, no. 87).

military affairs would remain in Inchiquin's hands, but he had to share the civilian government with Cork's son-in-law, the earl of Barrymore.[96]

The power-sharing exercise did little more than paper over the factional cracks which hampered resistance against the Catholic Irish in Munster; and although the Protestants came together to defeat the Confederate forces at Liscarroll in September 1642, the victory created further tensions, for, at the close of the day, the earl of Barrymore lay mortally wounded. With Barrymore dead, control of civilian as well as military affairs in Munster devolved to Inchiquin. Although Inchiquin wrote to Ormond in late September denying that he had any 'Ambitions of Governing alone here',[97] Cork for one suspected that Inchiquin was now close to securing the Munster presidency for himself. In response he delivered a blistering attack against Inchiquin's probity, on 8 October 1642 instituting an investigation which alleged that Inchiquin had colluded with the Confederate general, Viscount Muskerry, in gaining the return of intercepted letters to parliament which libelled Cork himself.[98] Inchiquin was quick to draw the connexion between this new attack and his appointment as governor: five days later he told Ormond that he feared his appointment 'will turne to my disadvantage & dishonor' as the lords justices in Dublin had withdrawn financial assistance from Munster, and 'that [is] all the reparation I am lyke to have, for the greate skornes and many affronts put on me by the Earle of Cork'.[99] By the end of October 1642 it was clear that whoever secured the presidency would first use it as a tool to destroy the rival faction. This brought an escalation which soon involved Westminster factions as well as the parties in Munster.

Once again, Broghill's part in the early months of the Irish rebellion cannot be separated from the wider policies and activities of his father. In military terms, he acted as the earl of Cork's subordinate as commander of the garrison at Lismore Castle, where he remained from December 1641 until November 1642, except for occasional involvement in joint operations, such as the Liscarroll campaign in September 1642.[100] Broghill's abilities as a soldier soon showed themselves. Hearing of a Catholic advance against Lismore in January 1642, he told Cork that he would ride out to meet them in the field 'if I am a third part of the[i]r number', but in any case his father was to 'feare nothing for Lismoore, for if it be lost it shall be with the Life of him that begs y[ou]r L[ordshi]ps blessings'.[101] These were no empty words of bravado. Broghill's valiant defence of the castle against Viscount Mountgarrett, who finally arrived before the gates in February 1642, was widely celebrated, not least for his

[96] Inchiquin to Ormond, 5 Aug. 1642 (Bodl., MS Carte 3, f. 398r–v).
[97] Same to same, 30 Sept. 1642 (ibid., f. 539v: 30 Sept. 1642).
[98] Examination of John Teige, 8 Oct. 1642 (Chatsworth, Lismore MS 23, no. 137).
[99] Inchiquin to Ormond, 13 Oct. 1642 (Bodl., MS Carte 3, f. 562r).
[100] Cork's accounts, 1641–5 (N.L.I., MS 6900, unfol.), entries for 12, 27 Dec. 1641, 6, 28, 29 Jan., 6 Feb., 4 June, 25, 31 Oct., 14 Nov. 1642.
[101] Broghill to Cork, 11 Jan. 1642 (Bodl., MS Carte 2, f. 284v).

defiance when summoned to surrender: 'the L[or]d of Broghell tould him [the envoy] that he knew not w[ha]t q[ua]rter meant & had them begin their assault when they would for he was ready for them'.[102] Although the threat of reinforcements forced the Catholics to retreat without attacking the castle three days later, the siege was not without personal loss for Broghill, whose wife was 'brought abedd of a child' during this time. The baby, 'a little son', died soon afterwards.[103]

Politically, Broghill was still little more than a foot soldier in his father's interest, and his own individual concerns, especially for military commissions, soon became incorporated into the wider struggle against St Leger and Inchiquin. Cork had pressed for Broghill to be given an official command (and to be paid, or at least have the promise of payment, by the government), but the matter had been put off by St Leger, and the desired commission was only granted at the end of June 1642.[104] In the meantime, Broghill was dependent on Cork as owner of Lismore and as paymaster for the troops there, and he naturally took orders from his father rather than from St Leger or Inchiquin. On 1 June 1642, for example, he promised not to react to news of enemy troop movements without his father's permission, saying that 'I will obay y[ou]r L[or]ds command, for noe Portent shall make me stirr without y[ou]r permission',[105] and later in the month he argued that once Youghal had been secured, the priority of Cork's troops in the area should be 'the gardinge of y[ou]r o[w]ne Plantations'.[106] As a soldier, Broghill was correspondingly critical of St Leger, whose 'necessity constraines us to give quarter to such peddelinge Castels, but we must never expect to doe any good upon the Rebels, till we march in two or three severall bodies'.[107] Inchiquin also came in for criticism, for his refusal to garrison Cappoquin (which commanded the River Blackwater between Lismore and Youghal): 'if it had bin left destitute as my Lo[rd] Inchequins wisdome desired, it would have bin the Ruin of this Co[u]ntry and in time the starvinge of yoghill'.[108] As he was bound by his membership of Boyle family, and by his duty to a father who doubled as a military superior, such comments in Broghill's correspondence with the earl of Cork may reflect a desire to please rather than his own, privately-held opinions. But the importance of this period for Broghill's political career later in the 1640s cannot be overstated: for, in the factional turmoil of Munster in 1641–2, the seeds of his later rivalry with Lord Inchiquin were sown.

---

[102] B.L., Sloane MS 1008, f. 61r.
[103] Fitzpatrick, *Waterford*, pp 123–4; *Boyle's correspondence*, i, 23.
[104] Cork to St Leger, 30 Jan. 1642 (Chatsworth, Lismore MS 22, no. 143); Broghill to Cork, 20 June 1642 (ibid., Lismore MS 23, no. 83).
[105] Broghill to Cork, 1 June 1642 (ibid., no. 62).
[106] Same to same, 26 June 1642 (ibid., no. 94).
[107] Same to same, 14 June 1642 (ibid., no. 78).
[108] Same to same, 26 June 1642 (ibid., no. 94).

III

In the winter of 1642–3, Broghill slowly began to emerge as a political player in his own right. On 16 November 1642, at the height of the row with Inchiquin over Muskerry, the earl of Cork sent Dungarvan and Broghill to lobby the English parliament. The journey may have been occasioned by Dungarvan's duty to return to Westminster, where he was M.P. for Appleby in Cumberland, but the primary mission of the brothers during the winter of 1642–3 was factional in nature: to discredit Inchiquin, and, if possible, to gain the presidency of Munster for Dungarvan.[109] Yet it soon became apparent that this factional squabbling was destined to be a mere side-show to the more pressing problem of gaining proper support from politicians in England for the Irish war in general. By signing the Adventurers' Act of April 1642, Charles I had allowed parliament to take executive control of the Irish war, raising money for the struggle by selling the lands of Irish rebels to English investors.[110] But the act, which had promised so much, had been subverted by the outbreak of civil war in England, and the men and supplies intended for Ireland diverted into the English war effort. As Inchiquin complained in December 1642, the English were 'soe involv'd in theyr owne danger that a word of Ireland will not be heard'.[111] The peace negotiations between king and parliament, which took place at Oxford during the first few months of 1643, raised hopes in Ireland that an English settlement would allow a united front against the Irish rebels.

The Boyle brothers were involved in these negotiations, and Dungarvan served as a representative of the commons in the parliamentary commission sent to Oxford to deal with the king in January 1643. The breakdown of these peace talks in April 1643 was a disaster for the Irish Protestant cause. Not only did failure reactivate the war in England; it also legitimised Charles I's efforts to strike a deal with the Irish rebels, in order to release Irish royalists for service in England (a plan which had been common knowledge since February 1643). The only hope lay in persuading the king to modify his policies, and accept parliament's claim (under the Adventurers' Act) to conduct the Irish war alone. In late April, therefore, there was a rush of Irish Protestants from Westminster to Oxford, where they attended the king and the lord lieutenant, the earl of Leicester.[112] Cork's friend, Viscount Ranelagh (now lord president of Connacht), attended the court at Oxford at this time, as did Inchiquin's

---

[109] Patrick Little, 'The political career of Roger Boyle, Lord Broghill, 1636–60 (unpublished Ph.D. thesis, London University 2000), pp 49–51.

[110] For the Adventurers' Act, see K. S. Bottigheimer, *English money and Irish land: the 'adventurers' in the Cromwellian settlement of Ireland* (Oxford, 1971).

[111] Inchiquin to Ormond, received 6 Dec. 1642 (Bodl., MS Carte 4, f. 83r).

[112] Robert Armstrong, 'Protestant Ireland and the English parliament, 1641–1647' (unpublished Ph.D. thesis, Trinity College Dublin, 1995), pp 87–98.

envoy, Sir Hardress Waller.[113] On 22 April an official parliamentary delegation, led by Sir Robert King, William Jephson and Colonel Arthur Hill was sent to Oxford,[114] in the hope that the king would give his official consent to an act to raise more money from the adventurers for a renewed expedition against the Confederates.[115] On 24 April Dungarvan was also given leave to travel to Oxford before returning to his father in Ireland.[116] Dungarvan, accompained by Broghill, had set out by mid-May, when Henry Croone wrote to the earl of Cork from London that 'for the newes in England I refer you to the Relation of the Ho[noura]ble Lord Broughall, whom I pray god send in Safety to yo[u]r honor'.[117]

Whatever the initial plan had been, Dungarvan and Broghill did not return to Ireland immediately, but stayed in Oxford for the whole of the summer, returning to Munster only in July 1643.[118] Although their activities at this time are irritatingly obscure, a later report made by Lord Inchiquin suggests that the Boyle brothers may have played an important part in bringing Munster into the Irish cessation of arms – the truce between the king and the Irish Confederates, intended to allow Protestant troops to reinforce the royalist war-effort in England, signed in September 1643. In June 1644 Inchiquin told Ormond that, in the previous July, the second earl of Cork (as Dungarvan had become) had returned to Ireland, and 'brought me his Ma[jes]tie l[ette]re willinge me to give Creditt to his relacon Importinge what he thought not fitt to write by reason of the danger of intercepcon'. Inchiquin added that 'My lord [Dungarvan] did then let me knowe that it was his Ma[jes]ties pleasure that I should contribute all the assistance I could to the forwardinge of the cessation, whereuppon I sent pr[e]sentlie to my Lord of Muskerie [Muskerry] to desire a conference wth hym before the Lords Broghill and Corke [i.e. Dungarvan]'.[119] The implication of this later report is that Dungarvan and Broghill acted as confidential (and trusted) messengers from the king to Inchiquin. Their role may have reflected a deep sense of despair within the Protestant community that the king and parliament would ever settle their differences; it certainly showed them taking a very different line to that of their father, who was vehemently opposed to dealing with the Catholic Irish.[120]

---

[113] Lord Ranelagh to Ormond, 24 Apr. 1643 (Bodl., MS Carte 5, f. 165r).

[114] C.J. iii, 57.

[115] John Rushworth, *Historical collections of private passages of state* (7 vols, 1721), v, 318; L.J. vi, 35. Charles's ambiguous refusal of 5 May drove Jephson, King and other Irish Protestants into the parliamentarian camp. See also Armstrong, 'Protestant Ireland', p. 97, Bottigheimer, *English money and Irish land*, p. 85.

[116] C.J. iii, 57.

[117] Henry Croone to Cork, 16 May 1643 (Chatsworth, Lismore MS 24, no. 26).

[118] Grosart, *Lismore papers*, ser. 1, v, 230.

[119] Paper enclosed in Inchiquin to Ormond, 13 June 1644 (Bodl., MS Carte 11, f. 242r).

[120] J. A. Murphy, 'The politics of the Munster Protestants, 1641–9', *J.C.H.A.S.*, lxxvi (1971), p. 9.

Indeed, it may not have been a coincidence that the cessation of arms was signed by Dungarvan, Inchiquin and others on 15 September 1643 – the very day that the great earl died.

IV

The first earl of Cork's death was bound to have a profound affect on Lord Broghill. For twenty-two years he had lived under his father's thumb. His up-bringing, education, marriage and experience in the wars were not independent actions: they formed only a small part of a greater plan, formulated and carried out by his father. The only time when Broghill deviated from this was in the summer of 1643 when he and Dungarvan were drawn into the negotiations which surrounded the cessation of arms. Cork's evident dismay at this attempt to make peace with the hated Catholic rebels, orchestrated by his long-standing enemy, the earl of Ormond, was palpable; and it may even have been the cause of his death. The old man's death certainly contributed to the increasing distance between Broghill and his elder brother, Viscount Dungarvan (who succeeded his father as second earl of Cork) over the next few months. Both brothers could claim to hold true to their father's memory. The second earl went over to the royal court at Oxford, where he renewed his allegiance to the king, and conducted a vigorous campaign to prevent the Boyles' rival in Munster, Lord Inchiquin, from gaining the presidency of the province. In this he was very successful; so much so that Inchiquin, who had also travelled to England, returned to Ireland in February 1644 empty handed, and 'as full of anger as his buttons will endure'.[121] In continuing the feud with Inchiquin, and in remaining loyal to the crown, the second earl could be seen as following in his father's footsteps. Yet Broghill, who remained in Munster, also followed his father, but in different ways. During the early months of 1644 he became increasingly disillusioned with the cessation of arms, which seemed to be a Catholic plot to leach strength from the Protestant garrisons while they negotiated a permanent peace with the king.

The ethical problem of conducting a truce with Catholic rebels was compounded by the knowledge that the further negotiations were being led by the new lord lieutenant, the now marquess of Ormond, whose motives were deeply suspect, not least because of the importance of his Catholic relatives (including Viscounts Mountgarrett and Muskerry) in the counsels of the Confederation. Broghill was in contact with Ormond's enemies in Dublin by the spring of 1644, a group which included his father's old allies from the 'Boyle group', Sir William Parsons and Sir Adam Loftus, both of whom had been imprisoned by Ormond for refusing to countenance the cessation. Indeed, Loftus's son, Sir Arthur Loftus, may have been instrumental in turning Broghill

---

[121] Arthur Trevor to Ormond, 19 Feb. 1644 (Bodl., MS Carte 9, f. 243r).

against the royalist cause in the summer of 1644.[122] In opposing the Catholics and Ormond, and in strengthening his links with the old Boyle group, Broghill's stance was at one with that of his father in the previous decades. The only problem was that, in siding with parliament, Broghill could no longer share his father's sense of duty to the crown; and, in the short term at least, becoming a parliamentarian meant throwing in his lot with the Boyle rival in Munster, Lord Inchiquin, whose plan to defect to parliament was put into dramatic effect in July of that year.

Broghill's dilemma in the spring of 1644 highlights the impossibility of maintaining the first earl of Cork's integrated world-view during the upheavals of the Irish rebellion. The old certainties of the 1620s and 1630s, which had allowed this integration, this consistency of thought, had gone. Instead, Broghill had to carve out a new position, dropping some elements, and retaining the most important. Broghill's choice, to stick to the Protestant interest in Munster, and seek aid from England, while opposing the Catholic threat with all his might, reflects his earlier record of agreeing with his father over fundamentals. The first earl of Cork's career was founded on his Calvinist beliefs and the harsh policies which they necessitated in the Irish context. In 1644 Broghill's decision to join parliament was motivated by similar principles. As the 1640s continued, Broghill's views increasingly centred on Protestantism, and with it on a closer relationship between Ireland and England – both important parts of the political agenda developed by Cork and his friends twenty years before. In the circumstances, it was no surprise that his most important allies later in the decade were the very men that had been so closely associated with the earl and his 'Boyle group' in earlier decades; nor that his increasingly radical political agenda was firmly rooted in the policies advocated by this group over a decade before.

---

[122] The two were in close contact in April 1644: see note by William Roberts, 10 Apr. 1644 (Petworth House, MS 13192, unfol.); also Cork's accounts, 1641–5 (N.L.I., MS 6900, unfol.), entry for 16 Apr. 1644. In early June Loftus declared his hand, saying publicly that Ormond would soon 'turne to the Rebbells': see Robert Moulton to Ormond, 9 June 1644 (Bodl., MS Carte 11, f. 161r).

2

The rise of the Irish Independents, 1644–9

The defection of the Munster Protestants under Lord Inchiquin's command was announced by a 'unanimous declaration' of 17 July 1644. This uncompromising document denounced the Catholics as plotting for 'a generall extirpation, both of the Protestants and their Religion', and justified the Protestants' own desertion of the king with reference to the 1642 Adventurers' Act, in which Charles I had promised not to make peace with the Irish without parliament's approval.[1] The declaration was dispatched to the king, parliament and the committee of both kingdoms, and an explanation was sent to the king's lord lieutenant, the marquess of Ormond, at the same time.[2] On 26 July the governors of Cork, Youghal and Kinsale expelled the Catholic inhabitants in a coordinated action, to pre-empt any 'treachery' after the towns had been taken into parliament's hands.[3] Once the cessation had been revoked, the Munster Protestants could expect no further supplies from an Irish-dominated Munster, and they soon looked for help from England.

Broghill was fully committed to the July defection. A signatory of the initial declaration, he issued orders, as governor of Youghal, to effect the expulsions in that town.[4] He also made a point of publicly severing his political ties with his elder brother, the royalist second earl of Cork. As early as 10 July, Broghill went to Lismore and forced Cork's steward, John Walley, to pay him £500 on Inchiquin's warrant, 'for the pressent releefe of the garrisons upon the intelligence of a great mischiefe intended to breake owt'.[5] On 22 July, John Langton, Cork's receiver in Bandon, was ordered to deliver all the earl's rents to the Munster government. Langton refused, but was astonished to discover 'that my Lorde of Brahill was one of the Councell of warr & did consent thereunto'.[6] In August and September Broghill again raided his brother's

[1] Declaration of Munster Protestants [17 July 1644] (B.L., Add. MS 25287, ff 4v–5v).
[2] Munster Protestants to parliament and Ormond, n.d. (B.L., Add. MS 25287, ff 7r–v, 8v); Cal. S.P. Dom., 1644, p. 357; Inchiquin and others to Ormond, 17 July 1644 (Bodl., MS Carte 11, ff 491r–2r).
[3] J. A. Murphy, 'The expulsion of the Irish from Cork in 1644', J.C.H.A.S., lxix (1964), pp 123–31.
[4] Proclamation, 26 July 1644 (B.L., Add. MS 25287, f. 13r).
[5] Cork's accounts, 1641–5 (N.L.I., MS 6900, unfol.), entry for 10 July 1644.
[6] Langton to John Walley, 22 July 1644 (Chatsworth, Lismore MS 28, no. 3).

reserves at Lismore, reducing the amount in Walley's hands to just £5 10s. by 13 September 1644.[7] Broghill was eager to assert his commitment to the Protestant cause, and it seems to have been this religious motive, as well as his experience of the failure of the local cessation in Munster, that lay behind his decision to break with his elder brother and join Inchiquin's defection. Broghill's role in the government of the port town of Youghal in the following months seems to confirm this: after the expulsions, Broghill ruled the town by decree, readying the townsmen in arms (27 July), organising work-parties to strengthen the defences (17 August), renting out Irish property in the town (17 August), making provision for poor relief (31 August), and regulating the soldiery (30 October, 8 November).[8] In November, Broghill issued a proclamation ordering all the officers and soldiers of Youghal to attend church services and sermons, and to observe fast days. Under Broghill's command, Youghal would become a renowned puritan bulwark against Irish popery.[9]

Broghill's religious zeal no doubt helped to secure him a favourable reception when he travelled to Westminster in the winter of 1644–5, leaving his uncle, Sir William Fenton, in charge of Youghal.[10] He attended parliament's main executive committee, the committee of both kingdoms, in December, and presented propositions to its Irish sub-committee, which had taken over effective management of Irish affairs earlier in the year.[11] By January 1645 Broghill had gained the committee's support for two important appointments: the presidency of Munster for Inchiquin, and the generalship of the Munster horse for himself.[12] Broghill's apparent sponsorship of Inchiquin for the position that his father and elder brother had coveted for so many years again shows how far he had distanced himself from his family's former factionalism at this time, and how far he pinned his hopes on parliament's intervention to turn the tide against the Catholic Confederates in Munster. On his return to County Cork at the end of January, Broghill brought £10,000, urgent supplies, and the promise of 2,000 reinforcements from Ulster.[13] The success of his mission – which provided a lifeline to a province long starved of funds – reveals the extent of his credit among the parliamentarian stalwarts on the committee of both kingdoms.

Yet soon after Broghill's return to Munster, the vulnerable state of the Protestant garrisons was again displayed, as the Confederate Catholics suddenly attacked Duncannon fort, which guarded the approaches to the city

---

[7] Cork's accounts, 1641–5 (N.L.I., MS 6900, unfol.), entries for 9 Aug., 2 Sept., 13 Sept. 1644.

[8] B.L., Add. MS 25287, ff 13v, 15r, 15v–16r, 16v, 19v, 20v.

[9] Proclamation, 8 Nov. 1644 (ibid., f. 20r); see below, ch. 9.

[10] Ibid., f. 23r.

[11] K. S. Bottigheimer, *English money and Irish land: the 'adventurers' in the Cromwellian settlement of Ireland* (Oxford, 1971), pp 87–8.

[12] *Cal. S.P. Dom., 1644–5*, pp 171, 172, 237, 245, 251, 271–2.

[13] Lynch, *Orrery*, p. 52.

of Waterford by sea. Duncannon fell on 18 March 1645, after a desperate ten-week siege, and the Confederate general, the earl of Castlehaven, immediately sent forces west, into Counties Waterford and Cork.[14] The outlying castles fell one by one: the Boyle seat of Lismore Castle was taken on 26 June; and Castlehaven's troops were before Youghal a few days later.[15] Broghill's reaction to these reverses shows that he remained confident of English interven-tion. In early June, as the threat to Youghal grew, he left command of the town in the hands of his kinsman, Sir Percy Smyth, and travelled to England in person. As Smyth told Sir Philip Percivalle, Broghill's trip was full of urgency: 'he now comes to take his farewell of England; I mean, with a resolution never to implore more aid if not now cheerfully relieved'.[16] Using his connexions with leading English politicians (almost certainly including his wife's kins-man, the earl of Northumberland)[17] as well as with the Irish Protestants who had taken refuge in London, Broghill was again successful in securing much-needed supplies, which he brought to the relief of Youghal in September 1645.[18] Broghill's shipment, and the subsequent efforts of the new committee of Irish affairs, were vital in ensuring the survival of the Munster towns until the Castlehaven threat had receded. In 1645 Broghill gave every impression of being a loyal lieutenant to the new president of Munster, Lord Inchiquin.

I

As we have seen, Broghill's support of Inchiquin – even to the extent of securing the presidency of Munster for him – was a radical departure from his father's policy in the region. But it was to prove merely a temporary expedient, and long before the relief of Youghal relations between the two men were becoming strained. Indeed, the old factional fissures, which seemed to have closed after the 'unanimous declaration' of July 1644, had reopened before the year was out, as Broghill came to distrust the president's motives, and question

---

[14] J. T. Gilbert (ed.), *History of the Irish Confederation and the war in Ireland, 1641–3* . . . (7 vols, Dublin, 1882–91), iv, 184, 204.
[15] James Touchet, *The earl of Castlehaven's memoirs* (Dublin, 1815), pp 76–88, is an account of the campaign; Castlehaven's summonses to the castles of Cappoquin, Mogeely and Temple Michael, Apr.–June 1645 (B.L., Add. MS 25287, ff 29v, 30r–v).
[16] *H.M.C. Egmont*, i, 257.
[17] Broghill to Northumberland, n.d. [c.17 July 1644](B.L., Add. MS 25287, f. 32v). This letter, which asked Northumberland to 'imploy yor power for that speedy relief w[hi]ch wee humbly desire' can be dated by internal evidence and comparison with ibid., ff 8v and 27r–v. Broghill was certainly in contact with Northumberland in 1645: see *H.M.C. Egmont*, i, 453.
[18] *Cal. S.P. Ire. 1633–47*, p. 435; Robert Armstrong, 'Protestant Ireland and the English parliament, 1641–1647' (unpublished Ph.D. thesis, Trinity College Dublin, 1995), pp 194–5.

his attachment to the Protestant cause. There were three points of conflict: Inchiquin's equivocal relationship with Ormond and the Irish rebels; the related question of allegiance, which centred on the parliament's newly imposed Solemn League and Covenant; and the rise of a distinct party, with a radical political and religious agenda, among the Irish Protestants, which soon became associated with the radical Independent faction in the English parliament.[19]

Broghill's behaviour in 1644 and 1645 was entirely consistent with his support of parliament and his rejection of the cessation of arms. Inchiquin's attitude was more ambiguous. The root of the problem was parliament's delay in sending proper supplies and reinforcements to Munster, as this forced Inchiquin to reopen links with both the royalists led by Ormond and the Confederate Irish, in an attempt to prevent an immediate attack on the parliamentarian garrisons. Barely two months after the dramatic defection of the Munster forces, Inchiquin was keen to be again included under the terms of the renewed cessation agreed by Ormond and the Confederates on 5 September 1644,[20] and he was prepared to extend this temporary truce 'if the Irish desire it'.[21] Ormond seems to have acted as broker in Inchiquin's efforts to form a truce with the Irish. In early November the lord lieutenant asked the confederation at Kilkenny to sanction regular communication between him and Inchiquin, by 'footman express'.[22] The Irish refused, as 'The [Confederate] Councell beleeves hee [Inchiquin] sollicitts to be admitted to enjoy the benefitt of the Cessacion', while still seeking military aid from parliament.[23] Despite official objections, the Irish commander in Munster, Viscount Muskerry (who was Ormond's brother-in-law), had made a deal with Inchiquin by Christmas 1644, agreeing to observe 'a fair quarter and correspondency' until 1 February 1645.[24] This local cessation was extended across the whole of County Cork, until the earl of Castlehaven launched his attack on the southern garrisons a few weeks later.[25]

Even then, Inchiquin's response to the renewal of hostilities was not to affirm his commitment to parliament; instead, he redoubled his efforts to court the royalists and the Irish Confederates, apparently in an attempt to halt the

---

[19] For the complexities of Irish politics in the mid-1640s see Micheál Ó Siochrú, *Confederate Ireland, 1642–1649: a constitutional and political analysis* (Dublin, 1999); Robert Armstrong, 'Ormond, the Confederate peace talks and Protestant royalism' in Micheál Ó Siochrú (ed.), *Kingdoms in crisis: Ireland in the 1640s* (Dublin, 2001), pp 122–40; Patrick Little, 'The marquess of Ormond and the English parliament, 1645–1647' in Toby Barnard and Jane Fenlon (eds), *The dukes of Ormonde, 1610–1745* (Woodbridge, 2000), pp 83–99.

[20] Gilbert, *Confederation*, iii, 273–5.

[21] H.M.C. *Egmont*, i, 236.

[22] Gilbert, *Confederation*, iv, 41.

[23] Ibid., pp 42–3.

[24] H.M.C. *Egmont*, i, 242.

[25] Ibid., pp 243–8.

new offensive. In April Inchiquin made approaches to Castlehaven, begging him 'to spare Doneriale [Doneraile, the seat of his relatives, the St Legers], and other houses and castles not tenable'.[26] Such embassies (and the vacillation which lay behind them) encouraged the Confederates to push for the voluntary surrender of the Cork garrisons, giving Castlehaven authority on 7 April 'to passe our publique ffaith, unto all and every of his Ma[jes]ties said Protestant subjects in the said province, who will take the annexed oath'.[27] By mid-May, the influential English courtier, George, Lord Digby, was optimistic of winning Inchiquin back to the king's side, and instructed Ormond to broach the subject, for 'It weare A happy service if any allurements could regaine him, And if the Presidentship of Munster will doe it, And that yo[u]r Exce[llency] think it fitt, yow may assure him of it'.[28] Other evidence also suggests that Inchiquin was ready to begin negotiations with Ormond in the summer of 1645. Using his brother-in-law, Dean Michael Boyle, as a go-between, Inchiquin made contact with the bishop of Cloyne at Dublin, and indicated his willingness to make peace if it could be done with honour and safety, both for himself and the Protestant interest.[29] The timing of these discussions, which coincided with negotiations between the king's envoy, the earl of Glamorgan, and the Confederates (concluded on 25 August 1645), makes them all the more suspicious.[30] Although Inchiquin's approaches to Ormond's friends came to nothing, the mere fact that parliament's lord president of Munster was prepared to discuss unilateral deals with the king's lord lieutenant reveals the ideological distance that had grown between Inchiquin and that convinced parliamentarian, Lord Broghill, by the autumn of 1645.

Worse still, Inchiquin's efforts, first to include the Munster garrisons in the renewed cessation from September 1644, and then to negotiate a peace deal with the Ormondists (and probably the Irish) in the summer of 1645, cut across Broghill's efforts to secure military and financial aid from parliament. Indeed, it may not be a coincidence that Inchiquin was most active in this respect while Broghill was out of the province, in England in the winter of 1644–5 and in the late summer of 1645. Moreover, far from sharing Inchiquin's trust in Ormond as a broker, in late 1645 Broghill denounced the king's lord lieutenant, saying that 'My Lord Ormonde has now declared himself so publicly for the rogues that I wonder he sticks at anything henceforward that may advantage them'.[31]

---

[26] Touchet, *Castlehaven memoirs*, p. 79.

[27] Confederate oath, 7 Apr. 1645 (B.L., Add. 25287, ff. 31v–2r).

[28] Lord Digby to Ormond, 13 May 1645 (Bodl., MS Carte 14, f. 525r).

[29] Patrick Little, 'The political career of Roger Boyle, Lord Broghill, 1636–1660' (unpublished Ph.D. thesis, London University, 2000), pp 63–4.

[30] T. W. Moody, F. X. Martin and F. J. Byrne (eds), *A new history of Ireland*, iii: *Early modern Ireland, 1534–1691* (Oxford, 1978), pp 315–16.

[31] H.M.C. *Egmont*, i, 266.

The growing differences between Inchiquin and Broghill were to emerge still more clearly in a particular issue which became a test of allegiance for both king and parliament: the subscription of the Solemn League and Covenant, agreed by parliament and their Scottish allies in September 1643. Michael Perceval-Maxwell has shown that the significance of the covenant in Ireland differed greatly from its importance in Scotland and England. The Ulster Scots delayed their adherence to the document until April 1644, but from then it became compulsory in Ulster among British and Scottish forces alike, 'not from a desire to see religious unity in the three kingdoms, but from a perception of the Covenant as a means of survival against the Irish' by harnessing 'the power of Scotland'. It also became the ultimate test of loyalty to the English parliament and their Scottish allies, and thus a sticking-point for royalists. This led to a series of confrontations between the Ulster garrisons eager to affirm their support for the Protestant cause, and their royalist commanders, who refused to commit themselves by signing the covenant.[32] A similar problem would soon afflict Munster.

Soon after the July 1644 defection, Inchiquin and Broghill had become publicly divided by their attitude to the covenant. Broghill, eager to hasten military aid from England,[33] imposed the covenant on the garrison at Youghal in August, and took the oath himself. This unilateral act threatened to upset the delicate negotiations of Inchiquin, who hoped to maintain good relations with the Irish and the royalists: on 26 August he issued a declaration stating that, although the Youghal commanders had subscribed to the covenant, he was 'very sorry for theyre rashnes in soe doeinge', and 'for his parte heere hee would not take the Covenant untill the Cessacon bee out'.[34] Although Inchiquin's circumspection was perhaps essential in keeping the Irish forces from assaulting the weak Munster garrisons, Broghill was also right to fear that parliament would not send support without proof of loyalty: some ships did reach Cork in late August 1644, but, as Inchiquin admitted, 'their coming hither is now chiefly to see in what condition we are in and how disposed'.[35]

As the autumn of 1644 progressed, parliament became increasingly concerned about the true allegiances of its Protestant forces in Ireland. On 21 October the committee of both kingdoms ordered that all officers in Ireland must take the covenant.[36] In early November, parliament sent an Independent divine, Sidrach Simpson, to investigate the loyalty of Inchiquin and his

---

[32] Michael Perceval-Maxwell, 'Ireland and Scotland 1638–1648' in John Morrill (ed.), *The Scottish National Covenant in its British context, 1638–51* (Edinburgh, 1990), p. 204.

[33] Broghill and his allies claimed that 'unless they had taken that Covenante . . . the Parliament would not helpe them': declaration of Inchiquin, 26 Aug. 1644 (Bodl., MS Carte 12, f. 192r).

[34] Ibid.

[35] H.M.C. *Egmont*, i, 235–6.

[36] *Cal. S.P. Dom., 1644–5*, p. 61.

officers. Simpson arrived in the midst of Inchiquin's attempts to deal with the Irish through Ormond, but the Munster president somehow managed to convince parliament's agent of his acceptance of the covenant and his willingness to impose it on his men.[37] In his subsequent dealings with Ormond, of course, Inchiquin gave the impression that no such undertaking had been made by the Munster Protestants.[38] Parliament's suspicions were again aroused in the spring of 1645, and on 22 April the committee of both kingdoms ordered the committee for examinations to investigate which Irish officers had taken the covenant.[39] Two days later, a list of 'those who have subscribed the covenant' was drawn up, which included Broghill, his kinsmen Sir Arthur Loftus and Sir Percy Smyth, and other Munster officers. Significantly, Inchiquin's name did not appear.[40] The suspicions of the committee of both kingdoms were apparently confirmed by revelations in the summer of 1645: Digby's letter to Ormond (of 20 March), expressing hope that Inchiquin could be won over to the king's side, was intercepted by parliament's forces, and made public in July.[41] As Inchiquin's ally, Sir Philip Percivalle discovered in November, money had been voted for Munster, 'yett there is noe creditt to be had there uppon (for reasons that you knowe) nor such perticuler care had of them as you would wish'.[42] Thus, at the very time that Inchiquin most needed outside support against the Confederates, parliament had become increasingly unwilling to send money or men to Munster. The only supplies to reach Munster in the second half of 1645 were through Broghill's personal intervention. Once the contacts between Inchiquin and Ormond had become known, his refusal of the covenant became more suspicious, and this cannot have helped relations between the president of Munster and his subordinate, Lord Broghill.

The situation in Ireland in the later 1640s was further complicated by the growth of factional divisions within the Irish Protestant community which echoed those emerging in the English parliament. The formation of the committee of both kingdoms in February 1644 was more than an attempt to coordinate the English and Scottish war effort: it was also a thinly-veiled attack on parliament's captain-general, the earl of Essex, whose handling of the war in England had been repeatedly called into question since the end of 1642. This attack broke apart the uneasy alliance fostered by John Pym and others of the 'middle group' in parliament, and brought divisions which would later produce two distinct parties at Westminster: the Presbyterians, who favoured early negotiation and compromise with the king, and the Independents, who

---

[37] *Three severall letters of great importance*, 6 Dec. 1644 (B.L., E.21(6)), p. 6.

[38] Gilbert, *Confederation*, iv, 49–50.

[39] *Cal. S.P. Dom.*, 1644–5, p. 425.

[40] Certificate of committee for examinations, 24 Apr. 1645 (Bodl., MS Carte 14, f. 425r). The survival of this list in Ormond's papers again shows how far the covenant had also become a negative test of royalist allegiance.

[41] *H.M.C. Egmont*, i, 248; *C.J.*, iv, 191.

[42] Percivalle to Sir Robert King, 20 Nov. 1645 (B.L., Add. MS 46929, f. 46r).

would only negotiate from a position of strength, once the war was won.[43] The committee of both kingdoms was controlled by future Independents, led by the younger Sir Henry Vane and Oliver St John in the commons, and Viscount Saye, the earl of Northumberland and their allies in the lords. Against this caucus, a group formed around Essex, which included his allies in the commons, Denzell Holles and Sir Philip Stapilton, and the earls of Warwick and Holland, amongst others, in the lords. These men would form the nucleus of the Presbyterian party in later years.

The make-up of these factions had important implications for Ireland.[44] The Presbyterians favoured a 'British' solution, which would include Ormondists and Scots as well as English forces. This was in part a personal decision. Essex's half-brother was the Irish Catholic peer, the earl of Clanricarde, who was one of Ormond's closest allies;[45] Denzell Holles also had kinship ties with Ormond, and his brother-in-law was Oliver Fitzwilliams, a notorious royalist Irishman.[46] Many Irish M.P.s at Westminster thus found sympathy with the Presbyterian grandees: Sir John Clotworthy was a client of the earl of Warwick in the early 1640s; William Jephson had served with other Presbyterians in the committee of Irish affairs before 1644.[47] Through men such as Jephson and his ally, Sir Philip Percivalle, and through his contacts with Ormond, Inchiquin naturally found a sympathetic response among the Presbyterian interest at Westminster. The rival, Independent faction, was more concerned with victory in England, but at an early stage it was closely allied to the Scottish interest, and was eager to reinforce Ulster. The Scottish alliance had soured by the beginning of 1645, however, and thereafter the Independents were keen to reduce the bargaining power of their former allies, and tried to remove them from any influence over Ireland; they were also hostile to the cessation, and to Ormond's influence as lord lieutenant. Independent dominance in the committee of both kingdoms translated into influence over Irish

---

[43] These should be understood as political, rather than religious, labels for the factions: see David Underdown, *Pride's Purge: politics in the puritan revolution* (Oxford, 1971), pp 45–75; see also John Adamson, 'The baronial context of the English Civil War' in *Transactions of the Royal Historical Society*, ser. 5, xl (1990), pp 105–16.

[44] For the factional alignments between Westminster and Ireland see Little, 'Ormond', pp 84–7.

[45] John Adamson, 'Strafford's ghost: the British context of Viscount Lisle's lieutenancy of Ireland' in Jane Ohlmeyer (ed.), *Ireland from independence to occupation, 1641–1660* (Cambridge, 1995), pp 131–2; Patrick Little, 'Blood and friendship: the earl of Essex's protection of the earl of Clanricarde's interests, 1641–1646' in *E.H.R.*, cxii (1997), pp 927–41.

[46] Correspondence between Ormond and Holles, Sept. and Dec. 1642 (Bodl., MS Carte 4, ff 116r, 178r); *C.J.*, v, 114; Patricia Crawford, *Denzil Holles, 1598–1680: a study of his political career* (Royal Hist. Soc., 1979), p. 6n.

[47] M. F. Keeler, *The Long Parliament, 1640–1641: a biographical study of its members* (Philadelphia, 1954), pp 136, 234.

policy, as its sub-committee for Irish affairs was staffed by Northumberland, Vane and their friends.[48] Through existing connexions, as well as common objectives, in their Irish policy the Independents came to rely on a group of disaffected Irish Protestants, led by Ormond's enemies within the Irish council, Sir William Parsons, Sir Adam Loftus and Sir John Temple, and it was with this group – which may be christened the Irish Independents – that Broghill became associated during the mid-1640s.

The Irish Independents were the political heirs of the 'Boyle group' – that alliance of New English politicians and landowners which had formed around the first earl of Cork in the 1620s and early 1630s. In the 1640s, as before, their stance was uncompromising. Ireland could only benefit from closer association with England, which would lead to a reformation of the Irish in both manners and religion. This could best be achieved through the suppression of Catholicism and extensive plantation. This harsh logic was as relevant in 1645 as it had been in 1625; and official parliamentarian policies, notably the Adventurers' Act, were entirely in agreement with it. A further important unifying force was the Boyle group's hatred of the marquess of Ormond. The first earl of Cork, with Parsons and others had attacked the power of Irish lordships, and had done their best to undermine the power of the Butlers in Leinster and Munster in a private, as well as a public, capacity. Ormond's growing influence in the king's counsels, his sponsorship of the repugnant cessation, his appointment as lord lieutenant, and his imprisonment of Parsons, Loftus and Temple in 1643, had rekindled this antagonism, and proved their earlier suspicions to be correct. By the mid-1640s, as we have seen, Broghill had his own suspicions of Ormond, to add to those inherited from his father and the Boyle group. And through his influence, their hostility towards Ormond was now extended to include another suspected quisling, Lord Inchiquin.[49]

II

The decision to appoint a new, parliamentarian, lord lieutenant of Ireland in the winter of 1645–6 brought factional matters to a head, cementing the alliance between the old Boyle group in Ireland and the English Independents at Westminster, and forcing Inchiquin and Ormond into a closer connexion with the Presbyterian party. The new lord lieutenant, Viscount Lisle, was an important member of the Independent faction; he also had long-standing

---

[48] *Cal. S.P. Dom. 1644*, p. 61; see David Scott, 'The "northern gentlemen", the parliamentary Independents, and Anglo-Scottish relations in the Long Parliament' in *H.J.*, xlii (1999), passim.

[49] Patrick Little, 'The Irish "Independents" and Viscount Lisle's lieutenancy of Ireland' in *H.J.*, xliv (2001), pp 945–7.

connexions with Broghill. The two men had studied together at Saumur in the 1630s; both had fought in Ireland earlier in the 1640s, when Lisle's father, the earl of Leicester, was lord lieutenant; and Lisle was the nephew and protégé of Broghill's main ally in the Independent party, the earl of Northumberland. The elevation of Lisle to the lieutenancy also had wider implications. From the English Independents' point of view, Lisle's lieutenancy was part of their more general attempt to reduce the political influence of the Scots, as it challenged Scottish hegemony over the Irish war effort (which had been conceded by parliament once the Solemn League and Covenant had been approved in 1643). For Broghill and his allies, Lisle's office was principally an attack on the position of the king's lord lieutenant, the marquess of Ormond, who had come to represent everything that was wrong with Charles I's Irish policy, with its moves to make peace with the Confederate rebels, apparently at any price. Despite this difference of attitude, the appointment of Lisle was of crucial importance to the Irish war effort. Hopes ran high that at last the English parliament would honour its commitment to reconquer Ireland.

During the spring and summer of 1646 the Irish and English Independents worked closely together.[50] Lisle's commission as lord lieutenant came into force on 9 April 1646, and within a month the English Independents had taken control of the Irish war effort. On 4 May Lisle and five English Independents were added to the Committee of Irish Affairs, and thereafter they commanded a majority at every meeting.[51] Their Irish allies, Sir William Parsons, Sir Adam Loftus and Sir John Borlase, were brought into the administration;[52] and in June the committee of Irish affairs began to promote Lord Broghill as a rival to Inchiquin in Munster.[53] In fact, Broghill was to prove the major beneficiary of the conjunction of the English and Irish Independents during this period. With backing from Westminster, Broghill proceeded to undermine Inchiquin's authority – with the ultimate intention of replacing him as lord president. When Inchiquin was away from Munster, Broghill was authorised to disburse money 'for carrying on the warre in that province' – a privilege he freely exercised until Inchiquin returned in late July.[54] With Inchiquin's return to Munster, Broghill left for Westminster, raising fears that the main aim of his visit was to turn parliament against the lord president.[55] Broghill's position was strengthened by news of the conclusion of Ormond's peace deal with the Confederate Irish in August, and from the end of the month, the Irish committee began to reduce Inchiquin's military strength further. On 28

---

[50] The following is based on Little, 'Irish "Independents"', pp 951–7, with permission from Cambridge University Press.
[51] *C.J.*, iv, 532; *Cal. S.P. Ire., 1633–47*, p. 446ff; Armstrong, 'Protestant Ireland', p. 228.
[52] Armstrong, 'Protestant Ireland', p. 229.
[53] Ibid., p. 236.
[54] P.R.O., S.P. 63/261, f. 141v; ibid., S.P. 16/539/3, ff 226r–31r, 510r–11r; ibid., S.P. 28/39/2, f. 120v.
[55] H.M.C. *Egmont*, i, 301, 305.

August the committee ordered the Munster commissary to 'lay up' all further arms and ammunition arriving in the province, until Lisle sent further instructions;[56] on 11 September the president's officers were ordered to return 300 pikes reserved for Lisle's army but already released to Inchiquin;[57] and in October there were complaints from Munster that a further shipload of arms had been withheld in order 'to shorten his lo[rdshi]p's power'.[58] Six thousand pounds allocated for Munster was not sent to Inchiquin, but kept in England, where it was disbursed by Broghill.[59]

In contrast to the restrictions placed upon Inchiquin, Broghill was rapidly promoted. On 6 September the Irish committee advised that Broghill should return to Ireland with 'some better command then that of a Colonell', suggesting that he should take control of four new regiments bound for Munster as 'a distinct Brigade from the rest of the Armie there'.[60] This was a direct attack on Inchiquin's authority as president of Munster. Broghill's commission, drafted by 26 September, made it clear that he was to accept instructions only from Lisle, or the Irish committee, or parliament, but not from Inchiquin. The final version of the commission, presented on 2 October, was passed by a committee made up solely of Independent M.P.s, led by Northumberland and Lisle.[61] Inchiquin was certainly justified in voicing his fear that a powerful coalition had formed against him, led by Broghill and his brother-in-law, Sir Arthur Loftus, but also involving English Independents, notably Viscount Lisle. In a letter to Percivalle, he used gender-swapping as a code, but his meaning was plain: 'It is but this day that I writ unto you of one of the Lady [i.e. Sir Arthur] Loftus's lies . . . tell the ladies that writ to the Lady Caesar [i.e. the viceroy, Viscount Lisle], that such things are practised every day, whereof my Lady Loftus gives an account at night to my Lady [i.e. Lord] Broghill, who does not appear in anything herself'.[62]

The close co-operation between the English and Irish Independents was also evident in the increasingly bitter libels against Ormond printed in the spring and summer of 1646, including Sir John Temple's notorious book, *The Irish rebellion*, which was produced in April, just after Lisle took up his position as lord lieutenant. For Temple, the original 'conquest' was that of Henry II, who had united Ireland (in an echo of language used by the Boyle group twenty years before) 'to the Imperiall Crown of England'. This had established the English settlers 'in point of interest and universall possession, owners, and

---

[56] *Cal. S.P. Ire.*, 1633–47, p. 502; H.M.C. *Egmont*, i, 309.

[57] P.R.O., S.P. 63/262, f. 107v.

[58] Ibid., f. 123r.

[59] H.M.C. *Egmont*, i, 283–4, 312; P.R.O., S.P. 28/41/5, f. 460r.

[60] P.R.O., S.P. 63/262, f. 103r.

[61] Ibid., ff 121r, 123r–v.

[62] H.M.C. *Egmont*, i, 317: for a similar example of gender-swapping from the 1640s see *The cuckoo's-nest at Westminster; of the parlement between the two lady-birds, Quean Fairfax and Lady Cromwell* (1648) (B.L., E.447(19)).

proprietors of the whole Kingdome of Ireland'; and Elizabeth I did not reconquer Ireland, but intervened simply to 'redresse the disorders of her subjects in Ireland', with the implication that a similar policy was needed now.[63] The main body of Temple's book concentrated on the early 1640s, and attacked the Old English of the Pale for joining the Gaelic Irish in rebellion, justifying the action of Lords Justices Parsons and Borlase, and defending the lieutenancy of Lisle's father, the earl of Leicester.[64] Temple was a close associate of Lisle, and an English Independent M.P.; but he had also been an associate of the Boyle group since the 1630s, and his approach to the Irish situation was that of an Irish Protestant. In October 1646 Temple's work was seconded by *Ormond's curtain drawn*, a pamphlet written by Adam Meredith, the son of another prominent Irish Independent, Sir Robert Meredith.[65] Meredith's attack on Ormond was more explicit. He praised the faithful councillors of 1641 – Parsons, Borlase, Loftus, Temple, Coote senior and Meredith (all associates of the Boyle group) – and added that problems only arose with the advancement of new councillors (who 'like Tares (sowne by the wicked one) suddenly over-top the good Corne'). There followed a sustained attack on Ormond, who showed favour to the rebels, obstructed the best military men (notably Sir Arthur Loftus and Viscount Lisle), and engineered the 1643 cessation of arms.[66] In concentrating on the period before the cessation, both works aimed to justify the lords justices and the old councillors, and to explore Ormond's role in negotiations with the Irish, which paralleled his deals with the Confederates in 1646. Like the rapid promotion of Broghill within the army, the propaganda of Temple and Meredith shows that the English and Irish Independent factions had effectively joined forces during 1646.

Yet the close co-operation between the Irish and English Independents disguised serious differences in their attitude to Irish affairs. For the Irish Independents, attacks on Ormond and Inchiquin constituted the very essence of their political programme; for the English Independents, such aims were subordinate to the need to defeat their factional rivals at Westminster, and to secure a favourable peace deal with the king. The crisis came soon after 14 September, when news of the collapse of Ormond's peace treaty with the Confederates reached London. Within a few days, the Presbyterians had seized the opportunity. Pamphlets were published defending Inchiquin, and voicing hopes that Ormond would at last 'declare himself for the Parliament'.[67]

---

[63] Sir John Temple, *The Irish Rebellion* (27 Apr. 1646) (E.508), pp 4–8.
[64] Ibid., pp 13–14.
[65] Armstrong, 'Protestant Ireland', p. 245n; Adamson, 'Strafford's Ghost', pp 140–2.
[66] Adam Meredith, *Ormond's curtain drawn* (5 Oct. 1646) (E.513(14)), pp 10–14, 23–4; Kathleen Noonan, '"The cruell pressure of an enraged, barbarous people": Irish and English identity in seventeenth century policy and propaganda' in *H.J.*, xli (1998), p. 173n.
[67] *A letter from a person of quality residing in Kinsale* (15 Sept. 1646), p. 1; *The Irish papers, containing the Lord Digbyes letter, and the Lord Inchiquins answer* (1 Oct. 1646), pp 6–7.

Presbyterian M.P.s seized control of the Irish committee, and on 8 October Broghill was told that the supplies for his men had been stopped, and that, until further notice, 'the Comissions intended to his Lo[rdshi]p are to be respited'.[68] Soon afterwards, Inchiquin's soldiers broke open the weapon stores denied them in August,[69] and the Presbyterians began to plan their new treaty with Ormond. In response, the Independents abandoned their Irish policies, in order to wrest the political initiative back from the Presbyterians. The new Derby House committee, set up on 12 October 1646 and manned by Independents, was specifically designed to take control of the negotiations with Ormond. Ormond, who had been attacked during the summer, was now courted by the Independents.

The Irish Independents reacted with confusion. Broghill, his hopes of an independent command dashed, even tried to mend fences with Inchiquin, calling on his few Presbyterian contacts to help effect a reconciliation with his former enemy.[70] He was helped in this by Sir William Parsons, who recommended Broghill in his own conciliatory letters to Sir Philip Percivalle and even to Ormond.[71] Broghill's allies also back-tracked, with Sir Arthur Loftus and Parsons reported to 'speak very honourably' of Ormond in early November.[72] In a world turned upside down, even reinforcing the suspect Ormond was better than the complete collapse of the Protestant interest in Ireland. This confused situation continued until the end of November, when news reached London that Ormond had finally refused to conclude a treaty with parliament's agents.[73]

The collapse of parliament's treaty with Ormond reopened the factional split within Protestant Ireland, and this allowed a patching up of the alliance between the Irish Independents and their English counterparts. On 28 November it was reported that 'the differences between Enchyquin and Broghill groweth greater' and on 11 December there were rumours that Broghill was again expecting a 'commission independent from In[chiquin]'.[74] But the trust which had grown up between the English and Irish Independents in the summer of 1646 had been seriously damaged. After the fiasco of October and November, the Irish Independents were no longer content merely to follow the Independents' lead. On 10 December Broghill's allies, Loftus, Temple and Parsons, working with Arthur Annesley and Inchiquin's former ally, Sir Hardress Waller, filed a report to parliament on the state of Ireland, which set out a detailed plan of action 'towards the restoring thereof to the

---

[68] P.R.O., S.P. 63/262, f. 128r.
[69] H.M.C. *Egmont*, i, 320.
[70] Little, 'Political career', pp 90–3.
[71] H.M.C. *Egmont*, i, 318, 334; Parsons to Ormond, 16 Nov. 1646 (Bodl., MS Carte 19, f. 402v).
[72] H.M.C. *Egmont*, i, 330–1.
[73] Little, 'Ormond', pp 90–3.
[74] H.M.C. *Egmont*, i, 338, 341.

due subjeccon & governemt: of the Crowne of England'.[75] Their first proposal, 'That the safety of their parties and places in Mounster be first taken into Care, and to that end, that the Lord Lieutenant: now residing here, be w[i]th all convenient speed dispatched ther',[76] not only indicated their focus on reinforcing Munster as opposed to aiding Ormond in Dublin or the Anglo-Scottish forces in Ulster, but also signalled their impatience with Lisle's lack of progress in the previous year. The arrival of Lisle in Munster would supplant the authority of Inchiquin as president of the province, and facilitate Broghill's independent command. The last point was suggested by an insistence on the three regiments of horse and four of foot already raised for service under Broghill, to be transported with Lisle to Munster. Other proposals betray the Irish Independents' dissatisfaction with Lisle's regime: money already promised must now be sent, followed by regular payments to the army; and Munster would again become the priority for parliamentarian assistance.[77] Although not directly involved in framing the document, Broghill probably influenced the programme promoted by his friends. Indeed, some aspects of the report echoed 'proposals' suggested by Broghill in August 1646, which denounced Ormond, requested a large army for Munster, and questioned Inchiquin's loyalty, by saying that without immediate and vigorous support, 'many of the Gentrie and others . . . will join with them [the Ormondists] heart and hand'.[78] In December, therefore, the other Irish Independents followed Broghill's logic, insisting that a strong, well-funded expeditionary force to Munster, led by parliament's lord lieutenant, would be the only way to begin a proper reconquest of Ireland. Such vigorous policies would also advance Broghill, neutralise Inchiquin, and reduce Ormond's bargaining power. And in putting forward a radical, Irish Protestant agenda, the Irish Independents were resurrecting the policies of the old Boyle group, which had in earlier decades called for harsh measures against Irish Catholics, a massive extension of plantation schemes, and ever closer ties between England and Ireland.

The Irish Independent demands of 10 December had an immediate effect at Westminster: on the same day the Derby House committee ordered Lisle to go to Munster as soon as possible;[79] and in the next few weeks an expeditionary force was prepared, ready to cross to Ireland from the south-west. The influence of the Irish Independents over Lisle's regime increased markedly in the intervening period. On 1 January, the Derby House committee appointed Lisle's privy council, including Loftus, Temple, Parsons, Borlase and Meredith

---

[75] Report, 10 Dec. 1646 (Bodl., MS Carte 19, f. 604r). Waller, now a New Model colonel, had turned against Inchiquin in 1645; Annesley's brief flirtation with the Independents ended in the summer of 1647: see their draft biographies, 1640–60 section, History of Parliament.

[76] Bodl., MS Carte 19, f. 605r

[77] Ibid., f. 605v.

[78] Bodl., MS Carte 67, ff 299r–301r.

[79] Cal. S.P. Ire., 1647–60, p. 727.

– all Irish Independents and Boyle associates.[80] Inchiquin and a few other Presbyterians were also included, but 'onely for the present . . . Till the Houses shall think fitt to adde any other'.[81] The Belfast Presbyterian, John Davies, was aware of the wider factional implications: 'I never doubted but Sir Will. [Parsons] and Sir Ad. [Loftus] would join with Sir Jo. [Temple]. Time will try all things, and if destruction doth not befall some of them, I know nothing. If Bro[ghill] doth embrace that business it will ruin him'.[82] The Irish Independents remained vehemently opposed to any compromise with either Ormond or Inchiquin. In late February 1647 Percivalle received reports of continuing opposition to new peace negotiations between Ormond and parliament, led by those 'whose fiery zeale hath so farre transported them, that they have said, it were better all those inocent people should perish, rather then hee should escape unpunished'.[83] While Ormond was slandered at Westminster, Inchiquin was confronted in Munster. Lisle embarked from Minehead on 18 February, accompanied by Sir Arthur and Sir Adam Loftus and Sir Hardress Waller, and on arrival at Kinsale he was met by Broghill.[84] Inchiquin, who said the expedition had 'the semblance rather of a conquest than of relief',[85] saw Broghill as the source of the vindictiveness of Lisle's brief rule in Ireland. On 5 March he complained that he had been excluded from Lisle's counsels, 'as well as all others of relacon to this Province formerly, except such only as my Lord of Broghill hath intimated to bee of that faction'.[86] A few days later, his situation was worse, as 'purposely to avoyd owing any-thing to my assistance, advice or intelligence they repose sol[e]y on my Lord of Broghill's, who assures them myne to bee of no value'.[87] On 29 March, Inchiquin again characterised Broghill as the ringleader of the Independents in Munster: 'my person and authority [are] daily affronted, my Lord of Broghill comaunding all things at his pleasure, so as my Lord Lieutenant puts the execution of my place in effect into his hands'.[88] Inchiquin seems to have been certain that, although Lisle was not quite a 'figurehead', in Munster he took his lead from his local subordinate, Lord Broghill.

Yet Broghill's moment of power over Inchiquin was to be shortlived. At Westminster, Independent control of Irish affairs had begun to weaken from the end of February 1647, when Ormond again offered to reopen peace

---

[80] Annesley and Valentia had turned against Temple and his friends by the summer: H.M.C. *Egmont*, i, 352.
[81] Bodl., MS Nalson 21, f. 111r.
[82] H.M.C. *Egmont*, i, 352.
[83] Edmund Smith to Percivalle, Feb. 1647 (B.L., Add. MS 46931/A, f. 70r).
[84] H.M.C. *Egmont*, i, 362.
[85] H.M.C. *Egmont*, i, 367.
[86] Inchiquin to Thomas Pigott, 5 Mar. 1647 (B.L., Add. MS 46931/A, f. 76v).
[87] Enclosed in Inchiquin's letter to Percivalle, 13 Mar. 1647 (B.L., Add. 46931/A, f. 99v: [printed with some errors in H.M.C. *Egmont*, i, 374]).
[88] H.M.C. *Egmont*, i, 380.

negotiations with the English parliament, and, as in September 1646, the renewed hope of peace wrong-footed the Independents, who were now forced to divert their energies, and the available funds, towards the recapture of Dublin.[89] With Lisle, Temple and other key Independents already on their way to Munster, the Presbyterian party was soon able to reassert its position at Derby House, and by late March they could rely on a majority in the committee.[90] This, and the corresponding resurgence of Presbyterian power in parliament, brought a hostile reaction to Lisle's conduct in Ireland, and on 1 April the renewal of the lord lieutenant's commission was blocked, with the government of Ireland being vested instead in two lords justices.[91] The removal of Lisle would damage the Independent party and would help to conciliate Ormond, whose lieutenancy rivalled Lisle's.[92] It also protected Inchiquin in the short term: Broghill's brother-in-law, Sir Arthur Loftus, had received a favourable hearing when presenting a list of accusations against Inchiquin to the Derby House committee in March; but in April William Jephson successfully intervened on Inchiquin's behalf, calling in support from other Presbyterians, to ensure that the charges were suppressed.[93]

The refusal to renew Lisle's commission strengthened the position of Inchiquin, who quickly asserted his right to rule alone as lord president of Munster.[94] Despite a last-ditch attempt to hold Cork city against Inchiquin's forces – spearheaded by Broghill's own regiment – the Independents were forced to relinquish control, leaving Munster soon after the expiry of Lisle's commission on 15 April. As one Irish Protestant, John Hodder, told Percivalle on 21 April: 'now thankes be geeven to god wee have the Command of all againe and I thinke my Lord of Inchequin will tourne out those that tourned out us'.[95] With Lisle gone, Inchiquin set about stabilising Munster ready for the summer campaign. He also punished those Munster officers who had supported the Independents, and, in a symbolic act of revenge, planned to reassign Broghill's post as general of the horse to William Jephson.[96]

Yet Broghill and his friends were not finished. Although the Presbyterians continued to dominate parliament and the Irish committees, and Inchiquin was once more in control of Munster, throughout the summer Broghill and his friends conducted a propaganda campaign against Inchiquin. On 23 April Sir Adam Loftus and Sir John Temple, newly arrived from Munster, sent the

---

[89] C.J., v, 136; P.R.O., S.P. 21/26, pp 10, 15–16; see Little, 'Ormond', pp 93–4.

[90] P.R.O., S.P. 21/26, pp 33–34; Adamson, 'Strafford's ghost', pp 152–3.

[91] C.J., v, 131.

[92] This was still an important consideration: see John Giffarde to Ormond, 15 Apr. 1647 (Bodl., MS Carte 20, f. 613r–v).

[93] H.M.C. Egmont, i, 383, 387.

[94] Sir Adam Loftus and Sir John Temple to Lenthall, 23 Apr. 1647 (Bodl., MS Nalson 6, f. 80r).

[95] Hodder to Percivalle, 21 Apr. 1647 (B.L., Add. MS 46931/A, f. 186r).

[96] Inchiquin's notes, c.22 Apr. 1647 (ibid., f. 190r).

speaker an account of the expedition 'to make knowne the Lord Inchequins carriage herein to ye Parl[iamen]t'.[97] For the first time, Inchiquin's Gaelic line-age was used against him, and on 18 May he reported news of an 'Instrument that Sr Ar[thur] Lo[ftus] indeavoured to gett the Officers to signe at Bristoll to desire that they might not be sent to be under the Comande of an Irish-man'.[98] Similar slights later in the month brought Inchiquin close to resigning his post, and he complained that only military success in Munster would prevent criticism of his integrity in England.[99] He was even directly implicated in the 'treasons' alleged by the English Independents against the eleven mem-bers – the leaders of the rival Presbyterian faction – in June. The 14th article of the Independent charges accused Clotworthy, Holles and Stapilton of suppressing 'many articles of high treason' against Inchiquin, and of conniving with him to destroy Lisle and remove all loyal officers from Munster.[100]

The removal of the eleven Presbyterian M.P.s brought the Independents back into control at Westminster, and Broghill and his friends immediately launched further attacks on the lord president's reputation. On 17 July, Percivalle was worried that both he and Inchiquin were to be slandered in Jephson's absence by Lisle, his brother Algernon Sidney, and Temple; he added that, although Loftus was not yet involved, Broghill was 'very hopeful' of the results.[101] On 22 July a pamphlet was published in London insulting Inchiquin as 'an Irish General, who starves his Army here [in Munster] to feed his good name in England', and voicing the complaints of the Munster garrisons, who 'must be Commanded by the natural Irish'.[102] Soon afterwards there were rumours that Broghill would be returned to the council of Munster by order of the Derby House committee.[103] By 27 July Percivalle could confirm the rumour: all future Munster initiatives were to be done 'by the advice and consent of the Lord Broghill and the rest of the Council, and to that end, Sir A[rthur] L[oftus] added when Col. Jephson was lately out of town'.[104] The future looked bleak for Inchiquin. As Viscount Valentia (the former Lord Mountnorris) wryly commented on 4 August, 'The Lord Inchiquin is like to be well counselled by those who accused him of treason'.[105]

[97] Loftus and Temple to Lenthall, 23 Apr. 1647 (Bodl., MS Nalson 6, f. 80r–v).

[98] Inchiquin to Percivalle, 18 May 1647 (B.L., Add. MS 46931/A, f. 234r).

[99] H.M.C. Egmont, i, 408–9; see also Richard Fitzgerald to Percivalle, 30 May 1647 (B.L., Add. MS 46931/A, f. 249r).

[100] R. Bell (ed.), Memorials of the Civil War, comprising the correspondence of the Fairfax family (2 vols., 1849), ii, 376–7; also William Prynne, A full vindication and answer of the xi accused members (15 July 1647) (B.L., E.398(17)), p. 25.

[101] H.M.C. Egmont, i, 428–30.

[102] A letter from Lieutenant Colonel Knight in the province of Munster (22 July 1647) (B.L., E.399(23)), pp 4, 12; see also the Presbyterian reply: A copy of a Remonstrance (24 July 1647) (B.L., E.399(33)).

[103] H.M.C. Egmont, i, 435.

[104] Ibid., p. 438.

[105] Ibid., p. 442.

The Presbyterian coup, or 'forcing of the houses', which began at Westminster on 26 July 1647 and lasted until the New Model Army and its Independent allies entered the capital by force on 6 August, brought the rival parliamentarian factions close to open warfare. Just as in the attack on the eleven members in June, so the continuing close links between Inchiquin and the Presbyterians in July presented Broghill with yet another opportunity to press home his assault on the lord president. On 26 July Percivalle had warned Inchiquin that 'Broghill is at the army' outside London, adding that he and Temple had been brought to the headquarters 'on invitation from Hard[res]s [Waller]'.[106] The triumph of the army over the Presbyterians in early August put Inchiquin in an increasingly awkward position, and from then on he became very defensive in his dealings with England. His secretary, Richard Gethings, defended his reputation in print, while others, including Jephson, tried to head off criticism in the House of Commons.[107] Despite their best efforts, however, after September 1647 relations between the president and the English parliament broke down almost completely. Although Inchiquin won a remarkable series of victories against the Confederates during the summer of 1647, sacking Cashel in County Tipperary, and destroying a Catholic army at Knocknanuss in County Cork, the Independents in the Derby House committee fell back into the old pattern of refusing him supplies, a tactic which had crippled the Munster war effort in 1646. By the end of January 1648 Inchiquin was desperate for relief, warning Lenthall that he would be forced to send troops back to England as he could not support them.[108] By early March Inchiquin had himself been forced to revert to his survival tactics of 1644–5, and was arranging a local cessation of arms with the Confederates.[109] After talks with the royal agent, Colonel John Barry, by the end of the month Inchiquin had defected to the king, and eagerly awaited the arrival of the viceroy, the marquess of Ormond, who had recently gone to France.[110] Inchiquin's defection may have been triggered by lack of supplies and increasing alienation from parliament; but both of these were provoked by Broghill's efforts to blacken the lord president's name in 1647–8.

---

[106] Ibid., p. 436.
[107] Little, 'Political career', pp 100–1.
[108] Inchiquin to Lenthall, 31 Jan. 1648 (Bodl., MS Nalson 6, f. 168r–v).
[109] John Barry to Clanricarde, 3 Mar. 1648 (Bodl., MS Carte 22, ff 37r–8r).
[110] Sir John Denham to Ormond, 30 Mar. 1648 (ibid., f. 53r); the Derby House committee learned of Inchiquin's defection on 13 April: P.R.O., S.P. 21/26, p. 153. For Ormond's position see Little, 'Ormond', pp 98–9.

III

In many ways, the vigorous political campaign against Inchiquin conducted by Broghill and the Irish Independents had been too successful. Forced into an ever tighter corner, the lord president had not resigned, nor was he replaced. Instead he defected back to the king. The defection of Inchiquin had serious consequences for Broghill, who found himself without a foothold in Munster, as he had been stripped of his military commands, and his remaining lands were now in royalist hands. It also greatly reduced Broghill's influence in London – a situation worsened by the outbreak of the Second Civil War, and the need to resist the Scottish invasion of England in Charles I's favour, which further reduced parliament's willingness to fund a proper expedition against Ireland.[111] In the face of parliamentary procrastination, Broghill, like other Irish Independents, became disillusioned with Westminster, and he retired to Somerset rather than be ignored in London. This was but the last in a long line of disappointments with English intransigence over Ireland. In 1642–3 Broghill had seen at first hand the way in which English affairs took precedence over the pressing needs of Ireland; in 1644–5 he had secured aid, but only after intensive lobbying; in 1646 the English Independents had betrayed their Irish counterparts by reopening negotiations with Ormond; and in 1647 the vagaries of English factionalism had stunted the Protestant war effort. As the Irish Protestants became increasingly reliant on English assistance to fend off the Confederate armies, so it became increasingly apparent that their influence in London was very weak, being dependent on English priorities – priorities that were seldom the same as those of the New English in Ireland. This realisation had two effects on Broghill. In the long term it encouraged him to try to increase Irish participation in Whitehall and Westminster – not as occasional lobbyists, but as equal members of a formally constituted union. Union would legally bind the English to live up to their imperial rhetoric when it came to Ireland. But the opportunity to implement such a unionist policy was a long way off. In the short term – that is, in 1648 and early 1649 – dissatisfaction brought a sense of disillusion, a feeling of impotence, which encouraged Broghill, in his desperation, to look elsewhere for a solution to the Irish problem.

Once in retirement in the country, Broghill came into contact with his former friends and relatives in the royalist camp. The first approaches may even have been made by Broghill himself: on 30 March 1648 Ormond was told that Broghill was 'unsatisfied' with the conduct of the war, and had

---

[111] Patrick Little, 'The English parliament and the Irish constitution, 1641–9' in Micheál Ó Siochrú (ed.), *Kingdoms in crisis: Ireland in the 1640s* (Dublin 2001), pp 118–20. For an alternative view see John Adamson, 'The frighted junto: perceptions of Ireland, and the last attempts at settlement with Charles I' in Jason Peacey (ed.), *The regicides and the execution of Charles I* (2001), pp 36–70.

resolved 'either wholy to decline the business' or to join Michael Jones and George Monck in Ireland, 'who he believes have the same resolution' to join the king.[112] Broghill, according to the same account, even offered to settle his differences with Inchiquin, but was unwilling that 'the secret of his intentions' should be revealed.[113] Both Ormond and the prince of Wales made initial approaches to Broghill in the summer,[114] but the matter was not pursued until November, when Ormond wrote to Broghill via his brother, Francis Boyle.[115] Ormond said that he already had notice 'of yor Lo[rdshi]ps inclinations to serve the king', but had delayed his reply until he was sure of his own authority to promise him 'all security & honour to your person'.[116] But, despite Ormond's assurances, once again no progress was made.

Efforts were renewed in the spring of 1649, on the intiative of the second earl of Cork, who had gone into exile with the court.[117] Secretary Nicholas told Ormond that 'The Earl of Cork saith he expects his brother the Lord Broghill here every day, and that he comes hither with intention to adhere to the King's friends in Ireland'.[118] Cork's efforts were supplemented by those of Broghill's sister-in-law, Lady d'Aubigny, who asked Ormond to show 'kindness to my brother Broughill', and had also lobbied the new king on his behalf.[119] Charles Stuart wrote to Ormond on 20 April, hopeful of the 'good affection of the Lord Broughell to the king our late father', and stating that Broghill would wait on him in Holland on his way to join the royalists forces in Ireland.[120] Ormond promised to welcome the new recruit with open arms.[121] This was the last evidence of contact between Broghill and the royalist court. Even the intervention of other members of the Boyle family could not make him change his mind. The obstacles were too great. After years of fighting against the Confederate Catholics, Broghill was not likely to accept a formal alliance between them and the king. Nor was he about to change his opinion of the slippery Ormond, who had brokered the treaty in January 1649. A further obstacle was the position of Inchiquin, especially after Prince Charles had granted him the presidency of Munster on 2 July 1648.[122] Secretary Nicholas admitted the danger in April 1649, implying that Broghill's desire to join the crown depended on reducing 'the great disaffection which is known to have been here between the Lord Inchiquin . . . and the Lord Broghill'.[123]

---

[112] Denham to Ormond, 30 Mar. 1648 (Bodl., MS Carte 22, f. 53r).
[113] Ibid.
[114] Ormond to Denham, 15 Apr. 1648 (ibid., f. 65r); H.M.C. Pepys, p. 297.
[115] Ormond to Broghill, 2 Nov. 1648 (Bodl., MS Carte 22 f. 552r).
[116] Ibid.
[117] Cork to Ormond, 2 Mar. 1649 (Bodl., MS Carte 24, f. 10r).
[118] Nicholas to Ormond, Apr. 1649 (ibid., ff 390r–1v).
[119] Lady d'Aubigny to Ormond, 10/20 Apr. 1649 (ibid., f. 403r).
[120] Charles Stuart to Ormond, 20 Apr. 1649 (ibid., f. 483r).
[121] H.M.C. Pepys, p. 297.
[122] Royal commission, 2 July 1648 (Bodl., MS Carte 67, f. 315r).
[123] Nicholas to Ormond, Apr. 1649 (Bodl., MS Carte 24, ff 390–1).

Charles referred to the same problem in his letter of 20 April: Ormond must 'settle a right understanding betweene the Lord Inchiquin our President of Munster and the said Lord Broughall'.[124] As long as Inchiquin remained lord president of Munster and Ormond lord lieutenant of Ireland, Broghill would side with parliament.

If the appointment of Inchiquin as president of Munster had given Broghill a reason to reject the invitation of the royalists, the appointment of Oliver Cromwell as lord lieutenant of Ireland in March 1649 gave him a very good reason to support parliament. Just as the decline in parliament's commitment to the Irish war in 1648 and early 1649 had encouraged Broghill to toy with the idea of supporting the Stuarts, so the vigour of parliament's new campaign, the decision to devote adequate resources, and above all the appointment of a proven general to command the army, soon brought Broghill back into the parliamentarian camp. As we shall see in the next chapter, efforts to persuade the Munster Protestants to abandon Inchiquin and once again defect to parliament were under way as early as April 1649 – the same month that Broghill dropped his negotiations with Ormond and the royalists in exile. The two events are surely linked. Broghill's transition from potential royalist to Cromwellian recruit seems to have been relatively smooth, and once again the circumstantial evidence weighs against accepting the story told by Thomas Morrice many decades later – that Broghill was intercepted by Cromwell en route for the continent, and was forced to make an agonising choice between imprisonment as a royalist or service against his Irish enemies.[125] With Broghill's career throughout the later 1640s borne in mind, this scenario becomes less and less credible. Broghill was unlikely to accept unconditionally the offers of the discredited royalists – whose only hope of victory in Ireland, in 1649 as in 1646, depended on an alliance with the hated Confederate Catholics – when the prospect of reconquest, and the fulfilment of the Irish Independent agenda, was at last on offer from the English parliament.

IV

Broghill's emergence as the leading 'Irish Independent' in the later 1640s was the culmination of various developments which can be traced through his early life. First, it shows the continuing influence of his father, the first earl of Cork. Cork's programme for the reform of Ireland was the forerunner of the Irish Independents' plans, with both demonstrating a hatred of Irish Catholicism, a suspicion of unreconstructed Old Englishmen such as the marquess of Ormond, and a trust in a closer relationship with England as an essential prerequisite for social, religious and political reform in Ireland. The

---

[124] Charles Stuart to Ormond, 20 Apr. 1649 (ibid., f. 483r).
[125] For problems with Morrice's reliability as a historian see above, Introduction.

proposals fielded by the Irish Independents in December 1646 were very close in detail, as well as tone, to the ideas put forward by the old Boyle group in the 1620s and early 1630s. This continuity is hardly surprising. Apart from Broghill himself, the leaders of the Irish Independents were old associates of the first earl of Cork, including Parsons and the Loftuses, or men from similar backgrounds who had joined them in their resistance against Ormond earlier in the 1640s, such as Temple and Meredith. Broghill was thus continuing a link with the personnel, as well as the policies, of the old Boyle group from twenty years before. His father's legacy also underlay Broghill's choice of enemies. The Butlers of Ormond had been targeted by the first earl of Cork by 1630, and this historic enmity seems to have influenced Broghill's later hostility to the marquess of Ormond. Cork's feud with Lord President St Leger and his son-in-law, Lord Inchiquin, had a direct influence on Broghill's attitude towards Inchiquin, which emerged stronger than ever in 1644–5, despite a short period of amity between them. In opposing Inchiquin and Ormond, and in championing radical solutions to the Irish problem, Broghill was returning to his father's agenda with a vengeance.

Broghill's rejection of Ormond and Inchiquin was not principally based on ethnic prejudice, but on their perceived political and religious unreliability. This was something that developed as the 1640s wore on. Ormond's cessation of arms with the Catholic rebels, and his repeated attempts to make a permanent peace with them, could be seen as a betrayal. Not only did it undermine the Protestant duty to oppose rebels, it also threatened to bring them into a league with Antichrist. Such thoughts influenced Broghill and his friends, who soon came to see Ormond as the principal obstacle to defeating the rebels in Ireland. Inchiquin's continued collaboration with Ormond reinforced fears that he was secretly working with the Confederates themselves. For Broghill, there was little difference. Where the ethnic dimension appeared, it was more complicated than has been allowed. Broghill's father had been sympathetic to the native Irish, as long as they could be converted to Protestantism and thus neutralised as a threat to the religious establishment and to the crown. The marriage policy of the Boyles, which happily incorporated Old English families such as the Fitzgeralds and Barrys, demonstrated Cork's commitment to the principle of inclusion. Broghill's godparents included Old English and Gaelic Irish nobles, but not English settlers. The Irish rebellion signalled the failure of this policy. Worse still, it looked like a betrayal. Cork's Irish acquaintances, such as Viscount Muskerry, became leading Confederates. Their defection cast doubt on everyone of Catholic stock, including Inchiquin and (especially) Ormond. This sense of suspicion explains the hostility of Temple and other writers towards the Old English, whose treachery they blamed for the success of the rebellion.

Broghill's attitudes had been inherited from his father; but they also underwent a further, crucial metamorphosis, through his experience of the war in Ireland. This made him even less tolerant of Catholicism, for example. Broghill was also involved in changes which affected the whole Irish Protestant community. Faced with annihilation at the hands of the Confederates, the Protestant families drew ever closer together, not only in the fortified towns of Munster, Ulster and the Pale, but also in the lodging houses of London, where so many Protestants were forced to take refuge. Toby Barnard is surely right to stress the impact of this time on the Protestant community as a whole.[126] In Broghill's case, the experience of the 1640s seems to have given him a strong sense of obligation towards the Protestant Irish, which in later years broadened to include Presbyterians and even former royalists, who could all be included within the political nation if they lived peaceably, and eschewed the Stuart cause. Rather than being a champion of a particular family, or affinity, or even province, Broghill became the guardian of the Protestant interest as a whole. This was an important development, and one which determined his actions in the longer term. It also tied in with his desire to have a greater influence over the decision-making process in England, upon which Protestant Ireland would stand or fall.

[126] Barnard, 'Protestant interest', pp 220–5.

Part II

The Rise and Fall of the Cromwellian Union

3

Ireland and England, 1649–55

I

Lord Broghill's relationship with Oliver Cromwell was the most important influence on his political career during the interregnum; but it was also the most recent. There is no evidence that the two men had any dealings with each other before 1649, although both had been aligned with the Independent party during the later 1640s, and they undoubtedly had friends in common, such as the Munster landowner and New Model colonel, Sir Hardress Waller.[1] What brought Broghill and Cromwell together was not their social con-nexions, or their former political allegiances, but the realities of war. For if Cromwell wanted his reconquest of Ireland to be a success, he needed to har-ness the support of the Irish Protestant community. Broghill, as one of the most important politicians and soldiers among the Irish Protestants, was an obvious man to win over, especially as his influence in Munster could rival, or even exceed, that of the royalist turn-coat, Lord Inchiquin. The exact date of Broghill's firm commitment to the Cromwellian venture, and the precise nature of his 'conversion' is uncertain. Once Thomas Morrice's fictional account of a confrontational meeting with Oliver Cromwell is discounted,[2] the evidence suggests that Broghill's decision was made slowly, over a period of weeks, during the summer and autumn of 1649, as the scale and success of the initial invasion became known. In early August 1649, although he was still in 'retir[e]ment' in Somerset, it is likely that he was already in touch with the Westminster government about Ireland, possibly using his siblings, Robert Boyle and Lady Ranelagh, as intermediaries. As Boyle told his sister on 2 August, for the previous '3 or 4 weeks' he had been in the south-west, '[to] wayte & wayte upon my deare Broghill'.[3] On 4 August, even before news of Ormond's catastrophic defeat at the Battle of Rathmines had reached London,[4]

---

[1] John Adamson, 'Oliver Cromwell and the Long Parliament' in John Morrill (ed.), *Oliver Cromwell and the English revolution* (1990), pp 49–92; for Waller see History of Parliament, 1640–60 section, draft biography.
[2] See above, Introduction and ch. 2.
[3] *Boyle's correspondence*, i, 80; Robert Boyle was delighted with Broghill's service in Ireland later in the year: ibid., pp 84–5.
[4] News of Rathmines arrived on 11 August: *Cal. S.P. Dom., 1649–50*, p. 273.

the council of state ordered that £500 be paid to Broghill, and a further warrant of 8 September makes clear that this was to facilitate his imminent journey to Ireland.[5] Cromwell's victory at the siege of Drogheda, and his rapid advance towards the south coast may have stiffened Broghill's resolve. Orders were issued to provide him with shipping on 16 October, and he had reached Munster by early November.[6]

The recruitment of Broghill was a key element in parliament's plan to win over the irresolute Protestant forces in Munster. As early as April 1649 Cromwell was planning to encourage the royalist garrisons to defect, and after Rathmines he redoubled his efforts, sending Colonel Robert Phaier to the province to make contact with known malcontents in Cork and Youghal.[7] By early October the garrisons were in a state of unrest. On 16 October the Cork garrison rose against its governor (Broghill's cousin, Sir Percy Smyth), in retaliation at the imprisonment of three colonels who had tried to stir up trouble in Youghal. Fearing that 'they would else bee slaves to the Irish', the Cork officers rallied their men, expelled the Catholic soldiers from the town, and appealed to parliament for assistance.[8] Robert Blake, who arrived in Cork harbour with a parliamentarian fleet on 5 November, assured Cromwell that the Cork garrison had 'a firme and sincere affectio[n] . . . to the English Interest and Army', and he was confident that the other towns would follow suit.[9]

Broghill, who arrived with Blake, soon began to use his local influence to ensure that this would happen. His first target was the old Boyle town of Youghal, which soon sent representatives to take advantage of the 'access of the Lord of Broghill' – their former governor – to treat with the parliamentarian forces under Blake. This delegation was led by the town's recorder, Broghill's kinsman and long-standing servant of the first earl of Cork, Joshua Boyle.[10] Other important defectors included Major Francis Foulke and Captain Henry Smithwick – both of whom had served under Broghill in the 1640s.[11] Broghill himself played an important part in the surrender of

---

[5] *Cal. S.P. Dom., 1649–50*, pp 584, 587.

[6] *H.M.C. Portland*, ii, 67; corporation of Youghal to Cromwell, 7 Nov. 1649 (B.L., Add. MS 25287, f. 39v).

[7] *Cal. S.P. Dom., 1649–50*, pp 77, 112, 121; Richard Caulfield (ed.), *The council book of the corporation of the city of Cork, 1609–43, 1690–1800* (Guildford, 1876), pp 1164–5, 1178–9.

[8] Richard Deane to Lenthall (Bodl., MS Tanner 56, ff 138r–9r); *H.M.C. Leyborne-Popham*, p. 48.

[9] Blake to Cromwell, 5 Nov. 1649 (Bodl., MS Tanner 56, f. 137r).

[10] Corporation of Youghal to Cromwell, 7 Nov. 1649 (B.L., Add. MS 25287, f. 39v).

[11] Richard Caulfield (ed.), *The council book of the corporation of Youghal* (Guildford, 1878), pp 560–1, 563, 565–7; for Boyle and Smithwick see petition of Munster forces to Ormond, 6 Oct. 1644 (Bodl., MS Carte 12, f. 439r); for Foulke see his History of Parliament, 1640–60 section, draft biography.

Youghal, according to Cromwell's report to the speaker of the commons, William Lenthall. On being presented with the town's terms, 'my Lo[rd] Broughall being on board the shippe answreing them it would be more for their honour and advantage to desire noe conditions. They said they would submitt: whereupon my Lo[rd] Broughall[,] Sr William Fenton and Coll Faire [Phaier] went to the towne and were received. I shall give you my Lo[rd] Broughalls owne words, wth all the reall demonstrations of gladnesse an overioyed people were capable off.'[12]

As the final arrangements were made at Youghal, the towns of Kinsale and Bandon made their own approaches to parliament's forces. Once again, Broghill proved an important influence on the townsmen's allegiances. The inhabitants of Kinsale had shown signs of defecting to parliament in early November, and had contacted Broghill and Phaier at Cork to discuss terms, but the garrison of the fort only surrendered when Broghill arrived in person.[13] Bandon, another town with traditional ties to the Boyle family, was also preparing to defect at this time, despite the strength of its Ormondist governor. On 25 November, Cromwell had heard that the townsmen had overthrown their commander, and therefore sent Broghill to take control.[14] But, as Broghill soon discovered, the town remained in the grip of royalist officers under Colonel Francis Courtenay. According to later accounts, on Broghill's approach to Bandon, the junior officers had 'contrived to seize on the guard' but had been thwarted. The inhabitants then sent envoys to Broghill, offering to open the gates if the royalists would not surrender, but Courtenay backed down, and Bandon was eventually delivered to Broghill without bloodshed.[15] With Kinsale and Bandon now secure, in early December Broghill marched eastwards into County Waterford, where he forced the town of Dungarvan to surrender on terms.[16]

In less than two months, five key garrison towns (and numerous smaller outposts) had defected to parliament, four of them owing to the direct intervention of Broghill. Cromwell was clearly impressed. In his reports back to Westminster, the lord lieutenant was fulsome in his praise of Broghill's activities: 'I must needs say', he wrote to Lenthall from Dungarvan in December, 'that in the bringing in of this garrison, Kingsale, the fort of Bandonbridge, Mallow and divers other garrisons, his Lordship hath been most eminently serviceable unto you'.[17] Cromwell rewarded Broghill by boosting his authority in the newly captured area. In mid-November Broghill and Fenton were

---

[12] Cromwell to Lenthall, 14 Nov. 1649 (Bodl., MS Tanner 56, f. 142r–v).

[13] Richard Caulfield (ed.), *The council book of the corporation of Kinsale, 1652–1800* (Guildford, 1879), pp 357–8.

[14] Cromwell to Lenthall, received 12 Dec. 1649 (Bodl., MS Tanner 56, f. 151r).

[15] Caulfield, *Kinsale*, pp. 361–2; see also J. T. Gilbert, *A contemporary history of affairs in Ireland from 1641–52* (3 vols, Dublin, 1880), ii, 322–3.

[16] Abbott, *Writings and speeches*, ii, 173–5; Gilbert, *Contemporary history*, ii, 334.

[17] Abbott, *Writings and speeches*, ii, 177.

appointed 'Commissioners for a temporary managem[en]t of affaires' in Cork;[18] and when two regiments were raised from the Cork and Youghal garrisons, Cromwell involved Broghill in the nomination of officers.[19] Significantly, on his arrival in Munster, Broghill had also been commissioned as colonel of a double regiment of horse, again drawn from the Old Protestants of the province.[20] This gave him not only a source of local patronage and a regular salary for himself, it also enhanced his military prestige, as a double regiment implied seniority, even precedence, among his fellow colonels. The appointment may even have been intended to emulate Cromwell's own command of a double regiment of horse in the Eastern Association army of the first Civil War.[21] Cromwell was also behind efforts to alleviate Broghill's financial problems, by requesting money-grants from Westminster: both the £200 awarded in December 1649 for Broghill's wife, and the £1,000 p.a. grant of lands (until his own could be retaken from the enemy) in January 1650, were secured through Cromwell's lobbying.[22]

Broghill's readiness to serve in Munster, and Cromwell's willingness to reward that service, soon brought the two men from an association of convenience to a close political alliance. While in winter quarters at Youghal, Cromwell was the guest of the Boyle family in their residence, the old college.[23] The favoured position of Broghill was reported in the London newsbooks. For example, in a letter released for publication by the council of state in the new year of 1650, London readers were told that

> my Lord Lieutenant came from Youghall (the head-Quarter) unto Corke, my Lord Broghill, Sir William Fenton, and diverse other Gentlemen, and Commanders, attending his Excellency, who hath received here very hearty and noble entertainement . . . This week I beleeve they will visit Kingsale, Bandon Bridge, and other places in the Province, who have lately Declared for us.[24]

The prominence of Broghill in this triumphant cavalcade underlined not only his crucial role in bringing in the Munster towns, but also the special relationship which he now enjoyed with the victorious Oliver Cromwell.

---

[18] Cromwell to Thomas Scot, 14 Nov. 1649 (Bodl., MS Tanner 56, f. 140r).
[19] Cromwell to Cork and Youghal corporations, 12–13 Nov. 1649 (B.L., Add. MS 25287, ff 40v–42r).
[20] Youghal officers to Cromwell, c.Nov. 1649 (ibid., ff 41v–2r); payment and list of troops in Broghill's regiment, 18 Dec. 1649 (P.R.O., S.P. 28/64/2, ff 273r, 275r).
[21] C. H. Firth and G. Davies, The regimental history of Cromwell's army (2 vols, Oxford, 1940), i, 5–6.
[22] Cromwell to Scot, 14 Nov. 1649 (Bodl., MS Tanner 56, f. 140r); Cal. S.P. Dom., 1649–50, p. 595; Abbott, Writings and speeches, ii, 177; C.J., vi, 344a.
[23] Caulfield, Youghal, p. liii. In the absence of the earl and countess of Cork, the invitation to use the college was presumably extended on their behalf by Broghill.
[24] A Briefe Relation, no. 17 (1–8 Jan. 1650), pp 215–6 (B.L., E.589(7)). I am very grateful to Dr Jason Peacey for drawing my attention to this reference.

Broghill's relations with Cromwell's subordinates were not so cosy. Public demonstrations of Broghill's alliance with Cromwell had heightened expectations (in Munster, at least) that he would soon gain a permanent position in the province's government. The notion was already current in the garrison towns in the closing weeks of 1649. As early as November 1649 the Youghal officers had petitioned Cromwell 'that the Lord of Broghill . . . bee Qualified with power to command the province'.[25] It seemed natural that Broghill, as undisputed leader of the Old Protestant interest in the province, would now be appointed lord president of Munster, not least because it would mark his crucial role in ousting the existing holder of the office, his old enemy, Lord Inchiquin. It was surely no coincidence that Broghill decided to make Inchiquin's house at Cork his own official residence in the winter of 1649–50.[26] Yet, only days after the triumphal progress around the Munster garrisons, parliament granted the presidency of the province to Cromwell's son-in-law, Henry Ireton.[27] The royalist agent, Sir John Grenville, soon heard reports that Broghill, 'discontented wth Cromwells refusing him the Goverment [sic] of Munster & disposing it to his sonne in lawe Ireton', planned to defect to the Ormondist camp.[28] There is no evidence to suggest that Broghill's loyalties were wavering, but Grenville's basic information was accurate: the appointment of Ireton could only be interpreted as a rejection of Broghill, as the most obvious candidate for the position, and Broghill's relations with the new lord president were distinctly cool after Cromwell's departure from Ireland in the spring of 1650.

There followed a series of affronts to Broghill's authority in Munster. In recognition of his service against the Irish in western Munster earlier in the year, and possibly on Cromwell's recommendation, on 28 June 1650 parliament resolved that the £1,000 p.a. previously granted to Broghill should become a permanent settlement on him and his heirs, in satisfaction of his pay arrears.[29] Yet in this new award there may have been an element of compensation: for, in early July 1650, Broghill was again passed over for promotion, this time as lieutenant-general of the horse in Ireland. Broghill had long coveted this position – which had been held by Michael Jones until his death in December 1649 – as it would compliment his role as colonel of a double regiment of horse, and give him a much-needed additional salary. But on 2 July the lieutenant-general's office was given to an outsider – the New Model colonel, Edmund Ludlow.[30] The promotion coincided with the nomination of Ludlow and

[25] Youghal officers to Cromwell, c.Nov. 1649 (B.L., Add. 25287, f. 41r).

[26] Caulfield, *Youghal*, p. liii.

[27] *C.J.*, vi, 344; *Cal. S.P. Dom.*, 1649–50, p. 476.

[28] Grenville to Robert Long, received 19 Apr. 1650 (B.L., Add. MS 37047, f. 78v).

[29] *C.J.*, vi, 434; for the importance of this grant to Broghill's financial position see below, ch. 8.

[30] Bulstrode Whitelocke, *Memorials of English affairs* (4 vols, Oxford, 1853), iii, 214.

another officer, Colonel John Jones, as new parliamentary commissioners to take control of the civil government of Ireland.[31] They were soon joined by two additional commissioners, Miles Corbett and John Weaver. Both civil and military government positions seemed to be slipping through Broghill's fingers.

In the circumstances, there is no reason to doubt Ludlow's own account of Broghill's reaction during the following months: 'The Lord Broghil, who had conceived great hopes of obtaining the command of the horse, or at least to be made a general officer, well knowing his own merit, and thereupon thinking himself neglected, made his complaint to the Deputy [Ireton] in a letter directed to him . . . wherein enumerating the services he had done, he declared his resolution not to obey the commands of any other but of General Cromwell and him.' Ludlow admitted that Broghill's indignation was justified, 'by reason of his interest and experience in the country; I being in those respects much inferiour to him'.[32] Broghill does indeed seem to have taken his rejection very hard, and other evidence supports the claim that he refused to co-operate in the military campaigns of the second half of 1650: the newsbooks, usually so avid in recounting tales of his exploits, are strangely silent about Broghill's activities in this period. According to Ludlow, relations remained strained until the new year of 1651, when Ireton met the newly-arrived parliamentary commissioners, to decide Broghill's fate: 'whether he should be wholly laid aside, or whether something should be done in order to content him for the present, by conferring upon him some office of profit, and the title of general officer'.[33] The meeting decided on the latter course, and in February 1651 Broghill was appointed lieutenant-general of the ordnance – as a counterpart to the mastership of the ordnance, which he had enjoyed since 1648.

Ireton and the commissioners do seem to have made an effort at keeping Broghill on board at this time. On 10 February they wrote to Speaker Lenthall in support of Broghill's request that his award of £1,000 p.a. from enemy estates be perfected, and problems with the legislation ironed out.[34] Some sort of reconciliation had evidently been effected by the spring of 1651, as Broghill again began to attract attention by his military service in Munster, and he defeated Viscount Muskerry in a decisive battle in June.[35] Yet, despite his successes against the Catholic Irish, Broghill's military authority was further eroded in the summer of 1651, when he lost the privilege of commanding a double regiment of horse. From the pay warrants issued by Ireton, it is clear that the nine troops mentioned regularly as forming Broghill's regiment from

---

[31] *Cal. S.P. Dom., 1649–50*, p. 228.
[32] *Ludlow memoirs*, i, 263–4. For Ludlow's reliability as a source see Blair Worden, *Roundhead reputations: the English Civil Wars and the passions of posterity* (2001), chs 1–4.
[33] *Ludlow memoirs*, i, 264.
[34] *H.M.C. Portland*, i, 557.
[35] *Mercurius Politicus*, no. 56 (26 June–3 July 1651), pp 896–7 (B.L., E.633(6)); Bodl., MS Tanner 54, f. 76.

late 1649 had been reduced to four by July 1651. Furthermore, in what may have been a deliberate snub, at least four of these reduced troops (those commanded by William Warden, George Bishop, Joseph Cuffe and Thomas Southwell) had now been incorporated into Ludlow's own horse regiment.[36] During 1652 there was the constant danger that Broghill's attempts to make Muskerry surrender upon articles of war would be misinterpreted,[37] especially after the row which followed Sir Charles Coote's alleged leniency to the Irish at the surrender of Galway.[38] In October 1652, for example, Broghill's decision to arm local farmers against attacks by Catholic robbers and tories came under hostile scrutiny.[39] It was therefore not much of a surprise when, in the reduction of the army during the summer of 1653 (when most of the Old Protestant commanders lost their positions), Broghill's horse regiment was disbanded altogether, leaving him with a single non-regimented troop. Although he retained his position as lieutenant-general of the ordnance, Broghill had thus been removed from any real influence in the Irish army.[40]

From January 1650, when he was presented as Cromwell's favourite, to the summer of 1653, when he lost his regiment, Broghill was subjected to a series of rebuffs from the civil administration and the military high command in Ireland. He had been denied the presidency of Munster and the position of lieutenant-general of horse; and as Ludlow's influence increased, Broghill's regimental command was halved, and then removed altogether. The wasting away of Broghill's military position was a sign of his worsening relations with the commonwealth regime in Ireland. This was more than merely a personal feud between Broghill and either Ireton or Ludlow and his colleagues in the parliamentary commission: it was symptomatic of a deeper malaise in Ireland, caused by tensions between the Old Protestants and the Englishmen in the government and the army. Competition for commands and civil appointments was exacerbated by deeper questions arising from the need to settle Ireland after the defeat of the rebels. As Ludlow admitted, 'those of the army showed great partiality' against the Irish Protestants when lobbying for an advantageous land settlement.[41] Religion was also a cause of tension, as radical Independents in the army became involved in Baptist (and, later on, Quaker) sects.[42] Such tensions were far from being unique to Ireland, and provided an early instance of how problems in the commonwealth tended to spread,

---

[36] P.R.O., S.P. 28/79/1, ff 91r, 103r, 235r; S.P. 28/64/2, ff 273r, 275r; S.P. 28/81/1, f. 143r; S.P. 28/86/1, f. 52r.

[37] Dunlop, *Ireland*, i, 116; *Mercurius Politicus*, no. 95, p. 1520 (B.L., E. 658(13)); Sankey to John Jones, 9 Mar. 1652 (Bodl., MS Tanner 55, f. 166r).

[38] William Basill to Lenthall, 12 Apr. 1652 (ibid., MS 53, f. 4r); parliamentary commissioners and army officers to Lenthall, 5 May 1652 (ibid., f. 20r).

[39] Dunlop, *Ireland*, i, 292.

[40] Firth and Davies, *Regimental history*, ii, 588.

[41] *Ludlow memoirs*, i, 338.

[42] See Henry Cromwell's comments in *Thurloe S.P.*, ii, 149.

affecting all the constituent nations equally.[43] This underlined what was already becoming evident to Broghill and other Old Protestants – that they desperately needed to influence the government in England.

II

Despite his worsening relations with the administration in Ireland, throughout the early 1650s Broghill was careful to maintain his good relations with Oliver Cromwell. Cromwell's timely departure from Ireland, soon after Broghill's failure to gain the presidency of Munster, meant that he was not implicated in the vindictiveness of Ireton or Ludlow, although he did little to intervene on Broghill's behalf. Cromwell, as lord lieutenant – and thus head of the Irish government even in his absence – became a focus for Old Protestants seeking a court of appeal against the partialities of the Dublin administration, and this encouraged suitors to cross the Irish sea for redress in England. Cromwell certainly used his influence to help individual Old Protestant claimants, but as he tended to act behind the scenes, possibly in an effort to avoid embarrassing the governors within Ireland, his moves are often obscure. Despite this, it is clear that Broghill's friends and relatives generally had a courteous reception from Cromwell, and it is through such case-studies that we can glean evidence of the continuing alliance between the two men in this period.

Broghill was able to intercede with Cromwell on behalf of the wider Boyle affinity in the early 1650s. The former royalist, Viscount Moore, who was related to Broghill through the first marriage of Broghill's sister, Sarah Digby, was allowed to return to his estates at Mellifont in May 1650 through Cromwell's intercession, after Broghill had championed his cause.[44] Likewise, the hand of Broghill may be detected behind Cromwell's efforts to protect the financial security of two of Broghill's brothers-in-law, Sir Arthur Loftus and the earl of Kildare, in 1649 and 1651 respectively.[45] Early moves towards the rehabilitation of Broghill's elder brother, the second earl of Cork, also seem to have owed something to his influence with Cromwell. In January 1651 the countess of Cork's agent in England reported that the family's interests were served 'beyond exp[ectation] by y[ou]r Sister R[anelagh] & y[ou]r br[others] R[obert] & Rog[e]r'.[46] In the same year, when the earl and his family were at last allowed to return to Ireland, the countess thanked Cromwell for

---

[43] For tensions between the army and parliament in England see Blair Worden, *The Rump Parliament* (Cambridge, 1974).

[44] Lynch, *Orrery*, p. 79; Dunlop, *Ireland*, i, 24.

[45] Abbott, *Writings and speeches*, ii, 116n, 165; *Cal. S.P. Dom., 1650–1*, p. 456: both had lost their commands in 1649, and suffered near bankruptcy thereafter: see below, ch. 8.

[46] W. Thornton to 'Richard Richardson' [Cork] at Caen, 14 Jan. 1651 (B.L., Althorp B6, unfol.).

supporting their cause, and reassured him that their activities in protecting their interests had been entirely above board, 'for my brother Broghill was therewith acquainted'.[47] As in all these cases, the implication was that Cromwell was working to ensure the survival of Cork principally on the request of Broghill.

Broghill's efforts were not entirely selfless, as his position in Munster was dependent on the collective power of the Boyles. After 1649 the family had seen its civil, as well as military, authority in the province go into decline, as control of County Cork came under the control of the Baptist governor of the precinct, Colonel Robert Phaier, and the chief justice of Munster, John Cook – neither of whom was favourable to the Boyle family.[48] This situation was mitigated by the decision of the English government to allow the return of the earl of Cork to his Munster estates in May 1651. The earl still had enormous social and landed influence within the province, and his return gave the Boyles the opportunity to try to reassert their dominance in Munster. This dimension was not lost on Broghill, whose cultivation of his brother's local influence is evident from the earl's diary. On his arrival in Ireland, Cork journeyed to Youghal, where 'My brother Broghill and the L[or]d Barrymore came to visit mee'. After the initial briefing, Cork joined Broghill at his camp at Castlelyons on 3 June, from whence the two brothers stayed at Broghill's castle at Blarney for a week. In early July Cork accompanied Broghill to the old family town of Bandon, 'where I was visited by the Provost and Burgesses'. In October Broghill and Cork attended Ireton in his headquarters before Limerick, passing through Kilmallock and other Boyle lands in County Limerick, before returning to County Cork in early November.[49] The itinerary, which took in much of the traditional Boyle area of influence, was perhaps designed to remind the locals that their overlord had returned. Just as important was Broghill's accompaniment of his brother, as such a tour emphasized the renewed unity of the Boyle clan after years of political disunity, just as the triumphal progress of Broghill and Cromwell had demonstrated their own alliance in late 1649. Broghill had a great deal to gain from the political and financial resurrection of the earldom of Cork, as we shall see.

Cork lost no time in making efforts to recover his estates in Munster. In August 1651, for example, he persuaded Colonel Phaier, the otherwise

---

[47] John Nickolls (ed.) *Original letters and papers of state . . . among the political collections of . . . John Milton* (1743), p. 85; see also Abbott, *Writings and speeches*, ii, 230–1.

[48] Although Broghill and Fenton had served as revenue commissioners for the county in 1649, by 1650 they had both been removed, and Phaier took over as chairman: compare order of revenue commissioners, 24 Nov. 1649 (Chatsworth, Lismore MS 28, no. 13) and order of revenue commissioners, 12 Oct., 1650 (P.R.O., S.P. 28/71/1, f. 13r). Broghill did not return to the commission until 1652: see B.L., Eg. MS 1762, f. 202v. For John Cook see T. C. Barnard, *Cromwellian Ireland* (Oxford, 1975), pp 273–4.

[49] Second earl of Cork's diary (Chatsworth, Lismore MS 29, unfol.), entries for 31 May, 3 June, 6 June, 27–8 June, 4 July, 30 July, 27–9 Oct., 3 Nov. 1651.

unsympathetic governor of the Cork precinct, to lift the suspension on his lands in the county.[50] But such moves attracted the hostile attention of the parliamentary commissioners, who were wary of allowing a former royalist (and Broghill's brother) too much leeway. On 4 October the commissioners issued an order stating that the Irish estates of all persons who, like Cork, had been sequestered for their support of the king in England, should be confiscated and the profits assigned to the government.[51] Cork, who had hoped that his subscription of the Dublin Articles in 1647 had saved him from such penalties, suddenly saw his position in Ireland under threat, and it was this that gave added urgency to his visit to Ireton at Limerick in late October. When the earl took leave of the lord deputy on 1 November he pressed his case, and received assurances that 'when hee met with the Commissioners of Parliam[en]t that hee wold remove all ruts in my busines'.[52] The case remained unresolved when Ireton died in November, however, and in the period of uncertainty that followed, Broghill became fearful that the commissioners would manage to increase their power in the Irish government. Writing to Bulstrode Whitelocke (who, as an English councillor, had some influence over Irish policy), Broghill bemoaned Ireton's death, fearing 'the Change Its like to produce In our affayres here'.[53] But, although the commissioners did pass resolutions maintaining their power, and appointing Ludlow as commander-in-chief,[54] their authority was not confirmed, as the English parliament delayed in naming a successor to Ireton, or instituting a new form of government for Ireland.[55]

This hiatus, and the assembling of a council of officers at Kilkenny in December 1651, provided Broghill with an opportunity to intervene on Cork's behalf. On 23 December, as Cork noted in his diary, 'My brother Broghill went towards Kilkenny to meete the Commissioners of Parliament'.[56] In a confrontation with Broghill, the commissioners were forced to admit that they did not have the authority to confiscate Cork's property, and that the Dublin articles might still be valid. As they later complained to the council of state's Irish committee, 'uppon the debate of that matter wee conceived ourselves under some difficultie how to proceede therin and in other cases of that nature without some further significacon of the Parliam[en]ts sense theruppon'.[57]

---

[50] Ibid., 28–30 Aug. 1651.

[51] B.L., Eg. MS 1779, f. 36r.

[52] Cork's diary (Chatsworth, Lismore MS 29, unfol.), 27–8 Oct., 1 Nov. 1651.

[53] Broghill to Whitelocke, 1 Dec. 1651 (Longleat, Whitelocke papers, vol. 11, f. 148r).

[54] B.L., Eg. MS 1779, ff 43v–44r.

[55] The commissioners demanded clarification on 2 December, and this was received on 9 December, but the matter was not even referred to the council of state for consideration until 13 January: see parliamentary commissioners to Lenthall, 2 Dec. 1651 (Bodl., MS Tanner 55, f. 99r); C.J., vii, 49a, 63b, 68a.

[56] Cork's diary (Chatsworth, Lismore MS 29, unfol.), 23 Dec. 1651.

[57] Parliamentary commissioners to Irish committee, 16 Jan. 1652 (Bodl., MS Tanner 55, f. 116r).

Apparently at a loss how to proceed, the commissioners seem to have capitulated to (or perhaps attempted to buy off?) the Boyles, and on 2 January they allowed Cork to enjoy the profits of his estate for two years, or until a permanent decision could be made.[58] In an equally extraordinary move, on the very same day the commissioners passed another order, that 'Baron Broghill to be added to Com[mission] of Rev[enue] at Cork' – the body given power to implement the order on the earl of Cork's behalf.[59] Thus reinforced, on 5 January Broghill returned to Youghal, presenting Cork with orders (in the earl's words), 'enabling mee to receive my rent notwithstanding their restriction issued the 4th 8ber [i.e. October] upon Security by mee given'.[60] His £2,000 bond was agreed with the revenue commissioners for County Cork – a body which now included Broghill – on 7 January, and was certified by them on 12 January.[61] The weakness of the parliamentary commissioners at this time had profound implications. Not only had Cork been reprieved, the decision had also set a precedent for other former royalists with Irish estates. Delinquents such as Viscount Conway had recognised as early as November 1651 that the fate of Cork would be a test case,[62] and a flood of claims followed the award in January, with Lord Montgomery of the Ards, Viscount Clandeboye, Conway, the Percivalles and other Irish Protestants all benefiting. This automatically reduced the amount of confiscated land free for reallocation to the army. Once the mistake had been realised, it was too late. As the commissioners later complained, 'by this Vote there is an hundred thousand pounds att least [lost] at one Clap'.[63]

The confused state of the Irish government was not resolved until the end of 1652. The source of the problem was parliament, and its worsening record of co-operation with the army and the Cromwellians.[64] After a long delay, John Lambert, who had been nominated as general of the army in Ireland in January, refused to serve in June, and the council of state nominated as commander-in-chief in his place Cromwell's son-in-law, Charles Fleetwood, who was appointed by parliament in July and arrived in Ireland in September – ten months after Ireton's death.[65] Although short-term gains had been made

---

[58] Dunlop, *Ireland*, i, 116.

[59] B.L., Eg. MS 1762, f. 202v. Broghill was also added to the commission for the administration of justice in the county on 2 January (ibid.). On the same day Broghill was granted £100 by the commissioners, for his expenses, and he was also given charge of setting up a new garrison in the Fenton townland of Fermoy: see Edward MacLysaght (ed.), 'Commonwealth state accounts, 1650–6' in *Analecta Hibernica*, xv (1944), p. 317.

[60] Cork's diary (Chatsworth, Lismore MS 29, unfol.), 5 Jan. 1652.

[61] Ibid., entry for 7 Jan. 1652; certificate of revenue commissioners, 12 Jan. 1652 (ibid., MS 28, no. 22).

[62] *Cal. S.P. Ire.*, 1647–60, p. 383.

[63] Parliamentary commissioners to Sir Arthur Hesilrige, 2 Nov. 1652 (Bodl., MS Firth c.5, f. 84v).

[64] Worden, *Rump Parliament*, pp 265–316.

[65] C.J., vii, 77, 79, 133–4, 142–3, 152; Barnard, *Cromwellian Ireland*, pp 17–18.

by the Boyles during this period of confusion, their long-term financial and political prosperity depended on a strong (and sympathetic) government. This explains the Boyles' guarded welcome of Fleetwood, who arrived in Ireland in late 1652. Cork and Broghill attended the new commander on his arrival at Waterford, and the earl extracted new promises of 'his best assistance in my purpose', in other words, the confirmation of his estates.[66]

Cork's position had already started to improve markedly during the late summer of 1652, when the council of state presented the matter to parliament, which referred it to the court of the articles of war in September.[67] Having already petitioned parliament, in October Cork lobbied the court of the articles, and on 6 October his cause was further advanced by Broghill, who had returned from another meeting with the parliamentary commissioners in Ireland bearing news that they had 'promised to leave my estate in the same condition it was of suspension untill the resolution concerning it twas taken in England'.[68] On 10 December the whole case was referred to the court of the articles, and on 7 January 1653 the earl was at last granted the right to compound under the Dublin articles, and the decision was extended to all royalists who had not actively supported the king after 1647.[69] In March 1653 Cork and Broghill again waited on the parliamentary commissioners in Dublin, and in April orders were passed to restore the earl to his estates.[70] The Cork estates, and thus the earl's social and political hegemony in Munster, now seemed secure.

The tireless activity of Broghill throughout the struggle to protect the earl's interests underlines the collective responsibility which had been fostered by the first earl of Cork, and remained an important factor within the Boyle affinity even after years of political difference and geographical separation.[71] It also shows just how important the recovery of the second earl of Cork was to Broghill's own ambitions in Munster in the 1650s. It was no coincidence that Broghill's political influence improved at the same time as Cork's financial fortunes. Although Broghill had lost much of his military authority by the spring of 1653, his involvement in the civil government increased. He was especially active on the local revenue commission,[72] which he seems to have controlled at this time: in April 1653 he was granted custody of lands in Imokilly by virtue of his role as revenue commissioner;[73] and in May 1653 he

---

[66] Cork's diary (Chatsworth, Lismore MS 29, unfol.), 15–16 Sept. 1652.

[67] Memorandum on Cork's estates, 10 Dec. 1652 (ibid., MS 28, no. 30).

[68] Cork's petition, Oct. 1652 (Chatsworth, Lismore MS 28, no. 26); Cork's diary (ibid MS 29, unfol.), 6 Oct. 1652.

[69] Orders of commissioners for relief upon articles, 7 Jan. 1653 (ibid., Lismore MS 28, nos. 34, 36).

[70] Cork's diary (ibid., Lismore MS 29, unfol.), 27–9 Mar. 1653; order of parliamentary commissioners, 11 Apr. 1653 (ibid., Lismore MS 28, no. 39).

[71] See below, ch. 7.

[72] Dunlop, *Ireland*, ii, 292.

[73] B.L., Eg. MS 1762, f. 207v.

was able to order the garrison commanders of north County Cork to protect the lands of his neighbour, John Percivalle (son of Sir Philip), and to help him distrain for unpaid rents – neither of them activities that came within their formal remit.[74] In August, Broghill was appointed to the standing committee for transplanting the native Irish to Connacht, and in October he was given charge of transporting 'beggars and idlers' from County Cork to the New World.[75] With the earl of Cork now re-established in Munster, Broghill was becoming increasingly confident of his own position in the province. The reprieve of Cork, and its knock-on effect for other former royalists, also confirmed Broghill's position as a defender of Old Protestant rights across Ireland. His only rival as overall leader of the Protestant Interest was the lord president of Connacht, Sir Charles Coote; but Coote's influence was closely tied in with his own military position, and he had thus suffered far more than Broghill from the 1653 reduction of the army. Moreover, Coote did not share Broghill's close connexion with Oliver Cromwell.

The importance of having friends in the English government was becoming increasingly apparent at this time. As Cork and Broghill reasserted their local pre-eminence, the future of Ireland was being decided at Westminster. The act of settlement and the act for stating soldiers' accounts, both passed in August 1652, had started the process of confiscation and reallocation of Irish land, but, despite extensive debate, the Rump did not fulfil expectations that more legislation would follow.[76] As William Dobbins reported to John Percivalle from London in March 1653, 'The Act for the Adventurers lies still asleep, and it is not known which way it will be settled when it goes on'.[77] The increasing radicalism of the army and the growing hostility of the parliamentary commissioners made such a settlement by statute crucial to the wider Old Protestant interest in Ireland. At stake was not only the allocation of land and the protection of Protestant estates, but also the pressing need to confirm the awards recently made to former royalists and to secure compensation for arrears of military pay owed to those who had fought for parliament in Ireland during the 1640s.[78] The desire to secure a permanent settlement seems to have overridden any religious qualms among some Old Protestants over supporting the Nominated Assembly (commonly known as the Barebone's Parliament) instituted in the summer of 1653 to replace the moribund Rump. Six M.P.s were returned for Ireland, three of whom were of established Irish families – Sir Robert King of County Roscommon, Alderman Daniel Hutchinson of Dublin, and the Cork landowner (and Broghill's colleague on the revenue

---

[74] H.M.C. Egmont, i, 519.

[75] Dunlop, Ireland, ii, 369–70, 375.

[76] A & O, ii, 598–612.

[77] H.M.C. Egmont, i, 516.

[78] Efforts by Cromwell and others to settle the pre-1649 arrears had been rebuffed by the parliamentary commissioners as recently as April 1653: Dunlop, Ireland, ii, 332–3.

commission), Vincent Gookin.[79] These three, collaborating with another Irish M.P., Oliver Cromwell's son, Henry Cromwell, formed an important lobbying group in parliament. William Dobbins soon reported that 'Our Parliament members of Ireland have been very active and are daily sitting in revising and finishing the Adventurers' Act':[80] this was the 'Act for the Satisfaction of the Adventurers', passed on 26 September 1653, which allowed the allocation of land to the Irish adventurers and the parliamentarian army of conquest. Crucially, it also allowed the settlement of military arrears incurred in Ireland before 1649, and the repayment of money lent, or supplies procured, for the forces loyal to parliament from 1641.[81] In theory, the financial position of Broghill and his fellow Old Protestants had thus been secured. The problem remained of making sure the act was implemented, and this meant overcoming significant obstacles in England as well as Ireland.

III

After the uncertainties of the previous years, the establishment of Oliver Cromwell as lord protector in December 1653 was broadly welcomed by the Old Protestant community. In early 1654 the Munster agent in London, William Dobbins, was effusive in his praise of the new regime: 'now the Lord Protector is settled, to the good liking of most judicious, honest, quiet-spirited men, we trust and are confident of the smoother and equaller proceedings and certainer periods and conclusions of differences'.[82] This sense of release made for a tumultuous reception for the new protector's son, Henry Cromwell, when he arrived in Dublin in early March 1654. In his own report of 8 March, Henry Cromwell attacked the 'peevishness and frowardness' of Ludlow and Jones, and added that 'sober men (not anabaptists) are overjoyed with hopes, that the time is now come of their deliverance from that bondage and subjection, which they were in'.[83] According to one witness of Henry Cromwell's reception in Dublin, even a large section of the army welcomed the change of regime in England, while others were pleased 'that religion, ministery, lawes, mens proprietys, are own'd and protected'.[84]

---

[79] Austin Woolrych, *Commonwealth to Protectorate* (Oxford, 1982), pp 179–83; for Gookin see Patricia Coughlan, 'Counter-currents in colonial discourse: the political thought of Vincent and Daniel Gookin' in Jane Ohlmeyer (ed.), *Political thought in seventeenth century Ireland: kingdom or colony?* (Cambridge, 2000), pp 56–82.

[80] *H.M.C. Egmont*, i, 524; Woolrych, *Commonwealth to protectorate*, pp 304–5.

[81] *A & O*, ii, 722–52.

[82] *H.M.C. Egmont*, i, 534, 537–8. Dobbins, formerly an ally of Inchiquin, was another Old Protestant who obviously had little problem in conforming to the new regime.

[83] *Thurloe S.P.*, ii, 149.

[84] Ibid., pp 162–3.

Among the Old Protestants who flocked to Dublin was Lord Broghill, who travelled from Munster twice, on 13 March (returning on the 25th) and 1 April 1654.[85] On both occasions, Broghill was evidently eager to renew his acquaintance with Henry Cromwell (who had been his colleague in the Irish wars in 1650–2), but there were also more immediate political reasons for staying in Dublin at this time. Not least was the need to influence the general council of officers which had been convened to sort out the division of land and the further reduction of the army.[86] Broghill seems to have pulled off something of a coup during his Dublin visits. He had been included in the commission appointed on 10 January 1654 to set out lands in County Cork for the disbanded forces in lieu of arrears,[87] and by February had succeeded in securing special treatment for the officers and men formerly of his own regiment in the barony of Kilmore and Orrery, an area in which he himself held land. Despite protests from other Munster Protestants (such as John Percivalle) who felt their own local interests threatened, this scheme went ahead.[88] On 11 April the parliamentary commissioners in Dublin issued an order 'being the desire of the Lord Broghills regiment, Sir William Fenton[,] Lt Coll Francis Foulk and other officers' allowing them half the lands in the baronies of Fermoy and Kilmore and Orrery. This order seems to have resulted from Broghill's lobbying the Dublin government – it was certainly no coincidence that its implementation was entrusted to the commissioners for setting lands in County Cork, a body dominated by Broghill and his uncle, Sir William Fenton.[89]

While Broghill was busy winning local battles over land allocation, the confidence of the Old Protestant community as a whole was dealt a serious blow by the sudden recall of Henry Cromwell to England. In early April it became clear that, contrary to expectations, Henry Cromwell was not going to take over running the Dublin administration.[90] As a result, the Old Protestants had lost 'the gentleman from whom so much was expected'.[91] Henry Cromwell's departure signalled that the affairs of Ireland would once again depend on English politics, especially as the form of the protectoral government in Ireland remained undecided, and so much still depended on the English council's deliberations on the Irish land settlement. This affected Broghill as much as his fellow Munstermen, and by early May 1654 he had himself travelled from Dublin to London, which would be his base throughout the following year.[92]

---

[85] Cork's diary (Chatsworth, Lismore MS 29, unfol.), 13, 25 Mar., 1 Apr. 1654.
[86] *Thurloe S.P.*, ii, 213.
[87] Dunlop, *Ireland*, ii, 391.
[88] H.M.C. *Egmont*, i, 536, 539.
[89] Bodl., MS Firth c.5, f. 150v.
[90] *Mercurius Politicus*, no. 203 (27 Apr.–4 May 1654), p. 3454 (B.L., E.734(6)).
[91] H.M.C. *Egmont*, i, 539.
[92] Broghill had left Dublin by 2 May: see Cork's diary (Chatsworth, Lismore MS 29, unfol.), 2 May 1654; H.M.C. *Egmont*, i, 540.

The formation of the protectoral government had made England a far more receptive place for Old Protestant lobbyists than it had been for many years. Before Broghill's arrival, a number of Irish Protestants had already made inroads into the counsels of the new government. William Dobbins, commenting in January 1654, recognised the importance of 'the Parliament men of Ireland' – the former Barebones' M.P.s, Sir Robert King, Vincent Gookin and Daniel Hutchinson – in on-going negotiations with the adventurers over the Irish land settlement.[93] Broghill quickly became part of this network on his arrival in London. The former clerk of the Irish council, Sir Paul Davies, asked William Dobbins to further his private business in England in consultation with 'the Lord Broghill, Sir Robert King and Alderman Hutchinson, on whom I now principally rely herein'.[94] John Percivalle, who also travelled to London in May 1654, presented his own petition to 'Lord Broghill, V. G[ookin], D. H[utchinson] and Sir J. C[lotworthy]', and agreed to be bound by Broghill's advice when approaching men of influence at Whitehall.[95] Although there were rumours in June that Broghill's 'interest is not so great as was believed' among government circles,[96] by the late summer he was again included in the roll-call of Irish 'fixers' in Westminster. On 25 July John Percivalle delivered a petition to Henry Cromwell 'by the hands of Bro[ghill], Mr [Arthur] Ans[ley], and Sir Jo[hn] Clot[worthy]', and later found his business retarded by Broghill's temporary absence from town, and Clotworthy's preoccupation with the adventurers' business.[97] Broghill had clearly become a central figure in the Irish network which sought to influence events in England. Moreover, he was not only working with his old allies among the Protestants who had sided with the Independents in the 1640s, but also with men who had, until recently, been his political opponents. After a period of estrangement from the republican regime, the former Presbyterian, Arthur Annesley, was back in London; and the return of Sir John Clotworthy, who had been impeached in 1647 and imprisoned in the early 1650s, is an important indication that the Old Protestant connexion was broadening to include Presbyterians and former royalists as well as those who had supported Viscount Lisle and the Independent party a decade before.[98] This was the next step in the development of a strong Old Protestant interest, which Broghill had initiated with his efforts earlier in the decade to rehabilitate former royalists (including his brother, the earl of Cork). For Broghill, the 'Old Protestants' had come to represent the whole of Protestant Ireland.

[93] H.M.C. Egmont, i, p. 534.

[94] Ibid., p. 540.

[95] Ibid., p. 541.

[96] Ibid., p. 542.

[97] Ibid., pp 551, 555.

[98] Clotworthy had been back in favour since April 1653, if not before: order of council of state, 4 Apr. 1653 (P.R.O.N.I., Foster-Massereene papers, D. 207/15/3).

This uniting of the Protestant interest was based on their common concern for land security and the settlement of the government of Ireland. Hopes of winning an ordinance of indemnity or 'oblivion' for the Munster Protestants had been on foot since 1653. The prime mover had been Broghill's neighbour from County Cork, Vincent Gookin, 'who hath exceedingly laboured in that business', and drafted the ordinance eventually submitted to the English council.[99] There is evidence that Broghill was also involved in this move. The council's committee only reported its recommendations on 8 May, perhaps hastened by Broghill's recent arrival in London,[100] and Broghill guarded the subsequent passage of the measure, warning other Irish Protestants not to press their own individual petitions for fear of jeopardising the general order.[101] Drafts of the ordinance were sent back to Dublin for consultation by Sir Paul Davies, Sir Gerard Lowther and other men of influence, and Arthur Annesley advised on matters in London.[102] Gookin's efforts finally paid off on 27 June, when the ordinance was passed by the protector's council, much to the relief of the Munster Protestants.[103] Its passage not only promised to protect landowners in the southern province: it also underlined the effectiveness of the Irish Protestant network as a lobbying tool in England, and highlighted Broghill's position at the centre of this Irish web of influence.

Broghill's political importance in 1654 was only partly dependent on the Old Protestant interest. Perhaps equally important was his continued ability to draw on support from the English government, and especially from key members of the protector's entourage. At least three prominent courtiers had connexions with Broghill, and he had been careful to cultivate such contacts since 1649. He remained associated with his old ally, the former lord lieutenant of Ireland, Viscount Lisle, and provided Lisle with intelligence from Ireland in the early 1650s.[104] Bulstrode Whitelocke, though absent on an embassy to Sweden for much of 1654, had been courted by Broghill since the beginning of 1650, and came to consider him a close friend.[105] The two men collaborated on various occasions in the following years.[106] By the summer of 1654 Broghill had also come into contact with Edward Mountagu – a relationship which

---

[99] H.M.C. Egmont, i, 544.

[100] Cal. S.P. Ire., 1647–60, p. 798.

[101] H.M.C. Egmont, i, 541.

[102] Ibid., pp 541–3.

[103] Cal. S.P. Ire., 1647–60, p. 804; H.M.C. Egmont, i, 546; Mercurius Politicus, no. 211 (22–9 June 1654), p. 3588 (B.L., E.745(6)).

[104] H.M.C. de Lisle, vi, 468.

[105] Whitelocke diary, pp 249–50.

[106] Broghill to Whitelocke, 1 Dec. 1651 (Longleat, Whitelocke Papers, vol. xi, f. 148r); Broghill to Whitelocke, 20 Dec. 1652 (ibid., vol. xii, f. 188r); Broghill reciprocated in September 1654, by supporting Whitelocke's claim to compensation for his ambassadorial expenses: see Whitelocke diary, p. 395.

would mature later in the decade.[107] As well as these connections, Broghill was also on intimate terms with the Cromwells, and during the summer of 1654 he became especially close to Henry Cromwell. As we have seen, John Percivalle and other Irish Protestants saw Broghill as their best chance to influence the protector's son, and some became suspicious that they were being deliberately distanced from the centre of power as a result.[108] There seems to have been some truth behind this slur. By the late summer of 1654 Broghill had wormed his way into a position of trust at Whitehall, and was able to control access to Henry Cromwell, who was, in turn, the best intercessor with an increasingly pre-occupied protector.[109] The duality of Broghill's political influence in the summer of 1654 – with the Old Protestants on the one hand, and the English 'court' on the other – was thus increased by his position as mediator between the two.

Much had been achieved by Broghill and his Old Protestant colleagues by the late summer of 1654. The principle had been conceded of including pre-1649 soldiers and settlers in the land allotments, and individual measures such as the ordinance for indemnity in Munster showed that the English government was less hostile to the Irish Protestants than the commonwealth had been. But a sense of insecurity remained, fostered by the knowledge that the English government could so easily reverse even these gains. The imminent parliament, set up under the terms of the Instrument of Government of December 1653, promised to settle many questions by enacting statutes as guarantees, and the inclusion of thirty Irish seats among the Westminster M.P.s meant that the Irish Protestants could at last hope to influence policy directly.[110] Yet these elections came close to not happening at all. Lord Deputy Fleetwood and the parliamentary commissioners, concerned at the growing influence of the Irish Protestants, pressed hard for the Irish seats to be allocated by the government, rather than elected by the people. In July 1654 John Percivalle reported with concern rumours that 'Lord Fleetwood . . . thinks Ireland not yet in a fit posture to elect their own members'.[111] Edmund Ludlow, in his memoirs, was more explicit: sporadic warfare and continued unrest in Ireland was being used by the Dublin government as a pretext to halt elections, for 'if the proprietors should chuse, they would return such as were enemies of the English [ie. the army] interest'.[112] The political balance of power could thus be tipped in the Old Protestants' favour. Fleetwood's advice seems to have fallen on deaf ears, however, and in late July writs of election were issued to the Irish boroughs and counties.[113]

---

[107] Broghill supplied Mountagu with information on the Irish revenues: see notes dated 20 July 1654 (Bodl., MS Carte 74, ff 90–1).

[108] H.M.C. Egmont, i, 543, 545–7, 550.

[109] Ibid., pp 551–2.

[110] S. R. Gardiner (ed.), The Constitutional documents of the puritan revolution, 1625–1660 (3rd ed., Oxford, 1906), pp 407–9.

[111] H.M.C. Egmont, i, 546.

[112] Ludlow memoirs, i, 387.

[113] Thurloe S.P., ii, 445.

There has been a tendency to see the Irish M.P.s elected to the first protectorate parliament as government placemen or military interlopers.[114] S. R. Gardiner asserted that the M.P.s 'were all supporters of the Government, the great majority of them being officers of the army', and likened the Irish seats to 'the Ministerial pocket-boroughs of the eighteenth century'.[115] Paul Pinckney, preparatory to his analysis of the 1656 elections, states that in 1654 the government decided all the places and 'most of those returned were Army officers'.[116] A close examination of the elections and the M.P.s returned suggests that the picture was in reality rather more complicated. The case of County Cork is instructive. All three M.P.s elected for the constituencies within the county were Old Protestants, and all seem to have been returned on the Boyle ticket. Broghill himself sat for the county; his neighbour, William Jephson, represented Cork and Youghal; Vincent Gookin was elected at Bandon and Kinsale.[117] The key figure in each of these elections was, in Broghill's absence, his brother, the earl of Cork. Cork visited Bandon on 24 and 25 July 1654 and was attended by the provost and burgesses, who asked him to name his own candidate for their borough; which, in his own words, 'I did the day after and nominated Mr Vincent Gookin, whom they afterwards upon my desier did choose'.[118] If Cork could choose his own man at Bandon, it is almost certain that he could influence the electorate at his home borough, Youghal. The return of William Jephson as M.P. for the latter, despite his prominence as one of Lord Inchiquin's allies in the 1640s, shows how far the new mood of consensus had penetrated even Munster society. Equally striking is the apparent absence of influence in these elections of the governor of Cork, the religious and political radical, Colonel Phaier.

The influence of the army was no more apparent in other areas. Factional divisions during the elections for Counties Kildare and Wicklow – where Major Anthony Morgan and Major William Meredith were elected against Lieutenant-General Ludlow, Major Salwey, Adjutant-General Allen and other candidates – may at first seem like an internal split within the army.[119] But, despite their military ranks, Morgan would become a close ally of Henry

---

[114] The Venetian ambassador (not the most reliable source for Irish information), stated in August 1654 that 'the majority [of Irish and Scottish MPs] are soldiers': *Cal. S.P. Ven.*, *1653–4*, p. 252.

[115] S. R. Gardiner, *History of the commonwealth and protectorate, 1649–56* (4 vols, 1903), iii, 173.

[116] P. J. Pinckney, 'A Cromwellian parliament: the elections and personnel of 1656' (unpublished Ph.D. thesis, Vanderbilt University, 1962), p. 232; see also Hugh Trevor-Roper, 'The union of Britain in the seventeenth century' in his *Religion, the reformation and social change* (3rd ed., 1984), p. 464.

[117] H.M.C. *Egmont*, i, 556; *Mercurius Politicus*, no. 218 (10–17 Aug. 1654), p. 3698 (B.L., E. 808(17)).

[118] Cork's diary (Chatsworth, Lismore MS 29, unfol.), 24–5 July 1654.

[119] H.M.C. *Egmont*, i, 553.

Cromwell, and Meredith was the son and heir of the Old Protestant chancellor of the exchequer, Sir Robert Meredith.[120] The ability of these two men to see off senior army officers also points to the influence of the Old Protestant interest in Leinster. A similar pattern can be discerned in Ulster and Connacht, where men such as Colonel Arthur Hill and Sir Charles Coote were able to return their own candidates in a number of seats. The crude identification of army officers with the Dublin government, as practised by both Gardiner and Pinckney, obscures the dominance of the Old Protestants and their English allies in the 1654 elections. Of the thirty M.P.s returned for Irish seats,[121] sixteen were of Old Protestant stock;[122] and a further three were elected due to Old Protestant electoral influence.[123] Four M.P.s were members of the army, but were not political or religious radicals.[124] One, William Halsey of Waterford and Clonmel, was an English civilian whose factional allegiances in 1654 are unknown. In fact, only five M.P.s can be positively identified with the army interest at this time.[125] With only a sixth of the M.P.s loyal to the army interest, compared with nearly two-thirds representing the Old Protestant interest, it becomes clear why Fleetwood and the commissioners had preferred to nominate members rather than allow elections. This imbalance was further justified by the result of the protector's insistence on keeping six senior officers in Ireland to cope with unrest during the parliamentary session. The order prevented the attendance of two important Old Protestants – Sir Charles Coote and Sir Hardress Waller – but it also excluded two members of the army interest: Colonels Axtell and Sadleir.[126] Once the dust had settled, one Baptist army officer, Quartermaster-General Vernon, denounced the Irish M.P.s as 'malignants within their hearts'.[127] He may have had a point. Of the M.P.s who crossed to England in August and September 1654 only three were allied to the army, while seventeen had links with the Old Protestant interest.

---

[120] Dunlop, *Ireland*, i, 68n.

[121] *Mercurius Politicus*, no. 219 (17–24 Aug. 1654), pp. 3709–10 (B.L., E.809(5)).

[122] These were Broghill, William Cadogan, Cole, Coote, John Fowke, Gookin, Hill, Hutchinson, Jephson, Theophilus Jones, Ralph and Sir Robert King, Meredith, Thomas Newburgh, Temple and Waller. For a full discussion of these elections see Patrick Little, 'Irish representation in the protectorate parliaments' in *Parliamentary History* (forthcoming).

[123] Thomas Scot junior (Cos. Westmeath, Longford and King's) on the interest of his father-in-law, Sir Henry Peirce of Tristernagh; Henry Ingoldsby (Cos. Kerry, Limerick and Clare) and William Purefoy (Cos. Limerick and Kilmallock) by Sir Hardress Waller.

[124] Robert Venables, John Reynolds, Anthony Morgan and Daniel Redman.

[125] Jerome Sankey, Thomas Sadleir, Daniel Axtel, John Hewson and John Clarke.

[126] *Thurloe S.P.*, ii, 558.

[127] *H.M.C. Egmont*, i, 555.

IV

The 1654 parliament was an important staging-post in Broghill's political career.[128] Before the parliament sat, Broghill had carefully fostered contacts with English courtiers as well as Old Protestants, and during the parliament he reaffirmed his alliance with both groups. Indeed, during the session, the objectives of the two 'interests' began to merge, as both reacted against the growing power of the army, and both looked towards a strong, centralised protectorate as a bulwark against political instability, religious radicalism and military rule. Broghill's view of the protectorate was not always in line with official policy. In religious affairs, in particular, he supported a limited settlement, rather then the broad toleration favoured by Cromwell. This created tensions which would influence Broghill's own political aims and goals not just in 1654–5, but also later in the decade, as he sought to make the protectorate less reliant on minority groups through a conservative reform programme. His activity in the 1654 parliament can be divided into three loosely associated parts: his attempt to influence the religious settlement; his support of the protectorate; and his moves to secure the Irish protestant interest through formal union with England.

The religious debate in the 1654 parliament centred on toleration. Cromwell's desire to promote liberty of conscience to the sectaries was challenged by the strong Presbyterian caucus in the commons, which tried to erect parliament as a guarantor of religious conformity, vesting it with powers which superseded those of the protector and his council, and imposing a formal confession of faith to be subscribed by all ministers.[129] Broghill was torn between his desire to support the government and his sympathy with the Presbyterian distrust of broad toleration. On 25 September he was named to the committee for ejecting scandalous ministers, and during its deliberations he seems to have favoured the government line: for during the division (on 6 November) on whether to suspend the old ordinance in favour of the new act, Broghill joined John Disbrowe as teller against the motion, in opposition to the Presbyterians in the House.[130] Guibon Goddard characterised the existing legislation as 'the former ordinance of the Lord Protector', and this vote may have been intended to assert parliament's right to annul such non-parliamentary legislation: an issue which would become important in later, secular, debates.[131] Despite this, Broghill seems to have veered from the

---

[128] For the 1654 parliament see Peter Gaunt, 'Law-making in the first protectorate parliament' in Colin Jones et al. (eds), *Politics and people in revolutionary England* (Oxford, 1986), pp 163–86. For Broghill's involvement in religious matters during this parliament see below, ch. 8.

[129] David L. Smith, 'Oliver Cromwell, the first protectorate parliament and religious reform' in *Parliamentary history*, xix (2000), pp 38–48.

[130] *C.J.*, vii, 382.

[131] *Burton diary*, i, pp lxii, xc–i.

government line on the 'enumeration of damnable heresies' towards the end of the session. He was named on 12 December to the committee on this part of the constitution, and on 3 January voted in favour of the heresies being decided by parliament,[132] although this was contrary to the wishes of the protector, who wanted to curb parliament's independent authority over religious matters,[133] and his actions may indicate a desire to limit toleration, at least on this point.[134] The setting of such limits was sensible, considering the Presbyterian majority in the commons and the unpopularity of the sects in all three nations; and the vote may also reflected Broghill's own adherence to a Calvinist orthodoxy and suspicion of radicalism.[135]

Broghill's personal preferences emerge most clearly in evidence of his involvement in consultations with a committee of divines, a body sanctioned by parliament in September, and up and running by the middle of November.[136] Broghill was a prominent member of the parliamentary committee chosen to deal with the divines: on 6 December he was one of four M.P.s instructed to attend the ministers each day; on 12 December he was ordered to thank them for their efforts;[137] and when parliament had first appointed the committee members, Broghill had 'named the Primate of Ireland, Archbishop Ussher'.[138] Broghill's choice was partly based on his family's long-standing friendship with Ussher; but it also suggests that he agreed with Ussher's efforts over the previous decade to find common ground between moderate Episcopalians and Presbyterians.[139] Ussher's attempts to reconcile the different parties seem to have appealed to Broghill, and it is significant that when he failed to persuade Ussher to advise the 1654 parliament, Broghill nominated instead the puritan divine, Richard Baxter, who shared Ussher's desire for unity, although Baxter included the Independent churches as well as the Episcopalians and Presbyterians in his scheme for Protestant unity.[140]

In the summer of 1654 Baxter became acquainted with Broghill, and the two became very close. Broghill gave him lodgings in his own house, and even gained permission for him to preach before the protector.[141] Broghill was also

---

[132] C.J., vii, 399, 412.

[133] *Burton diary*, i, pp. cxvi, cxviii.

[134] Smith, 'Religious reform', pp 41–2.

[135] See below, ch. 9.

[136] C.J., vii, 367, 385; *Burton diary*, i, p. xlvi.

[137] C.J., vii, 396, 399.

[138] Matthew Sylvester (ed.), *Reliquiae Baxterianae: or Mr Richard Baxter's narrative of the most memorable passages of his life and times* (1696), pp. 197, 206.

[139] Hugh Trevor-Roper, 'James Ussher, archbishop of Armagh' in his *Catholics, Anglicans and puritans*, p. 151; Barnard, *Cromwellian Ireland*, pp 91–2, 92n; Sylvester, *Reliquiae Baxterianae*, p. 62.

[140] Sylvester, *Reliquiae Baxterianae*, p. 197; for Baxter see W. Lamont, *Richard Baxter and the millennium: Protestant imperialism and the English revolution* (1979).

[141] Sylvester, *Reliquiae Baxterianae*, p. 205.

instrumental in bringing Baxter into contact with Ussher in early 1655 – a meeting which the older man had previously been unwilling to counte-nance.[142] Broghill's role as the catalyst to bring together Baxter and Ussher during the sitting of parliament shows his commitment to a broadly-based, Calvinist church, which would provide a strong foundation for a religious settlement in England as well as Ireland.[143] On this point he differed from Cromwell, whose idea of toleration encompassed Baptists and Quakers, but excluded Episcopalians as well as Catholics.[144] In this parliament, as in later years, Broghill was actively involved in encouraging the government to abandon the radical fringe, and to embrace the majority who held more moderate religious beliefs. He did so partly in the light of his experience in Ireland, where military power and radical religion had combined to exclude the Old Protestants from influence. He may also have recognised the need to court the Presbyterian majority in the commons to ensure the smooth passage of legislation. Well-placed religious concessions might buy co-operation in other matters – a tactic which he would use to good effect in 1656–7. In 1654–5, however, the religious scruples, and political inflexibility, of the stricter English Presbyterians soon led them to question the political authority of the protector, and hastened the dissolution of parliament.[145] This was not a path which Broghill could follow, for his doubts on religious policy were balanced by his consistent support for the existing protectoral constitution, and his personal loyalty to Oliver Cromwell.

Cromwell's attempt to pass the Instrument of Government into statute law dominated the 1654 parliament, and, alongside his anger at Presbyterian intolerance, his dissatisfaction with the efforts of the republicans and their allies (described by Ludlow as the 'Commonwealth-party') to limit the pro-tector's authority and to increase the constitutional powers of parliament would prove the main reason for his summary dissolution of the parliament in January 1655.[146] The earliest indication of Broghill's involvement in the con-stitutional question was his appointment to two committees in late September 1654: the first to bring in a bill for settling the government, and the second to draw up the 'recognition' of the protectorate, which was to be used as a test (or oath) for all M.P.s.[147] The debate on the constitution was then diverted to a committee of the whole house, where the divisions within parliament became more apparent. From this time the protector was clearly supported by

---

[142] Ibid., p. 206.

[143] See below, ch. 9.

[144] See J. C. Davis, *Oliver Cromwell* (2001), pp 128–36.

[145] Smith, 'Religious reform', p. 45.

[146] *Ludlow memoirs*, i, 390–1. Recent arguments that the short-lived proposal to crown Oliver Cromwell was 'the central point of contention' in this parliament are unconvincing: see Eric Porter, 'A cloak for knavery: kingship, the army, and the first protectorate parliament 1654–5' in *The Seventeenth Century*, xvii (2002), pp 187–205.

[147] *C.J.*, vii, 369, 370.

'the court party' and various army officers, and opposed by republicans and Rumpers.[148]

Broghill's collaboration with the courtiers became more obvious in early November, when the Instrument was debated in the commons. On 10 November the factional divisions within parliament flared up when an attempt was made to limit the protector's power to veto legislation, by allowing parliament to pass bills without consent after a twenty day delay. Broghill joined one prominent 'courtier', Sir Charles Wolseley, in opposing the proposal in division, but was defeated by twenty-four votes.[149] As the diarist, Guibon Goddard, recorded, the 'court-party' was furious at this defeat, claiming that 'this vote had destroyed the Government . . . We had, as much as a vote could do, unmade the Protector.'[150] Broghill joined in this outcry: 'so mortal was this wound to the Government, in the opinion of some, that one, a person of honour and nobility [ie. Broghill], did wish he could have redeemed that wound with a pound of the best blood in his body'.[151] The issue of the protector's right to control parliament re-emerged in another context on 14 November. The debate concerned a proposal to allow the protector to veto any attempt by parliament to extend its term beyond six months. The opposition objected that this implied 'an inherency of right as to such a negative to be in the Lord Protector', and that this was 'a new thing, and a new right, which was never before settled in the single person'.[152] Broghill and Wolseley again teamed up in support of the protector's veto, but again lost the division, this time by seventeen votes.[153] Once again, the 'courtiers' proved bad losers. After this latest rebuff 'They insisted upon it with as much earnestness, as they did upon the vote on Friday night [i.e. 10 November]'.[154]

The court party had more success on 2 December 1654, when the protector's right to nominate his own councillors (to be approved by parliament subsequently) was pushed through a divided house. Broghill and Wolseley told for the motion, winning the division and defeating John Bulkeley and Herbert Morley by thirty-two votes.[155] In January 1655, as the constitutional issue came nearer to some sort of resolution, Broghill continued to support the court party, joining Wolseley as teller against further amendments to the first article of the Instrument on 8 January,[156] and supporting another courtier, John Cleypole, in a further division on 17 January.[157] On 18–19 January, Broghill acted as

---

[148] *Burton diary*, i, pp. xxv–xxvii; such 'parties' were often 'shallow and shortlived' in nature: Gaunt, 'Law-making in the first protectorate parliament', pp 184–5.

[149] *C.J.*, vii, 384.

[150] *Burton diary*, i, p. lxvi.

[151] Ibid., p. lxvii.

[152] Ibid., p. lxxiv.

[153] *C.J.*, vii, 385.

[154] *Burton diary*, i, p. lxxiv.

[155] *C.J.*, vii, 394; *Burton diary*, i, pp civ–cvii.

[156] *C.J.*, vii, 413.

[157] Ibid., 419; *Burton diary*, i, p. cxxxi.

teller on minor issues with his old ally, Henry Cromwell – another indication of his support for the court party.[158] Despite the efforts of Broghill, Wolseley, Cleypole, Henry Cromwell and their allies to steer the Instrument through parliament relatively intact, on 20 January the opposition made a last bid to limit the protector's authority, by denying Cromwell the right to raise or use the militia without parliament's consent. Broghill and another Cromwellian, John Disbrowe, opposed this motion, but it was carried by twenty-seven votes.[159] For the protector, who had watched with dismay as his powers were whittled away by a hostile parliament, this was the last straw. Before the new constitution could be enacted, Cromwell dissolved the parliament, and returned to ruling in council, on 22 January 1655.[160]

Despite his own religious qualms, the 1654 parliament had seen Broghill reaffirm his trust in Oliver Cromwell: a trust which had not diminished despite his conflict with the Irish government after 1649. In his support of the protector, Broghill found himself once again in close alignment with the English court party. During this period he came closer to Henry Cromwell, with whom he seems to have worked in the commons, and, in a new departure, found common cause with some of the most prominent civilian supporters of the protector, including Sir Charles Wolseley. Building on his existing connexions within the protectoral court, during the 1654 parliament Broghill edged closer to the centre of power in England.

Broghill stands out as the Irish M.P. most deeply involved in the court party's attempts to increase Cromwell's political authority, but it would be a mistake to see his courtly objectives as separate from his Irish concerns. After all, it was not just Broghill who had been won over by Cromwell in 1649; nor was he the only Old Protestant to greet Henry Cromwell with enthusiasm in 1654. The confirmation of the protector's powers would have profound implications for the Irish situation, not least because it was hoped that Cromwell and his civilian council would act as a check on the army faction backed by Fleetwood and his allies. Certainly, there are strong indications that Broghill and the other Old Protestant M.P.s were collaborating on certain issues during the 1654 parliament. Of the nine Old Protestants who reached Westminster, Sir Paul Davies identified five as likely to work together, namely Broghill, Sir Robert King, Arthur Hill, Daniel Hutchinson and Theophilus Jones (brother to the deceased general, Michael Jones);[161] in September, others in Dublin saw that Broghill and the former Irish Independent, Sir John Temple, 'may be of good use' in promoting reform in Ireland.[162] To these men can be added William Jephson and Vincent Gookin – both elected on the Boyle interest in Munster – and William Meredith, son of the Irish

[158] C.J., vii, 420.
[159] Ibid., 421; Burton diary, i, p. cxxxiii.
[160] Ibid., p. cxxxiii.
[161] H.M.C. Egmont, i, 557.
[162] Thurloe S.P., ii, 633.

Independent, Sir Robert Meredith, who had opposed the army in the elections for Counties Kildare and Wicklow. A crude analysis of Broghill's committee appointments during this parliament suggests that he was indeed working within a broad Old Protestant alliance: of his twenty-two committee-appointments, Broghill was named to six in common with William Jephson and Arthur Hill, four with Sir Robert King, and three with Sir John Temple and Theophilus Jones.[163]

This apparent collegiality among the Old Protestant M.P.s was reinforced by their common political agenda. Before the start of parliament, various issues were causing concern in Ireland. The most prominent was the fear that the assessments, which paid for the army, would be raised to £10,000 per month, or even higher.[164] There was also mounting concern that the protectoral ordinances did not have the same force as parliamentary acts, raising the possibility that the recent Munster indemnity ordinance could be annulled by the acts of settlement passed in 1652 and 1653.[165] The need for administrative reform – reducing the charges of the government and the army, re-establishing the old courts of justice, and settling the government on a more regular basis – was also causing anxiety among the Old Protestants.[166] Such worries and concerns would provide a focus for the emerging Old Protestant party at Westminster in 1654–5.

In their reaction to the legislation that came before the 1654 parliament, Broghill and the Old Protestants seem to have been guided by their immediate concerns for Ireland. In October, Broghill was involved in measures to encourage trade in foodstuffs and to regulate customs – measures which would affect Irish trade and the economic position of the Protestant landowners.[167] On 27 November, when a committee was appointed to consider the article on qualifications for elections, an amendment allowed the exemption of Irish Protestants who had submitted to parliament before 25 December 1649.[168] This committee included Broghill, Hutchinson, Hill, Gookin and Theophilus Jones, and its report was accepted by parliament without a division.[169] The assessment question was also of great importance to the Irish M.P.s. When on 21 November the English rate was set at £60,000 per month, 'the Scots and Irish' moved that their rates should be included in a general settlement, for fear that if the tax proved insufficient to fund the army, 'all the rest that fell short would be laid upon them'.[170] The assessment act was

---

[163] C.J., vii, passim.
[164] H.M.C. Egmont, i, 549, 552–3.
[165] Ibid., p. 551: this concern was echoed by Lord Montgomery of the Ards in December 1654: see Cal. S.P. Ire., 1647–60, pp 543–4.
[166] Thurloe S.P., ii, 633.
[167] C.J., vii, 375, 380.
[168] Burton diary, i, p. xcvix.
[169] C.J., vii, 390–1.
[170] Burton diary, i, p. lxxxviii–lxxxix.

brought to a division on 29 November, Broghill acted as teller against changing (in effect, increasing) the general rate,[171] and on 2 December it was resolved to debate Irish and Scottish assessments separately.[172] The result was a further debate, in which 'Much was said by the members of both nations', and the Irish tax was eventually reduced from £10,000 to £8,000 per month.[173] Hand in hand with lowering the assessments was the need to further reduce the size of the English, Scottish and Irish armies maintained by the tax. Broghill was clearly involved in calls for a smaller standing army – for political as well as financial reasons. He was appointed to the committee which considered the size of the armed forces from 26 September, along with Jephson, Meredith, King, Temple, Jones and Hill: a line-up suggesting Irish interest in the question.[174] When it came to the Irish army, Cromwell seemed inclined to rely on Fleetwood, who strongly advised keeping the establishment as it was,[175] but Broghill seems to have hoped that the protector could be persuaded otherwise: in a division on 5 December he supported a proviso in the new constitution giving the protector sole control of the size of the army.[176] Perhaps in a corollary to this, in early January 1655 Broghill was named to a committee to discuss the revenue to be settled by the new constitution, and on 16 January he acted as teller in favour of freezing military expenditure for the next five years.[177] In reducing the assessments and pegging army spending, Broghill could relieve the tax burden on Ireland and curb the political ambitions of the army. Both objectives could be underwritten by placing more power in the hands of the protector.

The concerns of the Irish M.P.s at the beginning of the session seem to have begun to take clearer shape in the wake of the assessments debates. The legal and administrative reforms, widely discussed in Old Protestant circles before the parliament met, finally came into centre stage. On 14 December Broghill was named to a committee for settling probate law in Ireland, as part of a legislative programme which included an act to remove the Irish court of wards and *in capite* tenures, prompted by extra-parliamentary debates on changes to the legal system.[178] Such moves were not universally popular, as former civil officers, such as Sir Paul Davies, were worried that the old forms would be swept away to no advantage.[179] But the attempt to reorder the law courts, along with the suggested inclusion of the revenues within a 'British' format, was part of a much larger plan to bring Ireland in line with English practice.

---

[171] C.J., vii, 392.
[172] Ibid., p. 394.
[173] Ibid., p. 395; *Burton diary*, i, p. cvii.
[174] C.J., vii, 370.
[175] *Burton diary*, i, p. xciii; *Thurloe S.P.*, ii, 602–3, 733.
[176] C.J., vii, 395.
[177] Ibid., pp 415, 418.
[178] Ibid., pp 401, 407; *Thurloe S.P.*, ii, 633.
[179] H.M.C. *Egmont*, i, 564.

The culmination of this was the bill of union between England and Ireland, which took as its model the Anglo-Scottish union ordinance of 1654. The latter had promised to confirm the right of representation at Westminster, to make all taxes (including the assessment) proportionable across the commonwealth and to remove customs barriers, and it was followed by legislation concerning the legal system in Scotland.[180] Irish union legislation was introduced at the very end of the parliament: on 15 January 1655 the first reading was given to a bill 'for the uniting of Ireland into the Commonwealth of England, the re-establishing the Courts of Judicature there . . . and making a great seal and other seals to be used in Ireland'.[181] The link between reform of the legal apparatus and the union itself was thus made explicit,[182] and by analogy with the Scottish union, the assessments, customs,[183] and other taxation would also be made more equitable.[184] Time was allocated for a second reading on 22 January – the very day that Cromwell dissolved parliament – and so the precise form of the proposed union remains uncertain.[185] But it is clear that, after the various attempts to reform the Irish economic, tax and legal systems, and bring them closer to the English system, an act of union was the next logical step. It would also correspond closely with Broghill's efforts to increase the power of the protector in the new constitution, for under a united state the lord deputy of Ireland would be redundant, and under a settled government the army (and therefore the assessments) could be reduced. In short, union with England would guarantee the Old Protestant interest.

The act of union had become the ultimate aim of Broghill and his Old Protestant allies by the end of the 1654 parliament. The Scottish observer, Robert Baillie, recognised that the Irish M.P.s had some sort of hidden agenda, which influenced their support of the Instrument: for they were 'men who, for peace, were resolved to do or say anything they found tollerable to their own large mind and, I think were all so complying with the Protector as he would have wished'.[186] The army's supporters in Ireland were also aware of the significance of events in England. By mid-December Fleetwood was becoming concerned that 'Ther are some, who relate to Ireland (not of the souldiers) who doe ill offices in England, and heare, for us; which, if not tim[e]lly observed

---

[180] A & O, ii, 873, 883–4. For the origins of the union bill see Patrick Little, 'The first unionists?: Irish Protestant attitudes to union with England, 1653–9' in I.H.S., xxxii (2000), pp 45–9.

[181] Burton diary, i, p. cxxviii. The exact nature of the union bill is unknown, but see Gaunt, 'Law-making in the first protectorate parliament', p. 179.

[182] For the legal implications of the Irish union see Barnard, Cromwellian Ireland, p. 280.

[183] For the trade implications of the Irish union see T. C. Barnard, 'Planters and policies in Cromwellian Ireland' in Past and Present, lxi (1973), pp 62–5.

[184] A & O, ii, 873, 875–84.

[185] C.J., vii, 415, 416.

[186] Baillie letters, iii, 289.

and prevented, will prove unhappy'.[187] On the dissolution of parliament on 22 January, Fleetwood emitted an almost audible sigh of relief, and castigated those 'evill men [that] are very much dejected and disappointed in the late dissolution'.[188] In contrast, at the closure of the parliament the Old Protestants were left with the sense of a job only half finished. It was this which prompted the Dublin merchants to petition Henry Cromwell in May 1655, urging that, as 'by an act of parliament Ireland is declared to be of the commonwealth of England', customs might be removed and Ireland accorded 'equal privilege with Scotland'. Such equality, and the abolition of trade barriers in particular, had formed an important part of the union bill introduced in parliament earlier in the year.[189] The call for union legislation on similar lines was renewed by the Irish lobby in the 1656 parliament, and in 1659, despite statements that Ireland and England were so close they were 'naturally united', the lack of a formal union was felt to have relegated Ireland's constitutional status below that of Scotland.[190] Far from union with England having been merely an imperialist notion foisted on an unwilling population, the Irish Protestants welcomed it as a guarantee against further abuses by the Dublin government and its army supporters.[191]

Nor was Broghill's quest for a formal act of union between England and Ireland a purely constitutional concern. It also marked the maturation of a plan which had been developing over previous decades in the minds of the Boyle group and the Irish Independents, both of whom sought to underpin the hegemony of the Protestant Interest through the incorporation of Ireland into the 'English Empire'. By the 1650s this had become translated into unionism – the need for a formal, civilian, settlement between the two nations, underwritten by statute law. This constitutional aim was connected with a political campaign against the army interest in Ireland. During the winter of 1654–5 there was a highly co-ordinated effort by the Old Protestants to discredit Fleetwood's administration in Dublin, and to replace him with Henry Cromwell. Perhaps encouraged by the replacement of the parliamentary commissioners with an Irish council and by moves to reduce the army's role in the administration,[192] petitions denouncing Fleetwood were circulating in

---

[187] *Thurloe S.P.*, iii, 23.

[188] Ibid., 136.

[189] P.R.O., S.P. 63/286, ff 57v–58r; the signatories were headed by Daniel Hutchinson, M.P. for Dublin in 1654.

[190] *Burton diary*, i, 6, 12, 352; iv. 239–41.

[191] See Little, 'The first unionists?'. This argument counters the assumptions made in Derek Hirst 'The English republic and the meaning of Britain' in Brendan Bradshaw and John Morrill (eds), *The British problem, c.1534–1707: state formation in the Atlantic archipelago* (Cambridge, 1996), pp 194–5; and Sarah Barber, 'Scotland and Ireland under the Commonwealth', in Steven Ellis and Sarah Barber (eds), *Conquest and union: fashioning a British state, 1485–1725* (1995), pp 218–21.

[192] *Mercurius Politicus*, no. 219 (17–24 Aug. 1654), p. 3716 (B.L., E. 809(5)); no. 223

Ulster by December 1654, and soon there were similar attempts to undermine the lord deputy's authority in Munster.[193] More seriously, in early January 1655 an anonymous pamphlet was published in London which not only questioned the transplantation policy but also attacked the Dublin government and the political and religious influence of the army in Ireland.[194] The author was Broghill's fellow M.P., Vincent Gookin. Fleetwood's reaction shows that he interpreted Gookin's publication as a seditious act. Throughout this period, Broghill was kept abreast of developments in Ireland by the regular dispatch of letters from the earl of Cork, who had moved to Dublin shortly after the opening of the English parliament.[195] When all these factors are borne in mind, the introduction of an act of union should be seen as the culmination of a concerted effort to oust the lord deputy, and to replace him with the more trustworthy Henry Cromwell. Once more, Broghill's loyalty to the Cromwell family and his duty to the Old Protestant community seem to have been running on parallel lines.

V

The five-year period between the summer of 1649 and the spring of 1655 was a time of transition for Broghill and the Old Protestant interest. The heady days of co-operation with Cromwell in late 1649 were soon replaced by uncertainty, as the lord lieutenant's successors attempted to remove men such as Broghill from the army and local commissions, and a total collapse of Boyle influence in Munster was only prevented by the continuing support of Cromwell behind the scenes, aided by periodic crises of confidence which gripped the Dublin government and allowed the earl of Cork to re-establish his authority in the area. The violent fluctuations that characterised Irish politics before 1653 were largely resolved after the formation of the pro-tectorate. From 1654 the Old Protestant interest – which had held together during great adversity – became more politically active, whether in Dublin, in the council lobbies in England, or in the union parliament. Broghill was at the centre of this process, and it is through him that we can begin to see a common agenda among Irish Protestant politicians. Integral to this was a reaffirmation of Irish ties to the protectorate as a shield against the political

---

(14–21 Sept. 1654), 3780 (B.L., E. 812(8)); moves were made to reduce the army in size, and abolish military precincts in December 1654: see ibid., no. 235 (7–14 Dec. 1654), p. 4086 (B.L., E. 820(2)).

[193] Cork's diary (Chatsworth, Lismore MS 29, unfol.), 17 Feb. 1655; *Thurloe S.P.*, iii, 29, 70.

[194] [Vincent Gookin], *The great case of transplantation in Ireland discussed* (3 Jan. 1655) (B.L., E. 234(6)).

[195] Cork's diary (Chatsworth, Lismore MS 29, unfol.), 25 Sept., 4, 10, 18, 20 Oct., 10 Nov., 5, 16 Dec. 1654, 18 Jan. 1655.

excesses of the army faction in Ireland, and as an agent for an equitable land settlement and a stable economic climate in Ireland. The union, which seems to have lain at the heart of this programme, was at once a constitutional tool for stabilising Ireland and a political weapon to replace the suspect Charles Fleetwood with the more moderate Henry Cromwell as lord deputy.

Broghill's political manoeuvrings were subject to certain constant factors. The first of these was his loyalty to the Boyle family – which re-emerged strongly in the early 1650s despite the political divisions that had existed between its members in the 1640s. Broghill's sense of obligation towards his family, as much as his desire to re-establish his own power in Munster, lay behind his efforts to resurrect the financial and political fortunes of his brother, the second earl of Cork. Connected to this was Broghill's growing attachment to the wider Old Protestant interest. A coherent group of Irish Independents had continued to work with the commonwealth after the execution of the king, and from this kernel there developed a broader alliance which was able to absorb former Presbyterians (such as Sir John Clotworthy and William Jephson) and even former royalists (including the earl of Cork and Viscount Conway). Under pressure from the army and from a hostile regime in Dublin, this Old Protestant interest became a highly organised lobbying machine in Whitehall and Westminster, a development which would have important implications for Broghill's political activities later in the 1650s.[196] Under-pinning Broghill's efforts on behalf of his family and the Old Protestants was his investment in the Cromwellian court. Broghill's connexion with Oliver Cromwell survived the political upheavals of the early 1650s, and encouraged his support of the protectorate in the 1654 parliament.

Shortly after the closure of the 1654 parliament, Broghill was appointed lord president of the council in Scotland, a post which required his presence in Edinburgh, where he resided from the autumn of 1655. But the fate of Ireland continued to be one of Broghill's greatest concerns and he was careful to remain in close contact with Henry Cromwell, who had crossed the Irish Sea in July 1655. As lieutenant-general of the Irish army, and (from September 1655) *de facto* governor of the country while Fleetwood was in London, Henry Cromwell soon came to dominate the Irish government. He and Broghill saw eye-to-eye on most areas of policy. Unlike Fleetwood, who courted religious radicals and soldiers, Henry Cromwell tried to expand the popular base of the administration, by bringing Old Protestants and Presbyterians into the government and the church. He also revived traditional forms of local government and justice (especially j.p.s), and prevented the sequestration of former royalist landowners. As Toby Barnard has argued, Henry Cromwell's 'main interest was in the secure establishment of his father's protectorate in Ireland', and in this, as in the details of his reform programme, he was in broad agreement with

---

[196] See Barnard, 'Protestant interest', p. 219; for a fuller examination of these themes, see below, chs 7, 8.

Broghill.[197] Yet Henry Cromwell's own position was not entirely secure. He would not replace Fleetwood as lord deputy until November 1657, and in the meantime struggled to get his policies accepted at Whitehall, where the council's Irish committee was dominated by the absentee lord deputy, and his allies in the army interest, especially General John Lambert.[198] Under increasing pressure, in 1655 and early 1656 Henry Cromwell sent agents to lobby the council and the protector, and in the summer of 1656 even threatened to resign if his enemies continued to meddle in Irish affairs. As yet the protector was unwilling to intervene, and such issues remained unresolved.[199] The only comfort that Henry Cromwell could derive from this difficult situation was that Broghill, keen to implement similarly moderate policies in Scotland, faced exactly the same problems.

---

[197] Barnard, *Cromwellian Ireland*, pp 299–303.
[198] For Lambert's influence over Irish affairs in 1655–6 see *Cal. S.P. Dom.*, *1655*, pp 204, 256, 265, 303; Reynolds to Henry Cromwell, 11 June 1656 (B.L., Lansdowne MS 821, f. 156r); Morgan to Henry Cromwell, 19 Aug. 1656 (ibid., f. 234r).
[199] *Thurloe S.P.*, iv, 327, 348–9, 373–4; v, 176, 177, 196.

4

Scotland and 'Britain', 1655–6

If anything, Scotland was in an even worse state than Ireland in 1655. There were many similarities between the two: both had experienced political and economic ruin after more than a decade of civil war; both had been conquered by an English army; and both were expected to pay crippling taxes to finance the occupying forces. Yet there were other factors which made Scotland's position within the Cromwellian union even more difficult. A significant proportion of the Old Protestants in Ireland had sided with Cromwell, and like Broghill were able to ameliorate harsh policies against their royalist friends and relatives. But in Scotland the risings in support of the Stuarts between 1647 and 1651 had implicated almost all the Scottish Protestants (to a greater or lesser extent) as enemies of the regime. There were also serious divisions within the Protestant community in Scotland, centred on the disputes between the Resolutioner and Protester factions in the Kirk; royalists such as Middleton and Glencairn kept rebellion alive in the highlands until the summer of 1655; and, in the absence of a civilian ruling council, Scotland was governed by military men, Robert Lilburne and (from April 1654) George Monck.

The 1654–5 parliament, which included 30 Scottish M.P.s, was as unsatisfactory for Scotland as for Ireland, and on its dissolution there were immediate calls for reform and settlement. On 8 February 1655, for example, the Scottish M.P.s attended the protector, 'laying downe the heavy grievance of that nation by reason of a very numerous Army'.[1] The English council's decision to consider the government of Scotland, made on 28 February, was the belated response to this and other such demands for reform north of the border. The decision to send a civilian council – chaired by a lord president – had been taken by the end of March 1655, but it took over a month before the final membership list was decided. On 4 May it was finally announced that Broghill would serve as lord president, with a council of eight: two Scotsmen – John Swinton and William Lockhart – and six Englishmen – George Monck, Samuel Disbrowe, Charles Howard, Adrian Scrope, Thomas Cooper and Nathaniel Whetham. A ninth member of the council, Sir Edward Rhodes,

---

[1] 'G.D.' to Monck, 8 Feb. 1655 (W.C.O., Clarke MS 1/15, f. 44r).

was appointed subsequently.[2] The extent to which Broghill had a hand in the choice of these councillors is uncertain. There is evidence that he had been involved in Scottish affairs as early as 1654, and his salary was backdated to 1 March 1655 'in regard of his attendance in town from that time on that service'.[3] But it seems likely that prominent members of the English council (especially John Lambert, who dominated the Scottish committee at Whitehall), and General Monck himself, were also eager to select their own candidates, and this may account for the delay in producing the final list. The instructions for the Scottish council were also delayed. The first set, proposed in March, was only passed in July; and an additional paper in August. Broghill had a certain influence over these instructions. He was able to insert a clause confirming the articles of war (at the request of Monck), and, as Frances Dow has argued, it seems likely that he had some influence over the additional instructions.[4] It was only once these additional instructions had been passed that Broghill journeyed north, and the new council assembled in Edinburgh on 12 September 1655.[5]

I

For biographers of Broghill and students of Scottish history alike, Broghill's presidency of the Cromwellian council of Scotland has always been something of an inconvenience. Broghill was only in Scotland from September 1655 until August 1656, and the biographer is thus faced with coming to grips with the complexities of Scottish politics and religion for less than a year of his (or her) subject's forty-year career. Kathleen Lynch, in her study of Broghill, gives only a cursory glance north of the border – to which she devotes barely a page of her book – before returning, with evident relief, to English politics.[6] From the Scottish historian's point of view, the year of Broghill's administration interrupts the account of George Monck's stint as general, with its satisfying (and thoroughly 'British') denoument in the restoration of 1660. Frances Dow emphasises the continued importance of Monck in 1655–6,[7] and treats Broghill almost as an anomaly. She also relies on the old *Dictionary of National Biography* for a potted (and largely erroneous) biography of the president. In her words, 'The choice of Broghill to be President was, on the face of it, a

---

[2] Frances Dow, *Cromwellian Scotland, 1651–1660* (Edinburgh, 1979), p. 165; *Thurloe S.P.*, iii, 423.
[3] *Cal. S.P. Dom.*, 1655, p. 290.
[4] C. H. Firth, *Scotland and the protectorate* (Edinburgh, 1899), p. 295; Dow, *Cromwellian Scotland*, p. 167.
[5] Dow, *Cromwellian Scotland*, pp 165–8.
[6] Lynch, *Orrery*, pp 86–7.
[7] Dow, *Cromwellian Scotland*, pp 163–4.

surprising one: aged only 34, he had until six years previously been a staunch Royalist and his political experience had been confined to Irish affairs.'[8] Other historians have agreed.[9] The overall consensus seems to be that Broghill arrived in Scotland with no knowledge of, or interest in, a country which had never before heard of this ambitious young man. He might just as well have fallen from the sky as arrived by coach in the autumn of 1655. Such an attitude makes Broghill's success as governor of Scotland in the following year all the more astonishing. This chapter aims to look afresh at the problem of Broghill in Scotland, with the aim of elucidating not only his domestic policies there, but also the impact his year as governor had in broadening his political horizons. Before coming to Edinburgh, Broghill was an Anglo-Irishman; by the time he left, he had become a man of three nations. Far from being glossed over, 1655–6 must be highlighted as a crucial year in Broghill's development as a 'British' politician.

As a preliminary, it is necessary to challenge the view that Broghill was both a stranger to Scotland and a stranger in Scotland. Through the marriages of his siblings in the Boyle family, Broghill had an extensive network of contacts in the Irish and English peerages; through his wife's family, the Howards, earls of Suffolk, he had equally impressive connexions with the nobility and gentry of Scotland.[10] Lady Broghill's mother, the countess of Suffolk, was a Scotswoman: her father was George Home, earl of Dunbar, and her mother Elizabeth Gordon, daughter of Sir Alexander Gordon of Gight. Lady Broghill's sister, Catherine Howard, had married George, Lord d'Aubigny, the brother of the fourth duke of Lennox. After d'Aubigny's death in 1643, Catherine took as her second husband another Scot, Sir James Levingston, later earl of Newburgh.[11] Other Scottish relatives included James Johnstone, earl of Hartfell, whom Broghill acknowledged in 1656 as 'a kinsman of my wife's'; and he was even related, through the Homes, to the disgraced earl of Lauderdale.[12] To his wife's array of Scottish relatives, Broghill could add a significant one of his own. In 1639 his brother, Viscount Kinalmeaky, had married Elizabeth Feilding, sister of the marchioness of Hamilton. The sisters' cousin, Mary Villiers, was wife of the fourth duke of Lennox. Broghill thus had family ties with the Stuarts, Hamiltons, Homes, Maitlands, Levingstons, Gordons, Johnstones and through them with many other families of note within the Scottish aristocracy. The Scots were as obsessed with genealogy as

[8] Ibid., p. 165.

[9] Julia Buckroyd, 'Lord Broghill and the Scottish church, 1655–1656' in *Journal of Ecclesiastical History*, xxvii (1976), pp 362–3; L. M. Smith, 'Scotland and Cromwell: a study in early modern government' (unpublished D.Phil. thesis, Oxford University, 1979), p. 87; Hugh Trevor-Roper, 'Scotland and the puritan revolution' in his *Religion, the reformation and social change* (3rd ed., 1984), pp 433–5.

[10] For Broghill's relations with the Howards see below, ch. 7.

[11] *Complete Peerage*, s.v.

[12] *Thurloe S.P.*, v, 295.

the English or the Irish in this period.[13] They would have known all about Broghill's position in the Scottish social order long before he and his wife crossed the border.

This was more than mere genealogy. Broghill's sense of obligation towards his Boyle relatives was extended to his Scottish friends and relatives. Broghill had been forward in protecting the interests of his royalist sister-in-law, Lady d'Aubigny, throughout the 1640s, and after her death in 1650 continued to help her second husband, Sir James Levingston, and her son, the earl of Lichfield, to preserve their financial security.[14] It is also tempting to see Broghill as the main influence behind the English council's decision to waive a hefty fine against the earl of Hartfell, in 1655;[15] he certainly called on Hartfell's local influence in the south-west of Scotland during the parliamentary elections of the following year.[16] There is also some evidence that Lady Broghill's relatives within the Home family were also in contact with the president during the mid-1650s.[17] In 1656 Broghill and his lady were attended by Lady Halkett – the daughter of Thomas Murray, and wife of Sir James Halkett – who had been 'intimately acquainted' with the couple before the Civil War. Her suit on behalf of her husband was listened to with 'much freedom and kindnesse', and Broghill promised to help. Lady Halkett's story is incomplete, and we do not know whether Broghill's promises were finally put into action, but there is no doubt that she was encouraged in her approaches by the knowledge that 'what they acted now was more outt of a good designe then an ill, as was evident by the civility they shewed to all the Royallists'.[18] Lady Halkett's assertion that Broghill was a friend to the Scottish royalists in general accords with other evidence that Broghill's sympathies went far beyond his extended family. The earl of Lothian, for example, was assured of Broghill's support in August 1655, being told by his London agent that he was 'very confident his lordship wilbe very sensible of the equity of the case'; and in October of that year Broghill wrote to the earl with his own expressions of friendship, promising to assist him 'either in the publike businesse of debts, or in any privat affairs of your owne'.[19] The leniency shown to other nobles by the Scottish Council in 1655–6 may have been influenced by Broghill. There were certainly rumours in September 1656 that 'it would have stood hard with Glencairne's

---

[13] K. M. Brown, 'The Scottish aristocracy, anglicization and the court, 1603–38' in *H.J.*, xxxvi (1993), p. 551.

[14] For Broghill's connexions with Lady d'Aubigny and her family see below, ch. 7.

[15] *Cal. S.P. Dom., 1655*, pp 70, 319; *Cal. S.P. Dom., 1655–6*, p. 8.

[16] *Thurloe S.P.*, v, 295.

[17] James Sharp to Robert Douglas, Feb. 1657 (N.L.S., Wodrow Folio MSS, vol. xxvi, f. 152v).

[18] *The Memoirs of Anne, Lady Halkett and Ann, Lady Fanshawe*, ed. John Loftis (Oxford, 1979), pp 5, 86–7, 207.

[19] *The correspondence of Sir Robert Kerr, 1st earl of Ancram and his son William, 3rd earl of Lothian* (2 vols, Edinburgh, 1875), ii, 397–8; for Broghill's assistance to the family later in the decade see ibid., pp 410, 429.

life, had it not been the President's favour'.[20] Broghill's willingness to show favour to enemies like the earl of Glencairn, as well as to friends and relatives, again testifies that his relationship with the northern nation was complicated by personal and political considerations. Rather than being coldly aloof from the Scots, he was well known to them, and proved himself broadly sympathetic to their plight.[21]

II

The Presbyterian Church of Scotland was deeply divided in 1655. These divisions had their origins in the political upheaval which followed the defeat of the Scots at Dunbar in September 1650, when a minority of the Kirk ministers called for a purge of former Engagers and other offenders from church and state. This small group of hard-liners, known as the 'Remonstrants' or 'Protesters', led by the western ministers James Guthrie and Patrick Gillespie, was vigorously opposed by the 'Resolutioners' – the majority party led by Robert Douglas, James Wood and the Edinburgh clergy – who advocated leniency towards former royalists in order to unite the nation against Cromwell.[22] After the subjection of Scotland by the English in 1651–2, the divisions within the Kirk became set in stone. The Resolutioners, as un-repentant royalists, were suspected of inflaming rebellion, especially as they steadfastly continued to pray for Charles Stuart in public worship. The Protesters were more accepting of the Cromwellian regime, and had contacts with the Independent churches in England, although they remained wary of state intervention in religious matters. In 1654 the government managed to win over one faction within the Protester party, that led by Patrick Gillespie, and after consultations in August 1654 the English council passed an ordi-nance allowing the minority party extensive control over university education, the selection and payment of ministers, and the ejection of those deemed scandalous or unworthy. The terms of 'Gillespie's Charter' were rejected not only by the Resolutioners but also by others in the Protester camp (notably those led by James Guthrie), and by the summer of 1655 the scheme had collapsed. General Monck, who had tried to implement the Gillespie Charter throughout the previous year, now gave up, declaring himself disillusioned with both parties in the Scottish church.[23]

---

[20] *Baillie letters*, iii, 317.

[21] Broghill was not the only member of the Scottish council to favour the Scots: on 16 September 1656 – just before the new parliament opened – it was formally agreed that Charles Howard's sister would marry Lord Balgonie, the grandson and heir of the ex-royalist earl of Leven: Howard to Leven, 16 Sept. 1656 (N.A.S., Leven and Melville papers, GD 26/13/336); further contract, 2 and 4 July 1657 (ibid., GD 26/13/237).

[22] Buckroyd, 'Broghill and the church', pp 359–61; David Stevenson, *Revolution and counter-revolution in Scotland, 1644–51* (1977), pp 193–205.

[23] Dow, *Cromwellian Scotland*, pp 196–8.

The traditional account of Broghill in Scotland has seen his church policy as the greatest success of his term in office. While differing in emphasis, Frances Dow and Julia Buckroyd agree on the basic outlines of Broghill's attitude towards the church. Arriving with no restricting preconceptions about Kirk politics, Broghill gained a remarkable victory in the first weeks of his administration, by persuading the Resolutioners to abandon their prayers for the exiled king. He then tried and failed to unite the factions, before attempting to form a 'centre party' made up of moderate elements in both. The failure of this scheme forced Broghill to renew his approaches to the Resolutioners, and by the late summer of 1656 he had become their 'avowed champion'.[24] Both authors conclude that Broghill's policy was largely the result of his attachment to the Cromwellian regime and his detachment from the bitter wrangling of Scottish politics. For Buckroyd, Broghill was able to bring 'unprecedented imagination and initiative' to his church policy, but his ignorance of Scotland limited his success because of his persistence in 'underrating of the strength of the divisions and the bitterness of the antagonisms' within the Kirk.[25] Dow goes further. For her, Broghill was guided in church matters by 'not only the cold calculation of an "English" politician, but also the intellectual contempt of a man who cared little for the principles and interests of the parties he was manipulating'. Broghill 'came north with few preconceptions or illusions about the attitude of either party in the church'; and his own attitude to the clergy 'bordered at times on arrogance and contempt for the people he was dealing with'.[26] According to Dow, Broghill brought innovation, but, in the last instance, his agenda in church affairs was purely secular.

Yet, in its account of Broghill's motives, if not in its basic outline of the successes and failures of his policies, the line taken by Buckroyd and Dow is fundamentally flawed. For Broghill was not an impartial outsider. His own religious beliefs followed orthodox Calvinism; he had readily signed the Covenant in 1644; and had gone on to support Presbyterian attempts to limit religious toleration during the 1654–5 parliament. Privately and publicly he had a natural affinity to Scottish Presbyterianism.[27] We have already examined Broghill's links with the Scottish aristocracy, many of whom had strong connexions with other former royalists within the Kirk. Furthermore, there is direct evidence to suggest that Broghill had made contact with the moderate Resolutioner party even before his arrival in Scotland. It was these prior connexions and partialities – and the reaction against them displayed by other members of the government in England as well as Scotland – which dictated much of Broghill's church policy in his year of office.

---

[24] Buckroyd, 'Broghill and the church', pp 366–7; Dow, *Cromwellian Scotland*, pp 204–6.
[25] Buckroyd, 'Broghill and the church', pp 359, 367.
[26] Dow, *Cromwellian Scotland*, pp 195, 199, 210.
[27] See below, ch. 9.

Broghill had already been drawn into Kirk politics by the spring of 1654, over a year before his appointment as lord president of Scotland. In March 1654 Cromwell had summoned Patrick Gillespie and other Protester ministers to London to discuss the state of the church, and in May he extended this invitation to two prominent Resolutioners, Robert Douglas and Robert Blair. The refusal of the Resolutioners to attend left the way clear for Gillespie to secure his 'charter', which gave the Protesters official support in their attempts to rule the church, in August.[28] Broghill had been corresponding with the Edinburgh Resolutioners since early May 1654, and a letter to him from Robert Douglas, dated 23 May, suggests that Cromwell's request for Resolutioner participation in the debates may have been made on Broghill's advice.[29] In response to such approaches, Douglas addressed his official refusal to Broghill, 'since I know no other way of addresse', and begged him 'to present them, in a fair and favourable way, to the Lord Protector, least my stay be mis-constructed'. He added that he would wait before doing anything further, 'untill yow acguaint [sic] the Lord Protector herewith, and I receive a returne'.[30] In this crucial issue, Broghill – who had as yet no official interest in Scottish affairs – was already acting as a sympathetic intermediary between the Resolutioners and the protector.

Broghill's attitude to the Resolutioners may also have been influenced by the views of the Scottish theologian and advocate of Protestant unity, John Dury. Broghill and Dury were probably introduced by their common friend, Samuel Hartlib, whose association with the Boyles, and especially with Robert Boyle and Lady Ranelagh, is well known. This connexion was reinforced by Dury's marriage, in 1645, to the sister of the leading Old Protestant politician, Sir Robert King.[31] Dury's correspondence with Hartlib in the period after Broghill's appointment as president suggests that, despite his concern at the Resolutioners' inflexibility, he had high hopes of his friend's eventual success. On 13 May 1655 he wrote to Hartlib, 'I pray remember my humble service to my Lord Broghil, & present my wishes for his happie successe in his eminent employment; hee will have a difficult piece of work to deale with a stiff necked generation of men; but love Prudencie & patience will at last conquer all; & I hope God will open their eyes to see that which is most advantagious for themselves & the Gospell.'[32] The impression that Broghill had consulted Dury before leaving for Edinburgh is reinforced by a later letter from Dury to Hartlib, dated 11 December: 'how doe the Ministers in Scotland behave themselves

---

[28] Dow, *Cromwellian Scotland*, p. 196.
[29] Douglas to Broghill, 23 May 1654 (N.L.S., Wodrow Folio MSS, vol. xxvi, f. 7r); Cromwell's letter of invitation was enclosed in a letter from Broghill to Douglas dated 16 May 1654.
[30] Ibid.
[31] Toby Barnard, 'The Hartlib circle and the origins of the Dublin philosophical society' in *I.H.S.*, xix (1974–5), p. 71.
[32] Dury to Hartlib, 13 May 1655 (S.U.L., Hartlib MS 4/3/97A).

since my Lord Broghils arrivall: I would be gladde to heare that they would not meddle any more with state matters in the pulpit'.[33] Broghill may have derived valuable information on the Scottish situation during his discussions with Dury in the the the spring of 1655; he had certainly divulged his plans to change the accepted policy towards the Kirk, and to win the Resolutioner party for the Cromwellian government.

Another personal connexion which brought Broghill into contact with the Resolutioners before 1655 was his growing friendship with the Antrim planter and devout Presbyterian, Sir John Clotworthy. We have already seen the political collaboration between the two men which developed in the period before the 1654 parliament. This was reinforced by their common concern for the family of Arthur Jones, Viscount Ranelagh, who was brother-in-law to both Broghill and Clotworthy.[34] In early 1655, for example, a debt of £500 which Broghill and Clotworthy were jointly owed by Lord Paget was, by mutual assent, assigned to Ranelagh's two daughters as part of their marriage portions;[35] and in April of the same year Lady Clotworthy was reliant on Broghill to facilitate her financial requests to the government.[36] Sir John Clotworthy had been involved in Scottish affairs since the 1630s, and as a leading political Presbyterian in the 1640s had proved himself sympathetic to the covenanters in Scotland and Ireland.[37] He also had very close links with the London Presbyterian party and was a patron of the Antrim presbytery – both of which maintained connexions with the Scottish Resolutioners during the 1650s.[38] His wife even intervened with the authorities to help the imprisoned earl of Crawford attend suitable church services in 1655.[39]

Clotworthy and his wife seem to have been important figures in ensuring Broghill's amicable reception at Edinburgh. In early September 1655, as Broghill travelled north, Sir John and Lady Clotworthy were contacted by David Dickson and other Edinburgh Resolutioners, who asked them to present their case to Broghill. Sir John replied that he would write on their behalf,

> lest y[our] not beeinge knowne to his Lop should p[ro]duce somw[ha]t off a strangeness, w[hi]ch I prsume will not bee[,] yett to obviate any such inconvenience I have putt the inclosed into y[ou]r hand, w[hi]ch will geive my lord the knowledge

---

[33] Same to same, 11 Dec. 1655 (ibid., Hartlib MS 4/3/135B).

[34] Ranelagh's wife was Broghill's sister; his sister was Clotworthy's wife.

[35] 1655 indenture (N.L.I., bundle D. 22,017–22).

[36] *Thurloe S.P.*, iii, 395.

[37] Michael Perceval-Maxwell, 'Ireland and Scotland 1638–1648' in John Morrill (ed.), *The Scottish National Covenant in its British context, 1638–51* (Edinburgh, 1990), pp 196–7; Peter Donald, *An uncounselled king: Charles I and the Scottish troubles, 1637–41* (Cambridge, 1990), pp 191–6.

[38] See the minutes of the Antrim Prebytery, 1654–8 (P.R.O.N.I., D.1759/1A/1,) pp 44–5, 51, 95, 120, 122, 179, 218; see also St John D. Seymour, *The puritans in Ireland, 1647–1661* (Oxford, 1921), p. 98.

[39] Lady Clotworthy to Captain Lydcott, n.d. [1655] (Bodl., MS Rawl. A.32, p. 305); Lady Clotworthy to Thurloe, 10 Nov. 1655 (ibid., p. 327).

off y[ou]r beeinge the p[er]sons wee have formerly dyscourst off; And that, once sygnifyed I hope that acquaintance will soe usefully improve as itt may bee in order to a comfortable answear [to] such desyres as som who wish y[o]u well, have putt up in your beehalves . . . y[o]u will find him a man off cleere understandinge & well able to make a Judgm[en]t of w[ha]t is offer[ed].[40]

In other words, Clotworthy had already discussed Scottish affairs at length with Broghill, and now reassured the Resolutioners of a 'comfortable answear' to their approaches to the government in London through Broghill's intercession. This confirms the comments of another Resolutioner, Robert Baillie, that on his arrival in Scotland Broghill had already gained 'a good impression' of the Resolutioner party from his 'sister-in-law [sic], the Ladie Clotworthie'.[41] Influenced by the Clotworthys, by Dury, and by his own dealings with Douglas in 1654, Broghill came north not with 'few preconceptions', but with a strong bias in favour of the Resolutioners. This predeliction would become obvious enough immediately after Broghill's arrival in Edinburgh in September 1655.

In the aftermath of Glencairn's rebellion the government had become very jittery about ill-feeling towards the regime fostered by the Resolutioner ministers across Scotland. In February 1655 Cromwell had refused to make concessions to the delegation of Scottish M.P.s, precisely 'because the Ministery did preach uppe the interests of Charles Stuart'.[42] The Resolutioner ministers were themselves in talks with Monck in the summer of 1655, and were rumoured to be close to 'agreing with the Inglish to quyte [ie. quit] the King'.[43] The test of this professed desire to make peace with the Cromwellian regime was the ministers' willingness to abandon public prayers for Charles II, and it was this issue which brought negotiations with Monck to a grinding halt. Oppressive legislation against the Resolutioners – including the suspension of clerical salaries – would only be lifted if the prayers were abandoned; but the ministers would lose face if they were seen to bow to government pressure for their own benefit.[44] Within a few weeks of Broghill's arrival in Scotland, the Gordian knot had been cut. After a private meeting between Broghill and key Resolutioners, the Scottish council agreed to cancel punitive orders against the clergy, who were thus freed to abandon prayers for the king without dishonour. The Edinburgh ministers fell into line by early October, and by the end of 1655 many others had been encouraged to drop the controversial prayers.[45]

[40] Clotworthy to Dickson et al., 4 Sept. 1655 (N.L.S., Wodrow Folio MSS, vol. xxvi, f. 11r). When collecting his documents, Wodrow misread this letter as being dated 4 February, and annotated it accordingly. The original clearly reads '4 : 7bris : 55'.

[41] Baillie letters, iii, 295.

[42] 'G.D.' to Monck, 5 Feb. 1655 (W.C.O., Clarke MSS 1/15, f. 44r).

[43] Wariston diary, iii, 6; see also Baillie letters, iii, 295.

[44] Baillie letters, iii, 295; see Buckroyd, 'Broghill and the church', pp 363–4.

[45] Stephen, Register, i, 89–90; Thurloe S.P., iv, 56, 58, 73; Buckroyd, 'Broghill and the church', pp 363–4; Dow, Cromwellian Scotland, p. 199.

The speed and effectiveness of this solution startled Secretary Thurloe in London, who told Henry Cromwell that 'the Councell of Scotland have wrought a great wonder there, in perswading the ministers to leave praying for C. Stuart, which is accounted a great conquest; especially it being done by faire meanes'.[46] Thurloe's surprise is echoed by twentieth-century historians, who variously attribute Broghill's success to his masterful diplomatic and political flair, or his Machiavellian adeptness in manipulating the Kirk parties.[47] The truth behind this quick success is, however, rather more mundane. The issue of praying for the king had been current long before 1655: it had almost certainly formed part of the discussions on Scottish affairs between Broghill and Clotworthy in the spring of that year; and it was claimed that Broghill's willingness to treat with the Resolutioners on this issue was the result of Lady Clotworthy's intervention, as we have seen. It thus seems plausible that a solution had been worked out long before Broghill arrived in Edinburgh. Once there, he immediately arranged a private interview with Robert Douglas and David Dickson – the very same men who had corresponded at length with Broghill and Clotworthy in 1654–5.[48] In the circumstances, it was hardly surprising that a mutually acceptable deal was concluded in a matter of days. Broghill, a man with the right religious credentials and a track-record of favouring Resolutioners, had evidently used his influence to succeed in September 1655 where Monck had failed.

In the month after his arrival in Scotland, Broghill was pursuing a clear policy of winning over the Resolutioners, in the hope of settling the Kirk and stabilising the country politically. But this initiative was not sustained. During the autumn and winter of 1655–6 there followed a number of plans, most of which were directed towards the Protester faction, with the Resolutioners apparently left out in the cold. What was the reason for this sudden *volte-face*? Perhaps the key problem was that Broghill had fallen victim to his own success. Even in September 1655, when the plan to win over the Resolutioners was in full swing, Broghill realised that his efforts were not universally popular in government circles. There were rumours of 'som jealousies betwixt the President and General' soon after Broghill's arrival in Edinburgh.[49] A particular concern, as Broghill had foreseen, was that by 'nullinge the generall's and the judges declaration' against the Resolutioners, the new measures would affront various key members of the Scottish council.[50] There were also fissures opening along confessional lines. As one Resolutioner, Robert Baillie, put it, 'Generall Monck was irritat[ed] against us, as if we had yielded to Broghill what we had denied to him: and from that day, in all occasions, befriended openlie the

---

[46] *Thurloe S.P.*, iv, 88.
[47] Buckroyd, 'Broghill and the church', p. 364; Dow, *Cromwellian Scotland*, p. 200.
[48] *Thurloe S.P.*, iv, 73.
[49] *The diary of Alexander Brodie of Brodie*, ed. David Laing (Aberdeen, 1863), p. 154.
[50] *Thurloe S.P.*, iv, 56.

Remonstrants [or Protesters] to our prejudice'.[51] In fact, Monck was already well known for his sympathies with and connexions among the Protesters,[52] and more worryingly for Broghill, he seemed to be drawing closer to the pro-Independent party led by James Guthrie. In early September 1655, for example, when the Protesters unveiled their plans for a 'new covenant' as a solution to the Kirk problem, they received notice of 'Gen. Moncks taiking weal of our advertisement, and speaking very faire of friendship'.[53] Monck's support for the new covenant continued in later months, and he went out of his way to entertain and encourage members of the Guthrie faction through the winter of 1655–6, causing many to wonder 'to see the General so realye our freind as he was'.[54] Monck also seems to have protected the leader of this faction, James Guthrie, in person: in September 1655 he intervened when Guthrie was expelled from his church at Stirling, and ordered the military governor there to reinstate him and to prevent the Resolutioners from taking over;[55] in January 1656 he ordered the garrison at Stirling to reduce the number of its church meetings, as these were 'some inconvenience to Mr Guthrie & Mr Rule'.[56] Monck's favouritism towards the Guthrie faction was to become more pronounced as the months wore on.

The divergent opinions of Broghill and Monck, manifest in their favouring opposite parties in the Kirk, precipitated a split in the council chamber between the old Scotland hands and a group formed around the new men who came north with Broghill.[57] The leading Protester (and Guthrie's ally), Sir Archibald Johnston of Wariston, was deeply suspicious of certain members of the council. Chief among them was Samuel Disbrowe, Broghill's main ally at the board. Disbrowe openly obstructed the Protesters in December 1655, and by the summer of 1656 was denounced by Wariston as a 'great enemye to al our busines'.[58] Two other councillors with strong ties to Broghill, Charles Howard and Sir Edward Rhodes, were dismissed as 'Erastians' by Wariston.[59] Another probable ally was Nathaniel Whetham. The other members of the council were either Monck's military associates (Colonels Scrope and Cooper) or, like the Scotsmen Lockhart and Swinton, religious Independents appointed as judges by the earlier regime, who had already been insulted by

---

[51] *Baillie letters*, iii, 296.

[52] For Monck's religious views see Firth, *Scotland and the protectorate*, pp lviii, 185, 193; also Monck to Cromwell, 10 Jan. 1656 (W.C.O., Clarke MS 3/2, fo. 139r).

[53] *Wariston diary*, iii, 8.

[54] *Baillie letters*, iii, 297; *Wariston diary*, iii, 19.

[55] Monck's order, 8 Sept. 1655 (W.C.O., Clarke MS 3/10, unfol.).

[56] Monck's order, 9 Jan. 1656 (ibid.).

[57] For the individual councillors see History of Parliament, 1640–60 section, draft biographies.

[58] *Wariston diary*, iii, 18–20, 41; for Broghill and Disbrowe see *Thurloe S.P.*, iv, 57, 188–9; v, 295.

[59] *Wariston diary*, iii, 18, 20

Broghill's annulling of their orders against the Resolutioners.[60] Wariston seemed to think that he and the other Guthrie men could at least work with, and possibly win over, Monck's allies: in contrast, they had received a notably frosty reception from Broghill's friends.[61] The split in the council by the end of 1655 seems to have been five against five. With a divided council, Broghill was forced to delay his pro-Resolutioner policy, while he struggled for supremacy within the council.

In October 1655, therefore, Broghill reconsidered his tactics. Rather than pushing for even closer co-operation with the Resolutioners, and risking an open breach with Monck, he turned his attentions to the two Protester factions. Arranging a private meeting with seven Protesters from different parties, and (unlike the Resolutioner negotiations in the previous month) being careful to invite Monck and another observer, Broghill initially planned a debate on uniting the Kirk factions.[62] But from the start of the meeting it became clear that the agenda had changed, when Broghill announced his plans to put into effect the Gillespie Charter of 1654, for 'the hinderinge of unworthy men's admission' to the ministry.[63] This new move was a shocking departure from the pro-Resolutioner measures of September; but, more importantly, it also exacerbated existing divisions within the Protesters' ranks, by giving the president's public support to the Gillespie faction against that of Monck's friend, James Guthrie. The latter had rejected the Gillespie Charter in 1654, and his party's new covenant, produced in the summer of 1655 and supported by Monck, had already been touted as its successor. By reintroducing the charter as official policy, Broghill had found a cunning way of countering Monck's faction in Kirk and council. If challenged on this, Broghill could – and did – claim that he was merely enforcing a protectoral ordinance which the previous regime has signally failed to implement.[64] Predictably, when the text of the charter was published and the ordinance proclaimed on 24 October, Gillespie's faction co-operated, while Guthrie and his friends (still supported by Monck) continued to push for their new covenant.[65]

Despite Broghill's success in promoting the Gillespie Charter, and pushing the necessary orders through the Scottish council, during November and December there was little progress in religious affairs. The Guthrie faction continued to form the most vociferous lobbying group at the council during and after the cross-party conference designed to improve chances of a union

---

[60] Swinton was an Independent, and would later become a Quaker: see Dow, *Cromwellian Scotland*, pp 55–6.
[61] *Wariston diary*, iii, 18.
[62] *Thurloe S.P.*, iv, 127–8.
[63] Ibid., pp 128–9.
[64] Ibid., pp 557–8: in a later letter to Cromwell, surveying recent events, Broghill pointedly referred to the Gillespie Charter as 'your highnes ord[i]nance'.
[65] Dow, *Cromwellian Scotland*, p. 201.

of the Kirk.[66] Broghill's incapacity owing to a severe attack of gout from 27 November to 25 December further hampered efforts to reach a settlement.[67] In January tensions between Broghill and Monck seem to have increased, and, according to one commentator, 'their was som gumme among themselves in the Counsel'.[68] It was not until late January 1656 that the stalemate was broken, possibly as a result of the departure from Scotland of one of Monck's closest allies on the council, Colonel Cooper,[69] and it was only at this stage that Broghill, with a slight factional edge in the council, was able to introduce what seemed to be yet another change in church policy: an attempt to abandon the traditional factional divisions and create a 'centre party' in the Scottish Church.

On 29 January 1656 Broghill wrote to Secretary Thurloe, airing his frustration at the lack of progress in church matters and outlining his chosen solution: 'that we shall hardly doe our worke by buildinge with any one of thos two partyse [the Protesters and Resolutioners], but by composeing a third, extracted out of both, and consisting of the honnestest and most peaceable amongst them'.[70] In late February, in a letter to Cromwell, Broghill fleshed out his scheme. He proposed to join the more moderate Resolutioners with Gillespie's Protester faction and 'compose' a party which 'would only consist of the most sober, most honest, and most godly of this nation', in order to settle the Kirk and reduce support for royalist rebellion.[71] Both Julia Buckroyd and Frances Dow see the creation of this middle group as the defining moment of Broghill's church policy. This was 'a mark of his willingness to innovate',[72] and a sign of his continuing plan to divide and rule for secular ends.[73] According to this line, it was the attempt to implement such a policy which occupied Broghill's attentions between January and August 1656. Only the failure of this, the preferred solution, caused Broghill to consider a return to his negotiations with the Resolutioners alone in the late summer. Yet there is strong evidence to suggest that the centre party was never a serious plan; nor did it last beyond February 1656, when William Lockhart's departure for England (en route for France) left Broghill with a clear majority in the council. It was, in fact, merely a smokescreen to hide Broghill's dual aims during this period: to discredit Monck and the Guthrie party and to return to the policy he had favoured all along – the winning of the Resolutioners to the government's side.

---

[66] Ibid., pp 202–3.
[67] *Thurloe S.P.*, iv, 250–342.
[68] *Wariston diary*, iii, 26.
[69] Cooper went to Ulster in January 1656: see *Thurloe S.P.*, iv, 376, 407–8.
[70] Ibid., p. 479.
[71] Ibid., p. 557.
[72] Buckroyd, 'Broghill and the church', p. 365.
[73] Dow, *Cromwellian Scotland*, pp 204–5.

As we have seen, Broghill was well aware of the threat posed by Monck in the closing months of 1655, and it has been argued that his interest in resurrecting the Gillespie Charter in October of that year was in order to attack the general's friends in the Guthrie faction. Tensions over the rival Protester parties had been growing during December, and in the new year Broghill, now recovered from his illness, relaunched his campaign to silence Guthrie and his friends. Strengthened by a protectoral order of mid-January rejecting a petition by Guthrie in favour of a new covenant and reiterating the need to enforce the Gillespie Charter,[74] Broghill went on the offensive. On 29 January he wrote to Thurloe, outlining his centre party plan, which implicitly excluded the Guthrie group from consideration;[75] and on the next day he publicly rebuked Guthrie before the council, 'for treasonable words in the first paper [his petition] against the Ordinance'.[76] In his letter to Cromwell of 26 February, Broghill made the connexion between the 'centre party' and the need to destroy the Guthrie party more explicit. He told the protector that Guthrie and his friends were 'bitterly averse to your highnes authority . . . indeed by as much as I can recollect after severall discourses and meetinges with the lord Warresten and Mr Gutery, thos of their judgment are, as I may call them, Fifth-monarchy-presbiterians'.[77] By comparing Guthrie's party to the radical sectaries who attacked Cromwell in England, and by emphasising that Guthrie had already rejected the government's policy over the Gillespie Charter, Broghill was voicing his very real concerns at the divisive effect of radical religion within the Scottish system; and he was also playing on Cromwell's own deep-seated fear of sedition, which had been further heightened by fears of an alliance between the fifth-monarchists and the royalists in the previous winter.[78] The fifth-monarchy line was so good that Broghill could not resist using it again in the Scottish council a month later, causing Wariston to record angrily that 'Brochil called M[r] J[ames] G[uthrie] and me Fyft Monarchye men'.[79] Under cover of his plan to form a centre party, Broghill was able to score very damaging hits against his enemies in the Kirk, and their patrons in the council.

The centre party was also a useful device for Broghill to promote his allies in the Resolutioner party. In his letter to Cromwell of 26 February, Broghill did point out the problems of relying on the Resolutioners, but using very moderate terms: they were 'not inclyned' to the government, and some were

---

[74] *Wariston diary*, iii, 24.

[75] *Thurloe S.P.*, iv, 479.

[76] *Wariston diary*, iii, 26.

[77] *Thurloe S.P.*, iv, 557; significantly, Broghill seemed to have borrowed the phrase from a Resolutioner minister, George Hutcheson: see *Wariston diary*, iii, pp xix, 5.

[78] See J. C. Davis, *Oliver Cromwell* (2001), p. 144; Johann Sommerville, 'Oliver Cromwell and English political thought' in John Morrill (ed.), *Oliver Cromwell and the English revolution* (1990), pp 252–3.

[79] *Wariston diary*, iii, 28.

'not fitt' as ministers; but these were not insuperable obstacles.[80] Such mild criticism contrasted strongly with the violence of Broghill's language against the Guthrie party. Broghill went on to catalogue the benefits of fostering links with the Resolutioners. They were 'very much the greater number of the ministry, and best esteemed by the presbiterians in England and Ireland'; their support would help to quieten unrest in Scotland; and (perhaps echoing John Dury's arguments) a tolerant line would signal the sincerity of Cromwell's claim to champion Protestantism to 'all the reformed churches in Europe'.[81] Again, by emphasising the security aspects in all three kingdoms, and Cromwell's role as guardian of European Protestantism, Broghill was using his knowledge of the protector's attitudes to good effect. There is little doubt that Broghill's principal intention in this letter was to 'sell' the Resolutioners to Cromwell. By contrast, the other partners in the supposed centre group, the Protesters of Gillespie's faction, hardly received a mention. It is true that Broghill termed them 'pious sober men . . . frends to your government, and servants to your highnes',[82] and that, as the regime's most obvious allies within the Kirk, they were already familiar to Cromwell, but they do not seem to have been according equal status with the majority Resolutioners. Indeed, in the following months, while Broghill continued to court the Resolutioners, the Gillespie party was sidelined, and by June the charter had been dropped as official policy.[83] Once again, Broghill's support for the Gillespie party seems to have been merely a tool to undermine Guthrie's faction, and the whole centre party policy was a Trojan Horse – the means by which the president could reintroduce his pro-Resolutioner policy of September 1655.

The traditional account dates Broghill's decision to return to his policy of courting the Resolutioner party to August 1656 at the earliest. Yet the evidence shows that contacts between the president and the Resolutioners had been re-established (if they had ever been severed in the first place) by the end of January 1656. On 29 January, in the midst of Broghill's verbal assault on Guthrie, Wariston picked up rumours that 'M[r] Douglas, Mr Dikson and Mr J. Wood' had made 'undertaikings' to Broghill 'to declare their allowance of the Government, to preach and praye for itt; and that they wer to subscryve som paper about it'.[84] Such rumours were based on fact: on 30 January Douglas, Dickson and George Hutcheson sent Broghill a letter outlining their concerns at the 'secret suggestions and insinuations' of the Protesters in other quarters, and begging his support for the majority in the Kirk and 'our Covenanted

---

[80] *Thurloe S.P.*, iv, 557.

[81] Ibid.

[82] Ibid.

[83] [Broghill] to [English Council], 10 June 1656 (N.L.S., MS 7032, ff 82r–3r); see below, n.99.

[84] *Wariston diary*, iii, 25.

reformation'.[85] In February James Wood and three Edinburgh ministers petitioned the Scottish council to 'take off what restraints are putt upon the
exercise of our kirk discipline and government', and on the 20th of that month
a paper was presented to Broghill complaining about the withdrawal of clergy
stipends and other abuses.[86] These intercessions culminated in a letter to
Broghill of 23 February, from Douglas, Dickson, Wood and James Sharp. The
four Resolutioners were confident of a good reception from the president,
'being encouraged hereunto, not only by your Lordship's favourable condes-
cendencie in admitting us to propound our case freely unto you, but also by
the experience we have found of your tenderness towards us'; and they went
on to promise 'to live peaceably and inoffensively in our stations and con-
versations . . . and . . . to live under the present government'.[87] It was this final
communication from the Resolutioners, rather than a desire to erect a centre
party, which prompted Broghill's letter to Cromwell of 26 February. In
this letter Broghill not only praised the Resolutioners in general terms, he also
passed on the four ministers' offers to 'live inoffensively and peaceably' under
the government, highlighted their promise to purge 'unfitt ministers' by the
following April, and related their efforts to curb royalism in the ministry. By
the summer, Broghill asserted, 'all thes ministers, which hitherto have bin soe
averse, will openly pray for your government'. He went on to advise Cromwell
to write in person to six leading Resolutioner ministers, including his old
friends Robert Douglas and David Dickson.[88]

The months of inactivity which followed Broghill's letter to Cromwell of
26 February were not the fault of the president; rather they marked the strength
of opposition to Broghill's new pro-Resolutioner policy in Whitehall. On
11 March Broghill asked Thurloe to remind Cromwell of the seriousness of
the religious negotiations north of the border.[89] This call was repeated by a
Scottish agent working for the English government, David Drummond, who
warned Thurloe that 'your ho[nour] spoyles all, thatt you doe nott returne
his highnes answer to ther desyres sent by Broghill, that worthie man'.[90] On
15 April Broghill told Thurloe that the ministers 'I thinke may be woon if
well handled'.[91] On 13 May Broghill, close to despair at the level of inactivity
at Whitehall, demanded to be allowed three months' leave to return to
England to argue policy matters in person.[92] As the last request suggests, the
dithering of Cromwell was not the only reason for delay. Just as in late January

[85] Stephen, *Register*, i, 184–7.
[86] Ibid., pp 191–3, 194–7.
[87] Ibid., pp 198–201; see also *Wariston diary*, iii, 26.
[88] *Thurloe S.P.*, iv, 558–9.
[89] Ibid., p. 597.
[90] Ibid., p. 646.
[91] Ibid., p. 700.
[92] Ibid., v, 18.

1656 the Scottish council had become 'gummed' by political divisions, so in the spring of that year the English council was in the grip of the army faction inimicable to Broghill's policies. Of especial concern for Broghill was the fact that the Scottish committee of the council was still dominated by John Lambert and Charles Fleetwood, who were favourable to Monck and generally suspicious of Broghill, with whom they had crossed swords in the Irish council and the English parliament.[93] The delay in turning round business suggests that the Scottish committee was dragging its heels, in a deliberate attempt to undermine Broghill.[94] The growth of opposition to Broghill in London is attested by two other pieces of evidence: first, on 23 February 1656 the Guthrie faction was encouraged (possibly by Monck) to write 'supplications' to England against the Resolutioners, and targeted Lambert, Fleetwood and President Lawrence, all of whom were Broghill's enemies;[95] second, in his letter to Cromwell of 26 February, Broghill asked that the Resolutioners' offers should be kept secret with only 'your highnes, the generall heer, and mr. secretary' in the know, a request which in effect excluded Lambert and the Scottish committee.[96] Such restrictions were wise: Guthrie's party had accurate information on Broghill's dealings with the Resolutioners even before this letter was sent – suggesting a leak by Monck.[97] By early May, therefore, Broghill was preparing to travel to London to destroy the log-jam created by his enemies on both sides of the border.

After a further delay, Broghill was refused permission to travel, and was forced to remain in Scotland.[98] His only recourse was to send another strongly worded letter to the English council, dated 10 June.[99] In this letter Broghill urged that 'if som thinge that is speedy & effectuall be not done concerninge the ordinance of the 8th of Augt 54 [i.e. Gillespie's Charter] . . . the settlement of the affections of the ministry of this nation will be much retarded, if not worse'. Far from desiring an enforcement of the ordinance, Broghill called for a new system to protect the Resolutioners ('against whom, either for Life

---

[93] For the dominance of Lambert, in particular, in the Scottish committee see *Cal. S.P. Dom., 1655*, pp 126, 160, 227, 250, 277, 284, 352, 378–9; *Cal. S.P. Dom., 1655–6*, pp 5, 129, 173–4, 204, 297. Monck regularly consulted Lambert on Scottish affairs in 1654–6: see W.C.O., Clarke MS 3/2, ff 57v–140v.

[94] Broghill to English council, 8 Mar. 1656 (N.L.S., MS 7032, f. 73); one of Broghill's letters was referred to Lambert and the Committee on 8 March, but not reported to the Council until 16 May.

[95] *Wariston diary*, iii, 27.

[96] *Thurloe S.P.*, iv, 558.

[97] *Wariston diary*, iii, 26.

[98] Broghill to Cromwell, 27 June 1656 (Bodl., MS Rawl. A.39, p. 170).

[99] [Broghill] to [English council], 10 June 1656 (N.L.S., MS 7032, ff 82r–3r); the correspondent and recipients of this letter, dated from Pinkie House, can be identified with reference to *Cal. S.P. Dom., 1655–6*, 375; Broghill was at Pinkie from the end of May 1656: see Monck's order of 29 May for a guard at 'pinkey House during such time as the Lord President resides there' (W.C.O., Clarke MS 3/10, unfol.).

or Doctrine we have noe just exceptions, espetially now the whole boddy of the ministry have all left of[f] prayinge for C[harles] S[tuart]'), by giving the Scottish council 'Power to mannadg the business of stipends'.[100] As an incentive, Broghill pointed out that his negotiations with the Resolutioners had come so close to success 'thatt they must have owned the Civill magistrate in their Kirke affairs.. [or] Layde downe the Authority at the feete of the Remonstrators [ie. Protesters]'.[101]

The English council received this letter on 17 June, and referred it to the Scottish committee.[102] A further delay ensued, but on 31 July additional instructions were at last despatched to the council in Edinburgh, admitting the 'great inconvenience' arising by the failure of the Gillespie Charter, and announcing that the protector and council now agreed to the payment of stipends to all who 'live peaceably under the present Government'. The decision whether to admit ministers to the scheme lay with the Scottish council in liaison with local presbyteries.[103] This was a remarkable success for Broghill, who was able to tell the Edinburgh ministers in a private interview in August[104] that 'there was a new order come downe giving unto the Councill the full power for appointing mentenance unto intrants in the ministrie, which would take off restraints in the former ordinance complained of'.[105] Not all the Resolutioners were overjoyed, as the intervention of the state went against some of the Kirk's deepest convictions;[106] but Broghill's friends – including Dickson, Douglas and Wood – welcomed the initiative, and thanked Broghill for his efforts in securing a pragmatic solution.[107]

The arrangement to drop public prayers for the king and the agreement to allow the Scottish council (rather than the Protester party) to administer clerical stipends form the book-ends of Broghill's policy towards the Scottish Church in 1655–6. Both measures favoured the Resolutioners and therefore the majority of the Kirk's ministers, and brought them closer to accepting the political authority of the Cromwellian regime. Both had been achieved on Broghill's initiative, yet traditionally they have not been seen as indicators of his own personal preferences in church policy.[108] Rather, the unstable intervening period – between the late autumn of 1655 and the early summer of 1656 – has been seen as providing a truer reflection of the lord president's aims and objectives. It is hardly surprising that Broghill comes across in the

---

[100] [Broghill] to [English council], 10 June 1656 (N.L.S., MS 7032, ff 82r–3r).
[101] Ibid., f. 83r.
[102] Cal. S.P. Dom., 1655–6, p. 325.
[103] Cal. S.P. Dom., 1656–7, p. 48; this scheme was similar to that brokered by Clotworthy for the Ulster ministers in 1655: see Seymour, Puritans in Ireland, p. 98.
[104] Broghill to Douglas, 10 Aug. 1656 (N.L.S., Wodrow Folio MSS, vol. xxvi, f. 18r).
[105] Stephen, Register, i, 202; Thurloe S.P., v, 301–2.
[106] Baillie letters, iii, 315.
[107] Stephen, Register, i, 210ff.
[108] Dow, Cromwellian Scotland, pp 195, 199, 210; Buckroyd, 'Broghill and the church', pp 359, 367; for Broghill's religious views, see ch. 9 below.

current literature as a scheming, worldly governor, intent on dividing and ruling the Kirk parties. Yet, as we have seen, Broghill's successes should not be ignored when judging his motives. Broghill had personal contacts with the Resolutioners, which were formed long before his arrival in Scotland, and which contributed to his ability to win agreements with the Kirk where others had failed. His policies in the interim – uniting the factions, reviving Gillespie's Charter and creating a 'centre group' – were short-lived, and guided by political considerations: not least the need to block opposition in the Scottish and English councils. Once Broghill had asserted his control in Scotland, and increased his influence in England, he could return to his original policy of reconciling the Resolutioners to the Cromwellian administration. For much of his term of office, Broghill had to negotiate his way round various stumbling blocks in England and Scotland. This caused him to swerve and change direction in what was otherwise a clear, straightforward and consistent church policy.

The English council's ruling of 31 July on clerical stipends was a significant gain, but it was not a decisive victory. Broghill was acutely aware that political shifts in Scotland – and particularly in England – could quickly destroy his good work. He could not rely on the protector to resist the advice of Lambert or others in London, and this danger was heightened after 19 August, when the Protester ministers sent agents south to lobby for the 31 July order on stipends to be reversed.[109] On 22 August Broghill asked Thurloe to uphold the Kirk settlement as it then stood, and to 'prevayle with his highness to heere what I can say, ere any alteration be made, for thos, who sollicit it, are the bitterest enemyes against the government in all Scotland'.[110] When Broghill left Scotland in late August – ready to take up his place (as M.P. for Edinburgh) in the parliament called for the following month – he took with him James Sharp, who had been commissioned by the other Resolutioners as their agent in London.[111] Shortly afterwards, the Protesters sent their own representatives to England, and the stage was set for the bitter factionalism between the two parties, which provided a Caledonian sideshow to the main drama of the offer of the crown to Cromwell in the spring of 1657.[112] It is interesting to note that during 1657 the Protesters again received the backing of General Monck (who recommended them to Cromwell as 'better to be trusted then the . . . Generall Resolucion men'),[113] while the Resolutioners could rely on the help and advice from their long-standing friend and ally, Lord Broghill. As Broghill told Thurloe in the winter of 1656–7, 'Really I thinke the publike resolution-men will proove the honnester of the two'.[114]

---

[109] *Thurloe S.P.*, v, 323.
[110] Ibid., p. 336.
[111] Dow, *Cromwellian Scotland*, p. 207.
[112] See ch. 5 below.
[113] Firth, *Scotland and the protectorate*, p. 345.
[114] *Thurloe S.P.*, v, 656.

III

The conduct of church policy in 1655–6 had caused deep divisions in the Scottish council, and had created tensions between Broghill and the English council. The reforms in secular policy introduced during Broghill's presidency were less divisive. Rather than challenging the existing system (as he had done in church affairs), in many areas of secular policy Broghill seems to have been content to build on foundations laid by his predecessors, Robert Lilburne and George Monck. Thus Broghill's emphasis on using Scotsmen to administer their own affairs, and his desire to mingle civilian and military authority in the localities have rightly been seen as an extension of the pragmatic system established by his predecessors.[115] Yet beneath this general picture of co-operation, there were disagreements between Broghill and Monck in secular as well as religious policy during this period, founded on their fundamentally different approach to government. Monck saw the continuation of high levels of English involvement, and specifically the retention of an army of occupation, as the necessary precondition for stability; Broghill wanted to introduce to Scotland the kind of far-reaching civilian settlement which was being undertaken in Ireland by Henry Cromwell.

The problems facing the Scottish government in 1655 were urgent, and the possible solutions limited. The key issue was that of finance. In the summer of 1655 the Scottish finances were in a state of near-collapse. The continuing risk of rebellion necessitated a large and expensive occupying army; but the war had weakened the economy, and the country struggled to meet the heavy assessments levied to pay for the English garrisons.[116] In the spring of 1655 Monck complained to Cromwell that the £10,000 monthly cess or assessment, if enforced, would 'destroy the Country' and provoke further rebellions.[117] The tax shortfall was not met by the English government, which had financial problems of its own, and the soldiers' pay fell into arrears. As arrears mounted (reaching £86,000 by the summer), Monck found that he could not even disband troops to ease the burden, as no money was available to pay off the reduced companies.[118] It was in the face of this growing crisis that Monck requested the introduction of an excise, which would provide as much as £20,000 per mensem 'to make the sesse [i.e. cess] upp Monthly'.[119] He also urged that the collection of the new tax should be left to 'the Gentlemen of the shires and Magistrates of Burroughs' rather than English officials or soldiers. This innovation was approved by the protector and council in May 1655.[120]

---

[115] Dow, *Cromwellian Scotland*, pp 115–64.
[116] See for example *Baillie letters*, iii, 288.
[117] Monck to Cromwell, 27 Mar. 1655 (W.C.O., Clarke MS 3/2, f. 102r).
[118] Monck to Lambert, 3 July 1655 (ibid., ff 124v–5v).
[119] Monck to Cromwell, c.Apr. 1655 (ibid., f. 102v).
[120] Ibid.; Dow, *Cromwellian Scotland*, pp 168–9.

Monck's solution – to impose more taxes and to collect them more efficiently – became the bed-rock of Broghill's own financial programme, despite the unpopularity of such measures in the localities. On his arrival in Scotland, Broghill was anxious to put Monck's excise scheme into operation immediately, because, as he told Secretary Thurloe, 'every day's delay therin would be soe much loss to his highness'.[121] New commissioners were appointed to manage the excise, and, as Monck had suggested, the collection was done by Scotsmen.[122] Broghill's new reforms differed from Monck's only in degree. Thus, in his changes to the monthly assessment, he intended that savings were made on the collectors' fees by shifting the levying of this tax onto the local gentry, who would receive no payment for this concession to their political influence. Broghill told Thurloe that his inspiration came from across the Irish Sea (this was 'an expedient I got the gentlemen of my c[o]untry in Ir[e]lland to accept of') but the policy was little more than an extension of Monck's excise collection scheme.[123] The erection of a Scottish exchequer has been seen as 'Broghill's crowning achievement in the realm of financial administration', allowing a unified, civilian oversight over government finance.[124] Again, this was not a new departure. The English council had stipulated the necessity of such a court, and was busy instituting a similar body in Ireland; both used as their model the English exchequer system. That the final version in Scotland resembled the traditional Scottish rather than the English exchequer was due as much to the desire to continue Monck's use of native precedents than to Broghill's own administrative genius.[125] Broghill's main achievement was not in the framing of new financial reforms but in the implementation of an existing workable system, which could at least keep the government solvent and reduce the risk of further rebellions. The effects of this would only become apparent later in the decade, however, and in the summer of 1656 there were still problems with raising taxes, and fear among the Scots of heavier impositions to follow.[126]

In the field of the administration of justice Broghill's reform programme marked more of a departure. The reform of the central courts had been a serious problem for Monck, especially as it was necessary to balance English appointees by the retention of loyal Scots with a knowledge of the native legal system. Broghill also asked for English judges, and appointed Scots to the 'Inner House', even though there was a risk that a majority of the latter might

---

[121] *Thurloe S.P.*, iv, 48.
[122] Dow, *Cromwellian Scotland*, pp 169–70; see Monck to Broghill, 31 July 1655 (W.C.O., Clarke MS 3/2, f. 127v).
[123] *Thurloe S.P.*, iv, 127; Monck to Broghill, 31 July 1655 (W.C.O., Clarke MS 3/2, f. 127v).
[124] Dow, *Cromwellian Scotland*, pp 174–5.
[125] Ibid., p. 175.
[126] Monck to Morgan, 14 May 1656 (W.C.O., Clarke MS 3/10, unfol.); *Baillie letters*, iii, 318; *Cal. S.P. Dom.*, 1655–6, pp 249, 364.

start to influence the legal process overall.[127] On the local level, however, Broghill brought in a major innovation, with the establishment of commissions of the peace across Scotland. Although this had been suggested by Monck as early as April 1654,[128] after the suppression of Glencairn's rebellion he had lost confidence in the idea, and preferred to rely instead on military justice.[129] He had also undermined the circuit court system, and encouraged his officers to create a 'parallel system of administering justice' in the localities.[130] Broghill resurrected the scheme of appointing civilian justices, intending to give the new j.p.s 'the power such ministers have in England', but he was also eager to base the new appointments on similar commissions enacted by the Jacobean Scottish parliament.[131] A further influence was the effectiveness of the re-institution of j.p.s in Ireland since 1651, which had included local landowners and reduced the influence of the military over the judicial system.[132] His decision to make all justices into assessment commissioners was certainly influenced by Ireland, where separation of the powers of civilian j.p.s and predominately military assessment commissioners had caused tensions.[133] The Scottish j.p. system was a success. By April 1656 Broghill was able to report back to London that the arrangement 'does begin to take som life, [as] many considerable persons for interest and power have taken the o[a]th'.[134] As the example of the commission of the peace shows, Broghill was beginning to tease apart the military from the civilian functions of the government.

Broghill's administrative reforms were based on those of Monck, even though they sometimes exceeded the general's plans, and his emphasis on civilian involvement certainly exceeded that of Monck, who preferred to rely on the power of the military, especially in the administration of justice. There were, however, more serious areas of disagreement between Broghill and Monck, notably over the question of security.[135] Frances Dow has rightly seen 1655–6 as a period dominated by fears of invasion and royalist conspiracy, adding that 'Monck and Broghill had grossly overestimated the danger to Scotland from Charles's schemings abroad, and had been prone to take too

---

[127] Dow, *Cromwellian Scotland*, pp 176–7.
[128] Ibid., p. 178.
[129] Smith, 'Scotland and Cromwell', pp 170–1.
[130] Ibid., pp 155–60.
[131] *Thurloe S.P.*, iv, 57.
[132] T. C. Barnard, *Cromwellian Ireland* (Oxford, 1975), p. 257.
[133] Dow, *Cromwellian Scotland*, p. 172; *Thurloe S.P.*, iv, 342–3; Barnard, *Cromwellian Ireland*, p. 258.
[134] *Thurloe S.P.*, iv, 741; see Monck's order, 28 Sept. 1655 (W.C.O., Clarke MS 3/10, unfol.); Dow, *Cromwellian Scotland*, pp 178–9.
[135] The following section is based on Patrick Little, 'An Irish governor of Scotland: Lord Broghill, 1655–6' in Andrew Mackillop and Steven Murdoch (eds), *Military governors and imperial frontiers, c.1600–1800: a study of Scotland and empires* (Leiden, 2003), pp 79–97, with permission of Brill University Press.

seriously evidence of plans which had little hope of realisation'.[136] Beneath this shared sense of unease, the two men had rather different priorities, for while Monck was worried by support for the Stuarts from the continent, Broghill 'professed to discern a close connection between events in Ireland and in Scotland'.[137] The difference between the concerns of Broghill and Monck is not something Dow develops, but it is worth exploring. Evidence from Monck's order books shows that he did not share Broghill's fears about royalist plots bridging the Irish Sea. On 22 March 1655, for example, he reacted to reports of sedition by restricting passes for those going abroad, but on the same day he allowed a pass for 'one of Glencairn's p[ar]tie' to go to Ireland.[138] In July 1655 he resisted attempts by Colonel Barrow to prevent Scotsmen from travelling to Ulster 'without p[ar]ticular passes from the Gen[e]rall', arguing that this would hamper Scottish trade,[139] and only relented when Barrow was backed by the Irish lord deputy, Charles Fleetwood.[140]

Broghill's experiences in Ireland had taught him not to be so complacent. The Irish Confederates may have been defeated and their leaders banished to Connacht, but fears of a repeat of the rebellion, and massacres, of 1641, were still very real. Broghill agreed with Henry Cromwell that 'the Scotts comeinge into the north of Ireland' was 'a growing evill'.[141] Unlike Monck, he was ready to intervene to prevent such a conjunction, telling Thurloe in December of the Scottish council's intention 'to publish a proclamation against the Scotch of this country, transplantinge them into Ulster, whither they dayly resort in such thronges, that its apprehended both ther and heere ther is som ill intended therby'.[142] This proclamation was produced in early January 1656 – the same month that the former governor of Ayr (and Scottish councillor), Colonel Cooper, arrived in Ireland to take over as governor of Ulster.[143] Throughout January 1656 Broghill remained concerned that 'possibly Ireland and this place may understand each other better then we could beleeve', a possibility confirmed by news of agents 'to be sent from some lords in Scotland to some very considerable persons in Ireland'.[144] In response, Broghill was eager to work closely with Henry Cromwell and the Irish government, 'to prevent any breakings for the either frome Scots or Irish'.[145] In constrast, George Monck apparently showed little interest in the Irish dimension until August

---

[136] Dow, *Cromwellian Scotland*, p. 194.
[137] Ibid., p. 190.
[138] Monck's order, 22 Mar. 1655 (W.C.O., Clarke MS 3/9, unfol.).
[139] Monck's order, 9 July 1655 (ibid., MS 3/10, unfol.).
[140] Monck's order, 7 Aug. 1655 (ibid.).
[141] *Thurloe S.P.*, iv, 191, 198.
[142] Ibid., p. 343.
[143] Ibid., pp 403, 407–8, 418–19.
[144] Ibid., pp 372, 403.
[145] Ibid., p. 483.

1656, when there were fears that a Spanish fleet was trying to intercept troop ships from Irish and Scottish ports en route for the West Indies.[146]

In Broghill's eyes any contact between Scotland and Ireland was sinister, but the possibility of Irish Catholics making common cause with their Scottish counterparts raised his worst fears. Monck's attitude was less fanatical. For him, the Catholics were less of a threat than those Presbyterians who remained loyal to the Stuarts, and he was unsympathetic to the idea of allowing more jurisdiction to the kirk sessions, which traditionally dealt with religious misdemeanours, including recusancy.[147] While banning the meeting of the General Assembly and ordering local commanders to suppress ministers who prayed publicly for the king,[148] Monck was less zealous in his attitude towards the Catholics in the north and west, and he was attacked in April 1655 by 'some Ministers in those p[ar]ts [who] have given out that hee hath protected popish preists', because he refused to prosecute them.[149] Robert Baillie saw this leniency to papists as part of a wider scheme by a tolerationist government who let sectarians run riot, and he complained that 'Popery encreases more than these seventy years'.[150] In March 1656, once fears of royalist plots had died down, Broghill was eager to address the problem of 'the Increase & Grouth of Papists'. Implying that the fault lay with his predecessors, he complained that the 'usuall way of Discovering & Convicting of a Papist' had been removed with the suppression of the judicial function of the Kirk, and suggesting instead the introduction of an 'Oath of Abjuracon', as imposed in England.[151] The English council agreed to this proposal on 16 May,[152] and on 5 June Broghill ordered the local commanders to find all Catholics, take their weapons, and impose bonds for good behaviour.[153] He also allowed the kirk sessions to work alongside the new j.p.s to ensure that church discipline (including measures against Catholics) could proceed without jurisdictional conflict.[154] As with the attempt to isolate the Scottish and Irish royalists, the active suppression of Catholicism was very much Broghill's own policy, rather than a measure inherited from General Monck.

Broghill's greatest disagreement with Monck was over another, crucial, aspect of Scottish policy: the government's treatment of the greatest Scottish

---

[146] Dow, *Cromwellian Scotland*, pp 192–3.
[147] Smith, 'Scotland and Cromwell', pp 219–42.
[148] See Monck to Cromwell, 10 Jan. 1656 (W.C.O., Clarke MS 3/2, f. 139r); Monck's orders, 3 Nov. 1654, 10 and 20 Mar. 1655 (ibid., MS 3/9, unfol.); and 27 Apr. 1655 (ibid., MS 3/10, unfol.).
[149] Monck's order, 25 Apr. 1655 (ibid., MS 3/9, unfol.).
[150] *Baillie letters*, iii, 291, 304.
[151] Broghill to English Council, 8 Mar. 1656 (N.L.S., MS 7032, f. 73r–v).
[152] Report of Scottish committee (ibid., f. 79r).
[153] W.C.O., Clarke MS 1/16, ff 39v–40r; for the response of Resolutioners see Stephen, *Register*, i, 201–2.
[154] Smith, 'Scotland and Cromwell', p. 224.

lord, Archibald Campbell, marquess of Argyll. Seated at Inveraray, and with a mainland powerbase centred on Argyllshire, the Campbells had emerged after the collapse of the MacDonald Lordship of the Isles in 1493 as the dominant clan in the west of Scotland. During the sixteenth and early seventeenth centuries the earls of Argyll had extended their influence into the Western Isles, ousting the MacDonalds from Islay and Kintyre and undermining the MacLeans of Mull, their power relying on royal favour and the remarkable cohesion of the extended Campbell clan.[155] The marquess of Argyll, a prominent covenanter, had clung to power by siding with the Cromwellians in 1650, and soon became a valuable ally to the new regime in its attempt to quieten unrest in the west. The government's trust seemed to have been repaid in the mid-1650s, when Argyll sought to demonstrate his attachment to the Cromwellian regime by distancing himself from his royalist son, Lord Lorne, who openly supported the rebellions of Glencairn and Middleton.[156]

The policy of favouring Argyll was promoted by Lilburne and Monck, who were willing to turn a blind eye to irregularities in the government of the Western Isles and put aside their periodic doubts about Argyll's own loyalty to the protectorate. In 1654 Lilburne had allowed Argyll to increase his regional influence still further, by taking over Mull from the MacLeans, and endorsing the incorporation of the island into Argyllshire; he also endorsed Argyll's 'good affection' to the regime in his correspondence with Cromwell.[157] Monck was equally tolerant of Argyll. In April 1654, when he drew up a list of assessment collectors, the new general left a blank for Argyllshire, with a note that 'the blanke to bee fill'd by the Lo[rd] of Argyle'.[158] In May 1654 Monck thanked the marquess for his efforts 'in drawing your people together to oppose [Glencairn's] coming into the country', and recommended that Cromwell 'give a favourable hearing' to Argyll's agent in London, who sought financial rewards for his master.[159] In the summer of 1655, with Glencairn's rebellion suppressed, Monck continued to bolster Argyll's local position. In August he wrote to Cromwell in support of Argyll's latest suit, procured the marquess a pass to travel to London, and invited him to visit him in Edinburgh before travelling south.[160] On 28 August Monck made another significant concession to Argyll, allowing him to organise the supply of fuel to the key government garrison at Dunstaffnage (a castle which controlled the sea-lanes

---

[155] E. J. Cowan, 'Clanship, kinship and the Campbell acquisition of Islay' in *S.H.R.*, lviii (1979), pp 132–57; Jane Dawson, 'The fifth earl of Argyle, Gaelic lordship and political power in sixteenth century Scotland' in *S.H.R.*, lxvii (1988), pp 1–27; Gordon Donaldson, *Scotland: James V–VII* (Edinburgh, 1965), pp 228–31.

[156] For Argyll's career see A. I. Macinnes, *Clanship, commerce and the house of Stuart, 1603–1788* (East Linton, 1996), pp 94–115.

[157] Firth, *Scotland and the protectorate*, pp lx, 37–8, 61, 399–400.

[158] W.C.O., Clarke MS 3/5, f. 21v.

[159] Firth, *Scotland and the protectorate*, pp 104, 110–11.

[160] Monck's order, 17 Aug. 1655 (W.C.O., Clarke MS 3/10, unfol.).

around the Isle of Mull), and giving him a hand in the administration of the assessment for Argyllshire, which would now be paid directly to the garrison commander without passing through the Edinburgh coffers.[161] The degree of trust which had grown up between Monck and Argyll is further attested by the general's decision on 10 September not to attend a military conference, as 'the Marquess of Argyll is to bee heere with him his l[ordshi]p intending to goe for England'.[162]

Both Lilburne and Monck accepted Argyll's fundamental loyalty. They seem to have calculated that with the Campbells acquiescent, the English government could worry less about security in the Western Isles and the dangers of collusion between the Irish and Scottish rebels, and government troops could thus be redeployed against the northern highlands. In August 1655, for example, Monck recommended Argyll to Cromwell on the grounds that 'his Lo[rdshi]ppe hath bin alwayes ready & indeavoured to keepe those that belonged to him (Tenants & others) from going in Armes'.[163] Argyll's loyalty would be indeed have been a great asset to the government. But in Monck's case the friendship which developed between him and the marquess was singularly ill-advised. It would take the general another two years to admit it, but his subordinate officers already had firm evidence of the weakness of the Argyll's allegiance to the Cromwellian regime.[164]

Broghill arrived in Scotland just as Argyll left for England. The new president took against the marquess almost immediately, apparently swayed by information received from Secretary Thurloe's intelligence network – which seems to have been better informed than Monck's – and his own fears of the activity of Argyll's royalist son, Lord Lorne.[165] Broghill's suspicions of Argyll's involvement in stirring plots in Ulster, and memories of the first earl of Cork's violent hatred of autonomous lordships in Ireland, may also have played a part in turning the new governor against the Campbell interest on his arrival at Edinburgh. Broghill spent the next six months gradually undermining Argyll's hegemony in the west of Scotland, using the judicial and financial measures which he and Monck had recently introduced to good effect. On 27 November 1655, when the new j.p.s were nominated, Broghill 'hindred my lord Argile being made one', thus limiting the marquess's legal autonomy in Argyllshire.[166] By the end of 1655 the problems of Monck's decision to hand

---

[161] Monck's order, 28 Aug. 1655 (ibid.).

[162] Monck's order, 10 Sept. 1655 (ibid.); for more evidence of leniency to Argyll see Little, 'Irish governor', pp 85–8.

[163] Monck's order, 17 Aug. 1655 (W.C.O., Clarke MS 3/10, unfol.).

[164] Firth, *Scotland and the protectorate*, pp 411–15. Monck had turned against Argyll by the summer of 1657: see *Thurloe S.P.*, vi, 295, 306, 341.

[165] In November 1655 Broghill told Thurloe that he was prompted to move against Argyll in response to 'that touch you gave me about him': *Thurloe S.P.*, iv, 250; for Lorne see Dow, *Cromwellian Scotland*, p. 191.

[166] *Thurloe S.P.*, iv, 250.

over the assessment collection in the region to Argyll had become apparent; and, under pressure from the council, the general was forced to rescind his earlier agreement, as 'there is none of the Assesse of the shire of Argyll paid in to him [the governor of Dunstaffnage] according to the Agreem[en]t, w[hi]ch the Council take very ill'.[167] By 1 January 1656 Broghill had received intelligence that Charles Stuart was encouraging Lord Lorne to rebel once again by offering to confirm his family in the 'Justiciary of the Isles' and the perpetual sheriffdom of Argyllshire: news which prompted him to send an agent to find '[all] he can discover concerning any thing w[hic]h relates to the L[or]d Argiles Actinges or his sons'.[168] He also renewed his efforts to reduce the territorial power of the Campbells. On 9 January the council removed the collection of assessments from Argyll's men, and appointed a new, independent sub-collector.[169] There were also punitive measures. In February it was decided to abate the assessment for the region by only £74, because over £4,000 of the money due was oustanding, and 'in regard there is soe much behinde the Councill thinke that they have done the Marquess of Argyll a Curtesie therin'.[170] In March the army was ordered to enforce the collection of assessment arrears in Argyllshire.[171] Argyll, already in debt, was vulnerable to the council's decision to use assessments and abatements as a tool for local control. In March there were further moves to reduce Argyll's power, as the Scottish council urged its English counterpart to consider dividing the sheriffdom of Argyll: which could only be seen as an assault on the marquess's position as hereditary sheriff of the county.[172] In response, Colonel Brayne was given jurisdiction over parts of Argyllshire as sheriff, and the marquess was ordered to pay feu duties to him at Inverlochy.[173] In May the government extended its direct control over the region by placing the three garrisons of Dunstaffnage, Inverlochy and Duart under Lieutenant-Colonel Cotterell, with orders to bring in the assessments and to distrain defaulters, acting under directions from the Edinburgh council as well as Monck.[174]

In the late spring of 1656 Broghill's government started to interfere in Argyll's local powerbase in other ways. In April 1656 the laird of Glenorchy (himself a senior member of the Clan Campbell) had his assessment abated as a reward for his loyalty to the government; in May Daniel MacLean, the tutor

---

[167] Monck's order, 31 Dec. 1655 (W.C.O., Clarke MS 3/10, unfol.). In this, and subsequent orders, Monck invariably makes it plain to his subordinates that he was merely passing on orders passed by the Scottish council, whether he agreed with them or not.

[168] Broghill to Cromwell, 1 Jan. 1656 (Bodl., MS Rawl. A.27, pp 667–8).

[169] Monck's order, 9 Jan. 1656 (W.C.O., Clarke MS 3/10, unfol.).

[170] Monck's order, 7 Feb. 1656 (ibid.).

[171] Monck's order, 20 Mar. 1656 (ibid).

[172] Cal. S.P. Dom., 1655–6, p. 224; Gilbert Mabbott to Monck, 25 Mar. 1656 (W.C.O., Clarke 1/16, f. 12r); Firth, Scotland and the protectorate, pp 414–5.

[173] 'Orders for the Counsaill of Scotland', n.d. [1656] (Bodl., MS Rawl. A.34, p. 73).

[174] Monck's order, 30 May 1656 (W.C.O., Clarke MS 3/10, unfol.).

of Duart, and Argyll's old enemy, was authorised to collect the assessment on Mull, and to bring to justice those who refused to pay, including the Campbell laird of Cawdor; and in early August official backing was given to the claims of Ronald MacDonald of Tarsett to his clan lands at Lochaber, 'that hee may bargaine with the Marquesse of Argyll for the same'.[175] Other marks of favour were given to Sir James MacDonald of Sleat and the Captain of Clanrannald;[176] and by the end of the year the collection of the Argyllshire assessment, previously the prerogative of the marquess, had been put into Glenorchy's hands.[177] All these men were from families with complex relations with the Campbells of Argyll, whose overlordship they accepted, but not without resentment.[178] To promote them was not only in line with government attempts to advance middle-ranking landowners; it also constituted direct interference with the delicate balance of factions upon which Argyll's power rested. In response, when he returned to Scotland in the following year Argyll came down heavily on his clients, especially the laird of Glenorchy and (with less justification) the laird of Cawdor, who were penalised financially; and he summoned the tutor of MacLean to Inveraray (a meeting which MacLean prudently declined to attend).[179] As one 'honest gentleman of Argyllshire' reported to the government's local agent, 'our Lord since his returne from England is moir earnest to know the affection off his friends butt also off his nighbowrs', and had declared his intention to act 'against other who hes aney Correspondence with the Genorll [sic] or who hes aney way with the Englisse'.[180] Argyll's furious reaction is in itself a sign that the Campbell clan was starting to unravel, aided by government pressure. Broghill's part in this cannot be doubted. When parliamentary elections were held in August 1656, the president again intervened in the locality, for, as he told Thurloe, 'Argile has bin very industrious to be chosen, but we have put a spoke in his wheele'.[181] When parliament convened in September, the marquess of Argyll was not among its members, and the Argyllshire constituency was represented by John Lockhart, brother of the Scottish councillor, Sir William Lockhart.

---

[175] Monck's orders, 29 Apr., 16 May, 10 June 1656 (ibid.); 18 July, 24 July, 13 Aug. 1656 (MS 3/11, unfol.); for the various clans see Dawson, 'The fifth earl of Argyle', passim, and F. J. Shaw, 'Landownership in the Western Isles in the seventeenth century' in *S.H.R.*, lvi (1977), pp 34–45.

[176] Monck's orders, 25 Apr. 1656, 9 May 1656 (W.C.O., Clarke MS 3/10, unfol.).

[177] Joseph Witter to Glenorchy, 10 Nov. 1656 (N.A.S., Breadalbane papers, GD 112/39/101/14).

[178] See Macinnes, *Clanship*, pp 38–9, 60–5, 73–6, 95–7, 100–1; Argyll had recently faced the total collapse of the Campbell lordship during the campaigns of Alasdair MacColla and Montrose: see David Stevenson, *Highland warrior: Alasdair MacColla and the civil wars* (Edinburgh, 1994), pp 145–63.

[179] *Thurloe S.P.*, vi, 295, 306.

[180] Letter to David Drummond, 31 May 1657 (Bodl., MS Rawl. A.51, f. 70r).

[181] *Thurloe S.P.*, v, 295.

Broghill's systematic attempt to reduce Argyll's local power may have been guided by his fears of royalists in Ulster and the west of Scotland making common cause, and influenced by his own inherited distrust of independent Irish lordships; but it was given added urgency by the political intrigue conducted by the marquess during his sojourn in London. Argyll soon proved that his plotting in England was as much a threat to the Scottish government as his royalist sympathies might have been. Probably in response to Broghill's early moves against him, on 11 January 1656 Argyll petitioned Cromwell asking that the articles he had signed with General Deane in 1652 would be publicly approved by the English council.[182] These articles, approved by the protector and council in March, in effect reiterated the government's faith in Argyll's loyalty, and made Broghill's job all the more difficult.[183] Thereafter, Argyll concentrated on lobbying for the repayment of various sums, amounting to over £50,000, which he had been promised by the English and Scottish parliament during the covenanting wars. These would clear his debts and make him less vulnerable to government financial pressure in Scotland. In September 1656 the English council agreed to pay him £12,000, which was to come directly from the Scottish excise, a tax only made workable through Broghill's recent efforts in Edinburgh.[184] Even more annoying than the money lost to the Scottish revenues by such grants was the clear signal they sent to the Scottish council that despite their suspicions, Argyll still enjoyed enormous influence in England, where Broghill's enemies ruled the Scottish committee.

During his stay in London, Argyll also started to interfere in the affairs of the Kirk. Argyll's local influence had been increased by his dominance of the Argyll synod, which referred most of their important decisions to him, and he had also established connexions with the Glasgow synod, and the Protesters under Patrick Gillespie.[185] From January 1656, when Broghill was in the middle of his dispute with Guthrie and Wariston in Edinburgh, the Protesters of this faction were alerted to the possibility that Argyll might help in 'our busines', and that he 'had som favor tho not great' with those around Cromwell.[186] The Guthrie faction, who had their own suspicions of Argyll's motives, were at first reluctant to accept his approaches, but the marquess persisted, and as his credit at Whitehall grew, their objections receded. In June Argyll told Wariston of his meeting with 'the Lord Deputy [Fleetwood], President [Lawrence] and Lambert' – all enemies of Broghill – and that he had tried to gain personal preferment for Wariston himself. The diarist was

---

[182] *Cal. S.P. Dom.*, 1655–6, p. 111.
[183] Ibid., p. 222.
[184] *Cal. S.P. Dom.*, 1656–7, pp. 18, 107.
[185] D. C. MacTavish (ed.), *Minutes of the synod of Argyll, 1652–1661* (Edinburgh, 1944), pp 77–9, 83, 98, 117, 119–22, 132, 135–6, 143, 151–2.
[186] *Wariston diary*, iii, 25.

confident of Argyll's standing at court, and added that 'if the report of Argyle's taiking imployment hold treu he knows how seasonable it was'.[187] In October 1656 Argyll secured a pension for Wariston, through the influence of Fleetwood and Cromwell.[188] Broghill's friends in the Resolutioner party recognised the threat posed by Argyll's position in London, and they suspected that his interference in church matters was political in motive, so that 'he might to his advantage fall in w[i]t[h] the grandees, & to follow his old trade & play his game by making us subservient to his ends'.[189]

Argyll's 'game' continued for a few months more, as he gave considerable support to the Protester representatives who attended the English council, and tried to block moves by Broghill's Resolutioner allies. General Monck, who was also an active supporter of the Protesters in early 1657, seems to have continued to give the marquess the benefit of the doubt, but by the summer all had changed. On his return to Scotland, Argyll's client lords, who had become used to increased government intervention, passed on information about the marquess's nefarious activities to Monck and the Scottish council, and hinted at his royalist sympathies.[190] In June Monck had withdrawn his support from Argyll, complaining to Thurloe 'how ill he deserves the twelve thousand pounds that was given him [from the excise]', and recommending the younger laird of Glenorchy to Cromwell's beneficence.[191] By early 1659 Monck was Argyll's sworn enemy, and in 1661 he was instrumental in procuring the marquess's execution by Charles II's government.[192]

Broghill's attempt to undermine Argyll demonstrates the difference of approach between him and Monck in secular government, which is easily obscured behind the red tape of more mundane administrative reforms. Monck's efforts to introduce judicial and financial changes were ineffective because they were piecemeal, while Broghill was able to co-ordinate policy more effectively, but there was no great disagreement over policy in this area. Broghill also realised that certain fundamental problems had to addressed before reform could work effectively. As with the Kirk parties, the greatest threat came from those who were ostensibly on the government's side, in this case the marquess of Argyll. Once again, Broghill was forced to counter Monck's earlier policy (at the risk of affronting the general) and engage in factional politics in order to achieve a stable situation in Scotland. Tacit opposition from Monck was matched by a quickening of interest in England, where

---

[187] Ibid., pp 36–7.

[188] Ibid., p. 48.

[189] Sharp to Douglas, after Oct. 1656 (N.L.S., Wodrow Folio MSS, vol. xxvi, f. 145v).

[190] *Thurloe S.P.*, vi, 295, 306.

[191] Ibid., pp 341, 352; John Campbell, the younger laird, would marry the daughter of the earl of Holland (and niece of the influential earl of Warwick) by the end of the year: see Campbell to Glenorchy, 31 Dec. 1657 (N.A.S., Breadalbane papers, GD 112/39/102/7–8).

[192] Firth, *Scotland and the protectorate*, p. 411; for more on Monck's views of Argyll in 1659 see B.L., Eg. MS 2519, ff 19r–30r.

Broghill's enemies dominated the council. Worse still, Argyll's existing connexions with the Protesters meant that a secular row over local government
soon became embroiled in the religious row which was already brewing in
Edinburgh and London.

As we have seen, Broghill's support for the Resolutioner party in the Kirk
was not based on personal preference alone. His willingness to oppose Monck
and the English council over church policy again shows the difference in their
attitude to governing Scotland. Broghill, who had fought long and hard for
the Old Protestant interest in Ireland, came to Scotland with the intention
of winning the Kirk's support for the protectorate. The Resolutioners, as the
majority party, were immediately attractive as a political ally, and it is significant that from first to last Broghill was eager to get public statements of
their loyalty to the regime, whether over prayers for the king or over stipends.
The Protesters, on the other hand, were a minority group, with ideas unaccept-
able to the majority of Scots. The encouragement of such a group threatened
to destabilise the careful administrative reforms which Broghill was currently
putting into place. His personal inclinations towards the Resolutioners and
his aversion to the Protesters thus coincided with his long-term political
objective, to demonstrate that a moderate, civilian settlement was the solution
to the protector's Scottish problems. It was also becoming apparent that any
reforms would have to be 'British' in nature, involving far-reaching changes
in all three nations within the Cromwellian union.

IV

Broghill's government of Scotland fits into the more general pattern set by his
activities in Ireland in the early years of the 1650s. With his links with the
Scottish aristocracy and his friendship with the Resolutioners in the Kirk,
Broghill was more open to the possibility of creating a broadly-based
protectoral party in Scotland, in much the same way as he had helped to erect
an inclusive Old Protestant party in Ireland. In Ireland, such a policy had
brought Broghill (and later, Henry Cromwell) into direct conflict with the
army radicals and their allies in England; in Scotland Broghill was opposed by
Monck and the Protesters, who also looked to the English council for support.
Divisions along religious lines were matched by divisions over certain elements
of secular policy, and, as the dispute with Argyll shows, the two easily became
entwined. Alongside the practicalities of government, there are signs that
Broghill differed from Monck in his fundamental attitude to governing
Scotland, and that this difference was caused, at least in part, by his Irish
background and experience.[193] As we have seen, his reform of local justice and
the collection of assessments was based on Irish models, his opposition to

---

[193] For a development of this theme see Little, 'Irish governor', passim.

Argyll may have been prompted by his knowledge of Irish lordships, and his approach to security was guided by fear of the highlanders and the Ulster royalists joining forces. In his attitude to the Kirk, Broghill was guided by his own Irish background, by his co-ordination of policy with Henry Cromwell, and by his conviction that through winning over the Resolutioners 'the presbiterians of England and Ireland, who are not inconsiderable, might probably be wonn unto your highness'.[194]

Broghill's concern for Presbyterian sensibilities in England is revealing. For, as well as adding an Irish flavour to the Scottish government, Broghill's policies offered a critique of the very different policies enforced in England in the same period. In Ireland and Scotland, the years 1655–6 saw the establishment of moderate government, with the army's power reduced, radical religion discouraged, and more influence placed in the hands of the local landowners, including former royalists. In England, the same period saw the introduction of tighter military rule, and increased persecution of royalists, under the notorious major-generals. Christopher Durston, in his definitive study of the rule of the major-generals, has confirmed the radicalism of their agenda, and their deep unpopularity in the localities they governed. The scheme was 'a radical innovation with no real antecedents in earlier English history' which put 'socially obscure' soldiers in charge of 'large regional groupings'.[195] This contrasted strongly with the attempt by Henry Cromwell and Broghill (and indeed, by Monck) to return local government to the traditional ruling classes, and, where possible, to re-establish traditional forms of government. The major-generals were instructed to impose religious and moral reform on their areas, but failed because of their 'inability to forge a sufficiently close partnership with the county magistracy and parochial ministry' to ensure such reforms could be enforced.[196] In Scotland and Ireland, every effort was made to encourage moderate religion, fostering majority groups such as the Resolutioners, and again placing authority in existing structures or (at least) in the hands of local landowners. Finally, the major-generals were created in response to the royalist rebellion led by Colonel John Penruddock in 1655, and military rule was financed by a decimation tax on known royalists. This was, in Durston's words, to use 'what proved to be a highly unpopular sledgehammer to crack an already seriously weakened nut'.[197] Henry Cromwell, who presided over a systematic policy of winning over former royalists in Ireland, saw this attempt to 'lay a burden promiscuously upon all the old cavalieer party' would only create 'a perpetuall enmity' against the regime.[198] Broghill, who

---

[194] *Thurloe S.P.*, iv, 557.
[195] Christopher Durston, *Cromwell's major-generals: godly government during the English revolution* (Manchester, 2001), p. 230.
[196] Ibid., p. 228.
[197] Ibid., p. 228.
[198] Quoted in ibid., p. 229.

had encouraged the royalist Resolutioners and forged close links with royalist nobles in Scotland, would surely have agreed with such an analysis. In the early 1650s he had protected the estates of former royalists in Ireland (including those of his brother, the second earl of Cork);[199] in 1656 it was widely believed that he had intervened to save the life of the earl of Glencairn;[200] and in 1657 he became a fierce critic of the decimation tax in England.[201]

The moderate reforms of Broghill in Scotland and of Henry Cromwell in Ireland produced strong counter-currents to the flow of protectoral government in England, as typified by the major-generals. We have already seen this in the strength of opposition which the new governments in Scotland and Ireland encountered in the English council, dominated by the army interest which had promoted the appointment of the major-generals in the first place. Such tensions were nothing compared with the factional turbulence which emerged during the second protectorate parliament, as the English enemies of the major-generals (whether in the 'court' or the country) made common cause with the Irish and Scottish M.P.s to overturn not just the decimation tax but the Instrument of Government as well, and to create a new, civilian constitution for all three nations, under the Humble Petition and Advice. Broghill was well aware of the strength of opposition to the major-generals in England, and the threat that resurgent military rule posed to the fragile civilian governments in Ireland and Scotland. Fleetwood was still lord deputy of Ireland; Monck was still commander-in-chief in Scotland: the removal of Henry Cromwell and Broghill could have reversed their moderating policies overnight.

The parliament summoned to sit in September 1656 thus provided a serious danger, and a brilliant opportunity. It was hardly a coincidence that, on his journey south from Edinburgh in August 1656, Broghill took time to visit his influential relatives, the earl of Warwick and the earl of Suffolk, at their houses in Essex.[202] Both had strong connexions with the Presbyterian church in England and with the country gentry who had shown their ability to dominate parliament in 1654, and who now so vigorously opposed the major-generals. Their influence would be an important factor in the success of a 'British' response to the threat of increasing military and sectarian power within the Cromwellian union. In visiting Warwick and Suffolk, Broghill was not attending a family gathering but convening a council of war.

---

[199] See above, ch. 3.
[200] *Baillie letters*, iii, 317.
[201] See below, ch. 5.
[202] *Thurloe S.P.*, v, 336; see below, chs 7, 9.

5

The Union Parliament and the kingship debates, 1656–7

Historians have disagreed about the extent of Broghill's influence over the second protectorate parliament. Hugh Trevor-Roper saw his role as crucial in managing the passage of such important legislation as the militia bill and (most importantly) the Humble Petition and Advice, with an organised party, including sixty Irish and Scottish M.P.s, at his beck and call.[1] Others have questioned this portrayal. Carol Egloff suggests that Trevor-Roper 'over-estimated both the polished efficiency of Broghill's organisation and the effortlessness with which it carried all before him', and instead emphasises the role of the 'English moderates' – including the Presbyterians – in bringing down the military regime.[2] Peter Gaunt has also questioned Broghill's ability to manage the house, pointing out that

> Burton's parliamentary diary does not suggest that he [Broghill] led the House, either during the kingship debates or at other times during the session. According to the Commons Journals, Broghill served as teller just four times throughout the session, far less often than a host of well known and not so well known MPs, and an examination of the number of times he was nominated to committees compared to the records of other members reveals than he came a glorious thirty-sixth in a league table of nominations, again appearing far less often than many seemingly less distinguished MPs.[3]

Gaunt concludes that 'Broghill was more active and prominent in the first Protectorate Parliament than in the second', and he sees the initiative for

---

[1] H. R. Trevor-Roper, 'Oliver Cromwell and his parliaments' in his *Religion, the reformation and social change* (1967), pp 345–91.

[2] Carol S. Egloff, 'Settlement and kingship: the army, the gentry and the offer of the crown to Oliver Cromwell' (unpublished Ph.D. thesis, Yale University, 1990), pp 10–12; for a general critique of Trevor-Roper's ideas see Roger Howell, jr, 'Cromwell and his parliaments: the Trevor-Roper thesis revisited' in R. C. Richardson (ed.), *Images of Oliver Cromwell* (Manchester, 1993), pp 124–35.

[3] Peter Gaunt, 'Oliver Cromwell and his protectorate parliaments: co-operation, conflict and control' in Ivan Roots, (ed.), *Into another mould: aspects of the interregnum* (2nd ed., Exeter, 1998), p. 92.

reform as coming from the protector's council.[4] Yet neither Egloff nor Gaunt provide convincing alternatives to the Trevor-Roper thesis – preferring to see the 1656–7 sitting as 'ad hoc', 'unplanned' and 'without a detailed programme of business'.[5] Yet the characterisation of this parliament as chaotic and leaderless does not ring true; and the pivotal nature of Broghill's role cannot so easily be dismissed. Gaunt relies on the incomplete Burton diary, and the notoriously inaccurate method of counting committee appointments, to determine Broghill's influence in the house.[6] In fact, as we shall see, Broghill's activities were much more far-reaching than such sources suggest. His influence over events was as apparent outside the house as within; his interventions, while occasional, were usually decisive; and his patchiness in attendance can in part be explained by his absence for at least two separate months, suffering from gout: and even then he was able to control affairs by remote-control through his numerous allies. The resulting parliamentary 'interest' was not the well-oiled machine of Trevor-Roper's account – in reality it needed a great deal of effort to keep it on the road; but there is no doubt of its existence, nor of Broghill's place in the driving seat.

I

Integral to understanding Broghill's importance in the 1656 parliament is the identification of his friends and enemies at Westminster, and the extent to which he could expect their support or opposition in the commons. In his public career since 1649, Broghill had been drawn into collaboration or conflict with a wide range of important figures. His consistency on the need for political, religious and financial reform and his opposition to the army and religious radicalism was overlaid by his capacity to harbour personal feuds and to strike up firm friendships, which promised, in the autumn of 1656, to produce a clash of personality and policy on an unprecedented scale.

Broghill's enemies were of two types. First, the old 'commonwealthsmen', who had strongly supported the republican government of 1649–53 and who opposed the protectorate as the instrument of Cromwell's ambition. This group included such firebrands as Sir Henry Vane and Sir Arthur Hesilrige (with whom Broghill had had little contact) and, more immediately, the parliamentary commissioners who had ruled Ireland before 1654, notably Broghill's enemy, Edmund Ludlow.[7] In the later 1650s Ludlow and his allies viewed

---

[4] Ibid., pp 92–7.

[5] Ibid., p. 83.

[6] For the problems of committee lists as evidence of activity see C. R. Kyle, 'Attendance, apathy and order? Parliamentary committees in early Stuart England' in C. R. Kyle and J. T. Peacey (eds), *Parliament at work: parliamentary committees, political power and public access in early modern England* (Woodbridge, 2002), pp 43–58.

[7] See above, ch. 4.

Broghill, and his policy of supporting the protectorate, with growing disgust, but in 1656 they could only comment from the sidelines, as Sir Arthur Hesilrige, John Weaver, Thomas Scot and other troublemakers were excluded from parliament.[8] This residual hatred, rather than the lack of a reform policy in the early months of the parliament, may explain Broghill's support of Lambert as teller in favour of the exclusions on 22 September 1656.[9] Suppressed for the time being, the commonwealthsmen would renew their attack on Broghill and his allies in 1658–9.[10] The second group of Broghill's opponents, the army interest, was more of an immediate threat. The officers were loyal to Cromwell, and were influential in his counsels, but their political and religious radicalism went against the moderate stance of Broghill and his friends. General John Lambert, whose influence with the soldiers was second only to Cromwell's, had done his best to hamper Broghill's reforms in Scotland through the English council in 1655–6. As the architect of the Instrument of Government, and initiator of the major-general experiment in England, he stood for a form of military rule which was incompatible with Broghill's 'settlement' policy; he also hoped to succeed Cromwell as protector, and as a result was firmly opposed to any attempt to introduce hereditary rule.[11] Lambert's close ally, Lord Deputy Charles Fleetwood, had encouraged Baptists in the Irish army, and had supported Colonels John Hewson and Jerome Sankey (M.P.s for Guildford and Marlborough in 1656) in their attempts to discredit Henry Cromwell.[12] Lambert and Fleetwood received support from the president of the English council, Henry Lawrence,[13] and a number of civilian councillors, such as Sir Gilbert Pickering and Walter Strickland. Other fellow travellers included a coterie of senior military figures, such as William Sydenham, John Disbrowe, James Berry, John Clarke, Thomas Kelsey and Adam Baynes, as well as members of Lambert's northern interest (such as the Yorkshire M.P., Luke Robinson) who supported liberty of conscience and a retention of the pro-tectoral system. Lambert, Fleetwood, the major-generals and their allies all secured seats at Westminster in 1656, and would form a party solidly opposed to Broghill's programme of reform in religion and politics.

Unlike his enemies in the army interest, Broghill's friends in parliament were not a coherent group. Broghill hinted at this in April 1657, when he

---

[8] For a thorough examination of the exclusions (which weeded out suspected royalists as well as radicals) see C. S. Egloff, 'The search for a Cromwellian settlement: exclusions from the second protectorate parliament' in *Parliamentary History*, xvii (1998), pp 178–97, 301–21.

[9] C.J., vii, 426; cf. Egloff, 'Settlement and kingship', pp 64–5; Egloff, 'Exclusions', p. 303.

[10] See Patrick Little, 'The first unionists?: Irish Protestant attitudes to union with England, 1653–9' in I.H.S., xxxii (2000), pp 44–58.

[11] For Lambert, see David Farr, 'The military and political career of John Lambert, 1619–57' (unpublished Ph.D. thesis, Cambridge University, 1996), ch. 5.

[12] *Thurloe S.P.* v, 278.

[13] Henry Lawrence to Henry Cromwell, 9 Oct. 1656 (B.L., Lansdowne MS 821, f. 242r).

reportedly prefaced his opinion on the kingship 'party' with the comment that 'it is a thing impossible for any to particularize every individual reason which invites a parliament to pass any vote; for the parliament is a body consisting of many members'.[14] In England, Broghill's connexions were varied. He had long-standing friendships with civilian members of the protector's court, including Edward Mountagu and Bulstrode Whitelocke (whose son, James, also sat in 1656). In the 1654 parliament he had collaborated with English councillors, such as Sir Charles Wolseley, Philip Jones and John Cleypole, and from 1655 he had worked closely with Secretary Thurloe over Scottish affairs and the problem of Irish security. Broghill's religious attitudes had also brought him into contact with two other courtiers, Nathaniel and Francis Bacon (friends of the earl of Warwick, who both sat for Ipswich), and with important local figures such as Thomas Grove of Wiltshire, Sir John Fitzjames of Dorset, and (through Richard Baxter) with three West Midlands moderates, Edward Harley, John Bridges and Robert Beake.[15] He also had family connexions with the earl of Salisbury (the countess of Cork's uncle), whose clients in the house included Sir Richard Lucy.[16] All these men secured election for parliament in 1656, and were able to link Broghill into a wider network of Cromwellian courtiers and Prebyterian country gentlemen, many of whom he had already encountered at Westminster in 1654.[17]

Broghill's position in the 1656 parliament was, above all, reliant on his ability to mobilise support in Scotland and Ireland. As president of Scotland, he had won the support of a number of important councillors, including Charles Howard, Samuel Disbrowe, Sir Edward Rhodes and (by the end of 1656) Sir William Lockhart.[18] All four were returned as M.P.s (with Howard sitting for Cumberland), and Broghill is known to have intervened to secure the election of Disbrowe, at least.[19] Other candidates actively supported by Broghill included Judge George Smith, Colonel Edward Salmon, Scoutmaster-General George Downing (who eventually chose to sit for Carlisle), Robert Wolseley (the brother of Sir Charles Wolseley), and his old ally from Ireland, Henry Markham. To these can be added those whom he probably supported: Lord Cochrane, Andrew Ramsay, Sir John Wemyss, Godfrey Rhodes, and George and John Lockhart – the last three being relatives of Broghill's allies

---

[14] *The parliamentary or constitutional history of England* (2nd ed., 24 vols, 1743) [hereafter *Old parliamentary history*], xxi, 86.

[15] See below, ch. 9.

[16] Salisbury and Lucy, although initially excluded, were 'approved by the Councell' in late September and readmitted: see Gilbert Mabbott to mayor and burgesses of Hull, 25 Sept. 1656 (Hull R.O., Hull corporation letters 1635–62, L.628).

[17] See below, chs 7, 9.

[18] Lockhart, originally an ally of Monck, had drawn closer to the protectorate court since his marriage to Cromwell's niece, Robina Sewster (in February 1655: see N.L.S., Lockhart Charters, A.1, folder 2, no. 4), and he was ambassador to France from 1656.

[19] *Thurloe S.P.*, v, 295.

on the council. He himself was elected for Edinburgh – another indication of his high standing among the conservative councillors and Resolutioner ministers who dominated that city.[20] Altogether, at least nine (and possibly as many as fifteen) Scottish M.P.s had Broghill's seal of approval.[21] He evidently expected that this group would support him at Westminster: on 19 August 1656 he told Thurloe that he had met the M.P.s and 'I have spoken to them to be at London without fayle before the parliament begins'.[22]

Broghill's absence from Ireland did not reduce his electoral influence at home.[23] In 1654 the Old Protestants had performed well at the elections, with Broghill and his brother, the earl of Cork, apparently co-operating with Sir Hardress Waller, Sir Charles Coote and others with seats in their gift, to return at least nineteen Old Protestants and their allies. A similar picture emerges from the elections of 1656. The earl of Cork's diary for August and September 1656 – the period during and after the Irish elections – suggests that once again the Old Protestants were acting together. He was in close contact not only with William Jephson and others in County Cork, but also with Sir Hardress Waller, Major John King (son of Sir Robert King) and through him, Sir Charles Coote.[24] Locally, the earl of Cork influenced elections to the three county and borough seats of County Cork – no doubt assisted by the presiding sheriff, Peter Courthope, formerly a captain in Broghill's horse regiment – with William Jephson, Vincent Gookin, and Broghill himself being returned.[25] In Limerick, Sir Hardress Waller and his son, Walter, were duly elected, with their ally Henry Ingoldsby. In Connacht and Ulster the 1654 veterans Sir Charles Coote, Sir Robert King, Thomas Newburgh and Ralph King, with newcomers Tristram Beresford, Richard Blayney, John Davies and James Traill were all returned on the Old Protestant interest. In Leinster Sir Paul Davies, John Fowke and Theophilus Jones were returned, while in Dublin Richard Tighe secured the borough, and John Bisse saw off a challenge by John Jones and John Hewson for the county seat.[26] As might be expected, Henry Cromwell was also involved in these elections, backing his principal agents Sir John Reynolds and Anthony Morgan, William Aston, Henry Owen, Daniel Redman, John Bridges and possibly William Halsey. In all,

---

[20] Edinburgh election indenture, 20 Aug. 1656 (P.R.O., C 219/45, unfol.); M. Wood (ed.), *Extracts from the records of the burgh of Edinburgh, 1655–65* (Edinburgh, 1940), pp 30–2; Edinburgh City Archives, SL 1/1/19, ff 142r–v, 148r: Broghill was allowed £300 for his expenses by the burgh.

[21] P. J. Pinckney, 'The Scottish representation in the Cromwellian parliament of 1656' in *S.H.R.*, lxvi (1967), pp 98, 100–6, 110–14. See *Thurloe S.P.*, v, 295, 322.

[22] *Thurloe S.P.*, v, 322.

[23] T. C. Barnard, 'Lord Broghill, Vincent Gookin and the Cork election of 1659' in *E.H.R.*, lxxxviii (1973), p. 354, n.

[24] Second earl of Cork's diary (Chatsworth, Lismore MS 29, unfol.), entries for 11, 18, 19, 21 Aug. and 9, 10, 22, 23, 26 Sept. 1656.

[25] *Thurloe S.P.*, v, 327; N.A.I., Ferguson MS 10, p. 3.

[26] *Thurloe S.P.*, v, 327.

the Old Protestant interest again mustered nineteen M.P.s, Henry Cromwell as many as seven, and the army interest a bare four (Daniel Abbott, Thomas Cooper, Thomas Sadleir and John Brett).[27] Coote, Waller, Ingoldsby and three soldiers were kept in Ireland for security reasons; John Davies and Sir Paul Davies were excluded; and Sir Robert King and Thomas Newburgh were too ill to attend at Westminster; but between them the Cromwellians and Old Protestants mustered at least nineteen active M.P.s in 1656–7.[28]

Broghill's immediate circle at Westminster can thus be identified as a disparate collection of courtiers, country gentry and men returned for Scotland and Ireland. The only thing the different groups had in common was their direct connexion with Broghill. At its widest, Broghill could call on the direct support of perhaps fifty members – a tenth of all those elected – all of whom seem to have broadly shared his desire for religious moderation and political reform.[29] This was a very large parliamentary connexion for one man, but in September 1656 it did not constitute a political 'party'; nor was Broghill yet acknowledged as its head. His relationship with Henry Cromwell, Bulstrode Whitelocke, Sir Charles Wolseley and others was as an ally, not a leader. Each had his own network of clients, just as Broghill had a solid core of supporters in Ireland and Scotland. For example, Philip Jones, the Cromwellian courtier and Welsh supremo, influenced the election of a number of M.P.s in South Wales, and in March and April 1657 there would be a similar number of Welsh supporters of kingship (or 'kinglings') as those from Scotland or Ireland.[30] In addition, there were other, overlapping groupings centred on the lawyers, London M.P.s and those from individual regions.[31] Above all, gaining a majority in the Commons depended on the support of the Presbyterian M.P.s. These men had angered Cromwell through their attempt to hijack the Instrument of Government in 1654–5, introducing dramatic changes to the political and religious settlement, and forcing the protector to dissolve parliament early. Broghill, whose religious sympathies with the Presbyterians had been apparent in 1654, was in a better position to harness their votes in 1656–7 after the success of his religious policy in Scotland, and his wooing of

[27] For details of these men see History of Parliament, 1640–60 section, draft biographies; for an overview see Patrick Little, 'Irish representation in the protectorate parliaments' in *Parliamentary History* (forthcoming).

[28] *Thurloe S.P.*, v, 336, 398–9; *Burton diary*, i, 288–9. Henry Cromwell intervened to prevent the exclusion of Tighe, Bisse and Beresford, who all sat from late October. See *Thurloe S.P.*, v, 477; C.J., vii, 427, 439, 445. Ingoldsby remained in Limerick throughout the first sitting of this parliament: see his letter to Henry Cromwell, 31 Mar. 1657 (B.L., Lansdowne MS 822, f. 17r–v).

[29] There were 458 serving members in 1656: see Sarah Jones, 'The composition and activity of the protectorate parliaments' (unpublished Ph.D. thesis, Exeter University, 1988), p. 42.

[30] A. H. Dodd, *Studies in Stuart Wales* (Cardiff, 1971), pp 149–71; *A Narrative of the Late Parliament* (B.L., E.935(5)), pp 22–3.

[31] Jones, 'Protectorate parliaments', pp 129–30; for an example of the problems inherent in trying to identify and label exact parties see ibid., pp 115–17, 136, n.

the Presbyterian interest became a crucial feature of his activity in parliament. If the various groups could be persuaded to work together, reforming legislation could be pushed through by sheer weight of numbers, and in this the skilful management of Broghill would prove crucial. Broghill's opponents in the army interest may have been tightly knit and ideologically united, but they would have difficulty in winning the numbers game in parliament. The inequality of the struggle would become more than evident as political tensions rose during the next nine months.

II

Broghill's political power base was built on the Irish and Scottish members, and much of his time and energy was devoted to the management of the affairs of Scotland and Ireland. Such concerns preceded, and concided with, the great debates on the militia bill and the Humble Petition and Advice, and provide an essential context within which to understand his activities on the wider stage. As we have seen, Ireland and Scotland also provided the immediate impetus for Broghill's policy of securing 'settlement' in all three nations. Broghill's role in Scottish affairs was particularly important. Although he had abandoned his immediate duties in Edinburgh to attend parliament, Broghill remained president of Scotland throughout this period, and many of his conciliar allies (including Samuel Disbrowe, Sir Edward Rhodes and Charles Howard) joined him as M.P.s. The councillors naturally expected to influence Scottish policy at Westminster, and their ability to call on around fifteen votes among the M.P.s for Scotland gave them an effective lobby group with which to realise this expectation. Broghill's need to manage Scottish affairs was made all the more pressing by the continuing influence of his enemies on the English council's Scottish committee. Lambert and Fleetwood, who had done so much to hamper Broghill's policies in the previous year, now tried to use their position on this committee to foil his plans in parliament.

Broghill's work as a parliamentary manager in this area is obscured by the fact that most routine business – as well as important legislation such as the union and assessment bills – was conducted through parliament's committee for Scottish affairs. Set up on 23 September 1656, this committee included a number of Broghill's enemies (notably Lambert, Major-Generals Kelsey and Whalley, and Scottish M.P.s opposed to his policies, such as the earl of Tweeddale and John Swinton) but many more of its members were his supporters. The initial committee list included Charles Howard, Sir Edward and Godfrey Rhodes, Samuel Disbrowe, George Downing, George Smith, Andrew Ramsay – all Scottish contacts of Broghill – as well as courtiers such as Philip Jones, John Thurloe, Nathaniel Fiennes, Bulstrode Whitelocke and John Glynn.[32] In the following weeks they were joined by John and George

---

[32] C.J., vii, 426.

Lockhart, and Broghill's Irish client, Henry Markham.[33] It is difficult to know exactly who attended this committee, but it seems that Broghill could command a majority. This would account for the relatively smooth passage of Scottish legislation through the house when he was not incapacitated by illness. The Scottish union bill promised to rework the terms of the original union ordinance of April 1654, extending free trade and burgh rights among other measures, and was of central importance to Broghill's plan for integration between the three nations. The bill received its first reading on 25 October, quickly moving through the second reading and into the committee stage in early November.[34] In Broghill's absence, during his attack of gout, the bill ran into trouble, and from the end of November meetings of the committee were repeatedly postponed in favour of other issues – the recusancy bill, the Nayler case, the militia bill, and even minor business, like the need to settle a minister on the Isle of Wight.[35] Broghill's close ally, Bulstrode Whitelocke, made a special effort to attend to 'advance' the bill through the commons, and other allies, including Samuel Disbrowe, George Downing, George Smyth, Sir Edward Rhodes, Charles Howard and Lord Cochrane, tried to hasten the bill through parliament or spoke in favour of union in the debates on 4 December and 14 January.[36] Despite their efforts, the initiative, lost during Broghill's illness, was never regained. The union with Scotland, when enacted later in the sitting, was an elevation of the existing ordinance, not a renegotiation of the relationship between the two countries.

Ironically, the very failure of the Scottish union bill demonstrates Broghill's vital influence over the committee of Scottish affairs; and this impression is reinforced by the surviving examples of his direct intervention in the day-to-day business handled by the committee in 1656–7. He was active in attempts to solve the thorny problem of settling the rival claims of the Scottish landowners and their creditors. In late October and early November 1656 he was teller with Sir Edward Rhodes against rejecting a general debtors' bill (which had obvious Scottish implications), and in December or early January he intervened on behalf of George Monck in the bill to secure his donative from the Hamilton estates, receiving grateful thanks from the general. In April 1657 he was named to a committee for settling Scottish estates (the conclusions of which Samuel Disbrowe reported to the commons) and brought in the bill for pardoning the former royalists, the earl of Callander and Lord Cranston, a measure which attracted support across the political divide.[37] In this business, which sought to implement compromise agreements made in

---

[33] Ibid., pp 428, 442, 474.

[34] Ibid., pp 445, 450, 452–5.

[35] Ibid., pp 456–7, 466, 473; *Burton diary*, i, 6, 215, 223–4.

[36] *Burton diary*, i, 12–18, 223–4, 346–7; *Whitelocke diary*, pp 451–2, 454 (1, 8, 12 Nov. 1656, 13 Jan. 1657).

[37] C.J., vii, 447, 449, 476, 488, 526–7; Monck to Broghill, 8 Jan. 1657 (W.C.O., Clarke MS 3/3, f. 2v).

the English council in the summer of 1656, Broghill seems to have been acting in his official role as Scottish president rather than as a private individual.[38]

Broghill's importance as a parliamentary manager of Scottish business can best be seen in his attempt to extend the franchise, through the fourth article of the Humble Petition and Advice, in 1657.[39] The original Remonstrance did not single out the Scots, and offered rehabilitation in vague terms to all who had served parliament or given 'signall testimonyes of their good affections'.[40] Clarification was required. In response, Broghill and his allies in the commons tried to introduce a clause allowing voting rights to all Scotsmen who had lived peaceably under Cromwell from 1652 (thus including all who had sided with Charles Stuart in 1651, and excluding only those who had joined Glencairn in 1653–4). Broghill was named to the committee which introduced this clause on 6 March 1657; Henry Cromwell's agent, William Aston, reported from this committee; and the measure was passed by seven votes on 9 March.[41] Broghill and Wolseley then acted as tellers against a motion to allow the opposition to present a paper suggesting amendments to the clause; and the fourth article passed on 11 March, and was duly included in the final version of the Humble Petition, which was passed on 25 May.[42] The majority was small, but it is clear that Broghill was still able to control Scottish affairs at Westminster. In June, however, the decision was reversed, with the Scottish franchise once again restricted to those who had remained loyal to the regime since 1649, thus excluding the Resolutioners and other supporters of Charles Stuart in 1650–1. On 15 June the position of Scotland was reviewed as part of the Additional Petition and Advice, and Lambert's allies, Adam Baynes and Stephen Winthrop, were tellers in favour of amendments to the original wording. Later attempts to overturn this vote failed, with Lambert and Strickland forcing through the amended franchise by four votes. The more restricted franchise was thus included in the Additional Petition passed on 26 June.[43] The reasons for this reverse are not hard to find. Broghill's ability to command a parliamentary majority had declined since Cromwell's refusal of the crown, and, for three weeks (and certainly until 26 June),[44] Broghill had once again been absent from parliament suffering from gout. Johnston of Wariston, who opposed the extension of the franchise, saw this as providential: 'Blissed be the Lord that hes layd asyde thes 3 weekes Brochil by the goutt, or els he had stopped both our publik and privat busines.'[45] The

---

[38] Dow, *Cromwellian Scotland*, pp 182–5.

[39] For the background of this issue see Ellen Goldwater, 'The Scottish franchise: lobbying during the Cromwellian protectorate' in *H.J.*, xxi (1978), pp 27–42.

[40] Draft of Remonstrance, n.d. [Feb. 1657] (Bodl., MS Clarendon 54, f. 118v).

[41] *C.J.*, vii, 499, 500.

[42] Ibid., pp 500, 501, 502; *A & O*, ii, 1049–50.

[43] *A & O*, ii, 1183.

[44] *C.J.*, vii, 543–76.

[45] *Wariston diary*, iii, 84.

removal of Broghill had caused organised resistance to the army interest to collapse; this, in itself, is a testament to his earlier importance as a leader of the house.

The successes and failures of Broghill's secular policy were reflected in his attempts to defend his church reforms at Westminster and Whitehall. When Broghill left Scotland in August 1656 he had just secured a pro-Resolutioner settlement, which had reduced the influence of the rival Protester party in clerical appointments. But this new policy remained untested. On 22 August Broghill asked Secretary Thurloe to be vigilant 'ere any alteration be made' to his hard-won reforms.[46] Broghill's open support for the Resolutioners brought him into immediate conflict with Lambert and his friends in the English council, who supported the Protesters just as openly. The main plank of Broghill's Kirk reforms – the scheme for clerical appointments and salaries – soon became the focus of a bitter of dispute in the English council. By October Broghill was advising James Sharp on his tactics on this issue; and when he succumbed to gout in late November, he recommended the Resolutioner cause to Thurloe's care.[47] In December the Edinburgh ministers lobbied Councillors Disbrowe, Whetham and Lockhart, and asked Broghill to 'continue to leave good impressions of our principles and way with those in power'.[48] The Resolutioners also called on their Presbyterian friends in England (including prominent ministers such as Edmund Calamy, Simeon Ashe and Thomas Manton) and in the English council received encouragement from Philip Jones, Fiennes and Wolseley.[49] In retaliation, the Protesters called on the support of a variety of Independent divines in England, and on important councillors including Lambert, Fleetwood, Pickering and Strickland.[50] The sides were drawn. On 12 February 1657 Sharp, coached by Broghill and Jones, attended the protector and defended the Resolutioners against charges of royalism.[51] On 13 March (immediately after Broghill's successes in parliament over the Scottish franchise) the debate resumed, with attention turning to the ministry at Stirling, where Broghill had supported Matthias Simpson as a rival to the arch-Protester, James Guthrie, and his colleague Robert Rule.[52] As Sharp recounted, after another confrontation in the council chamber, 'L[ord] Broghill took the papers, and told me he had sent to the L[ord] Lambert not to proceed in that bussines', but to no avail.[53] What

---

[46] *Thurloe S.P.*, v, 336.

[47] Stephen, *Register*, i, 220–2; *Thurloe S.P.* v, 655–6.

[48] Stephen, *Register*, i, 240–8, 255–63.

[49] Ibid., pp 232–9, 276–88, 348–9; ibid., ii, 20–1; Sharp to [Edinburgh ministers], [Oct. 1656] (N.L.S., Wodrow Folio MS vol. xxvi, f. 146r); *Baillie letters*, iii, 325–31, 339–40.

[50] Stephen, *Register*, i, 20–8.

[51] Ibid., ii, 21.

[52] For the Stirling dispute see ch. 5, above; see also the order in Simpson's favour, 3 Sept. 1656 (W.C.O., Clarke MS 3/11, unfol.).

[53] Stephen, *Register*, ii, 21.

had originally been a matter of Kirk organisation had become a challenge to Broghill as president of Scotland.[54] The next day, as the Stirling debate continued, Broghill brought Wolseley, Jones and Disbrowe to the council, and afterwards swore that 'the [Scottish] Councill would justify what they had done'.[55] On 17 March, as Broghill told Sharp, the situation boiled over: '"Yesterday", sayed he, "we had a bustling to purpose. My L[ord] Lambert and I fell very hott: that the Councill's proceedings in Scotland being just, ought not to be thus questioned . . ."'.[56] After months of tension, Broghill and Lambert had finally squared up to each other.

Broghill's management of Scottish affairs was not completely successful. On several key issues he had failed to win the day: a new union bill had not been passed, leaving the existing arrangements to be continued by default; and his initial victory over the franchise had been reversed in his absence. Despite this, the Scottish debates provide important evidence of Broghill's ability to manage parliament, through personal intervention in the house, and through his authority in committee. Indeed, the main problem was his absence during periodic bouts of gout, which allowed his enemies to regain the initiative, despite the intervention of allies such as Whitelocke and Thurloe on his behalf. Indeed, the inability of even these prominent courtiers to sway the house underlines Broghill's crucial importance as a manager. Broghill's involvement in Scottish affairs also demonstrates the consistency of his political agenda. His encouragement of the Resolutioners and endorsement of the compromise on debtors show that the reconciliation of former royalists lay at the heart of his plans for the Cromwellian regime. The attempt to force through such policies increased existing tensions between Broghill and Lambert, and added to their growing sense of personal rivalry.

The management of Irish affairs presented similar problems to Broghill and his allies. The English council's Irish committee was dominated by the absentee lord deputy, Charles Fleetwood, backed by John Lambert (who was described as the 'cheife' of that committee), and both men did their best to resist the reforms introduced by Henry Cromwell in Dublin, and to slow the progress of controversial business from the council to the commons.[57] Their personal influence in parliament would become obvious as the session progressed. An alternative focus was provided by parliament's own committee for Irish affairs, formed on 23 September. Although Fleetwood, Lambert and a few of their allies were named to this committee, their numbers were more than matched by Henry Cromwell's agents (including Anthony Morgan, William Aston and Sir John Reynolds), Broghill's friends (notably Vincent

---

[54] Ibid., pp 22, 25.

[55] Ibid., p. 25.

[56] Ibid., p. 31.

[57] Anthony Morgan to Henry Cromwell, 19 Aug. 1656 (B.L., Lansdowne MS 821, f. 234r); see above, ch. 4.

Gookin, William Jephson, Henry Markham and George Downing) and a further seven Old Protestant M.P.s.[58] As in the case of Scotland, the committee for Irish affairs had an important role in forwarding business in the Commons. The Irish union bill, various land cases and the pre-1649 arrears petition were overseen by this committee.[59] It also provided the power base for Henry Cromwell's agents to take charge of Irish legislation: Sir John Reynolds, William Aston and Anthony Morgan managed the four Irish bills promoted by the government (those for union, attainder, the settlement of estates and assessment), bringing in the bills, attending and reporting from committees, and taking the lead in debates.[60] Morgan and Reynolds kept in close contact with Dublin during the parliament,[61] with Reynolds, in particular, impatiently pointing out how the intense debate over the Humble Petition was delaying the Irish bills.[62]

Unlike Reynolds and his friends, Broghill was not involved in the day-to-day organisation of Irish business in parliament. Yet his general absence from the parliamentary records belies his importance in the formulation of policy. Other evidence shows that Henry Cromwell relied on Broghill for political guidance throughout this period. In a draft letter from early 1657, he admitted: 'My Lord I must & will steere your Course, wherefore have a Care how you lay it.'[63] The two men corresponded regularly during the first sitting of this parliament,[64] and for two periods (8 November to 3 December 1656 and 12 April to 6 May 1657) the earl of Cork attended Henry Cromwell at Dublin on his brother's behalf. On 11 November 1656, Cork recorded, 'I supt privately with my Lord Cromwell and had with him much discourse in private about Broghill'. On 3 December, during Broghill's illness, Cork again dined with Henry Cromwell, who was uncertain whether to travel to Westminster, 'and that it was Broghill that engaged him in comming over, and that if hee left him now in the sudden and came not over to assest him hee was to blame'. On 16 April 1657 Cork again dined with Henry Cromwell, and 'had some discourse about the publique'.[65] It seems clear that Broghill, either by letter

[58] C.J., vii, 427, 437, 439, 445, 446, 461, 477; the Old Protestants included Ralph King, Richard Tighe, Richard Blayney, Theophilus Jones, Walter Waller, Tristram Beresford, John Bisse.

[59] Ibid., pp 452, 472; Burton diary, i, 203; Whitelocke diary, p. 467.

[60] Burton diary, i, 12, 95, 127, 148, 150, 288–9, 338, 367; ii, 124, 155, 157, 162, 169, 196, 200–1

[61] B.L., Lansdowne MS 821, ff 296r, 314r, 316r, 330r, 356r; ibid., MS 822, ff 9r, 21r, 31r, 45r, 47r, 53r, 55r, 63r, 71r, 84r.

[62] Reynolds to Henry Cromwell, 24 Feb., 3 Mar. and 17 Mar. 1657 (ibid., Lansdowne MS 821, ff 296r, 316r, 356r).

[63] Henry Cromwell to Broghill, c. Apr. 1657 (ibid., Lansdowne MS 823, f. 328r).

[64] Henry Cromwell to Broghill, c. June 1657 (ibid., Lansdowne MS 822, f. 126r); same to same, undated draft letters (ibid., Lansdowne MS 823, ff 328–38).

[65] Cork's diary (Chatsworth, Lismore MS 29, unfol.), 11 Nov., 2 Dec. 1656; 16 Apr. 1657.

or through his brother, was a major influence on Henry Cromwell, and (by extension) on Irish policy, during this parliament. This helps to explain his apparent lack of involvement in key issues, including the Irish union bill, which promised to give Ireland free trade, legal reform, proportionate taxation and a guarantee of representation within a union parliament.

Broghill had championed Irish union in the 1654 parliament, but the premature dissolution had prevented the bill reaching even its second reading.[66] In 1656 there was a more concerted effort, and the fate of the Irish bill followed a very similar pattern to that of Scotland – suggesting that the two were now closely connected in the minds of proponents and opponents alike. The bill was introduced by the Irish committee in mid-November, and was quickly read twice and committed on the nineteenth of that month.[67] Broghill's absence, crippled by gout, seems to have had a devastating effect on the progress of the bill. With Lambert's ally, Luke Robinson, in the chair, the committee stage soon became bogged down, and the union was constantly pushed aside by other business, resurfacing only on 17 January 1657, when it was at last debated. Thereafter, despite the efforts of Aston, Reynolds and other allies, the Irish union bill failed to make much headway.[68] While the Scots could cling to the 1654 ordinance (now made into an act), the Irish M.P.s came away from the sitting with no formal union of their own.

Broghill's presence, as much as his absence, could also have a decisive impact on Irish policy. A particular concern was the Irish land settlement, which, as we have seen, would have profound consequences for the Old Protestant community, the Boyle family, and Broghill himself. In the winter of 1656–7 Broghill was named to four committees for settling Irish lands on adventurers and Old Protestants – all of which became test cases for the general land settlement;[69] and he was actively involved in two similar cases, those of the Irish 'donatives', and the city of Gloucester. The donatives were lands granted to a number of leading Old Protestants, including Sir Charles Coote, Sir Hardress Waller and members of the family of Michael Jones, who still waited for land grants awarded by the Long Parliament. Initially, their case was attached to that of the Scottish creditors. Broghill was named to the committee appointed to deal with both matters on 28 April 1657; his Scottish ally, Samuel Disbrowe, reported its findings to the house; and on 29 April the Irish donatives were referred to a separate committee, which included Broghill, Morgan and Aston, and five other Irish M.P.s.[70] From

---

[66] For a detailed investigation of Irish union legislation during this period see Patrick Little, 'The first unionists?', pp 49–53.

[67] C.J., vii, 452–5.

[68] Ibid., pp 458–9, 464, 466, 468–9, 480, 482, 486, 500, 519; Burton diary, i, 95, 127, 215, 352–3.

[69] C.J., vii, 477, 491, 494, 505.

[70] Ibid., p. 526.

then on, Broghill took charge, acting as reporter to the commons on 1 May.[71] In his report Broghill urged that the original grants should be upheld, for 'They are the gifts of the Long Parliament to your faithful servants, and those orders are all that they or their widows have to show for them. It takes nothing from you; it only makes them a better title, and it is but just and reasonable you should confirm them.'[72] Whitelocke and Wolseley supported Broghill, in the face of opposition by Denis Bond and John Disbrowe, who tried to delay proceedings by calling for copies of the original orders.[73] In the end the house accepted Broghill's report, leaving the matter to be incorporated into the general bill confirming former acts and ordinances, passed on 16 June, when the land grants were at last secured.[74] Broghill's intervention, and the weakness of his opponents' response, indicates his control of Irish affairs, and also points to his continuing role as guardian (and political leader) of the Old Protestant interest at this time.

The Gloucester land settlement was far more acrimonious. On 11 December 1656 the citizens of Gloucester, who had been promised compensation in Irish land for damage caused to their property by the royalists in the 1640s, petitioned the Irish committee of the English council.[75] The matter was brought into parliament on 22 December, and immediately caused controversy, as Lambert's allies (led by Major-General Whalley and Luke Robinson) pushed for the inclusion of other English towns, which had also suffered in the wars. Morgan and Markham tried to counter this, and tempers flared, with Markham being 'very angry with Mr Robinson for interrupting him', and after the debate ended 'they were at very high words both in their seats and at the door'.[76] The bill received its second reading on 19 February, and was committed.[77] There were very real fears that this bill would open the floodgates to English claims regardless of the rights of the adventurers, soldiers and Old Protestants: on 14 April Morgan told Henry Cromwell that 'the Gloster bill if it pass as it is now ordered to be engrossed will engage all the land & houses in Ireland'.[78] As yet, Broghill had played no part in this business (he had not even been named to the committee stage), but on the third reading of the bill, on 5 May, he joined the fray. Brushing aside Lenthall's claims that 'we desire not by this Bill to intrench upon the rights of others, of any of the soldiery', Broghill argued that 'those lands in Ireland have been first settled upon by the soldiers, who did you hard service . . . I move that you would declare that you intend not to make any intrenchment upon what was settled in relation to those ends;

---

[71] Ibid., p. 529.
[72] *Burton diary*, ii, 95–6.
[73] Ibid.
[74] C.J., vii, 558.
[75] *Cal. S.P. Dom.*, 1656–7, p. 194.
[76] *Burton diary*, i, 203, 204, 208.
[77] C.J., vii, 494.
[78] Morgan to Henry Cromwell, 14 Apr. 1657 (B.L., Lansdowne MS 822, f. 45r).

that your poor army there may not be disappointed'.[79] In the ensuing debate Broghill was opposed by Lenthall, Highland and Clarges, but received support from William Aston, and from two members of the army interest, Jerome Sankey and Thomas Cooper, both of whom had their own Irish land claims. In keeping the issue as broad as possible, Broghill had avoided divisions between the army, the adventurers and the Old Protestants; but the veneer of unity was soon stripped away by Broghill's ally, William Jephson, who proclaimed: 'We that served you in the heat of the day were cast behind. Those that had the swords in their hands after, got good satisfaction and were cast there . . . I have done you as good service as another, but had never a penny yet.' Jephson's speech makes it clear that, beneath the surface, Broghill's main concern was to protect the rights of the Old Protestants. In this, he was reasonably successful. The amendments were accepted, and the proviso added to the bill.[80]

As Jephson had hinted, the payment of military arrears incurred before 1649 was a major financial issue facing the Old Protestants. Broghill had received little by way of compensation for his eight years of active service before the arrival of Cromwell, and he was not alone in this.[81] On 22 January 1657 the English council considered a petition from the pre-1649 officers asking for their inclusion in the land settlement in lieu of arrears. On 5 February this was referred to the council's Irish committee, where (unsurprisingly) it stalled.[82] Approaches were made to courtiers and to the protector himself in the spring, and in late May the commons referred the matter to its committee of Irish affairs,[83] just at the time of Broghill's second attack of gout. On 7 June, Broghill wrote to Whitelocke to use his influence to secure the arrears, as 'we have Drawne up a bill . . . [and] That is a business of soe much Justice, It cannot receive ye le[a]st opposition, Thoe I must humble beg yor Lo[rdshi]p: (beinge my selfe Confyned to my Chamber) to get the Speaker to read the letter to morrow & then to Present the bill.'[84] With Broghill out of action, the reading of the letter was postponed until 15 June.[85] On 15 June Broghill again asked Whitelocke to 'have particular regard to the buisnes of the Irish Armies arrears', and Whitelocke did his best.[86] His repeated failure to make headway again shows the importance of Broghill's personal intervention in securing the passage of controversial measures through parliament. It was only on 26 June – with Broghill once again in the commons – that the letter was read, and the commons resolved to accept in principle the demands of the pre-1649 officers.[87]

---

[79] *Burton diary*, ii, 107–8.
[80] Ibid., pp 108–11; C.J., vii, 530.
[81] For Broghill's financial position, see below, ch. 8.
[82] *Cal. S.P. Dom.*, *1656–7*, pp 248, 266.
[83] *Whitelocke diary*, pp 462, 467.
[84] Broghill to Whitelocke, 7 June 1657 (Longleat, Whitelocke papers 18, f. 64r–v).
[85] C.J., vii, 550.
[86] *Whitelocke diary*, p. 469.
[87] C.J., vii, 576; Broghill was in the commons earlier the same day: see ibid., p. 576.

Broghill's influence over Irish affairs was apparent in the House of Commons, in its committees, and the private chambers of Whitehall and Dublin. Broghill's closeness to Henry Cromwell (by letter and through the earl of Cork) corresponded with his close collaboration with the Dublin government's agents in parliament. Together, they were able to mount a coherent Irish policy, which concentrated on securing a land settlement favourable to the Old Protestants and the English government, in the face of mounting opposition from Lambert and Fleetwood and their allies, who tried to retard such initiatives through the English council and its Irish committee. This dynamic, of a reformist, civilian lobby entrenched in parliament, facing concerted opposition from the army and its allies in the English council, was the same in Irish and Scottish affairs. Indeed, the personnel were remarkably similar in each case. In Scottish affairs Broghill could call on the support of Henry Cromwell's agents, such as William Aston, and in Irish affairs he was supported by Samuel Disbrowe, George Downing and others from the Scottish council. The courtiers who had supported Broghill in the committee of Scottish affairs were equally involved in Irish matters – with Whitelocke as a case in point. Their opponents were drawn from a small pool of men attached to Lambert and Fleetwood, and, again, Irish and Scottish issues had a tendency to coincide. The reports of the Scottish Protester, James Guthrie, being seen arm-in-arm with Henry Cromwell's enemy, Jerome Sankey, came as a nasty shock to Broghill and his friends;[88] but the incident was only symptomatic of a wider process. The Scottish and Irish union bills were steered through the commons in parallel, were supported and opposed by very similar groups of M.P.s, and both became bogged down in late November and early December 1656. By this time it was abundantly clear that Irish and Scottish affairs were not discrete: the religious settlement in Scotland would have Irish implications, and the land settlement in Ireland would influence policy towards the Scots. And both nations would ultimately stand or fall by the wider political and constitutional debates which would decide the future of the Cromwellian union as a whole.[89]

III

The lengthy debate on the fate of the notorious Quaker, James Nayler, and the acrimonious exchanges which led to the defeat of the militia bill and the rejection of the major-generals in December and January 1656–7 have rightly been seen as important precursors of the kingship debates. It was these issues which focused the minds of the Presbyterians and country gentlemen who

---

[88] *Wariston diary*, iii, 84; Stephen, *Register*, ii, 30.
[89] For the connexion between unionism and the Humble Petition see Little, 'The first unionists?', pp 49–53.

formed the majority in the house, encouraging them to back the programme of constitutional reform advanced by Broghill and others in the following spring.[90] But it would be wrong to see Nayler's case and the militia bill as arising independently from the agenda of Broghill and the 'settlement' party. As in Irish and Scottish affairs, the parliamentary debate soon became the vehicle for a power struggle between the two main political factions, and for a personal feud which was steadily growing between the two main protagonists, Broghill and Lambert.

The alleged blasphemies of James Nayler, who had re-enacted Christ's entry to Jerusalem through the streets of Bristol in October 1656, caused political as well as religious consternation when it was brought before the House of Commons. Although he had been named to the original committee on Nayler on 31 October 1656,[91] Broghill was prevented from any direct involvement in the December debates by his first attack of gout, which kept him out of parliament from late November until 22 December. But his absence did not mean that he was uninterested, or disinterested, in the dispute. Nayler's case raised two important questions, both of which were of profound importance to Broghill. The first was the desirability of a policy of religious liberty and toleration, which had allowed not just Quakers, but also Baptists, Fifth Monarchists and other radical groups to challenge the scripture-based orthodoxy which Broghill and his friends held so important for the political as well as the religious stability of the state. Broghill's own Presbyterian sympathies had been clearly articulated in the 1654 parliament and afterwards in the English council, particularly in Scottish affairs, and later in the 1656 parliament he was named to the committee set up after his two Scottish allies, Lord Cochrane and Sir Edward Rhodes, had defeated a motion to allow a softening of the conditions of Nayler's imprisonment.[92] On other occasions Broghill continued to direct political affairs from his sick-bed, and it is likely that he was encouraging Nayler's critics in December 1656. Broghill's allies were certainly prominent in their condemnation of Nayler's blasphemy. William Jephson was especially outspoken: 'I hope God will stir up your zeal in a matter that so eminently concerns the cause of God . . . For my part, I am clearly satisfied that, upon the whole matter, this person deserves to die.'[93] He was supported by a number of Irish and Scottish M.P.s: Judge Smith, Lord Cochrane, Henry Markham, George Downing, John Bisse and Richard Tighe; as well as the Bacon brothers and other English Presbyterians, all of whom had links with Broghill.[94] Unsurprisingly, Jephson and other hard-liners were opposed by Lambert and his allies, in a polarisation identical to that which

---

[90] Egloff, 'Settlement and kingship', pp 172, 207.
[91] C.J., vii, 448.
[92] Ibid., p. 497 (28 Feb. 1657).
[93] Burton diary, i, 88
[94] Ibid., pp 31, 34, 35, 52, 54, 86–7, 131, 168–9.

would split the English council over the religious settlement in Scotland. In the Nayler case there was more at stake than the fate of one man.

As the Nayler debate continued, a second question emerged which was even more politically charged: whether parliament could exercise the judicial function of the old House of Lords, and if so how that would square with the terms of the Instrument of Government.[95] John Glynn's arguments that 'Whatsoever authority was in the House of Lords and Commons, the same is united in this Parliament' were countered by Lambert in person, who protested that 'You are jurors, judges, and all, in this case'.[96] On 6 December the leading Presbyterian, Philip Skippon, launched a related offensive against the Instrument of Government, which had allowed toleration to religious sects.[97] This was more than a religious disagreement. Lambert, the architect of the Instrument,[98] would be damaged politically if his constitutional plan were to be undermined by parliament. On 8 December his friends, Baynes and White, defended the Instrument; and Downing and Skippon again attacked the articles which now served 'to bolster up blasphemies'.[99] Broghill's only recorded speech on the Nayler case, on 30 December 1656, concentrated on the constitutional question: his assertion that 'we have done as a parliament' indicated his broad approval of the judgement; he went on to discuss precedents for such actions, arguing that they should accept evidence 'only from such precedents as were, when both constitutions were in peace and unity'. Broghill's statement implied that the Instrument of Government was not the final word, and that other standards (from before the protectorate) should apply. Lambert responded by attacking the judicial role of parliament, which he branded as 'an arbitrary power'.[100] This was an ideological division between those who wanted to keep the Instrument, and those who wanted to replace it with a new, more conservative, constitution; but it was also a political dispute. Lambert's reputation was linked to Nayler's fate, and he had increasing cause to wonder if, in due course, parliament's new-found judicial role would be turned against himself.[101]

The militia bill, introduced on 25 December 1656, exacerbated the constitutional and religious divisions raised by the Nayler case, and sharpened the political quarrel between Broghill and Lambert. The bill was introduced on Christmas Day by John Disbrowe, one of Lambert's closest allies.[102] Although

---

[95] Ivan Roots, 'Lawmaking in the second protectorate parliament' in Harry Hearder and H. R. Loyn (eds), *British government and administration* (Cardiff, 1974), p. 134; T. A. Wilson and F. J. Merli, 'Nayler's case and the dilemma of the protectorate', *University of Birmingham Historical Journal*, x (1965), pp. 44–59.

[96] *Burton diary*, i, 30, 33.

[97] Ibid., pp 49–50.

[98] Farr 'Lambert', pp 269–73.

[99] *Burton diary*, i, 58–63.

[100] Ibid., pp 274, 281–2.

[101] Farr, 'Lambert', p. 281.

[102] *Burton diary*, i, 230.

framed as legislation to fund the militia through the taxation of royalist estates, the underlying issue was the survival of the rule of the major-generals over the English and Welsh localities.[103] There were various reasons for Broghill to oppose this motion. The first was personal. During the early 1650s Broghill had struggled to protect the landed interests of his royalist relatives, most notably the earl of Cork, in England and Ireland. In the early months of the 1656 parliament, Cork was fearful that he would be penalised if the decimation tax was introduced, telling one creditor that 'in case I sholdbe decimated, or put to compound, that I will free him and the E[n]glish from paying any thing in respect of either'.[104] Cork's exemption from sequestration, secured in 1652–3, had become a test case for other Irish royalists, including Viscount Conway, whose fate still concerned Broghill in October 1656.[105] These personal influences were closely connected to the general sense of obligation Broghill felt towards former royalist landowners in Ireland and Scotland, which had guided his own reforms and those of Henry Cromwell. The attempt to heal and settle Ireland and Scotland was related to the success of similar policies in England, and, more importantly, to the removal of the army interest from all three kingdoms. This ties in with Broghill's existing links with the Presbyterians in England: it is significant that his Irish ally, Vincent Gookin, was deep in negotiation with the London Presbyterians at the time of the militia bill.[106] Their friends among the Presbyterian gentry had a vested interest in removing the military presence from the shires and shared Broghill's distrust of Lambert, who had been the main instigator of the major-generals scheme. As a result the militia bill, like Nayler's case, saw a convergence of opposition elements, and soon became a vote of confidence in Lambert's influence in the Cromwellian regime.[107]

Broghill's keynote speech against the militia bill, delivered on 7 January in support of John Cleypole, makes this convergence explicit. The speech is recorded in Burton's diary, and the heads appear in a document in the Tanner manuscripts, with the latter mistakenly attributing two points to Broghill which Burton ascribes to the Welsh Presbyterian, John Trevor, and the courtier-lawyer, Bulstrode Whitelocke, an error which perhaps reflects Broghill's position as a political mediator between the Presbyterian and court interests.[108]

---

[103] *Thurloe SP*, vi, 8; Egloff, 'Settlement and kingship', pp 203–4; for background to militia bill, see Christopher Durston, 'The fall of Cromwell's major-generals' in *E.H.R.*, cxiii (1998), pp 18–37.

[104] Chatsworth, Lismore MS 29, unfol.: 16 Oct. 1656.

[105] *Thurloe S.P.*, v, 520.

[106] Ibid., vi, 19–20.

[107] Farr, 'Lambert', p. 281.

[108] Heads of Broghill's speech [7 Jan. 1657] (Bodl., MS Tanner 52, f. 186r–v); *Burton diary*, i, 311–13, 314–15, 317–18: heads 11 (with its reference to Charles VII of France) and 12 (which cites King John, Edward I and Henry III) belong to Trevor and Whitelocke respectively. A further copy of the 'heads' can be found in the Surrey History Centre, Loseley MS LM/1331/56.

Despite the slight differences in the accounts, both agree that Broghill attacked the injustice of decimation, reminding parliament that they were 'Judges of those whome we have conquer'd', and therefore had a duty to abide by their own articles of war and the 1652 act of oblivion, which allowed many royalists a fresh start. He went on to cite Scripture, echoing the speech of a prominent Presbyterian, Thomas Bampfield, made on 25 December: 'The Gibbeonites had tearmes & Conditions w[hi]ch being broken by Saule, God revenged theire Cause, not only in saule & his ffamelie, but on the whole Nation.'[109] The parallel was apposite: Israel was punished by God because Saul had murdered the defeated Gibeonites, who had trusted his earlier promises of peace. Broghill's decision to borrow the idea from Bampfield is further evidence of his closeness to the Presbyterians at this time.[110] It also suggests that the example struck a chord with his own approach to reform: the deliberate intrusion of religion into an apparently secular debate (which mirrored the confusion of issues in the Nayler case) was not just a concession to the religious sensibilities of some M.P.s or of Cromwell; it fitted with Broghill's own providential views, and revealed how far his reform policy was undergirded by his religious beliefs. Broghill continued his speech by referring to the injustice of casting all royalists as malefactors, and (in a repeat of his earlier arguments about Scottish policy) reminded parliament that 'Men of noe ffortune & desperate Condition may Rebell, & Gentlemen of sober principles & practices must beare the punishment'.[111] Broghill had thus attacked the major-generals, urged parliament to maintain its power, and related the situation in England to that in Scotland and to the workings of divine providence. He had also signalled his closeness to the Presbyterians and country gentry in England – a fact which caused one royalist commentator to suspect Broghill of disloyalty to Cromwell, until it became clear that many of the civilian courtiers agreed with him.[112]

The strength of the alliance between Broghill and the other opponents of the army can be seen throughout the debate. The courtiers were united in rejecting the militia bill. Royalist observers ranked Thurloe, Cleypole, Whitelocke and Lenthall alongside Broghill as principal opponents of the bill, and this line-up is supported by Burton, who records the same men as speakers against the motion.[113] The English Presbyterians were also prominent, with

---

[109] Bodl., MS Tanner 52, f. 186r–v; Durston, 'Major-generals', pp 24–5; for Bampfield's speech see *Burton diary*, i, 238. This biblical passage (2 Samuel, xxi) had been cited by George Smith in his work in praise of Cromwell's providential rise to power, *Gods unchangeableness* (15 Jan. 1655) (B.L., E.824(4)), p. 17.

[110] Broghill had already seconded Bampfield's introduction of a bill for the Lord's Day on 2 January: see *Burton diary*, i, 295.

[111] Bodl., MS Tanner 52, f. 186r–v.

[112] *Cal. Clar. S.P.*, iii, 242, 245; Egloff, 'Settlement and kingship', pp 207, 226–8.

[113] *Cal. Clar. S.P.*, iii, 239; *Burton diary*, i, 233–4, 310, 317–18; see also *Thurloe S.P.*, v, 786.

Bampfield, Trevor and Francis Drake in opposition.[114] As before, Broghill could command considerable support from the Irish and Scottish M.P.s. Jephson spoke against the bill on 25 December, and Gookin, who commended the 'anti-decimators' for 'moral justice and prudence', noted that 'The major-generalls are much offended at the Irish and Scottish members, who being much united do sway exceedingly by their votes.'[115] On 28 January, when a vote was taken whether to continue the debate on the bill (which, by this stage, was evidently going against the major-generals), Broghill's Scottish ally, Lord Cochrane, and his Irish friend, William Jephson, acted as tellers in favour of pressing on. The motion was carried by a majority of 36 votes.[116] Against this apparently well-organised group, Lambert could muster a number of influential supporters – notably Disbrowe, Sydenham, Baynes and Robinson – but not enough to win divisions.[117] The militia bill was finally rejected by parliament on 29 January,[118] and Broghill had scored his first major success against Lambert and the army interest.

The militia bill, coming on top of the debate on Nayler's case, had drawn together a number of interest groups, with Broghill's Irish and Scottish allies being supported by a number of councillors, lawyers and Presbyterians. The demise of the major-generals had whetted their appetite for further reform. It had also heightened tensions within parliament, and hardened the factional divisions in the protector's council. When Dr William Stane told Edward Mountagu about the new bill on 8 January he commented, 'I guesse it is to keep up the Reputaccons of the Maj[or] Genalls & so a Revolucon feared'.[119] Others agreed that the militia bill, in particular, had raised fundamental questions about the future of the Cromwellian state – not least because the protector remained unwilling to intercede to save Lambert's constitution, or his major-generals.[120] Vincent Gookin recognised that Lambert's future was at stake, telling Henry Cromwell on 27 January that 'if any others have pretensions to succeed him [Oliver Cromwell] by their interest in the army, the more of force upholds his highness living, the greater when hee is dead will be the hopes and advantage for such a one to effect his ayme, who desires to succeed him. Lamb &c [ie. Lambert] is much for decimations.'[121] The opposition to the militia bill was caused not only by hatred of the army but also by fear of Lambert's ambitions to succeed Cromwell.[122] The alternative was clear to Gookin, at least: in a letter of 3 February he wrote of the power

---

[114] *Burton diary*, i, 237–8, 314–15.
[115] Ibid., p. 233; *Thurloe S.P.*, vi, 20–1, 37.
[116] *C.J.*, vii, 483.
[117] *Burton diary*, i, 230–43, 310–19.
[118] *C.J.*, vii, 483.
[119] Stane to Mountagu, 8 Jan. 1657 (Bodl., MS Carte 73, f. 22r).
[120] Farr, 'Lambert', p. 281.
[121] *Thurloe S.P.*, vi, 20.
[122] *Cal. S.P. Dom.*, 1656–7, pp 257, 271.

of the army and its hostility to parliament 'which will I believe sudenly occasion a reducing of the goverm &c to kingship, &c.'.[123]

IV

There were manifold reasons for M.P.s to support a Cromwellian monarchy. The first was negative: without a hereditary succession, it was feared that Cromwell would be succeeded as protector by the leader of the army interest, John Lambert. Although not himself a religious zealot, Lambert supported Baptists and other sectaries who posed a threat to the restricted religious settlement which Broghill and Henry Cromwell (among others) were anxious to enforce in the three nations. Broghill, whose feud with Lambert was already far advanced, had personal reasons for excluding the army from Cromwell's counsels, and for promoting a hereditary succession which excluded his rival from power. The second reason for desiring a return to monarchy was a constitutional one: a king was a known quantity, with powers circumscribed by custom, whereas a protector (and especially a military dictator) was without such safeguards. With a monarchical settlement, parliament could return to a bicameral structure, which would solve the problems of judicial authority raised by Nayler's case. Any resultant restrictions on Cromwell's power would be more than balanced by the third factor: that a hereditary monarchy would vest permanent power in the House of Cromwell. Oliver Cromwell had great personal authority, but on his death all this would evaporate unless it was associated with a permanent office, like that of king. Stability depended on the crown, and it was this desire for stability which had prompted Broghill to support political and religious reform in Ireland and Scotland earlier in the decade (as well as successive union bills in parliament), and which had encouraged him to ally with the courtiers and the Presbyterians in the Nayler and militia bill disputes.[124] Unionism also had a direct influence on the decision to introduce a monarchical constitution in the new year of 1657. A mixture of political opposition and Broghill's ill-health had ruined both the Irish and the Scottish union bills in the previous weeks, and with them was lost the chance to renegotiate the relationship between the three nations. In the meantime, however, the terms of the debate had shifted, from a settlement based on a parliamentary union to one founded on a united kingdom. For the new constitution, by making Oliver Cromwell king of England, Scotland and Ireland, would provide union by another means, with the *de facto* political union reinforced by the union of the crowns, and all guaranteed

---

[123] *Thurloe S.P.*, vi, 37.
[124] For foreign perspectives on this debate, see *Cal. S.P. Ven.*, *1655–6*, pp 57–8, 132, 183, 241, 244; *Cal. S.P. Ven.*, *1657–9*, p. 2; and the Bordeaux correspondence (P.R.O., PRO 31/3/100, ff 81v, 85v, 108r).

by parliamentary statute.[125] In short, for Broghill and his friends, the union itself could best be preserved by the crowning of Cromwell.

Broghill's support for a Cromwellian monarchy, founded on political and constitutional calculations, was also influenced by his private concerns. At the heart of these was his sense of personal loyalty to Cromwell, which had grown up during his years of service in Ireland and Scotland, and was encouraged by his experiences in the 1654 parliament. This loyalty was mixed with a belief that the protector's promotion would have religious implications. The link between religion and a return to the 'ancient constitution' had been made by others in Broghill's circle, notably Richard Baxter, who commented on the opening of the 1656 parliament that 'I looke not for any [religious] setlement to purpose till we have agayne the ancient forme, of King Lords & Commons'.[126] Such pragmatic considerations could also be supplemented with providential arguments, which singled out Cromwell as an instrument of divine will. Like Gustavus Adolphus in the early 1630s, Oliver Cromwell was often seen in providential terms, and, for some, there was no doubt that 'God hath a great work for him to do'.[127] Similar views were prevalent within the Boyle circle, and were probably shared by Broghill, whose sense of the workings of providence was acute.[128] Such attitudes fit so closely with Broghill's long-standing interest in international Calvinism, and his belief in providence as revealed in the Bible, and it is tempting to suggest that his allegiance to the protector was therefore rather more than merely a matter of politics. These overtly religious motives provide the counterpart to concerns among the opponents of kingship that Cromwell's ambitions would anger God and bring calamity to Britain.[129] A final factor was one of personal finance. Since the foundation of the protectorate, Broghill's shaky financial situation had greatly improved largely because he now received a substantial salary, and there is much evidence to substantiate the view of hostile contemporaries that Broghill, like other kinglings, was motivated by self-interest. The extent to which this was the overriding factor in prompting Broghill's support for a permanent civilian settlement is less certain.[130] Nevertheless there are strong indications that the offer of the crown was the culmination of a great deal of investment, financially, intellectually and emotionally, as well as politically.

---

[125] Little, 'The first unionists?', pp 49–53.

[126] N.H. Keeble and G.F. Nuttall (eds), *Calendar of the correspondence of Richard Baxter* (2 vols, Oxford, 1991), i, 222, 224–5.

[127] Smith, *God's Unchangeableness*, sig. A2v. It seems likely that Broghill was familiar with Smith's work, as his later speeches echoed the biblical passage cited therein.

[128] See below, ch. 9.

[129] For the impact of providentialism on protectoral politics see Blair Worden 'Oliver Cromwell and the sin of Achan' in Derek Beales and Geoffrey Best (eds), *History, society and the churches* (Cambridge, 1985), pp 125–45.

[130] See below, ch. 8.

The idea of crowning Cromwell did not originate with Broghill. Various schemes were fielded even before the formation of the protectorate, and rumours of an imminent coronation reappeared periodically throughout 1654, 1655 and 1656,[131] and earlier in the 1656 parliament the hereditary succession, and the Cromwellian monarchy, were hotly debated even while other issues took precedence.[132] Much of the controversy was caused by those in Broghill's circle. On 28 October 1656, 'an Irish gentleman' moved for parliament 'to take into consideration the 31st [i.e. 32nd] article of the government', which stipulated that the protectorate would be elective not hereditary.[133] The motion was dropped in the face of strong opposition from the army interest, but the attempt was significant, not least because the speaker was William Jephson, Broghill's close ally.[134] On 25 November another Irish M.P., John Bridges, told Henry Cromwell that the army officers had opposed 'a settlem[en]t', but had been countered by '5 greate psons'; he had then been drawn into an argument with Major Generals Berry and Disbrowe about the succession, and had penned his own set of arguments in favour, in which he stressed the need 'to settle uppon the olde bottome'.[135] On 19 January 1657 a leading Presbyterian M.P., John Ashe, again brought up the issue in parliament, moving that 'his Highness would be pleased to take upon him the government according to the ancient constitution'.[136] Ashe was supported by Broghill's ally from the Scottish administration, George Downing, but once again the matter was dropped in the face of opposition from the army officers.[137] Tensions about the succession were running high, and the army interest was leading attempts to prevent a full debate in parliament. Ranged against them were a number of Irish and Scottish M.P.s, members of the council, and Presbyterians, many of whom had close connexions with Broghill. This raises the possibility that these were co-ordinated attempts to raise kingship as a question, preparatory to the introduction of a far-reaching reform programme. With issues such as the militia bill still to be decided, even in January 1657 the time was still not right.

---

[131] For a survey see Egloff, 'Settlement and kingship', ch. 4; also Eric Porter, 'A cloak for knavery: kingship, the army, and the first protectorate parliament, 1654–5' in *The Seventeenth Century*, xvii (2002), pp 187–205.

[132] For the parliamentary debate before February 1657 see C. H. Firth, 'Cromwell and the crown' in *E.H.R.*, xvii (1902), pp 429–42.

[133] *Thurloe S.P.*, v, 525.

[134] Bordeaux to Brienne, 9 Nov, 1656 [n.s.] (P.R.O., PRO 31/3/100, f. 85r–v); for Jephson's identity see *Ludlow memoirs*, ii, 20; and *Burton diary*, iii, 160; see also Firth, 'Cromwell and the crown', p. 433.

[135] Bridges to Henry Cromwell, 25 Nov. 1656 (B.L., Lansdowne MS 821, f. 250r–v); see also Bridges to Berry, 25 Nov. 1656 (ibid., Lansdowne MS 823, f. 318r–v); Egloff speculates that the five great persons might be Wolseley, Mountagu, Oliver St John, Philip Jones and Broghill ('Settlement and kingship', p. 296).

[136] *Burton diary*, i, 362.

[137] See ibid., pp 362–6 for the debate.

On 23 February 1657 the brake was at last released. On that day, Sir Christopher Packe, a London M.P. with contacts with the Presbyterians and the court, introduced the Remonstrance – a new constitution with two houses of parliament and a king. There seems little doubt that Packe was a front-man, rather than the author of the Remonstrance. Indeed, as Morgan told Henry Cromwell, Packe 'gave some advantage ag[ains]t himselfe by privatly confessing to one sate by him that he had never read it', causing Colonel Sydenham to demand that 'a Com[mi]ttee might be appointed to find out the contrivers of this remonstrance'.[138] Contemporaries suspected that Packe was influenced by a small group of prominent 'courtiers', or civilians, in the protector's council. Edmund Ludlow said that the 'new form' of government was 'prepared by his [Cromwell's] creatures'.[139] The M.P. for Coventry, Robert Beake, was more specific, saying that the 'new Goverm[en]t' was the work of a 'caball', comprising 'Ld Fines Sr Ch: Wolesley Col: Jones Mr Secretary Ld Mountagu Ld Broghill Ld Cheife Justice', who, 'wth singuler Industry did they prepare the thing wthout doores & wth as much prudence managed it wthin doores'.[140] Four of these seven – including Broghill – have been identified with the '5 greate p[er]sons' who had opposed the army over the succession in November 1656; and, as Beake claims, all played an active part in the kingship debates which followed. The leadership of this cabal is as problematic as its exact membership. There are hints that Broghill was the principal sponsor of Packe's proposals. Bulstrode Whitelocke said that once the Remonstrance had been introduced, 'then Wh[itelocke] & the L[ord] Broghill & Glyn & others of their friends putt it forward', although he admitted that Broghill and others had brought him into the design in the first place. Adam Baynes, in a speech against the new constitution in February 1659 recorded by the diarist, Thomas Burton, stated that the Remonstrance had been 'brought in irregularly . . . by a gentleman that found it by the way as he came from Lord ——'.[141] Burton's blank is a further reminder that Broghill cannot be identified with certainty as the creator of the Remonstrance introduced on 23 February. In his management of the ensuing debates in the commons, however, there is a strong case for seeing him as the sculptor of its modified form – the Humble Petition and Advice.

Surviving texts of the Remonstrance show it to be a very different document from the Humble Petition.[142] It was a much shorter, containing twelve, rather than eighteen, articles; and of these twelve, six were substantially changed by

---

[138] Morgan to Henry Cromwell, 24 Feb. 1657 (B.L., Lansdowne MS 821, f. 294r–v).
[139] *Ludlow memoirs*, ii, 21.
[140] Robert Beake to Leonard Piddock, 28 Mar. 1657 (Coventry City Archives, BA/H/Q/A79/302).
[141] *Whitelocke diary*, pp 463–4; *Burton diary*, iii, 216.
[142] Two versions of the Remonstrance survive: Bodl., MS Clarendon 54, ff 118r–119v is a royalist copy, and the most complete; an intriguing Scottish version can be found at N.L.S., Wodrow Folio MSS, vol. xxx, ff 126r–7r. For the final, protectoral, version of the Humble

the commons before the Humble Petition was passed on 25 March. In its original form, the Remonstrance was much more monarchical, and much less parliamentary, than the Humble Petition would become. In many ways, the original Remonstrance offered Cromwell powers similar to those enjoyed by Charles I before 1642. Parliamentary checks on the ruler were removed. There was no provision for parliamentary consent in such matters as changes in the membership of the privy council or the Other House, nor would parliament be consulted about appointments to the offices of state; the new king would not need to take an oath, nor would he undertake to keep the present parliament in being. All these provisions would be inserted in the Humble Petition. Other changes are also significant. The role of the privy council in excluding M.P.s was reduced in the Remonstrance, and the Other House was allowed the wide legal jurisdiction of the traditional House of Lords. The Remonstrance greeted Cromwell in providential terms, saying that the new order had been sanctioned by 'God who putts downe one and setts up another, & giveth the Kingdomes of the World to whomsoever he pleaseth', who had 'by a series of Providences raysed you to be a deliverer to these Nations'.[143] Such overtly religious acclamations were quietly dropped in the Humble Petition. The religious settlement in the Remonstrance was much broader than that of the Humble Petition, allowing differences in 'Doctrine, Discipline or Worship' without any agreed confession of faith, and thereby providing for much greater parity between the denominations. The rules excluding certain people from voting or sitting in parliament were much more relaxed, and, crucially, provision was made for an oath to restore former royalists to full participation in the life of the country. This last clause was later removed from article thirteen of the Humble Petition. Other changes included the introduction of the phrase 'these nations' instead of 'this nation' in the Humble Petition: both had been used, willy-nilly, in the Remonstrance. Overall, the modifications which changed the Remonstrance into the Humble Petition suggest that Broghill and the other members of the 'caball' were coming under intense pressure not only from the army interest (who opposed the whole project) but also from those whom they expected to support a return to the 'ancient constitution', the Presbyterians. Indeed, it soon became apparent that the erection of a Cromwellian monarchy without parliamentary safeguards, and the establishment of a religious settlement without concessions to the conservative, Presbyterian, interest, would cause an immediate split within its natural constituency in the commons. Yet a toned down, less monarchical, and more intolerant constitution would prove more difficult to sell to another interested party – the protector himself. The awkwardness of this situation determined the course of the kingship debates, in parliament and without, for the next three months.

Petition see S. R. Gardiner, *The constitutional documents of the puritan revolution, 1625–1660* (Oxford, 1889), pp 447–59.
[143] Bodl., MS Clarendon 54, f. 118v; N.L.S., Wodrow Folio MSS, vol. xxx, f. 126r.

The transition from Remonstrance to Humble Petition was not an easy one. For several weeks the individual articles were discussed in detail, and many passed with a rapidity which suggests some hard work was being done behind the scenes. Broghill soon became involved in discussions on the more problematic articles, which dominated the business of the house.[144] As in Scottish and Irish affairs, his interventions were selective but decisive. During the debate on the important fourth article of the Remonstrance, concerning the classes of delinquents to be refused the franchise (on 6 March) he was named to the committee to revise the clauses concerning Scotland and Ireland, the report from which was presented three days later by Henry Cromwell's agent, William Aston.[145] Broghill returned to Scottish and Irish affairs in committees appointed on 10 and 20 March.[146] On 12 March he was appointed to the committee which considered the controversial issue of the judicial role to be exercised by the Other House (an issue which had dominated the Nayler case in the previous months); and on 16 March was involved in discussions on the equally problematic question of the powers to be enjoyed by the new council.[147] Both articles were subjected to substantial changes by the commons on the advice of these committees. On 19 March Broghill was included in the committee which considered the thorny problem of the wide degree of religious toleration allowed under the tenth article (which became the eleventh article of the Humble Petition).[148] According to Whitelocke, Broghill was one of the four M.P.s who drafted the final version of this article so that 'any man might believe it, and never hurt his conscience', which was passed on 20 March in the teeth of Presbyterian opposition.[149] As in 1654, religion was an issue which could destroy the alliance between the courtiers and the country M.P.s, and which would also have an impact on Oliver Cromwell's acceptance of the new constitution. Broghill, despite his personal inclinations towards Presbyterianism, did his best to accommodate 'tender consciences' of all denominations, in order to preserve the internal unity of the reform party, and to appease the protector.[150] This he managed despite constant attempts by prominent Presbyterians to restrict toleration only to those who would subscribe to a strict Confession of Faith , a matter which was

---

[144] Firth, 'Cromwell and the crown', p. 54.

[145] C.J., vii, 499, 500.

[146] Ibid., pp 501, 508. For a full account of his activities in Irish and Scottish affairs see above, pp 130–9.

[147] C.J., vii, 502, 505.

[148] Ibid., p. 507.

[149] *Whitelocke diary*, p. 459; B.L., Harl. MS 6848, f. 146r.

[150] Thurloe was optimistic at the result: 'I cannot see that there can be any great difficultie to come to a just settlement if the basis of religion can be well agreed' (*Thurloe S.P.*, vi, 123); but it is clear from the division (which saw Broghill's Presbyterian allies, Henry Markham and Sir John Fitzjames telling against toleration) that the Presbyterian–courtier alliance was severely strained by the religious question: C.J., vii, 508–9.

eventually left optional, rather than compulsory, in the Humble Petition.[151] Broghill's skilful management of the most controversial articles of the Remonstrance, as it slowly became the Humble Petition, is palpable. It was with some justification that John Bridges told Henry Cromwell (on 10 March) that 'My Lord Broghill had gained to himselfe much honor by his prudent & dextrous deportm[en]ts. in the House.'[152]

Yet Broghill's influence over the progress of the new constitution was much greater than is suggested even by a survey of his committee appointments. As in Irish and Scottish affairs, much of the donkey-work was delegated to trusted friends and clients. The prominence of Broghill's friends active in the house during this period is striking. Anthony Morgan saw the supporters of kingship as including 'L[or]d Pres[i]d[en]t Lawrance Phils Jones, Mountegue, Sr C Wolsly, Ld ffines, Skippon Thurlow . . . all the long robe . . . [and] Ch: Howard'.[153] The committee lists suggest that the activity of these courtiers was matched by Presbyterians such as Nathaniel and Francis Bacon, Grove, Bampfield and Trevor: all of whom had previous connexions with Broghill.[154] They were backed by a strong 'British' contingent: at least fifteen Irish and Scottish M.P.s were appointed to committees concerning the Remonstrance before the end of March, and 28 were later included in the list of 'kinglings'.[155] Contemporaries saw the 'British' involvement as particularly important in voting through the Remonstrance: 'The Irish all for it, but Cooper, Huson, & Sanky' according to one;[156] while Henry Cromwell was told that 'the Irish officers stand to their principles';[157] and Broghill (with the help of Wolseley and Jones) intervened in early March to prevent Gookin and Markham from being recalled from Westminster to their administrative posts in Ireland.[158] Broghill was at the very centre of this overlapping set of political circles, and

---

[151] The compromise was considered 'better then what we yet have had though the text may seeme badd', by the prominent Presbyterian, Robert Beake: Beake to Piddock, 28 Mar. 1657 (Coventry City Archives, BA/H/Q/A79/302); the phrase 'what we have yet had' probably refers to the Remonstrance, rather than the Instrument: cf. C. S. Egloff, 'Robert Beake: a letter concerning the Humble Petition and Advice, 28 Mar. 1657' in *Historical Research*, lxviii (1995), pp 233–9.

[152] Bridges to Henry Cromwell, 10 Mar. 1657 (B.L., Lansdowne MS 821, f. 326r–v).

[153] Morgan to Henry Cromwell, 24 Feb. 1657 (B.L., Lansdowne MS 821, f. 294v).

[154] *C.J.*, vii, 499–514.

[155] Ibid.: Cochrane, Ramsay, Howard, Clarges, Samuel Disbrowe and Broghill himself for Scotland; Morgan, Aston, Reynolds, Tighe, Meredith, Theophilus Jones, Ingoldsby, Fowke and Cooper for Ireland; including Walter Waller and John Brett; see *A narrative of the late parliament* (Feb. 1658), pp 22–3.

[156] Morgan to Henry Cromwell, 24 Feb. 1657 (B.L., Lansdowne MS 821, f. 294v); by the end of the month Cooper had changed his mind (see *Thurloe S.P.*, vi, 157), and Hewson and Sankey, though Irish officers, in fact sat for English seats in parliament.

[157] Richard Cromwell to Henry Cromwell, 7 Mar. 1657 (B.L., Lansdowne MS 821, f. 324r).

[158] Gookin to Henry Cromwell, 3 Mar. 1657 (ibid., f. 308r).

his very presence helped to keep the differences between them (notably on religious toleration) from becoming causes of division.

This alliance, and Broghill's central position within it, can be seen in the important votes which determined the overall success of the attempt to modify the Remonstrance. The vote on 23 February whether to read Packe's paper saw the courtier, Sir Charles Wolseley, and the Dorset Presbyterian, Sir John Fitzjames, telling in favour, and Lambert's allies, William Sydenham and Luke Robinson, telling against.[159] Wolseley and Fitzjames made strange bed-fellows, but both had connexions with Broghill: Wolseley had been his ally in the 1654 parliament, and Fitzjames was an associate of Broghill's friend, Thomas Grove. On 2 March the motion to postpone the discussion of the first article (on hereditary succession and the royal title) was opposed by Broghill's ally on the Scottish council, Charles Howard, and the Irish M.P. and agent of Henry Cromwell, Sir John Reynolds.[160] On 9 March, when a rival paper was submitted by Colonel Matthews, Broghill and Wolseley stepped in to oppose it.[161] Broghill was also involved in the debate on the first article on 23 March, working with Whitelocke to answer the arguments of Major-General Disbrowe.[162] The crucial vote of 25 March, on whether to accept the first article and thus the title 'king', saw Reynolds and Howard again telling for the motion. The vote was passed by 123 votes to 62.[163] At each stage, Broghill and his close associates were involved in the successful attempt to push the new constitution through parliament relatively intact. The wording of the revised constitution, renamed the Humble Petition and Advice, was drafted by a committee of seventeen M.P.s, including Broghill and nine of his friends, on 26 March,[164] and controversial side-swipes at the army's influence were omitted from the preamble.[165] On 31 March, when the Humble Petition was presented to Oliver Cromwell by a committee of M.P.s which included Broghill and all the leading 'kinglings',[166] Thurloe noted the spirit of euphoria (and sense of relief) which pervaded the reform camp:

the liberties of the nation and those of the people of God are met, and doe embrace each other in this paper, and that it doth carrye with it a better foundation of settlement then hitherto hath beene propounded.[167]

[159] C.J., vii, 496.
[160] Ibid., p. 498.
[161] Ibid., p. 500.
[162] Reynolds to Henry Cromwell, 24 Mar. 1657 (B.L., Lansdowne 822, f. 3r).
[163] C.J., vii, 511.
[164] Ibid: Glynn, Thurloe, Jones, Whitelocke, Reynolds, Wolseley, Mountagu, Nathaniel Bacon and Aston had all worked with Broghill before.
[165] See the original Remonstrance: Bodl., MS Clarendon 54, f. 118r.
[166] C.J., vii, 514.
[167] Thurloe S.P., vi, 156–7.

Once the Humble Petition had been presented to Cromwell, a new phase in the kingship debates began. For nearly six weeks from 31 March, the political focus would be on the council chamber and the protector's private apartments, not on parliament. This shift was provoked by the leaders of the army interest, who, finding that resistance in parliament was difficult, put pressure on the protector instead. After an initial furious reaction against the Remonstrance, Lambert, Sydenham and other officers began to absent themselves from the house, and repeatedly attended Cromwell with their complaints about developments at Westminster during February and March.[168] Their alarm was heightened by Cromwell's apparent enthusiasm for the original version of the Remonstrance, which he saw as a way 'to come to a settlement and lay aside arbitrary proceedings'. Although he dismissed kingship as 'a feather in a hat', he did not reject the offer outright, and commended the authors of the Remonstrance as 'honest men' who 'have done good things'.[169] By contrast, Cromwell's reaction to the modified form, the Humble Petition and Advice, was frosty. In the course of the debates, parliament reduced the ruler's power, increased the role of parliament, and curbed the wide degree of toleration of the original – in a process which looked very similar to the conservative changes to the Instrument of Government which had so angered the protector in 1654–5. On receiving the Humble Petition, Cromwell refused to give a reply immediately, but said he 'would seeke God for his direction, and hop't hee should soe receyve it in an unbiast heart, as that neyther the vaine fancyes of some, nor the lust of others might divert him from giving an awnswer sutable to the mind of God'.[170]

In the face of Cromwell's cool response, the army became more optimistic, and the 'kinglings' lost heart. As John Bridges told Henry Cromwell in early April, Cromwell's delay in accepting the new constitution had 'caused many of or best frends to absent themselves from the s[ai]d Howse, as Lord Broghill, Sr Cha: Woosley, Ld Cheife Justice [Glynn], & others, w[hi]ch was noe small discouragem[en]t to us, that attended'. In fact a close vote (on 4 April) on whether to adhere to the old petition brought Broghill and his friends hurrying back to the commons.[171] Something of Broghill's personal disillusion can be seen in Henry Cromwell's letters to him during April 1657:

---

[168] Bordeaux to Mazarin, 15 Mar. 1657 [n.s.] (P.R.O., PRO 31/3/101, f. 88v); Bordeaux to Brienne, 29 Mar. 1657 [n.s.] (ibid., f. 119r); *Thurloe S.P.*, vi, 93, 107; Morgan to Henry Cromwell, 24 Feb. 1657 (B.L., Lansdowne MS 821, f. 294v); same to same, 3 Mar. 1657 (ibid., f. 314r–v).

[169] Abbott, *Writings and speeches*, iv, 417–18.

[170] Jephson to Henry Cromwell, 31 Mar. 1657 (B.L., Lansdowne MS 822, f. 19r); for the army's confidence see *Burton diary*, ii, 4.

[171] Bridges to Henry Cromwell, 7 Apr. 1657 (B.L., Lansdowne MS 822, f. 29r–v); *Cal. S.P. Dom., 1656–7*, pp 327–8; the tellers in favour were Broghill's allies, Jephson and Howard: *C.J.*, vii, 520.

I neither know what to doe or say upon this issue of affairs, certainly as you said The Lord hath yet a further controversy to decide with this poore Nacon. . . . Neither am I a little strengthened in this p[er]suasion that you have yet heart enough not to quitt all, w[hi]ch I desire you and all honest men not to doe, least the predominant gent[lemen] obtrude w[ha]tsoever they please upon us.[172]

A further letter from the same period was consoling: 'Remember that tis not Names or words that governe the world, but Things'.[173] Above all, Henry Cromwell seems to have appealed to Broghill not to let his anger cloud his judgement: 'Pray stand fast not onely in the house, but also improve your Interest wth his H[ighness] to keepe him in mind of these excellent things you hinted, nor lett the humor of o[u]r illwillers grow past cure. Bee not quite discouraged till things grow desperate for as long as there is life there is hope.'[174]

Despite his sense of frustration at Cromwell's prevarication, Broghill remained committed to the reform programme. During April five committees were appointed to arrange times to attend Cromwell, and to prepare arguments to convince him to accept the crown, and Broghill was named to all of them.[175] The delegation which attended Cromwell on 11, 16 and 22 April consisted of seven courtiers (Whitelocke, Glynn, Lenthall, Jones, Fiennes, Oliver St John and John Lisle), one Presbyterian (Sir Richard Onslow), and Broghill.[176] The arguments on both sides were recorded, and later published. The reliability of the published account is open to question, but internal evidence (and especially the repetition of ideas and imagery used in other contexts by the participants) adds a stamp of authenticity. Certainly, Broghill's two speeches at the meetings on 11 and 16 April seem to be genuine, and therefore deserve close scrutiny. On 11 April he seconded the legalistic arguments of Whitelocke, Lenthall, Glynn and others, by asserting that 'the title of King is that which the Law takes notice of . . . and that the old foundations that are good, are better then any new ones', and that a monarchy would bind the people to the government once they 'knew their dutie to him and he the dutie of his Office towards them'.[177] Cromwell's refusal of the crown would strengthen the royalists, but with a stable government under a new monarch 'it would be little less than madness, for any of them to cast off the blessings, onely in order to obtain the same end under another person'.[178]

---

[172] Henry Cromwell to Broghill, n.d. (B.L., Lansdowne MS 823, f. 328r). All these letters seem to have been written between March and May 1657.

[173] Henry Cromwell to Broghill, n.d. (ibid., f. 335r).

[174] Same to same, n.d. (ibid., f. 338r)

[175] C.J., vii, 519, 520, 521, 521, 523.

[176] Burton diary, ii, 5; Old parliamentary history, xxi, 65, 89; CJ vii, 521, 522.

[177] [Bulstrode Whitelocke?], Monarchy asserted, to be the best, most ancient and legall form of government (1660), p. 26.

[178] Ibid., p. 27.

He ended by reminding Cromwell that the Humble Petition, as passed by parliament, already carried 'very great force and authority', and that the new constitution itself contained 'many other excellent things, in reference to our civil and spiritual Liberties'.[179] Broghill's constitutional and political arguments on 11 April were consistent with his experiences in previous years: stability could only be achieved through a monarchical constitution, guaranteed by parliament, which would safeguard the people's liberties and allow the reconciliation of former royalists to the regime. This was Cromwell's president of Scotland (and the chief adviser of Henry Cromwell in Ireland) arguing for healing and settling in the grand manner.

Broghill's advice to Cromwell on 16 April repeated many of these themes, but he also introduced a religious element. This was partly in response to Cromwell's own doubts, expressed to the delegates, that Providence had laid aside kingship in 1649, and that the revival of the crown would provoke God. Earlier on, Jones and Onslow had argued that Providence was not clear on this matter, and that the designs of God could not be known for certain; but only Broghill met Cromwell's objections head-on. 'I cannot believe, if that office were blasted by the hand of God, that the Parliament would advise and petition you to take it up.'[180] If kingship was cursed, then so was government by a single person – the protectorate; and if destruction meant divine disfavour, how could any parliament sit after the Rump had been dissolved in 1653? He could not believe that the kingly government had been rendered unlawful by the 'word of God'.[181] In response to the protector's fears that kingship would offend the godly, Broghill reminded him that only those who submitted to 'Gospel-Ordinances' were worthy of consideration, and he cited the story of the death of King David's child in the Second Book of Samuel:

> The case of David when his child was sick may possibly parallel the case of such good men as are herein unsatisfied; while as the child was sick he was very earnest with the Lord for the restoring of it to health, but God was not pleased so to doe, and the child died, his servants being of another principle then himself, thus reasoned, if his trouble and grief were so great, while yet the child was not dead, what will it be now it is dead[?]; but David reasoned that, while there was hope, I wrestled with God, but since his will is declared I chearfully submit to it. I hope as scrupulous good mens cases in the particular of Kingship, is a parable to the History, so it will likewise prove in the event.[182]

At first sight, this seems an odd choice of biblical allusion. But in returning to 2 Samuel – which had featured so prominently in his speech against the militia

---

[179] Ibid., p. 28.
[180] Ibid., pp 69–72.
[181] Ibid., pp 73–4.
[182] Ibid., pp 75–6.

bill in January – Broghill was making a direct (and flattering) comparison between Cromwell and King David.[183] Moreover, Broghill seems to have been relying on Cromwell's thorough knowledge of the Bible to make further connexions: with the death of his child, David immediately begot another son, who would become the wise and successful King Solomon. Did he intend to draw an allegorical parallel between the fate of King David's children and that of the Instrument of Government (feared by Cromwell's servants 'of another principle'), which had died, only to be replaced by the wiser Humble Petition? At the risk of stretching the point too far, it is interesting that, at the end of the same chapter, King David destroyed the city of Rabbah: 'And he took their king's crown from off his head . . . and it was set on David's head.'[184] Bearing in mind Cromwell's obsession with discerning God's will through Scripture (which reached a high point during the kingship debates), the reference to 2 Samuel makes perfect sense.[185] Broghill had lost none of his old skill in manipulating the protector.

Broghill and his allies had appealed to Cromwell's heart as well as his head; but still the effect of such arguments remained difficult to gauge. On 14 April Sir John Reynolds told Henry Cromwell that 'we are at present in suspense . . . what the issue will be, none can declare'.[186] Even Secretary Thurloe was uncertain of the protector's attitude, reporting on 21 April that 'His highness keepes every body in suspence as to his acceptance of the Advice'.[187] On 29 April nothing had changed: 'I can take noe measure of his minde therein', bewailed Thurloe.[188] In the face of this intransigence, the pressure on Cromwell from both sides was maintained. In Whitelocke's words, in early May 'the Prot[ecto]r often advised with Wh[itelocke] about this & other great buisnesses, & severall times he would send for the L[ord] Broghill, Pierrepont, Wh[itelocke,] S[i]r Charles Oulseley [i.e. Wolseley] & Thurlo & be shutt up w[i]th them 3 or 4 hours togither in private discourse'.[189] In the meantime, other problems arose. Cromwell's delay in responding heightened existing tensions between the different groups within the 'kingship party'. On 24 April the Presbyterians, led by Bampfield, Godfrey, Trevor, the Bacon brothers and Griffith Bodurda, objected to moves to grant the protector a permanent revenue, asserting instead the right of parliament to control

---

[183] John Lisle had already referred to King David's enthronement (2 Samuel v, 3) in discussions with Cromwell on 11 April: see *Old parliamentary history*, xxi, 86. Broghill may also have been making a deliberate reference to George Smith's pro-Cromwellian tract, *Gods unchangeableness*, which cites 2 Samuel, v twice (pp 31, 39) as an example of submitting to God's providential designs.

[184] 2 Samuel xii, 15–23; Solomon's conception is ibid., 24; the defeat of Rabbah, ibid., 30.

[185] See Worden, 'Sin of Achan', pp 141–5.

[186] Reynolds to Henry Cromwell, 14 Apr. 1657 (B.L., Lansdowne MS 822, f. 47r).

[187] *Thurloe S.P.*, vi, 219.

[188] Ibid., p. 243.

[189] *Whitelocke diary*, p. 464; see also *Thurloe S.P.*, vi, 281.

taxation. Broghill and his allies, recognising the threat this posed to a central tenet of the Humble Petition, effected a compromise in which the revenue grant was limited in time; and the measure was eventually passed.[190] On 28 April religious toleration again became a political issue, as moves to confirm the ordinance for the approbation of preachers provoked Bampfield and his friends to champion parliament's right to decide individual cases. Broghill again intervened, 'to help to secure this', moving a proviso to allow parliament's approval of nominations, and this motion was agreed despite the continuing objections of some Presbyterians.[191] The unity of the 'kinglings', sorely tested, had held firm thanks to Broghill's activities. But his influence over the protector was not as strong.

In his final reply to parliament on 8 May, Cromwell accepted the Humble Petition, and commended its measures for 'settling the nation on a good foot, in relation to civil rights and liberties . . . [and] in that great, natural, and religious liberty, which is liberty of conscience' but added, 'I cannot undertake this government, with that title king'.[192] Cromwell's reasons were at heart religious. Ignoring the flattering parallels made by Broghill and others between his own rise and that of King David, Cromwell's inclination towards taking the crown was stayed by an acute awareness of the danger of angering God through his personal ambition, thus repeating the sin of Achan, who 'took the cursed thing', bringing calamity to the Israelites after the fall of Jericho. As Cromwell told parliament, 'I would not seek to set up that that providence hath destroyed and laid in the dust, and I would not build Jericho again.'[193]

Cromwell's refusal of the crown was a bitter blow to Broghill. On 19 May he joined Sir John Hobart, Sir Richard Lucy and Sir William Roberts in an attempt to vote down the change of title in the Humble Petition from king to protector.[194] This was only a symbolic act of resistance, but it showed Broghill's continued public support for the revival of monarchy. The revised bill was passed on 25 May, and a committee presented the new constitution to the protector. Broghill was conspicuous by his absence.[195] Indeed, whether through gout (which affected him until the end of June) or disappointment, Broghill was absent from parliament for most of the next month, and made no recorded contribution to debate even when he was present.[196] A general depression overtook his Irish and Scottish friends. On 27 May Jephson suggested, with heavy irony, that as the letters 'k-i-n-g' were so offensive to some, 'we must,

---

[190] *Burton diary*, ii, 24–31.
[191] Ibid., pp 50–5.
[192] C.J., vii, 533; *Thurloe S.P.*, vi, 267.
[193] Abbott, *Writings and speeches*, iv, 473; see Worden, 'Sin of Achan', pp 141–5.
[194] C.J., vii, 535.
[195] Ibid., pp 538, 538, 539.
[196] He was named to only three committees from 26 May–26 June (see ibid., pp 540, 543, 576) and makes no further appearance in *Burton diary*.

I think, have an Act to expunge them out of the alphabet'.[197] His disillusion was shared by many English M.P.s, whether courtiers or country gentlemen. On 12 May, Thurloe noted that 'I perceive this hath strucke a great damp upon the spirits of some . . . I finde the countrye gentlemen are very averse from this.'[198] As Sir Francis Russell told Henry Cromwell, the passing of the revised Humble Petition on 25 May caused not rejoicing, but dismay:

> Will Perepoint and General Montague will never trust to politiks any more, and the little Secretary [Thurloe] tells me that he seeth now that nothing is so considerable in any busynes as simplicity. [T]he truth is your father hath of late made more wise men fooles than ever, he laughs and is merry but they hang downe they're heads and are pittyfully out of countenance. [A]ll the lawyers are turned Quakers, who before boasted they would make penknifes of the soldyers swords . . . little Hampden, Sr John Hubbart [Hobart] and Jack Trevor I doubt are very angerey, they had strong dreames of being lords, but now they are awake find themselves but country Gentlemen.[199]

Worse was to come. Without the restraining influence of Broghill, the Presbyterian M.P.s and their former allies openly opposed each other in parliament. On 8 June a motion granting Irish lands as a reward to Fleetwood – supported by Morgan, Aston and other courtiers eager to heal the rifts in the government – was vigorously opposed by 'Bampfield Godfrey Grove & their gang'.[200] The attempt to set proportionate assessments reopened deep divisions. On 10 June, in a series of votes on Irish and Scottish assessments (introduced by Downing, MacDowell and Aston), reductions were opposed by the Presbyterians, led by West, Bordurda, Lucy, Robert Barrington, Francis Harvey and Isaac Puller. Ominously, the Presbyterians were supported in debate by Lambert, Sydenham and Baynes.[201] Two days later the Irish M.P.s petitioned against their assessment rates, 'but the example of it being disliked generally by the House, the petition was withdrawn'.[202] The opponents of this measure were Onslow, Trevor, Bordurda, Robert Shapcott, John Goodwin and others who had supported a 'British' approach earlier in the parliament.[203] Broghill, crippled by gout, was unable to intervene effectively to stop these divisions worsening. Leaderless, and without the common goal provided by the offer of the crown, Broghill's 'kingship party' had started to unravel.

As Broghill's alliance collapsed, the army interest was given its chance. The dispute over Broghill's own land grant in early June was indicative of the

---

[197] *Burton diary*, ii, 140.
[198] *Thurloe S.P.*, vi, 281.
[199] Russell to Henry Cromwell, 25 May 1657 (B.L., Lansdowne MS 822, f. 75r).
[200] Morgan to Henry Cromwell, 9 June 1657 (ibid., f. 84r); *Burton diary*, ii, 197–200.
[201] *C.J.*, vii, 554; *Burton diary*, ii, 207–13.
[202] *C.J.*, vii, 555.
[203] *Burton diary*, ii, 224–8, 245–7.

factional element which had re-emerged in the commons after the failure of the kingship proposals. A bill to confirm Broghill's original grant of £1,000 p.a. had been read for the first time on 2 April 1657, two days after the Humble Petition and Advice was presented to the protector, and at the height of Broghill's influence in parliament.[204] It received its second reading three days before the amended Humble Petition was finally accepted, and Downing reported amendments on 1 June.[205] Yet by the final reading, on 5 June, Broghill's friends were no longer in charge of the house. Instead of passing without dispute, the Blarney grant provoked 'great debate', with Lambert, Sydenham, Kelsey, and other army officers opposing a proviso to increase the grant by 2,000 acres (to make up a shortfall in the land survey) which had been championed by Broghill's allies, including Thurloe, Jephson, Lenthall, Morgan, Wolseley, Samuel Disbrowe and Jones.[206] When the question was brought to the vote, it was passed unanimously, but Lambert, Fleetwood, Sydenham and John Disbrowe insulted Broghill by withdrawing from the vote.[207] Worse was to follow: from 15 June Lambert and his allies systematically destroyed the concessions to Scottish royalists secured by Broghill in the previous March. Unlike in November/December 1656, in June 1657 it seems that Broghill no longer had sufficient power to influence parliament from his sick-bed. His return to the house on 26 June just salvaged the measure protecting the interests of the pre-1649 Irish officers, but it was already clear that his moment of political supremacy had passed. The refusal of the crown in May had effectively destroyed Broghill's 'party' in parliament. His personal faith in Cromwell had been shaken; and the chances of further 'settlement' in the three nations looked remote.

V

The failure of the offer of the crown to Cromwell should not detract from Broghill's achievements in the parliament during 1656 and 1657. An influential adviser of Cromwell even before the parliament began, he had used his authority and personal connexions to construct a broad alliance of Irish and Scots, Presbyterians, country gentlemen and courtiers, all of whom had good reason to oppose the military government typified by Lambert, Fleetwood, Disbrowe and the army interest. In Irish and Scottish affairs he had demonstrated an ability to manage policy, in the face of considerable opposition, within parliament and the council. These factional conflicts were replicated in the Nayler case and the militia bill, and allowed Broghill to cement his

---

[204] C.J., vii, 517.
[205] Ibid., pp 537, 543.
[206] Burton diary, ii, 175–8.
[207] Ibid., p. 178.

existing contacts with the Presbyterians and the moderate courtiers, and to secure a remarkable parliamentary majority when the new constitution was introduced in February 1657. During the kingship debates, Broghill guided this alliance with skill, intervening to prevent dissension, managing the change from the Remonstrance to the Humble Petition, and uniting the M.P.s behind one goal – the Cromwellian kingship. For Broghill, as for Cromwell, this was more than a mere title: it was an essential ingredient for a settlement, and a symbol of authority which had religious, as well as legal, implications. Cromwell's refusal was a personal disaster for Broghill, and a political reverse which destroyed the carefully constructed coalition, and allowed the army interest to reassert its position in parliament. Broghill, disillusioned and gout-ridden, was left with little to show for his Herculean labours.

6

From King Oliver to King Charles,
1657–79

The central focus of this book has been Lord Broghill's support for the Cromwellian union, and especially his importance in the political process which led to the offer of the crown to Oliver Cromwell in 1657. The dramatic events which followed the kingship debates, including the failure of the protectorate in 1659, the restoration of Charles II in 1660, and the new world of Carolean politics in the decades that followed, are largely outside the scope of this work. Having said that, there is a need to follow the story through, to see how Broghill's career in later years sheds light on his activities during the Civil War and interregnum. Above all, it is necessary to explore a central conundrum: as we have seen, Broghill's determination to encourage 'settlement' within the three nations had caused him to support the House of Cromwell – even to the extent of trying to change the elective protectorate into a hereditary monarchy – and the necessary corollary of this was the total exclusion of the Stuart dynasty. Yet within three years of the rejection of the crown by Cromwell, Broghill was outwardly reconciled to the restoration of Charles II. How was he able to switch so quickly and apparently easily from support for King Oliver to support for King Charles?

I

Cromwell's rejection of the crown had a lasting impact on Broghill. The Humble Petition, with its proposed Cromwellian monarchy, was not just a political programme. Broghill's desire for financial security and his private religious beliefs had increased his commitment to permanent constitutional change. More to the point, Broghill's honour and prestige had become identified with his policies; and his political influence was now dependent on his relationship with the protector. The offer of the crown, delivered to Cromwell by a large parliamentary majority, was the high-water mark of Broghill's political career. But with the crown rejected, the tide quickly began to ebb, and Broghill was soon in danger of being left stranded. In the closing weeks of the 1657 parliamentary sitting, Broghill's opponents regained the initiative and began to dismantle the Humble Petition. From then on, Broghill and his allies were forced to halt further reforms while they mounted a long and weary defence of the newborn constitution. Their policies became reactive, their factional battles were now rearguard actions. The euphoria of the first few months of 1657 would not return.

Broghill's disillusion is apparent as early as the summer of 1657. He had scored a number of successes in the weeks after the adjournment of parliament: the confirmation of the Blarney grant and the doubling of his Scottish salary had improved his financial position;[1] the sacking of Lambert from the army and the council had removed his principal rival at Whitehall. But the expected political rewards did not come. Thurloe was made a privy councillor, but there was no seat on the English board for Broghill.[2] Nor was there any discernible move to press on with the further settlement of the three nations, and, ominously, men like Fleetwood, Disbrowe and Sydenham were still influential in the council and its Irish and Scottish committees.[3] Far from securing the Old Protestant interest (and that of the majority of Scots), the 1656 parliament had done little more than confirm the status quo. It is indicative that shortly after parliament adjourned in July 1657, Broghill resolved to return to Ireland, rather than kick his heels in England. He took his leave of Whitelocke on 3 August, promising to return to London by early November.[4] Lady Broghill went to stay at the earl of Suffolk's house at Audley End.[5] After a delay caused by contrary winds, Broghill sailed from Milford Haven on 20 August, and arrived at Lismore at the end of the month.[6] The situation in Ireland was little better than that in England. Since the end of June, Henry Cromwell had repeatedly pressed for the settlement of Ireland to be taken seriously.[7] A particular concern was the passing of the long-expected order replacing Fleetwood with Henry Cromwell as lord deputy. Broghill had repeated conferences with Henry Cromwell at Clonmel, Kilkenny and Dublin in the autumn, and wrote to Thurloe urging haste.[8] Yet the orders appointing the new lord deputy were not sent out until early November, and Broghill told Mountagu, with a bitterness born of personal experience, that: 'if all things moove at the Rate our settlement of Ireland has Done, I shall thinke the boddy Politike has got the Goute'.[9] Even the news of Henry Cromwell's promotion and his own appointment to the 'Other House' did not revive Broghill's enthusiasm:

---

[1] See below, ch. 8.

[2] *Cal. S.P. Dom.*, 1657–8, p. 26.

[3] Fleetwood was appointed to the Scottish committee in Lambert's place: ibid., p. 27; see also Sir Francis Russell to Henry Cromwell, 4 July 1657 (B.L., Lansdowne 822, f. 132r); *Thurloe S.P.*, vi, 665.

[4] Broghill to Whitelocke, 3 Aug. 1657 (Longleat, Whitelocke papers 18, f. 75r).

[5] Broghill's accounts, 1657 (Petworth, Orrery MS 13192, unfol.).

[6] *Cal. S.P. Dom.*, 1657–8, pp 408–9; *Thurloe S.P.*, vi, 469; Second earl of Cork's diary (Chatsworth, Lismore MS 29, unfol.), entry for 29 Aug. 1657.

[7] *Thurloe S.P.*, vi, 404, 506, 526.

[8] Cork's diary (Chatsworth, Lismore MS 29, unfol.), 1, 3, 9, 24 Sept., 26 Oct. 1657; *Thurloe S.P.*, vi, 563, 572.

[9] Broghill to Mountagu, 6 Nov. 1657 (Bodl., MS Carte 73, f. 143r).

'I confes Retirement is soe much my Desyre, thatt I can hardly bringe (with a good will) any inducements against it . . . I finde I do more oblidge my Poore Famyly at home; then I can serve the Publike abroade.'[10] It was with great reluctance that Broghill prepared to return to England for the second sitting of parliament.

Parliament, which reopened in January 1658, did nothing to lift Broghill's spirits. In terms of Irish policy, the most pressing need was the reform of finances to allow the payment of arrears and a reduction of the army, with security matters being placed in the hands of local militia. Henry Cromwell relied on Broghill to push this through, aided by his old allies, Philip Jones, Mountagu and Wolseley, and with promises of support from other councillors.[11] Henry Cromwell was full of optimism that Broghill's influence, 'like the philosopher's stone, will turne into gold' the Irish financial question.[12] The Irish M.P.s were encouraged to attend, although their influence had been weakened by the deaths of Sir Robert King and Sir John Reynolds, the absence abroad of William Jephson (as Cromwell's ambassador to the king of Sweden), and the removal of Broghill from the commons into the Other House. Hopes of a repeat of the management coup of the previous year were soon dashed by the behaviour of the commonwealthsmen – the republican element excluded in 1656, but able to return in the 1658 sitting under the terms of the Humble Petition and Advice. This group, led by Sir Arthur Hesilrige and Sir Henry Vane, used spoiling tactics in an attempt to discredit the protectorate and its new constitution. While the commons erupted into chaos, the Other House became increasingly irrelevant, and Broghill was left discussing minor bills, such as the naturalisation of the Dutch wife of a London merchant.[13] Parliament was closed after only a few weeks, with the settlement programme still incomplete. The failure of parliament was more than a missed opportunity: its immediate result was to put more power into the hands of Disbrowe and Fleetwood, and their allies in the army interest. Henry Cromwell even speculated that the dissolution of parliament had been contrived, as 'the refusall [of the crown] in the last sessions was managed in the like manner'.[14] Broghill related rumours of Disbrowe's imminent appointment as general of horse, which (in the lord deputy's words) 'discovers the intentions, which have been industriously masked'.[15] On 10 March 1658 Henry Cromwell replied to a letter from Broghill which had brought even worse news: 'The intimacy you mention of Fleetwood and Disbrowe with Lambert I do not like; for when such as they dare correspond with such as hee, it argues their power to be greater than one

---

[10] Broghill to Mountagu, 20 Nov. 1657 (ibid., f. 156r).
[11] *Thurloe S.P.*, vi, 648–51, 661–2; Fleetwood to Henry Cromwell, 19 Jan. 1658 (B.L., Add. MS 43724, f. 23r).
[12] *Thurloe S.P.*, vi, 745.
[13] H.M.C. *House of Lords MSS*, n.s., iv, 503–23.
[14] *Thurloe S.P.*, vi, 811.
[15] Ibid., p. 790.

would wish.'[16] As the army interest increased its influence, more moderate voices at court were sidelined. According to one royalist agent, writing in early March:

> Broghill, Wolsley Pickering & all of that partie are entertayned wth the triviall business of the Councell. St John[,] Pierpont & that faction, are strangers to the prsent affayres, communicated to none save ffleetwood, Disbrough Whalley, Goffe, & Thurloe, His [Cromwell's] only ayme being to pr[e]serve (if possible) the Army intire to Him.[17]

This climate of distrust worsened Broghill's sense of failure; and his reaction was characteristic. In the closing days of March, he once again announced his retirement to Ireland, this time on grounds of ill health.

Henry Cromwell, learning of Broghill's decision on 7 April, reacted with horror. He told Thurloe that he did not believe that illness was the genuine reason, speculating that worries about Broghill's Irish lands and desire for military employment in Ireland might have had an influence, and more likely, that 'either he is not consulted well enough in England, or that such as doe not like him are more, or that his highnes is averse from makeing use of, though not from hearing his advise, or that som present melancholy has seized him'.[18] Writing to Broghill, Henry Cromwell begged him not to abandon Thurloe and Philip Jones to fight it out alone; warned him of the risk of 'the intrusion of worse counsels upon his highness' in his absence; and reminded him of just how close they were to the promised land of permanent settlement: 'why should your lordship, whose courage and faith has been always eminent, now faint in the way, and dye like Moses upon mount Nebo, before you enter into the land of Canaan?'[19] In reply, Broghill protested that he was indeed suffering an attack of gout, and assured Henry Cromwell that 'his highnes disproportionable esteem' was not a cause of his departure from London.[20] As if to prove that this was true, at first he only went as far as the west country, where he stayed throughout the summer, visiting friends; but by late July he had slipped off to Ireland 'to put his own affairs into some order',[21] arriving at Lismore on 14 August.[22] Broghill's actions suggest that Henry Cromwell's instinct had been right: illness was not the principal cause of his removal from London. Like other Old Protestants, he seems to have become increasingly dissatisfied with a Cromwellian regime which had not lived up to his high

[16] Ibid., p. 858; for another account of the importance of Fleetwood and Disbrowe (and the estrangement of Broghill and Wolseley) see Cal. Clar. S.P., iv, 19.

[17] Brodrick to Hyde, 1 Mar. 1658 (Bodl., MS Clarendon 57, f. 175v).

[18] Thurloe S.P., vii, 56.

[19] Ibid., pp 56–7. The reference is to Deuteronomy, xxxiv.

[20] Ibid., pp 72, 87, 101, 115.

[21] Ibid., p. 295.

[22] Cork's diary (Chatsworth, Lismore MS 29, unfol.), 14 Aug. 1658.

expectations. Irish hopes of trade privileges, as enshrined in the proposed union bills of 1654 and 1656, had receded, as the new customs' farm began to have an impact; and the hoped-for militia had received a cold reception at Whitehall.[23] Throughout 1658 Henry Cromwell became increasingly concerned about the disaffection of key Old Protestants, including Sir Hardress Waller and Sir Charles Coote, and pressed his father to reward them with land or titles and places on the Irish council.[24] Broghill was not the only Old Protestant to feel that his loyalty to the House of Cromwell had not been reciprocated.

Oliver Cromwell's death on 3 September 1658 forced Broghill back into the political arena. This was a political disaster, as well as a private bereavement. Henry Cromwell, in the midst of his expressions of personal loss, told Thurloe that 'If wee may speak as men, if no settlement bee made in his lifetime, can wee be secure from the lust of ambitious men?'[25] Broghill remained stoical (at least in his letter to Thurloe of 17 September), recalling once again his favourite biblical passage concerning the death of King David's child, for 'when God's pleasure was declared, he knew it 'twas a duty cheerfully to yeeld unto it'.[26] His sister, Lady Ranelagh, was less phlegmatic. 'I must owne not to have received the news of his highness's death unmovedly . . . I doubt his loss wil be a growing affliction upon these nations, and that we shal learne to value him more by missing him.'[27]

It was obvious to all in the government that Oliver's successor, his eldest son, Richard Cromwell, did not share his father's influence over the army; but Broghill was hopeful that his regime might still survive, 'if his friends stick to him'.[28] Parliament had already been called, and there were fears that the army interest would be able to dominate the assembly, reverse many of the reforms instituted through the Humble Petition, and seize power for themselves.[29] Alongside the military men, significant numbers of commonwealthsmen and crypto-royalists made use of the lifting of the council's powers to exclude M.P.s under the Humble Petition to seek election, with the intention of bringing down the protectorate once and for all.[30] In the face of such strong opposition elements, Henry Cromwell and Broghill set about arranging the Irish elections in the same manner as in previous years.[31] Of the 29 identifiable M.P.s returned for Ireland, only three (Thomas Sadleir, John Duckenfield and John Brett)

---

[23] Barnard, 'Protestant interest', p. 234.
[24] *Thurloe S.P.*, vi, 734, 773–4; ibid., vii, 155, 176.
[25] Ibid., p. 376.
[26] Ibid., p. 399.
[27] Ibid., pp 395–6.
[28] Ibid., p. 399.
[29] Ibid., p. 369. For the increasing influence of Fleetwood, Disbrowe, Sydenham and their allies see ibid., pp 146, 192, 269, 490.
[30] Ibid., pp 550, 588–9.
[31] Ibid., pp 553, 573–4.

can be classed as supporters of the army interest. Of the remainder, sixteen were Old Protestants and ten were Englishmen supported by Henry Cromwell or by Old Protestant grandees. Broghill's own interest group included the Cork M.P.s, Francis Foulke and Maurice Fenton, and he probably had a hand in the election of four Englishmen: William Halsey, Henry Markham, Thomas Stanley and Thomas Waller (the last elected through Broghill's influence with Sir John King in Sligo, Leitrim and Roscommon).[32] All was not entirely plain sailing, however. There were worrying signs of disunity among the Old Protestants during and after the elections. Broghill found his authority in County Cork challenged by his former ally, Vincent Gookin, who tried to get his own men elected;[33] and during the parliamentary session, Arthur Annesley, M.P. for Dublin, broke ranks, and joined the republicans in calling for a separate Irish parliament – against the unionist line promoted by Broghill and Henry Cromwell.[34] But overall, the Irish M.P.s still formed a united body, which could muster as many as 24 votes in favour of Richard Cromwell's government.

The Irish members were backed by a solid core of Scottish M.P.s. Broghill's electoral influence in Scotland was much less than it had been in 1656, although he still corresponded with the Resolutioners at Edinburgh, and promised Thurloe 'to doe what lyes in me, wher I have any interrest in Scotland' as well as Ireland.[35] More importantly, George Monck had by now changed his political views, coming closer to the stance of Broghill, even to the extent of trying to exclude the troublesome marquess of Argyll from sitting at Westminster.[36] With Monck's careful management, the returns for Scotland included reliable Scotsmen and members of the administration, but also a number of eminent London lawyers and relatives of the House of Cromwell.

---

[32] See History of Parliament, 1640–60 section, draft biographies for details; for Stanley see Cork's diary (Chatsworth, Lismore MS 29, unfol.), 6 Jan. 1659; for Waller see Broghill to Cork, 23 Jan. 1659 (ibid., Lismore MS 30, no. 72); and *Thurloe S.P.*, vii, 593, 597.

[33] T. C. Barnard, 'Lord Broghill, Vincent Gookin and the Cork elections of 1659' in *E.H.R.*, lxxxviii (1973), pp 352–65. Gookin's relations with the Boyles had been tense since 1658, when he sought to prevent the earl of Barrymore from securing his lands in Co. Cork: see Thomas Herbert to Thurloe, 27 Oct. 1658 (Bodl., Rawl. A.61, ff 380r–5v).

[34] Patrick Little, 'The first unionists?: Irish Protestant attitudes to union with England, 1653–9' in *I.H.S.*, xxxii (2000), pp 54–7.

[35] *Thurloe S.P.*, vii, 573; for Broghill's contacts with Scotland in this period see Robert Wood to Hartlib, 13 Oct. 1658 (S.U.L., Hartlib MS 7/116/1A); same to same, 3 Nov. 1658 (ibid., Hartlib MS 33/1/30A); for his continuing contacts with the Resolutioners see Stephen, *Register*, ii, pp 137, 148–9.

[36] Monck to Samuel Disbrowe, 24 Mar. 1659 (B.L., Eg. MS 2519, f. 19r); *Thurloe S.P.*, vii, 584. See also ibid., p. 388, where Monck advises Richard Cromwell to reduce the army, encourage the Presbyterians, and bring Broghill and other former 'kinglings' into his council.

As in 1656, they promised to provide a solid phalanx in support of the regime.[37] The enemies of the protectorate were in no doubt of the significance of this group 'chosen by the Pretender's Interest . . . most of them being chosen at Whitehall, whereof some had hardly been ever nearer Scotland than Grayes-Inn', and sought to question the legality of their sitting in a parliament which, according to the Humble Petition, was elected under the pre-1653 franchise.[38] The concern of the commonwealthsmen was heightened by memories of the impact of the Irish and Scottish votes in 1657, when they had acted as Broghill's shock troops. But the 1659 parliament proved much more difficult to manage, as Broghill would soon discover.

The third protectorate parliament marked the Indian summer of Broghill's relationship with the Cromwellian state. His arrival in London was delayed by the Cork election dispute and another attack of gout, but he took his seat in the Other House on 1 March.[39] He soon became a powerful figure in Whitehall, with far more influence with Richard Cromwell than he had ever enjoyed with Richard's father. On 15 March 1659 Lady Ranelagh told the earl of Cork of the position of Broghill, 'to whom H[is] H[ighness] is very oblige-ing visiting him at his owne lodgings telling him his thoughts wth great freedome, & sending for him wh[e]n he thinks [he] has need of advise, he much invites him to fix in this Country & has offered to make him of his Council here'.[40] Lady Ranelagh's comments support those of Edmund Ludlow, who identified Broghill as one of three men who constituted Richard's Cromwell's 'cabinet council'.[41] Broghill was a regular attender at the Other House,[42] and he supported Henry Cromwell over a controversial court martial case from mid-March,[43] but his ability to initiate legislation was severely hampered by the refusal of the commons, stirred up by the commonwealthsmen, to agree to any transactions with the Other House.[44] This dispute provoked a long and

[37] J. A. Casada, 'The Scottish representatives in Richard Cromwell's parliament' in *S.H.R.*, li (1972), pp 124–47.
[38] Slingsby Bethell, *Narrative . . . of the late parliament* (9 June 1659), pp 7, 11; for the problems of the franchise see Patrick Little, 'Irish representation in the protectorate parliaments' in *Parliamentary History* (forthcoming).
[39] Broghill to Cork, 11 Jan. 1659 (Chatsworth, Lismore MS 30, no. 63); Lady Ranelagh to Cork, 18 Feb. 1659 (ibid., no. 95); *Thurloe S.P.*, vii, 600; *H.M.C. House of Lords MSS*, n.s., iv, 543.
[40] Lady Ranelagh to Cork, 15 Mar. 1659 (Chatsworth, Lismore MS 30, no. 99).
[41] *Ludlow memoirs* ii, 61. The others were Philip Jones and the protector's brother-in-law (and future bishop of Chester), Dr Wilkins. I am grateful to Dr Beverly Adams for discussion of this point.
[42] *H.M.C. House of Lords MSS*, n.s., iv, 543–66; he is only mentioned as taking an active role twice (ibid., pp 551, 563).
[43] Morgan to Henry Cromwell, 22 and 29 Mar. 1659 (B.L., Lansdowne MS 823, ff 265r, 278r); *Thurloe S.P.*, vii, 639.
[44] For factionalism see Lord Aungier to Henry Cromwell, 15 Feb. 1659 (B.L., Lansdowne MS 823, ff 218r–9r); Sankey to same, 8 Mar. 1659 (ibid., f. 247r–v); Derek Hirst, 'Concord and discord in Richard Cromwell's House of Commons' in *E.H.R.*, ciii (1988), pp 339–58.

furious debate about the right of Scottish and Irish M.P.s to sit at all, as they had (predictably) been almost unanimous in their support of the government.[45] The parliamentary union was dissected, and English hostility to both the Scots and Irish came to the fore in an acrimonious debate. In this climate, a new Irish union bill (prepared by Dudley Loftus, probably on Henry Cromwell's instructions) could not even be introduced into the commons.[46] Meanwhile, the protector's supporters were threatened from another front, as the army officers, Fleetwood and 'the parties of Desborough and Lambert', set up their own council, in an attempt to put pressure on the government.[47] Broghill led moves to resist the army, opposing them 'so effectually' that 'it was appre-hended he had broken their design'.[48] Such hopes were short-lived, however. With Broghill and the traditional business managers confined to the emas-culated Other House, and the commonwealthsmen and crypto-royalists increasingly dominant in the commons, the protector's position in parliament became untenable. On 21 April Richard Cromwell held an emergency meeting 'w[i]th the L[ord] Broghill Fiennes, Thurlo, Woolsey, Wh[itelocke] & some others, whether it were not fitt to dissolve the present Parlem[en]t'.[49] Following the counsel of his advisers, Richard Cromwell closed parliament on 22 April. By 6 May, the protectorate had been abolished in favour of a renewed commonwealth, the old Rump Parliament had returned to Westminster, and a committee of safety, chaired by Fleetwood, would soon have a firm grasp on the reins of power.

The dissolution of the 1659 parliament, the collapse of the protectorate, and the growing power of the army interest in England, caused something close to panic among the Old Protestants. The re-establishment of a commonwealth regime awoke unhappy memories for Broghill and his allies, raising once again the spectre of military government in Ireland, the loss of land rights, free trade and hard-won legal and religious privileges, and the destruction of everything else that the Cromwellian union had promised. The speed with which Broghill returned to Ireland may indicate his not unreasonable fear of arrest by the new regime: he left London on 29 April, without having time to take leave of Whitelocke or Thurloe;[50] landed at Waterford on 9 May, met the earl of Cork

---

[45] Bethell, *Narrative . . . of the late parliament*, pp 5, 7, 9–11.

[46] Little, 'The first unionists?', pp 54–6.

[47] *Thurloe S.P.*, vii, 612.

[48] *Boyle's Works*, vi, 121; the detailed account of Broghill's confrontation with the army officers provided by Thomas Morrice, in which Richard Cromwell is portrayed as Broghill's puppet, cannot be corroborated, and must be treated with caution (Morrice, *Memoirs*, pp 27–31).

[49] *Whitelocke diary*, p. 512; see also C. H. Firth (ed.), *The Clarke papers: selections from the papers of William Clarke* (4 vols, 1891–1901), iii, 212; *Cal. Clar. S.P.*, iv, 176.

[50] Broghill to Whitelocke, 29 Apr. 1659 (Longleat, Whitelocke papers xviii, f. 129r); *Thurloe S.P.*, vii, 665. Thomas Stanley remained in London to attend the protector on Broghill's behalf: see Stanley to Henry Cromwell, 11 May 1659 (B.L., Lansdowne MS 823, f. 316r).

(who had hurried south from Dublin) outside Clonmel on 18 May, and attended Henry Cromwell in Dublin soon afterwards.[51]

There was no question of seeking a 'three nations' solution to this situation. Necessarily, Broghill's priorities centred on Ireland. His main concern was to reinforce Henry Cromwell's position, calm the army officers, and maintain the stability of the country.[52] As he told Lady Ranelagh on 25 May, 'blessed be god wee are stil in peace & through his mercy like to be for being unsencible how probably any divisions amo[n]gst ourselves might open too large a doore for any old Com[mo]n enemye to enter in'. He said he had persuaded the officers to moderate their petition to the newly restored Rump, and now he was confident that 'the Parl[iamen]t may expect al due obedience from hence', he considered that his responsibility to keep the peace in Ireland had finished, and 'I am to morow return[ing] home to live a quiet country life w[hi]ch I much preffer to that of either a courtier or statesman'.[53] The resignation of Henry Cromwell as lord lieutenant on 15 June confirmed Broghill's decision to retire.[54] When he wrote to Whitelocke from Ballymaloe in County Cork on 23 June, he described himself as one who 'now talkes with no other but his Thoughts, his small Library, his Wife & children, his Plowmen, & shepherds. & yet . . . would not change that life, for a kings, or wh[at] is more a Gen[era]lls'.[55] Even accounting for the exaggeration of Broghill's account, it is significant that, for the third time in two years, he had announced his determination to withdraw from the political process. The arrival of a hostile parliamentary commission and the appointment of his old enemy, Edmund Ludlow, as commander-in-chief in the next few months – both events horribly reminiscent of the early 1650s – did little to change Broghill's mind.[56] The fall of the protectorate had deepened the sense of disillusion which had characterised his political career since Cromwell's rejection of the crown in 1657.

---

[51] Chatsworth, Lady Burlington's Journal, 1656–88, unfol.: 9 May 1659; Robert Wood to Hartlib, 11 May 1659 (S.U.L., Hartlib MS 33/1/57B); Cork's diary (Chatsworth, Lismore MS 29, unfol.), 28 May 1659.

[52] For the similarity of Henry Cromwell's view with that of Broghill, see *Thurloe S.P.*, vii, 674.

[53] Broghill to Lady Ranelagh, 25 May 1659 (Longleat, Whitelocke papers xix, f. 129r).

[54] *Thurloe S.P.*, vii, 683–4.

[55] Broghill to Whitelocke, 23 June 1659 (Longleat, Whitelocke papers xix, f. 31r).

[56] Aidan Clarke, '1659 and the road to restoration' in Jane Ohlmeyer (ed.), *Ireland from independence to occupation, 1641–60* (Cambridge, 1995), pp 243–4.

II

In May 1659 Broghill had told Lady Ranelagh that his greatest worry was that disunity in the British state could give opportunities to the 'old Com[mo]n enemye' – the Stuarts. But the royalists on the continent had already marked Broghill as a potential ally, and a likely supporter of the restoration of Charles Stuart as Charles II.[57] On 13 May there were reports that Broghill might prove useful 'if his hearte dare walke with his tongue'; and in June there were rumours that 'Broughill and Coute [i.e. Sir Charles Coote], etc., are in ye heade of 6000 men, declareinge against this present government'.[58] In fact, it was not difficult for Broghill to make contact with the royalist court in exile, and, as in 1648–9, such contacts should not be assumed to indicate support for the royalist cause. Many of these links with the continent were first established through Cromwell's own spy network. As president of Scotland Broghill had collaborated with Thurloe and others in running an intelligence system which gathered information from the continent, and as early as April 1656 he was planning his own initiatives to get agents into Spain.[59] After 1657 he was kept informed of developments by his ally from the Scottish administration, George Downing, who was now envoy in Holland. Among his agents in Flanders in 1656–8 were Sir Robert Walsh (or Welsh), an Irishman who was recruited 'to live in the King Court, & certify to him the truth of that businesse', and was finally arrested in Brussels in June 1658.[60] He also employed a Scottish colonel, Henry Blackadder, as an agent,[61] and an 'intelligencer' at Bruges called Owen.[62] Broghill discussed plans to send Blackadder and another Scotsman, James Borthwick, to Portugal in September 1657.[63] In May 1658 Broghill received several letters from Holland.[64] Such channels of communication could easily be reversed, as the royalists in exile began to court Broghill in 1659–60.

---

[57] The earliest possible contact (after 1649) is a letter from Charles II to Broghill, provisionally dated to March 1654 (see *Cal. Clar. S.P.*, ii, 329), but this seems to have elicited no response.

[58] G. F. Warner (ed.), *The Nicholas papers: correspondence of Sir Edward Nicholas, secretary of state* (4 vols., 1886–1920), iv, 140, 162; see also *Cal. Clar. S.P.*, iv. 210.

[59] *Cal. S.P. Dom.*, 1656–7, p. 375; *Thurloe S.P.*, iv, 700, 725–6.

[60] Broghill to Walsh, 17 and 21 Nov. 1656 (P.R.O., S.P. 77/31, ff 429r, 430r); relation of Walsh's 'carryage' in England, c.Feb. 1657 (ibid., ff 449–53); see also receipts for Walsh, Nov. 1656 (P.R.O., S.P. 18/154, ff 226v, 298r, 300v); *Thurloe S.P.*, vii, 188; *Cal. Clar. S.P.*, iii, 291, 366–7. I am grateful to Dr Andrew Barclay for drawing my attention to the third of these references.

[61] *Thurloe S.P.*, v, 655; receipts for Blackadder (P.R.O., S.P. 18/154, ff 226v, 301r).

[62] *Cal. Clar. S.P.*, iv, 366–7; *Cal. S.P. Dom. 1656–7*, p. 294.

[63] *Thurloe S.P.*, vi, 538; for Blackadder see Edward Jenks, 'Some correspondence of Thurloe and Meadowe' in *E.H.R.*, vii (1892), p. 738.

[64] Broghill's accounts, 1658 (Petworth, Orrery MS 13192, unfol.).

His contacts with the continent were also personal. Again, these con-nexions could be equivocal. Thomas Howard, the earl of Suffolk's brother and brother-in-law of Lady Broghill, was a notorious double-agent. In early 1657 Howard was already suspected by the royalists of passing information to Broghill, through ciphered letters which were immediately passed on to Cromwell.[65] In August 1658 his private papers, including information of his 'journey into England', fell into the hands of George Downing at The Hague, who recruited him for the Cromwellian intelligence service.[66] From then on, Downing received information from Howard, who continued to have access to the Stuart court.[67] Other, less uncertain contacts included Broghill's sister-in-law, Lady Kinalmeaky, who was influential in court circles throughout the 1640s and 1650s. The Boyles had tried to protect Lady Kinalmeaky's Irish estates during the Irish wars, and she had been involved in attempts to win Broghill over to the royalist side in 1648–9.[68] As a confidante of Henrietta Maria, and a friend of the duke of Buckingham and Lord Jermyn (among others) in the 1650s, Lady Kinalmeaky was a figure of some importance in the exiled court at Paris, and in the days before the restoration she corresponded with the marquess of Ormond in Flanders.[69] She was also on friendly terms with another of Broghill's political associates, the ambassador to France, Sir William Lockhart.[70]

With the fall of the protectorate, such connexions became of greater importance. We know that in the early summer of 1659 Broghill was able to establish regular communications with the exiled court through three main routes. The first of these was through another Thomas Howard, son of the earl of Berkshire, who was close to the royal court in exile. Thomas Howard had been in Broghill's group of friends before the Civil War, and they had fought a duel over the hand of Mrs Harrison in 1640;[71] by the late 1640s he had been appointed master of horse to the Princess Royal on the continent;[72] and in June 1656 he was arrested while spying in England.[73] His brother, Henry Howard, had already been given a pass to go to France in 1655 on Broghill's request,[74] and it was probably this Thomas Howard (rather than Suffolk's

[65] *Cal. Clar. S.P.*, iii, 240.

[66] *Thurloe S.P.*, vii, 347–8.

[67] Ibid., pp 444–5, 457.

[68] See above, ch. 2.

[69] *Thurloe S.P.*, i, 735; Warner (ed.), *Nicholas papers*, i, 174; ii, 297, 335; iii, 286; *Cal. Clar. S.P.*, iii, 94, 207; iv, 90; Lady Kinalmeaky to Ormond, 30 Apr. 1660 (Bodl., MS Carte 214, ff 81–4).

[70] Lockhart to duchess of Hamilton, 10 Feb. 1658 (N.A.S., Hamilton papers, GD 406/1/2532).

[71] *Cal. S.P. Dom.*, 1639–40, p. 365; Grosart, *Lismore papers*, ser. 1, v, 121.

[72] *Cal. S.P. Dom.*, 1645–7, pp 525, 577.

[73] *Thurloe S.P.*, v, 169.

[74] *Cal. S.P. Dom.*, 1655, p. 580.

brother) who was in contact with Broghill in the early summer of 1659. On 3 June, Howard wrote to Charles Stuart, saying that 'I am by my Lord Broughill desired to come for Ierland and [he] assurs me he will doe all things that may advance your service.'[75] Both Thomas and Henry Howard were implicated in Sir George Booth's royalist rebellion in 1659, and by the end of the year, Thomas had returned to Flanders.[76]

In the early summer of 1659 Thomas Howard had been in close touch with Broghill's younger brother, Francis Boyle (now Viscount Shannon).[77] Francis had made no secret of his support of the Stuarts since the 1640s, and in the early 1650s moved freely between England, Ireland and the royalist court in exile.[78] He may have owed his freedom of movement to his brother's influence, but it was nevertheless a strange situation, especially as Francis's wife was one of Charles II's early mistresses.[79] In the late 1650s Francis's principal role now seems to have been as an intermediary between Broghill and the royal court. In May 1657 he was taken to Holland by a government ship,[80] and in June 1658 he approached Downing for help in a project to send horses to a 'friend' to serve the elector of Brandenburg. Despite the suspicions of Brandenburg's connexions with the Stuarts (not to mention the House of Austria), Downing asked Thurloe to grant the request, because Francis was Broghill's brother.[81] Francis was still in Holland in October,[82] but was back in Ireland by the end of the year: he met Cork and Broghill at Youghal in December 1658, and dined with them on 27 January 1659.[83] He remained in Ireland until April 1659, when he crossed to England,[84] and by the end of May had gone back to Holland, where he met Downing to discuss the situation in England.[85] Sir Daniel O'Neill told Hyde the details of this last encounter, which Francis had relayed to him only 'an hower after', with its intimations that not only Admiral Mountagu, but also Downing himself, were 'resolved never to serve those that governed' in England.[86] The collaboration between Broghill's friend, George Downing, and his brother, Francis Boyle, shows the intricacy of the network which Broghill could have exploited. More

---

[75] Howard to Charles Stuart, 3 June 1659 (Bodl., MS Clarendon 61, f. 87r–v).

[76] Bodl., MS Eng. Hist. e. 309, p. 5; *The letterbook of John Viscount Mordaunt, 1658–60*, ed. Mary Coate (1945), pp 37, 80; David Underdown, *Royalist conspiracy in England, 1649–60* (1979), pp 280–1.

[77] Howard to Charles Stuart, 3 June 1659 (Bodl., MS Clarendon 61, f. 87v).

[78] *Cal. S.P. Dom.*, 1650, p. 482; *Cal. S.P. Dom.*, 1651–2, p. 558.

[79] Warner (ed.), *Nicholas papers*, i, 174; she had borne the king an illegitimate daughter in 1650: see *Complete Peerage*, vi, 706.

[80] *Cal. S.P. Dom.*, 1656–7, pp 382, 388.

[81] *Thurloe S.P.*, vii, 182.

[82] *Cal. Clar. S.P.*, iv, 88.

[83] Cork's diary (Chatsworth, Lismore MS 29, unfol.), 11 Dec. 1658, 27 Jan. 1659.

[84] Cork's diary (ibid.), 19 Apr. 1659.

[85] *Cal. Clar. S.P.*, iv, 211.

[86] O'Neill to Hyde, 27 May 1659 (Bodl., MS Clarendon 61, f. 19r).

remarkable than his range of royalist contacts was the fact that they remained largely unused.

Broghill's reluctance to support royalist intrigue can best be seen in his relations with his wife's brother-in-law, Sir Edward Villiers. Villiers had been heavily involved in the royalist conspiracy known as the Sealed Knot since the early 1650s, and was one of the leaders of the Booth rebellion. As early as April 1659 Villiers claimed that he had made 'some progres in discoursing at [a] distance with Ld. Broghall . . . and having vowed secrecy on[e] to the other you may not impart it to any but the King there and to none here not any of our Knott'.[87] According to Underdown, Villiers fell out with Sir Edward Hyde in 1659 because of his refusal to negotiate directly with Broghill, a position he maintained until March 1660, when he reluctantly agreed to persuade his brother-in-law to join the Stuart cause.[88] But the surviving correspondence suggests that the problem lay less with Villiers' hesitancy than with Broghill's reluctance to go out on a limb. In early June Henry Cromwell was targeted by royalist agents, hopeful that he would 'refuse' to join the new commonwealth regime, 'and rather than fayle to defend himself, arme both the Scotch & Irish',[89] joining with Monck in Scotland, Mountagu (with the fleet) and Lockhart (governor of Dunkirk) in support of the Stuarts. Ireland was to be the base for an invasion of England: 'Many men wish hee could transport Himself either to Chester or Levirpoole, & his Friends in Munster to Bristol, and that the risinge weer concurrent to the expectation of his landing.'[90] As the last comment suggests, Broghill was a key player in such an invasion, and Hyde told Villiers on 10 June that 'the King lookes upon Lord Brahall as a Person who may be most instrumentall to do him service there', instructing Villiers to go to Ireland immediately, 'and that you would assure Lord Brahall of all that hee can wish for from the king'.[91]

The royalist plan was hugely ambitious, and equally unlikely to succeed. With support from Henry Cromwell and Broghill in Ireland and Monck in Scotland, and with assistance from Mountagu's ships and the Dunkirk garrison, the English royalists and Presbyterians would rise against the new regime – in what would become Sir George Booth's rising in August – and bring about the restoration of the Stuarts by force. The failure of similarly grandiose strategies in 1648 and 1651 did not dent the enthusiasm of the armchair generals in France and Holland; but to Broghill and other experienced commanders, it must have looked dangerously unrealistic. In the event, Aidan Clarke is surely right to say that 'Broghill had sought an accommodation with the new regime early' – he sided with the commonwealth at the latest by the end of

---

[87] Villiers to Hyde, 11 Apr. 1659 (ibid., MS Clarendon 60, f. 340r).
[88] Underdown, *Royalist conspiracy*, pp 81–2, 220, 232, 270, 279, 290–1, 308.
[89] Brodrick to Hyde, 8 June 1659 (Bodl., MS Clarendon 61, f. 134r).
[90] Ibid.
[91] Hyde to Villiers, 10 June 1659 (Bodl., MS Clarendon 61, f. 154v).

May – and any remaining inclination on Broghill's part to join such royalist plots was smothered by Henry Cromwell's decision to submit to parliament on 15 June.[92] By July, Hyde had heard from Villiers of Broghill's failure to move further: news, he admitted, 'which wonderfully amazes us, his friends haveinge alwayes magnifyed his intencon to serve the Kinge in a proper season'.[93]

The leaky royalist intelligence service may itself have prevented Broghill from acting alone. The new government certainly had its suspicions. On hearing of Booth's royalist revolt in England, Ludlow summoned Broghill and his officers to Dublin 'to give satisfaction touching their acquiescence under the present government'.[94] There is no evidence of any direct connexion between Broghill and Booth, but many of his English relatives were implicated, including his brothers-in-law, the earl of Suffolk and Lord Goring.[95] There was even talk in royalist circles that the earl of Warwick (another brother-in-law, Charles Rich, who had succeeded to the title earlier in the year) might be drawn into the conspiracy.[96] In Munster, Broghill and his immediate family certainly monitored the situation in England with great interest. On 10 August Cork recorded that 'My Brother Broghill . . . broght mee newes of the rising in Engld by Sr Ge. Booth and others', and the next day Broghill set off for Dublin, returning on 21 August. Six days later speculation was ended with 'The newes came hither of the defeate of Sr George Booth'.[97] In the end, it is impossible to know whether Broghill and his family were merely impartial observers, or whether they intended to join Booth's uprising if it should prove successful. At the fall of the protectorate their range of political options had suddenly increased, to include the possibility of joining the royalists; but Broghill's obvious lack of enthusiasm for the Stuarts was to continue to be a stumbling-block.

Clarendon saw Broghill's eventual decision to support Charles II in factional terms: 'though he had great wariness in discovering his inclinations, as he had great guilt to restrain them, yet hated Lambert so much that he less feared the king, and so wished a safe opportunity to do him service'.[98] This was a shrewd comment. Broghill's disillusion with the protectorate had been caused, in part, by the continuing influence of Fleetwood and his cronies at Whitehall, and the likelihood of Lambert regaining the power he had lost in 1657. In 1659, the restored Rump could be tolerated by Broghill, but the attempt by his old enemies in the army interest, led by Lambert, to seize power in October 1659 seems to have roused him and his allies into action. News of the 'forcing'

[92] Aidan Clarke, *Prelude to restoration in Ireland: the end of the commonwealth, 1659–60* (Cambridge, 1999), p. 50.

[93] Hyde to Villiers, 11 July 1659 (Bodl., MS Clarendon 62, f. 54r).

[94] *Ludlow memoirs*, ii, 107; Clarke, *Prelude*, pp 71–2; others defended his reputation: see *Cal. S.P. Dom., 1659–60*, p. 13.

[95] Bodl., MS Eng. Hist. e. 309, pp 40, 42.

[96] *Mordaunt letterbook*, pp. 19, 21.

[97] Cork's diary (Chatsworth, Lismore MS 29, unfol.), 10–27 Aug. 1659.

[98] *Clarendon's history of the rebellion*, ed. W. D. Macray (6 vols, Oxford, 1888), vi, 213.

of parliament reached Munster on 22 October, and the increasing power of the army interest caused growing alarm in Ireland and Scotland over the next few weeks.[99] On 13 December a group of Old Protestant officers, supported by Sir Hardress Waller and Sir Theophilus Jones, seized Dublin, and went on to refuse Ludlow permission to land at Ringsend.[100] Broghill was in Munster at the time, but the involvement of a number of his friends in the Dublin coup, and the success of Old Protestant efforts to secure Munster garrisons in the days that followed, suggests that he was at least aware of events in the capital. By the end of December the Dublin officers had asked Broghill to join them in person, and from then on his influence over the army council was palpable.[101] On 11 January Broghill, newly arrived in Dublin, and other Irish officers wrote a letter to parliament, reporting their actions against Ludlow, and asserting their loyalty,[102] and at the end of the month Broghill was appointed to the army commission which replaced Ludlow.[103] Broghill also made contact with his old colleague from the Scottish council, George Monck, who had already declared against Lambert.[104] Monck commended his actions in 'putting the army into honest and sober hands', and thanked Broghill for offering military support for his campaign.[105] Confident that the Irish army had been neutralised, Monck advanced into England, where he found that Lambert's support had evaporated, leaving the road to London clear. His troops arrived in the capital on 3 February 1660. Meanwhile, apart from a dangerous incident when the regicide, Sir Hardress Waller, suddenly lost his nerve and tried to stage a counter-coup, the unity of the Old Protestant community continued to hold.[106] Once Waller had been arrested, Broghill and his allies declared their support for a 'free parliament' in England, and summoned their own 'General Convention' to sit in Dublin at the beginning of March.[107]

The General Convention confirmed Broghill's influence in Ireland. In the elections, Broghill himself was returned for Dublin University, and was able to secure seats for his friends and clients across the country. Munster was almost entirely under Boyle control, as Aidan Clarke has found: 'with the exception of an O'Brien family retainer in Clare, all of the Old Protestants belonged to one or more of three categories: they were relatives, former companions in arms or clients of the Boyle family'.[108] The only Old Protestant to rival Broghill was Sir Charles Coote, whose firm grip over Connaught and much of

[99] Cork's diary (Chatsworth, Lismore MS 29, unfol.), 22 Oct. 1659.
[100] Clarke, '1659 and the road to restoration', pp 250–3.
[101] Clarke, *Prelude*, pp 1, 117–19.
[102] Firth (ed.), *Clarke papers*, iv, 241–3.
[103] Clarke, *Prelude*, p. 146.
[104] Firth (ed.), *Clarke papers*, iv, 225–7.
[105] H.M.C. *Var. Coll.*, vi, 438–9.
[106] *Cal. S.P. Dom.*, 1659–60, p. 398.
[107] *Thurloe S.P.*, vii, 817–20.
[108] Clarke, *Prelude*, p. 236.

Ulster had continued despite the changes in government. The result of these elections determined the character of the General Convention, which was seen by contemporaries as 'variously a contest or partnership between Coote and Broghill'.[109] Most of its business was constructive, including an attempt to settle religious divisions and ensure the protection of property. Other matters – especially the status of the Stuarts – were carefully avoided for the time being, as threatening to divide the Protestant community, or to jeopardise its relations with Westminster. As the royalist, Marcus Trevor, told Ormond on 7 April, the whole nation was eager to accept the king, but that 'our 2 lords [Broghill and Coote] keep all things upon a very slow motion'.[110] He also suspected that Coote, rather than Broghill, was the man to be trusted by the royalists.[111]

Trevor's reservations are supported by other contemporary evidence. In his letters to Thurloe in mid-March, Broghill still protested that they had no intention 'to make Ireland a back door to let in Ch. Ste[wart] into England'.[112] In the same month, the royalist agent, Sir Edward Villiers, again made contact with Broghill, telling Hyde that 'I am renewing my negotiation with Ld Broghill though in Ireland who probably may be of great consideration again'.[113] In April Villiers was able to report that he had received assurances that Broghill 'will never decline me', and hoped their former friendship might work in the king's favour.[114] But by early May his efforts had come to nothing, and had aroused the suspicions of Hyde and others at court, leaving him to protest that 'I should comport my self in all perticulars as you required nor doe I make any perticular proffer to my Lord Broghill untill I see greater demonstration of his perticular affection'.[115] As in 1659, in the early months of 1660 Broghill had the opportunity to begin dialogue with the king, but he did not take it. Aidan Clarke is probably right to suggest that while Broghill was not prepared to resist the restoration of the Stuarts, he was wary of the implications of such a change for the Protestant interest in Ireland. Broghill approved of the 'Presbyterian Knot' at Westminster (whose members he described as 'eminent old Patriots') and agreed with their attempt to defend the gains of the 1650s (and especially the Irish land settlement and the more overtly Protestant church) in any deal with the new king. He also renewed his contacts with the Resolutioner ministers in Scotland, who were equally concerned at the religious settlement that might be forced upon them on the restoration of the Stuarts,[116] and who wrote to Broghill at the end of March

---

[109] Ibid., p. 239.
[110] Trevor to Ormond, 7 Apr. 1660 (Bodl., MS Carte 30, f. 559).
[111] Clarke, *Prelude*, p. 278.
[112] *Thurloe S.P.*, vii, 859.
[113] Villiers to Hyde, 2 Mar. 1660 (Bodl., MS Clarendon 70, f. 66r).
[114] Same to same, 13 Apr. 1660 (ibid., MS Clarendon 71, f. 284v).
[115] Same to same, 1 May 1660 (ibid., MS 72, f. 121r).
[116] Clarke, *Prelude*, pp 276–7, 287–90.

1660 'as a good friend to the true Interests of Jesus Christ' who would ensure 'a blessed settlement upon foundations of religion & righteousness'.[117] As the weeks went by, the chances of a preferential settlement receded, and, as a result, Broghill continued to have little enthusiasm for the return of the Stuarts, leaving the initiative to others, notably his old associate, George Monck.

Broghill's indolence in the early months of 1660 contrasted with the activity of his brother, the earl of Cork.[118] Cork had left Ireland for England in late November 1659, arriving on 2 December.[119] He had acted as Broghill's eyes and ears in Dublin on previous occasions: now he would keep his brother informed of developments in London. Broghill had other friends in London, including Thurloe,[120] but Cork was his principal agent at this time. The earl's contacts in England were exceptionally good: apart from family members (notably Lady Ranelagh and Robert Boyle, with whom he 'consulted about my brother Broghills affayres' on 28 January) his social circle in early 1660 included the countesses of Devonshire and Sussex, the marquess of Dorchester, the earls of Manchester, Warwick and Newport.[121] Manchester and Warwick had both been identified as royalists in earlier months;[122] and Newport would introduce Cork to Monck in early April 1660.[123] Soon afterwards, Cork was in contact with Sir Edward Villiers in London,[124] and had also established direct links with the royal court, sending letters to Ormond's secretary and Francis Boyle.[125] Cork's relations with Francis were particularly close at this time.[126] With his own royalist contacts at home and abroad, this group might have provided Broghill with a wide range of influence with Charles II when the time was right. But it was not as a go-between but as an intelligence agent that Cork would prove of most use to Broghill. In the six months between December 1659 and May 1660, Cork's diary revealed that he wrote at least

---

[117] Dickson et al. to Broghill, 28 Mar. 1660 (Petworth, Orrery MS 13223(3)).

[118] Barnard, 'Cork', pp 183–4.

[119] Chatsworth, Lady Burlington's Journal, 1656–88, unfol.: 2 Dec. 1659.

[120] *Thurloe S.P.*, vii, 911–12.

[121] Chatsworth, Burlington's Journal, unfol.: 2 Dec. 1659–5 Mar. 1660, passim.

[122] *Mordaunt letterbook*, pp 8, 19, 21. Another former parliamentarian with continuing links with Broghill was the earl of Northumberland, who supported Broghill's unsuccessful candidacy for Cockermouth in the Convention Parliament in April 1660: see letters of burgesses of Cockermouth to Hugh Potter and earl of Northumberland, 10 Nov. 1660 (Cumbria R.O. (Carlisle), Leconfield MSS, D/Lec/107, unfol.). I owe this reference to Dr David Scott.

[123] Chatsworth, Burlington's Journal, unfol.: 5 Apr. 1660.

[124] Villiers to Hyde, 13 Apr. 1660 (Bodl., MS Clarendon 71, f. 284v).

[125] Cork to Sir George Lane, 12 Apr. 1660 (ibid., MS Carte 30, f. 563); Chatsworth, Burlington's Journal, unfol.: 12 Apr., 8 May, 17 May 1660.

[126] Ibid., entries for 3 Mar., 12 Apr., 8 May, 17 May 1660; according to Villiers, Cork was certainly passing intelligence from Broghill to the royal court at this time (see *Cal. Clar. S.P.*, iv, 659).

twenty-seven letters to Broghill in Ireland. These included weekly reports and news of specific events. He wrote to his brother on the day after Monck's arrival at Whitehall on 3 February, and on 11 February, after Monck's warm reception in London, 'I wrot to Broghill this newes'. Similarly, Cork wrote to Broghill on 21 February (the day after the secluded M.P.s were readmitted to parliament) and 17 March (the day after the Rump was dissolved). On 21 March the earl of Manchester came to Cork's house, occasioning another letter to Broghill, and on 1 May, when parliament voted to recognise Charles II as king, 'I did give my brother Broghill notice of this excellent newes.' As a sign of royalist goodwill, on 11 May Cork forwarded to Broghill his commission as president of Munster, which had been ordered by the English council of state four days earlier, and presented Broghill with a post which he had coveted for fifteen years.[127] Finally, on 19 May 1660, Cork noted 'I wrote to my bro[ther] Broghill inviting him speedily to come over in case hee co[u]ld leave the governement there in power to act.'[128] Having left it perilously late, in late May Broghill at last signalled his support of the Old Protestants' declaration for Charles II, and prepared himself to come over to England, with the hope that his royalist connexions were strong enough, and his usefulness to the new regime sufficiently obvious, to outweigh his previous support of the 'usurper'.

Broghill had monitored the situation in England and on the continent for more than a year before making his move. Apart from his role in creating the General Convention in Dublin (which was not in itself a sign of royalism), throughout the pre-restoration period Broghill had chosen to be a passive observer rather than an active participant. In the spring and summer of 1660 he had refused royalist blandishments, preferring to wait and see. As Aidan Clarke has commented, there is is little doubt that Broghill's acceptance of the restoration was pragmatic at heart, rather than borne of any enthusiasm for the restored king.[129] In promising peace and stability after a year of chaos, Charles Stuart's restoration had obvious practical advantages for Broghill and his kind. But something was missing. Whereas Broghill had been fully committed to the Cromwellian monarchy, with its providential overtones, its advantageous political and religious policies, and the prominence it promised not only for himself but also for the Irish Protestant interest and their friends in Scotland, his attitude towards the restoration of the Stuarts was decidedly lukewarm. His active support for a monarchical solution in 1657 had given way to a passive acceptance in 1660. Broghill certainly had the personal connexions with the court in exile which would have allowed him to commit himself much earlier than he did; he also enjoyed the influence within the political and military structures in Ireland to make such a gamble likely to

---

[127] Chatsworth, Burlington's Journal, unfol.: 11 May 1660.
[128] Ibid., dates as specified.
[129] Clarke, '1659 and the road to restoration', p. 263.

succeed, perhaps as early as December 1659. But he remained uncommitted until the restoration was a foregone conclusion. For a man known for his decisive actions and strong views, his reticence in 1660 speaks volumes.

III

From the spring of 1660 Broghill found himself with little choice but to submit to the inevitable, and work with the restored monarchy of Charles II. At first, he found his reception by the new king and his advisers rather cool, possibly as a result of Sir Charles Coote's attempts to play up his own part in the restoration, at the expense of his rival. Viscount Shannon was on hand to put his brother's case, however, and with the intervention of the earl of Cork and his friend Sir Edward Hyde (now lord chancellor and earl of Clarendon), Broghill was eventually allowed to attend the king in August. In the next few months, Broghill's fortunes began to change, and he was confirmed as lord president of Munster on 21 August, created earl of Orrery on 5 September, and on 26 October given a share in the caretaker management of Ireland as lord justice – a post his father had held thirty years before. As lord justice, the new earl of Orrery organised the Irish parliament which met in 1661, and he had some control over Irish policy in general until the arrival of the lord lieutenant, the newly elevated duke of Ormond, in July 1662. Despite his removal from his role in the Dublin administration, Orrery seems to have remained in royal favour until the fall of Clarendon in 1667. Thereafter, he became involved in a faction-fight with Ormond, which drew in the big guns within the English court, and resulted in both the duke's dismissal as lieutenant and Orrery's impeachment by the English parliament in 1669. Successive lords lieutenant remained suspicious of Orrery's influence, and in 1672, with the earl of Essex newly arrived at Dublin Castle, Orrery's local authority was curtailed with the abolition of the presidency of Munster. Ormond's re-appointment as lord lieutenant in 1677 angered Orrery, and the last two years of his life were marked by increasing tension between him and the Dublin government, not helped by the earl's worsening temper as he gradually succumbed to the gout which had plagued him throughout his adult life. He died, aged 58, on 16 October 1679.[130]

In the years after 1660, certain themes recur, and an exploration of these helps to explain Orrery's earlier activities as Lord Broghill. Surprisingly little close work has been done on his career as the earl of Orrery. Toby Barnard has teased out certain aspects, usually as part of studies of other nobles (notably Ormond and the second earl of Cork) or of the 'Protestant interest' as a whole, but has yet to attempt a study of the man in his own right.[131] Other historians

---

[130] This paragraph is based on Lynch, *Orrery*, pp 106–234.
[131] See Barnard, 'Protestant interest' and 'Cork', passim; also Toby Barnard, 'Conclusion.

have either relied on the unsatisfactory biography penned by Thomas Morrice (which is as unreliable after 1660 as before), or have resorted to the arcana of literary criticism, whose exponents have searched Orrery's published works, and especially his 'rhymed heroic plays', for clues as to his private attitudes during and after the restoration.[132] These eight plays, which were mostly written between 1662 and 1672,[133] have been studied by Kathleen Lynch, Mita Choudhury and Nancy Klein Maguire, all of whom are interested in using them as autobiographical sources, revealing Orrery's conscious, subconscious and even unconscious preoccupations. For Lynch, 'these heroic plays . . . offer a valuable insight on Orrery's character'.[134] Maguire goes further, claiming that 'the sub-genre of the rhymed heroic play is his biography'.[135] All three follow Morrice's line that Orrery was a penitent, a former royalist who had served Cromwell reluctantly, and after 1660 was able to return to his true vocation, as a loyal subject of the Stuarts. From then on, the interpretations differ. Choudhury has portrayed Orrery as a propagandist for Charles II,[136] while Maguire sees his dramatic work as marked by an overwhelming sense of guilt: 'Orrery apparently was forced to write his confession in his plays . . . [his] rhymed heroic plays neurotically repeat the themes of usurpation and restoration until they are sufficiently worn down to be forgotten', and his writings as a whole represent 'an exorcism, in ritualistic reparation' for his past sins.[137] Recently, the work of John Kerrigan has provided a more measured approach to the plays, taking greater account of Orrery's Irish Protestant identity, and concluding that his aim was not to eulogise Charles II, nor to exorcise his own demons, but to exert political influence over the new regime: 'Orrery strikes me as calculating: both critical of Carolean policy and cannily defensive.' According to Kerrigan, Orrery's targets were the former Irish Catholic rebels who now sought to regain their influence (and estates) in Ireland, and the increasingly pro-French foreign policy favoured by the monarch himself.[138]

Settling and unsettling Ireland: the Cromwellian and Williamite revolutions' in Jane Ohlmeyer (ed.), *Ireland from independence to occupation, 1641–1660* (Cambridge, 1995), pp 265–91; Toby Barnard, 'Introduction: the dukes of Ormonde', in Toby Barnard and Jane Fenlon (eds), *The dukes of Ormonde, 1610–1745* (Woodbridge, 2000), pp 1–53; Toby Barnard, 'The political, material and mental culture of the Cork settlers, c.1650–1700' in P. O'Flanagan and C. G. Buttimer (eds), *Cork: history and society* (Dublin, 1993), pp 309–67.
[132] Raymond Gillespie, 'The religion of the first duke of Ormond' in Barnard and Fenlon (eds), *Dukes of Ormonde*, p. 105.
[133] Apart from the 'heroic' plays, and the romance, *Parthenissa*, Orrery published two comedies, poetry, and, in 1677, his *Treatise on the art of war*: see Lynch, *Orrery*, pp 146–60.
[134] Lynch, *Orrery*, p. 159.
[135] N. K. Maguire, 'The rhymed heroic apology of Roger Boyle, earl of Orrery' in her *Regicide and restoration: English tragicomedy, 1660–71* (Cambridge, 1992), p. 164.
[136] Mita Choudhury, 'Orrery and the London stage; a loyalist's contribution to restoration allegorical drama' in *Studia Neophilologica*, lxii (1990), pp 43–59.
[137] Maguire, 'Orrery', pp 175, 178, 188–9.
[138] John Kerrigan, 'Orrery's Ireland and the British problem, 1641–1679' in D. J. Baker and

Thus, a play such as *The Generall* was aimed at the perfidious Irish rebels, while *Henry V* and *The Black Prince* were arguments in favour of hostility towards France.[139]

Kerrigan's arguments can be extended beyond the dramatic works to include Orrery's published or unpublished prose, when it directly addresses the events of the previous decades. Orrery's justification of the Old Protestants' actions in the 1640s and 1650s, published in 1662, was also a robust defence of his own behaviour. Like other Irish Protestants, Orrery saw his service in the parliamentarian forces in Ireland as being authorised by the Adventurers' Act of 1642 – to which Charles I had assented – which he described as 'that Royal Authority which first commissionated the Protestants' to reconquer Ireland. During the 1650s the Protestants 'only served under the Usurpers, but to bring the Irish Papists to those terms which without the force of English swords they would never have been brought unto', and the decade ended happily, as the Protestants 'when they were in power . . . [sought to] restore his Majesties Authority, with circumstances almost as dutiful as the Action itself'.[140] Nor did Orrery shy away from criticising Charles II directly, as well as dramatically. His opposition to the increasing leniency shown to Catholics, and his insistence on continuing to persecute them in Munster, lost him the presidency in 1672; in the 1660s he opposed the Dutch war; and in the 1670s he openly criticised the alliance with Catholic France. Although he died soon after the furore arose over the Popish Plot, there can be no doubt that Orrery believed in it, and suspected that the king's closest advisers were involved in it.[141] Again, Orrery's opposition was on behalf of Protestant Ireland as well as himself. As Toby Barnard puts it: 'Had the Dublin Parliament sat in the 1670s, as was several times proposed, the politicians who spoke on behalf of an alarmed Protestant interest, notably Orrery, might well have hastened the anti-Catholic laws, which were in the event only enacted after 1695.'[142] Orrery's attempts to advise Charles II were often unsubtle, as can be seen in an incident in November 1675, when he presented to the king his poem entitled 'A Vision', in which the headless Charles I warns his son not to risk everything by allying with the French.[143] His 1677 *Treatise on the Art of War* was dedicated to the king, but its subtext was strongly critical of the French alliance, and

Willie Maley (eds), *British identities and English Renaissance literature* (Cambridge, 2002), p. 209.

[139] Ibid., pp 208–11, 215–16.

[140] Roger Boyle, *Answer of a person of quality* (Dublin, 1662), pp 13–14, 38–40; see also Roger Boyle, *The Irish colours displayed* (London, 1662), pp 12–15; Patrick Little 'The English parliament and the Irish constitution, 1641–9' in Micheál Ó Siochrú (ed.), *Kingdoms in crisis: Ireland in the 1640s* (Dublin, 2001), pp 109–10.

[141] S. J. Connolly, *Religion, law and power: the making of Protestant Ireland, 1660–1760* (Oxford, 1992), p. 32.

[142] Barnard, 'Settling and unsettling', p. 266.

[143] Maguire, 'Orrery', p. 168; Kerrigan, 'Orrery's Ireland', p. 213.

it may be significant that a second volume of the work (to be published 'if the 1st pleases your Majesty') failed to appear.[144]

Orrery's actions, as well as his writings, demonstrate an opposition to Charles II's policies which grew directly from his earlier career. The post-restoration compromises over Catholicism were completely at odds with the agenda the Irish Protestants had developed through the trauma of the 1640s and the opportunities of the 1650s. There were limits to how far Orrery and others could continue to pursue this earlier agenda without provoking accusations of sedition, and once he had lost his position in the Dublin administration in 1662 he had little chance of influencing policy on a national level. His authority as president of Munster did, however, give him some scope for private initiatives – as the presidency of Scotland had done in the 1650s – and it is in his tense relations with the various lords lieutenant through the 1660s and early 1670s that the continuities in Orrery's political attitudes can best be seen.

Orrery's relationship with the duke of Ormond was never likely to be straightforward. The Boyles had been hostile to the Butlers since the 1620s, and Orrery inherited his father's distrust of this, the greatest Old English family in Ireland. This distrust was also shared by Orrery's elder brother, the second earl of Cork, whose 'hereditary rivalry' towards the Butlers re-emerged periodically after 1660.[145] Ormond's peace negotiations with the Confederates in the 1640s marked him, in Orrery's eyes at least, as a Catholic sympathiser and as an apostate from the Protestant interest. This was a charge periodically brought against Ormond after he was reappointed lord lieutenant in 1661. Whether or not Orrery coveted the lieutenancy, he certainly resented his demotion from the lord justiceship, and his subordination to his former enemy as president of Munster. At first, the two men worked together on many aspects of the adminstration, especially during the Irish parliament which sat between 1661 and 1666. The elections to this entirely Protestant assembly were organised by Orrery, with assistance from his fellow justice, Sir Charles Coote (now earl of Mountrath), and after Mountrath's death later in 1661, the management of parliamentary business was largely conducted by Orrery alone, in a reprise of his political performance on the wider stage of Cromwellian Westminster. In this he worked closely with Ormond, steering through such difficult measures as the act of settlement, which diminished the land gains secured by the Old Protestants in the 1650s, and in Toby Barnard's words 'without Orrery's management, the Irish parliament might well have broken up in disorder' before anything had been achieved.[146]

---

[144] Lynch, *Orrery*, pp 160–1.
[145] Barnard, 'Cork', pp 189–90.
[146] *A collection of the State Letters of the Rt Hon. Roger Boyle, the first earl of Orrery* (1742), pp 18–90 (of the second pagination); Barnard, 'Cork', p. 175.

Yet even during this period of relative harmony, tensions were growing between Orrery and Ormond. During the Irish parliament, Ormond had once again been accused of favouritism to Catholics, and by 1666 there were suspicions that Orrery was trying to poison Ormond's reputation both in Ireland and at the royal court.[147] With the fall of Clarendon (whose strong connexions with both Boyles and Butlers had encouraged a truce between the two families), hostility between the two men flared up.[148] In 1668–9, working with the duke of Buckingham, Orrery successfully edged Ormond out of the lieutenancy. Ormond, who suspected his rival's part in the faction raised against him, drew parallels with earlier tensions between them, saying that 'these times do too much resemble those, wherein he was very active, & learnt his politiques'.[149] Orrery's success was not complete – Charles appointed the unsympathetic Lord Robartes as Ormond's successor, followed by the pro-Catholic Lord Berkeley – [150] but Ormond still looked for revenge, joining Arlington in launching an attack on Orrery which ended with impeachment proceedings being brought against the earl in the English House of Commons. Orrery's record as president of Munster was dissected, and he was accused both of corruption and sedition, including the allegation that he had been behind the 1663 plot against the lord lieutenant himself. Orrery was saved by the intervention of the king, who moved to prorogue parliament before the impeachment could be concluded.[151]

Something of a truce followed, and there is no evidence to suggest that Ormond was behind the suppression of the Munster presidency in 1672,[152] but with the duke's reappointment as lord lieutenant for the third time in 1677, daggers were once again drawn. In the next two years, Orrery was constantly sniping at Ormond, insinuating that, under the influence of Catholic friends and relatives, he was not ruling Ireland with a firm hand. Orrery's comments led Ormond to suspect that he would eventually make a formal complaint, and 'charge the Government with neglect, weakness or worse'.[153] Ormond's son and deputy, the earl of Ossory (who slandered Orrery as 'the Charlatan of Munster') warned his father of Orrery's malice in 'alarming all persons in Ireland and [England] with his informations of the dangerous posture of affairs by the desperate condition the Protestants and English took themselves to be in by the multitude and evil designs of the Irish'.[154] With rumours of a popish

---

[147] Barnard, 'Settling and unsettling', pp 272–4; Lynch, *Orrery*, pp 125–6.
[148] *State Letters of Roger Boyle*, pp 319–23.
[149] Quoted in Lynch, *Orrery*, p. 132.
[150] James McGuire, 'Why was Ormond dismissed in 1669?' in *I.H.S.*, xviii (1972–3), pp 295–312.
[151] Lynch, *Orrery*, pp 135–8.
[152] Liam Irwin, 'The suppression of the Irish presidency system' in *I.H.S.*, xxii (1980–1), pp 21–2.
[153] *H.M.C. Ormonde*, n.s., iv, 220.
[154] Ibid., 243, 282.

plot, tensions increased still further. As Ormond complained in December 1678 to the earl of Burlington (as the earl of Cork had become), Orrery now intended 'under the secure pretext of zeal for the British interest and Protestant religion in himself, to insinuate a want of it in me . . . and the inference can hardly be other than that here was a combination against the English interest and Protestants, of which I was the head'.[155] The personal hatred between the two men, which stretched back to the 1640s, had reappeared in the late 1670s with renewed vigour. But this was more than a personal feud. As Ormond recognised, Orrery saw himself as the champion of the 'British' (or 'English') interest and of the 'Protestant religion', and attacked Ormond as a secret enemy of both. In this, Orrery had not moved on from the politics of the Irish 'Independents' of thirty years before, and his position was not dissimilar to that of his father, twenty years before that. At stake was not only who ruled Ireland but also the policies they pursued, and for Orrery there could be no place for leniency to Catholicism, or for any other policy which jeopardised the Protestant interest. This was still the bottom line.

It would be a mistake to see Orrery as entirely inflexible in his religious bigotry or personal feuds. His relationship with Catholics seemed to ebb and flow, depending on the political situation, leading one historian to accuse him of 'double standards' for maintaining social contacts with Catholic nobles, including the future earl of Tyrconnell, in the 1660s.[156] Orrery despised Catholicism, but was less severe in his judgement on individual Catholics, and acknowledged in print that it would be wrong to lump those 'worthy persons of that Nation and Religion' loyal to the king, with the 'Irish Papists' who were a threat to Protestant Ireland.[157] Even apostates could be accommodated. One long-standing feud which was brought to an end during the 1660s was that between the Boyles and the O'Briens. Broghill's views on Lord Inchiquin in the 1640s have already been examined at length; and from 1648 onwards the head of the O'Briens merely conformed to his suspicions, siding with the king and Ormond, abandoning Ireland altogether, and then, in 1657, converting to Catholicism. Yet in the 1660s the two found common ground, especially when trying to keep order in Munster, and in 1665 Orrery's daughter married Inchiquin's son and heir. The marriage alliance seems rather odd, until it is remembered that Orrery shared his father's long-term attitude to the assimilation of the Irish nobility through marriage and conversion. Inchiquin's heir was also the heir to the St Leger dynasty, and had been brought up as a Protestant by his half-Dutch mother. The mother had strongly resisted attempts to convert her eldest son, and for Orrery, such a match was not only advantageous in terms of land and social networks in Munster: it also 'saved'

[155] Ibid., 286–7.
[156] Connolly, *Religion, law and power*, p. 19.
[157] Boyle, *Answer of a person of quality*, pp 2–3; see also Barnard, 'Settling and unsettling', p. 285.

the Inchiquin heir from the penalties of his father's apostasy. In the weeks before his death, Orrery repeated the experiment, marrying his second son to Inchiquin's youngest daughter.[158]

Relations with another pre-1660 rival, Arthur Annesley, earl of Anglesey, were more complicated. Again, the Boyles and the Annesleys had a tradition of hostility stretching back to the 1620s, when the first earl of Cork and Anglesey's father, Lord Mountnorris, had headed rival factions within the Dublin administration. Broghill and Annesley had come into conflict period-ically in the later 1640s and again in 1659, when Annesley challenged Broghill's unionist agenda in parliament. The two families were not irreconcilable, however. In 1646 Annesley, as parliamentary commissioner in Ulster, was entrusted with the management of Robert Boyle's estates in neighbouring Connacht.[159] Both Broghill and Annesley had an interest in the prosperity of the earls of Kildare, serving together as 'donees of trust' for the young seventeenth earl after 1657;[160] and they shared a hatred of Catholicism born of their Calvinist opinions and shared experience of the Irish wars.[161] Politically, their relationship was that of rivals, not ideological opponents. After 1660 Anglesey rose to prominence in the English government on Ormond's coat-tails, and in 1668, when Orrery moved against Ormond, he first targeted Anglesey, who, as vice-treasurer of Ireland, shared responsibility for corruption within the Irish revenue system. Like Ormond, Anglesey thought he had lost his place as a result of Orrery's allegations; and like Ormond, he sought revenge, perhaps playing a role in engineering the suppression of the Munster presidency in 1672.[162] The bitter exchange of letters which followed, where each raked over the other's record of collaboration in the 1650s, was unedifying, and potentially very dangerous, reflecting the level of distrust which still survived after nearly fifty years of feuding between the two families. Yet the personal animus between the two men should not obscure their basic agreement on many issues. As Toby Barnard, summing up their relation-ship, says, 'Annesley and Broghill alternated between co-operation and ill-concealed rivalry until their friendship spectacularly exploded in 1672'; and later in the decade Anglesey, like Orrery, found himself in opposition to the foreign policy, and religious tendencies, of Charles II's regime.[163] Distrust between the two was based not on ends, but means. Like his father, Anglesey was a master of political expediency, whose links with the Old English made

---

[158] Lynch, *Orrery*, p. 229.

[159] *Boyle correspondence*, i, 29–30.

[160] P.R.O.N.I., Leinster papers, D. 3078/1/4/14; see also ibid., D. 3078/1/3/4; for Orrery and the Kildares see *Cal. S.P. Ire.*, *1660–2*, pp 536–7, 677; *State Letters of Roger Boyle*, pp 188–90 (of 2nd pagination).

[161] See Patrick Little, 'Providence and posterity: a letter from Lord Mountnorris to his daughter, 1642' in *I.H.S.*, xxxii (2001), pp 560–1.

[162] Lynch, *Orrery*, pp 133–4; Irwin, 'Irish presidency system', pp 30–1.

[163] Barnard, 'Protestant interest', pp 232–3, 237, 240.

his true adherence to the 'Protestant interest' suspect to hardliners like Orrery, despite their shared hatred of Catholicism. Perhaps Orrery compared Anglesey, like Ormond, to himself, and found him wanting.

Orrery's notion of the 'Protestant interest' – which had developed through the 1640s and 1650s – remained at the heart of his political beliefs after 1660, and it was this, rather than any sense of guilt, which governed his relations with Charles II and his ministers. In later years, two elements became essential to Orrery's idea of a Protestant interest. The first was the implementation of harsh policies against the Irish Catholics, who were seen as a fifth column within the Irish state. In his 1662 pamphlet, *The Irish colours displayed*, Orrery argued that 'the contention . . . will never have an end', as it was based on 'hereditary' animosity between the English and Irish, sharpened by religious differences after the reformation, which had left an 'implacable enmity' between Irish and English.[164] In the mid-1660s he feared further rebellions by the native Irish, backed by Catholic France.[165] Such fears prompted tough action. As president of Munster, Orrery went far beyond the Dublin government's requirements in implementing penal legislation against the Catholics. In 1669, for example, he told Viscount Conway that on his return to Munster from England he had found papists living in the cities of Limerick and Waterford against his express orders, and had immediately purged all the garrison towns of such unreliable inhabitants. He was equally shocked to discover that 'many convents' had been built surreptitiously, but added tersely 'I am now pulling them down'.[166] Orrery's provocative stance against Catholicism was increasingly risky after 1670, when the secret Treaty of Dover allied Britain to France, and later measures, such as the Declaration of Indulgence in 1672, brought the Munster administration into direct conflict with the policy of leniency promulgated by Whitehall and Dublin. Ignoring warnings from his superiors, Orrery again expelled all Catholics from the Munster towns and prohibited the saying of mass in public. His refusal to toe the governmental line was a major reason for the dissolution of the Munster presidency in 1672.[167] Orrery was not being confrontational for the sake of it: he was continuing the time-honoured Irish Protestant policy of subduing Catholics. His father, as lord justice in 1629–33, had been notorious for closing religious houses and persecuting the Catholic clergy, while advocating financial penalties against their lay counterparts. Orrery had himself used such measures as expelling Catholics from garrison towns in the 1640s, and with his Irish Independent allies promoted radical anti-Catholic policies throughout Ireland. Anti-Catholicism was something that had wedded Orrery to the Cromwellian government in the 1650s; and his sectarian convictions were

[164] Boyle, *Irish colours displayed*, pp 2–4, 6–7.
[165] *State letters of Roger Boyle*, pp 141, 149–52.
[166] *Cal. S.P. Ire.*, 1669–70, pp 267, 285.
[167] Irwin, 'Irish presidency system', pp 27–30.

little different in the 1660s and 1670s, despite the friction this caused with the weathercock king and his self-serving advisers.

Upholding the Protestant interest also involved giving the settler community control over the defence of Ireland and (as a corollary of this) increasing its share of Irish land. In the 1650s, Orrery had recommended the creation of a Protestant militia in Ireland, to take power away from the English standing army; and in the 1660s and 1670s he returned to the scheme, but this time with the emphasis on a militia as the best security against Catholic insurrection.[168] The militia's role in providing stability was reinforced by efforts to make sure the land settlement after 1660 confirmed the advantages gained by the Irish Protestants under the Cromwellian regime. Attempts to hold the government to promises made in 1660, and especially the lobbying of the pre-Cromwellian '49 officers' to secure land grants in lieu of military arrears, encouraged the Protestant community to close ranks, and increased Orrery's sense that he was representing the interests not only of himself and the Boyle family, but of settler families across Ireland.[169] His sense of championing the Protestant cause marked his dealings with Ormond in the political uncertainties of the late 1670s. Orrery drew an unfavourable comparison between Ormond's back-sliding and his own 'zeal for the British interest and Protestant religion', and argued that 'in such times as these all who love the true religion, their gracious King, or their poor country . . . ought to unite and serve all three'.[170] Orrery's call for Protestant unity against the threat posed by Catholics at home and abroad echoed not only his own views during the Civil War and interregnum but also the bellicose statements of his father in the late 1620s or early 1640s. One of Orrery's last letters, to his cousin Archbishop Boyle, dated 28 February 1679, could have been written by his father fifty years before. Although their external sponsor had changed from Spain to France, there was still an enormous threat from the Catholics of Munster,

> For the heads of their septs live amongst them, though for the last rebellion they have forfeited their estates. And in such parts generally the Romish clergy of this province, who have disobeyed the late proclamations by not removing out of the Kingdom, conceal themselves. And when the bulk of the common people are influenced by their lay chiefs and by their spiritual guides, how ready will they be for rebellion[?][171]

Orrery's concern for the Protestant interest did not only lead to tension with Ormond and the Dublin government; it also influenced his attitude to

---

[168] Barnard, 'Protestant interest', pp 235–6.
[169] J. G. Simms, 'The restoration, 1660–85' in T. W. Moody, F. X. Martin and F. J. Byrne (eds), *A new history of Ireland, iii: Early modern Ireland, 1534–1691* (Oxford, 1976), pp 420–53.
[170] *H.M.C. Ormonde*, n.s., iv, 286, 294.
[171] Ibid., p. 336.

the king. Again, his opinions after 1660 echo those of earlier decades. When faced with a choice between the Protestant cause and allegiance to the crown in 1644, Orrery had chosen the former, rejecting the cessation of arms brokered by Ormond on Charles I's behalf and siding with parliament. In 1649 he had declined offers to join Charles II in exile mainly because of his concern for the Protestant position in Ireland. In 1659–60 his reluctance to accept the restoration of the Stuarts was again based on his fears about its effect on Ireland. During the 1660s and 1670s Orrery's allegiance to the restored king was under increasing tension, as the king's policies cut across the interests of the Protestant community in Ireland. His letter to Ormond of November 1677 – before the Popish Plot raised further doubts as to the king's motives – laid out Orrery's priorities: 'I would, next to the service of God, wholly dedicate the rest of my life to make our religion safe (not oppressive), and to settle the Kingdom so firmly to the Crown of England, that it should be as much the interest as it is the duty of every honest subject to sink and swim with the Royal line.'[172] While asserting his loyalty to the crown, Orrery drew a revealing distinction between the interest of the subject and that of the king. Subjects had a 'duty' to be loyal, but it was not always in their interest to be so. There are parallels between Orrery's comments in 1677 and the funeral sermon read by his chaplain, Thomas Morrice, over his coffin before it was interred in his father's tomb in St Mary's Church, Youghal, two years later. Morrice's emphasis was not on Orrery's loyalty to the crown, but on his role as a 'Patriot of his Country' – meaning Ireland, or possibly Munster. He repeats the phrase four times, and on the last occasion echoes Orrery's earlier comments about the incompatibility of duty and interest: 'as he was a most faithful loyal subject to his Prince, so he was a good Patriot of his Country, making his Princes interest and Countries good, two inseparable Companions . . . He never would or could be brought to betray the one, or act against the good of the other.'[173]

Morrice's tone is very different from that of his later biography of the earl, which portrayed undivided loyalty to the crown as the hallmark of Orrery's career. In Youghal in 1679, in front of an audience of Munster dignitaries, including the earl's widow, Morrice may have been articulating the views not only of Orrery but also of many within the Irish Protestant community. Loyalty to the crown was an ideal, but it could be rivalled, and even superseded, by the good of the Protestant interest. Within this context, Orrery's plays and poems look more like warnings to the government than expressions of guilt. This distinction between loyalty to the crown and loyalty to Protestant Ireland shows how far the post-restoration era had departed from the confident world of the first earl of Cork, who explicitly linked duty to crown and duty to God as the bedrock of the Protestant interest in Ireland. By the 1650s, the duplicity

---

[172] Ibid., p. 65.
[173] Sermon preached at the funeral of . . . Roger, earl of Orrery (1681), pp 25, 26, 36–8; I owe this reference to Professor Jane Ohlmeyer.

of the Stuarts – both Charles I and Charles II – had severely compromised this harmonious ideal, leaving Broghill to try to square the circle by putting the crown into the hands of the godly Oliver Cromwell. If his later years were characterised by any emotion, it was not guilt but regret. This can be seen in his often abrasive relationship with authority after 1660. And like his often confrontational policies as president of Munster, Orrery's dramatic works repeatedly thrust before the king an alternative (and better) form of kingship. *Tryphon*, written in 1668, returns to the question of usurpation, and is far from hostile to Cromwell.[174] In writing the opening speech, Orrery sailed very close to the wind:

> But how men gain their Pow'r the Gods do not
> So much regard, as how 'tis us'd when got,[175]

and he went on to justify the character of Tryphon, the usurper, who was resolved

> . . . my reign shall be so good
> As shall outweigh my want of right by Blood.[176]

These were comments on Charles II as much as on Oliver Cromwell.

---

[174] Lynch, *Orrery*, pp 155–7, 159.
[175] Quoted in Maguire, 'Orrery', p. 186.
[176] Quoted in Lynch, *Orrery*, p. 156.

Part III

Broghill in Context

7

Family

The first two parts of this book followed a chronological pattern, in an attempt to trace a clear path through Broghill's often tortuous political career. The third part is thematic, considering the private preoccupations which underlay Broghill's public role, and helping to explain his personal commitment to the policies he pursued during the 1640s and 1650s. These preoccupations can be grouped into three categories: the social context provided by the extended Boyle family; the crises and opportunities which affected Broghill's finances; and the religious underpinning, which made so many of his activities a matter of faith.

It is appropriate that an examination of Broghill's private motives and assumptions should start with the Boyle family. The Boyles provided the most important constant in Broghill's political and social life, and moulded his attitudes to financial dealings and questions of religion. As a preliminary, it should be emphasised that this exploration of Broghill's family context is not designed to engage with the historiographical debate about the nature of the family in the early modern era. Nicholas Canny, in his chapter on 'The family life of Richard Boyle' has outlined the major contributions to this debate made by Lawrence Stone and Philip Greven, but after a long discussion of the Boyles is forced to conclude that such studies remain 'but highly stimulating hypotheses', adding that 'as with all such hypotheses, they are not sufficiently complex to accommodate the wealth of evidence that is available to us in the particular instance of the Boyle family'.[1] It is not necessary to go through the same painful process (and undoubtedly come to the same conclusion) here.

I

At the heart of the spider's web that was the extended Boyle family lay the first earl of Cork. Cork was conscious of the importance of his role as the *paterfamilias*, and scrupulous in his attention to family life and the upbringing of his many children. Professor Canny has asserted Cork's conscious part in creating a 'patriarchal' family, whose many members were encouraged, obliged

---

[1] Canny, *Upstart earl*, p. 123.

(even forced) to pledge their primary allegiance to the earl himself. For example, the errant Mary Boyle, whose courtship of Charles Rich incurred her father's anger, was also 'exposed to the collective wrath of the family', which 'identified openly with the patriarch until they forced the erring member to bend to his wishes'.[2] Canny's view of Cork's familial overlordship is convincing; and it fits with the picture of the earl's coherent pattern of religious and political beliefs as portrayed in chapter one, and as I have examined elsewhere.[3] Yet there is one aspect that Canny did not pursue: the earl's desire for loyalty not only vertically – from his children (or their spouses) to himself – but also horizontally, between the family members. Thus, in his final will, drawn up in 1642, Cork certainly emphasised the duty which his children owed to him; but he also made another explicit demand: that the Boyle children should work together for their mutual benefit and the future prosperity of the family in general:

> that my said Younger Sons be and Continue observant respective kind and Loving unto their Eldest Brother and that He will be helping Comfortable and assistant unto them and they Lodged and Entertained by and with him in his House in Dublin and when their several Occasions draw them thither and he or his Heir be there Resident and that all his younger Brethren do hearken unto incline and follow all such good Council and Advices as he . . . from time to time shall give them.[4]

Cork's desire to promote unity among his children was understandable. From 1620 the earl used his landed wealth and growing political influence to secure important marriages for his children with a wide range of aristocratic families in England as well as Ireland, creating a kinship group which was disparate both politically and geographically.[5] At first Cork concentrated on building his connexions in Ireland, marrying his daughters into the Barrys of Barrymore, Moores of Mellifont and Digbys of Geashill in the 1620s.[6] These marriages were followed in the early 1630s by matches for other daughters with Arthur Jones (son of Viscount Ranelagh), the earl of Kildare and Sir Arthur Loftus of Rathfarnham.[7] From 1632 Cork sought a marriage for his son and heir, Viscount Dungarvan, with Elizabeth Clifford, the heiress of an ancient English family and the niece of Viscount Wentworth, the newly appointed

---

[2] Ibid., pp 104, 107.

[3] See above. Also Patrick Little, 'The Geraldine ambitions of the first earl of Cork' in I.H.S., xxxiii (2002), pp 151–68.

[4] Dorothea Townshend, *The life and letters of the great earl of Cork* (1904), pp 504–5.

[5] T. O. Ranger, 'Richard Boyle and the making of an Irish fortune, 1588–1614' in I.H.S. x (1957), pp 257–97.

[6] Canny, *Upstart earl*, pp 61–2.

[7] Ibid., pp 48–53; see also Michael Perceval-Maxwell, 'Protestant faction, the impeachment of Strafford and the origins of the Irish Civil War' in *Canadian Journal of History*, xvii (1982), pp 235–55.

lord deputy of Ireland.[8] Dungarvan's marriage to Elizabeth Clifford, solemnised in July 1634, was not an immediate political success, as Wentworth seemed determined not to allow his family connexion with the Boyles to interfere with his campaign to reduce Cork's political influence in Ireland;[9] but there were considerable long-term advantages, not least because the Cliffords were related to such prominent courtiers as the earls of Salisbury, Pembroke and Northumberland.[10]

Cork's ambitions to connect himself to the English court had been apparent as early as 1629, when his daughter, Lettice, married the son of Lord Goring, Henrietta Maria's master of horse. Despite disputes with the Gorings over finances, and the continuing row with Wentworth, in the later 1630s Cork's marital policy was again focused on England. In 1639 he secured a marriage for his fourth son, Francis, with Elizabeth Killigrew, one of the queen's courtiers, and a few weeks later his second son, Viscount Kinalmeaky, married the earl of Denbigh's daughter, Elizabeth Feilding.[11] Cork's marriage policy shifted with the political tide. In 1639 alliances with the royal household were advantageous, but as the political crisis deepened, Cork began to associate with the opposition peers.[12] His marriage policy changed accordingly. Broghill's own match, with Margaret Howard, the sister of the third earl of Suffolk, in January 1641, brought him into contact with the opposition elements within the powerful Howard clan. In late July 1641 Broghill's sister, Mary Boyle, married Charles Rich, the second son of the earl of Warwick, and nephew to the earl of Holland. Although ostensibly against Cork's wishes, this match fitted very well with the earl's political manoeuvrings at the time.[13] By August Cork was also negotiating the marriage of his youngest son, Robert Boyle, with the daughter of another opposition peer, Lord Howard of Escrick.[14] This last, abortive match, would have been the keystone in Cork's new alliance with the opposition elements among the English peerage.

[8] Canny, *Upstart earl*, p. 56; C. V. Wedgwood, *Thomas Wentworth, 1st earl of Strafford, 1593–1641: a revaluation* (1961), pp 21–4, 32, 43–4.

[9] In fact, Wentworth would prove remarkably lenient to Cork (compared to his treatment of Lords Mountnorris and Loftus, or the earls of Clanricarde, for example): see Patrick Little, 'Family and faction: the Irish nobility and the English court, 1632–42' (unpublished M.Litt. thesis, Trinity College Dublin, 1992), pp 8–58.

[10] Ibid., pp 36–55.

[11] Grosart, *Lismore papers*, ser. 1, v, 112, 119.

[12] Patrick Little, 'The earl of Cork and the fall of the earl of Strafford, 1638–41' in *H.J.*, xxxix (1996), pp 627–8.

[13] Canny, *Upstart earl*, p. 89; Mary Boyle's later account of her marriage (B.L., Add. 27357, ff 5r–18v), and her father's initial opposition to it must be balanced by his generosity in the marriage portion (of £7,000), and the early date of the indenture of agreement (25 June) – see P.R.O., C 54/3267 – which suggest that he recognised the usefulness of the match to his political career.

[14] Townshend, *Cork*, p. 485; Grosart, *Lismore papers*, ser. 1, v, 184, 185–6. The match had failed by 1645, when Anne Howard married Charles Howard: see *Boyle's correspondence*, i, 27.

By the end of 1641 Cork's children were married into a wide range of important families in England and Ireland: from critics of the crown such as the Howards and the Riches to courtiers and future royalists such as the Feildings, Killigrews and Gorings; from the Old English Barrys and Fitzgeralds to the New English Jones and Loftus families. This variety was to prove an important resource for Broghill in later years, and would play a vital role in his survival, allowing him to change political complexion with a chameleon-like facility.[15] Yet, from Cork's point of view, the marriage policy had created a political and social connexion which, while useful, was formless. Perhaps in response to this situation, Cork tried hard to ensure that all his children, their spouses and offspring, owed a primary loyalty to what one might call the 'Boyle affinity'. He was particularly eager to promote symbolic displays of family unity. The funeral of the countess of Cork, who died in 1630, demanded a full turn-out of Boyle relatives, and the five Boyle daughters resident in Ireland formed the chief mourning party.[16] The ornate tomb erected for the countess in St Patrick's Cathedral, Dublin, contained statues of the earl and countess and all the Boyle children.[17] After 1630, Cork's diary gives the impression that the earl was making a conscious effort to bring members of his disparate family into contact with each other, and in his peregrinations around Ireland he seems to have made a point of taking his family – and especially his most impressive sons-in-law, the earls of Kildare and Barrymore and Lord Digby of Geashill – along with him.[18] When Cork left for England in July 1638 he travelled with the earl and countess of Barrymore and Kildare's son and heir, and Cork encouraged friends and relatives to join the lively household which he maintained at Stalbridge in Dorset: in August 1639, when Cork visited the earl of Bristol at Sherborne, he brought with him Broghill, Kinalmeaky, Barrymore, Arthur Jones and another prospective son-in-law, James Hamilton, son of Viscount Clandeboye.[19]

Yet the cohesion of the Boyle family was not purely a contrivance of the patriarch. Cork's children soon developed their own internal loyalties and affections within the extended family: in the early 1630s Dungarvan (while

---

[15] It also had an impact of Broghill's policy for the marriages of his own children after 1660: he chose a prestigious English match for his son and heir, influential New English noblemen as grooms for two daughters, and an ancient Gaelic (but Protestant) family for both his second son and youngest daughter: see Lynch, *Orrery*, pp 113, 122, 124, 217, 229, 239; for a similar spread of interests chosen by the second earl of Cork see Barnard, 'Cork', p. 192.

[16] B.L., Add. 4820, ff 114v–115v.

[17] See Canny, *Upstart earl*, p. 43; see also Clodagh Tait, 'Colonising memory: manipulations of death, burial and commemoration in the career of Richard Boyle, first earl of Cork (1566–1643)' in *Proceedings of Royal Irish Academy*, ci (2001) Sect. C, pp 107–34; Amy Harris, 'The funerary monuments of Richard Boyle, earl of Cork' in *Church Monuments*, xiii (1998), pp 70–86.

[18] Grosart, *Lismore papers*, ser. 1, iii, 98, iv. 52, 112, 123.

[19] Ibid., v, 56–7, 104–5.

abroad) kept up a regular correspondence with his sister, Lady Digby;[20] in 1633 Kinalmeaky associated with Dungarvan, Digby and his sisters when studying in Dublin;[21] Lettice Goring looked after Broghill and Kinalmeaky when they visited the court in 1636, and her husband and father-in-law were instrumental in presenting the young lords to the king and queen.[22] Broghill and Kinalmeaky spent several years together in Europe, as did Robert and Francis Boyle, who left for the continent having studied together at Eton during the mid-1630s. Events surrounding the marriage of Mary Boyle to Charles Rich in 1641 demonstrate the intimacy of the Boyle children. Broghill and Dungarvan mediated between Mary and her father,[23] and despite Cork's public disapproval of the match, after the wedding Mary could still rely on her 'dearest Sister Ranelaugh', who, with her brother, Robert Boyle, remained her most intimate friend thereafter.[24]

During the late 1630s and early 1640s the cohesion between the siblings was further strengthened by the shared martial experiences of the Boyle brothers and various brothers-in-law, as they took part in the Bishops' Wars and attempts to suppress the Irish rebellion. In the new year of 1639 there was great excitement in the Boyle circle at the prospect of war, and members of the family seem to have egged each other on, to see who could approach the coming conflict with greatest panache. Dungarvan and two of his brothers-in-law, the earls of Barrymore and Kildare, left Cork's house at Stalbridge in Dorset and travelled to London together on 29 January, in order to offer their services to the king.[25] Dungarvan raised a troop of Irish horse, and its officers included his two brothers, Kinalmeaky and Broghill, Lady Digby's brother-in-law, John Digby, and a more distant relative, Richard Power.[26] Barrymore's own contribution to the war effort was more extravagant: in March 1639 he had secured a commission to raise 1,000 Irish foot at his own expense.[27] And his efforts to do so were hampered by the earl of Kildare, who made even more extravagant promises 'to offer his prince thousands of Irish, and he saies they shalbe all Geraldines', while secretly plotting to poach Barrymore's recruits.[28] The mixture of co-operation and rivalry between the three noblemen attests

---

[20] Dungarvan to Lady Sarah Digby, June–July 1633 (Chatsworth, Lismore MS 17, nos. 146–54).

[21] Kinalmeaky to Cork, 1 Oct. 1633 (ibid., no. 166)

[22] Grosart, *Lismore papers*, ser. 1, v, 157; Broghill to Cork, 16 Mar. 1636 (Chatsworth, Lismore MS 18, no. 123*).

[23] B.L., Add. MS 27357, ff 12r–16r.

[24] Ibid., f. 18v; *Boyle's correspondence*, i, 133, 136.

[25] Grosart (ed.), *Lismore papers* ser. 1, v, 74; Arthur Jones also expected to fight against the Scots: see ibid., ser. 2, iv, 71–2.

[26] Ibid., ser. 1, v, 88–9; Lady Offaly to Cork, 18 Apr. 1639 (Chatsworth, Lismore MS 20, no. 9); see above, ch. 1.

[27] P.R.O., S.O. 1/3, ff 126v, 128r.

[28] Arthur Jones to Cork, 10 June 1639 (Chatsworth, Lismore 20, no. 53).

to the horizontal ties between the members of the Boyle affinity. Later conflicts were more serious, and less indulgent, but the same sense of unity can also be seen. The Irish rebellion of 1641 demanded a very different response, as the Protestant forces soon became isolated in small pockets of resistance centred on towns or castles scattered across Ireland. The Loftuses were confined to the area around Dublin, the Digbys defended their castle at Geashill in King's County, Kildare fortified Maynooth, the Joneses were stuck in Connaught; four of the Boyle brothers, and the earl of Barrymore, led the resistance in the enclave around the Munster ports. The last five were all present at the battle of Liscarroll in September 1642, where Kinalmeaky was killed and Barrymore mortally wounded.[29] The bonds between the different family members, facing the same enemy, were now sealed in blood.

The death of the first earl of Cork in September 1643 removed the central pillar of the Boyle affinity, but it did not bring the whole structure crashing down. There were obvious tensions between members of the family during the 1640s, but these were political more than personal in nature, and none was the cause of long-standing animosity, as we shall see. An inventory of Cork House in Dublin, made in November 1645, shows that chambers were still set aside for Dorothy Loftus and the countess of Kildare, that the young Lord Digby had a store room there, and that the second earl of Cork's coach had been removed to Rathfarnham on Dorothy's orders.[30] This was exactly the kind of arrangement which the first earl had demanded of his heir when writing his will three years before, when he had stipulated that the whole family should be 'Lodged and Entertained by and with him in his House in Dublin'. The itinerary of the youngest son, Robert Boyle, during 1648–9 again shows the coherence of the Boyle family, despite rising political tensions in England as well as Ireland. In February 1648 he went to Holland with Francis Boyle, returning in the spring; in August he was staying with Mary Rich at Leighs in Essex; in March 1649 he was with Broghill at Marston Bigot in Somerset, where he returned in November, having visited Bath and London in the meantime. During the same period he exchanged written correspondence with Lady Ranelagh, the countess of Cork, and Broghill, the last of whom had retired to Somerset in disgust at parliament's inactivity in the Irish war.[31] Broghill was at the same time being courted by the royalists, eager to secure his return to Ireland in support of the Stuarts, and these approaches were aided by members of his own family, including the earl of Cork and Francis Boyle, his sister-in-law, Lady Kinalmeaky, and his wife's sister, Lady d'Aubigny.[32] In return, Robert Boyle and Lady Ranelagh seem to have been instrumental in confirming Broghill's attachment to parliament.[33] Such ambassadors were

---

[29] Lynch, *Orrery*, p. 44.
[30] Inventory, 16 Nov. 1645 (Chatsworth, Lismore 28, no. 4).
[31] *Boyle's works*, i, p. xlv; ibid., v, 45–52.
[32] See above, ch. 2.
[33] *Boyle's correspondence*, i, 80.

well chosen by both sides. Broghill, despite his continued retirement from politics, could not turn away his own kinsmen.

Once the war had ended, the social round of the Boyles in Ireland in the 1650s resembled that of the 1630s, even without their father as master of ceremonies. The second earl of Cork's diary provides details of numerous gatherings and family events, which echo those recorded by his father twenty years before. The Loftuses of Rathfarnham, for example, remained an important part of the social circle. In October 1653 Lady Loftus and her daughter visited Broghill's castle at Blarney, and then waited on Cork at Lismore; Broghill and Loftus visited Cork in January 1654; and in November 1656 Cork, Lady Ranelagh and the earl of Kildare's sister, Lady Shaen, stayed with the Loftus family at Rathfarnham.[34] Another Boyle sister, Alice, dowager countess of Barrymore, was also part of the circle. In April 1657 the young earl of Kildare visited her at Castlelyons, accompanied by his uncle, the earl of Cork; Cork, his lady, and Lady Ranelagh were entertained by the countess in May 1658; and in June 1659 Lady Barrymore was staying with Lord Broghill at Bally-maloe.[35] Similar itineraries can be reconstructed for each member of the Boyle family, whether in Ireland or England, and the second earl of Cork's diary provides incontrovertible proof that the Boyle affinity was alive and well, ten or even twenty years after the first earl's death.

The parallels could be very close indeed. On 7 December 1658 Cork recorded that he had 'spent much of this afternoone in composing some differences betweene S[i]r Ar[thur] Loftus and his wife';[36] and the earl's anger is plain in an earlier entry, when he visited his brother-in-law, the wayward earl of Kildare, to force him to attend to his family's affairs:

there I found him, in bed, his whore being newly gone from him, and thogh I used all arguments I co[u]ld to perswade him to settle his estate for payment of his debts and maintenance of his children yet I co[u]ld prevayle noething.[37]

The second earl of Cork's comments about the failings of these in-laws are remarkably similar to remarks made by his father twenty years before. In 1633 the first earl had bemoaned his attempts to make 'the ill-guided Earle' of Kildare settle his finances, adding bitterly, 'god amend him, & better direct him'. Two years later he noted 'a veary unpleasing passadge' with the young Arthur Loftus 'towching a slight unkindnes he had taken against his wiffe, and exprest himself heddy and untractable therin, to my great discontent'.[38] The

---

[34] Second earl of Cork's diary (Chatsworth, Lismore 29, unfol.), entries for 7 Oct. 1653, 16 Jan. 1654, 12 Nov. 1656.

[35] Cork's diary (ibid.), 6 Apr. 1657, 31 May 1658 and 17 June 1659.

[36] Cork's diary (ibid.), 7 Dec. 1658.

[37] Cork's diary (ibid.), 4 Dec. 1656. The countess had died the previous March (ibid., 11 Mar. 1656).

[38] Grosart, *Lismore papers* ser. 1, iii, 212; ibid., iv, 88.

social cohesion of the 1630s remained in the 1650s; and Cork's injunctions to his children, whether *pre* or *post mortem*, were being observed to the letter.

II

Much of the social contact between the Boyle siblings involved Broghill directly, and he shared the financial and religious bonds which drew the family together. But this social unity also had an influence on Broghill as a politician, a phenomenon best seen by looking at his relationship with two siblings: his elder brother, Richard, second earl of Cork, and his sister, Katherine, Lady Ranelagh. Broghill's relationship with Cork was not as close as with other members of the family, but it was probably the most important. Cork was nine years older than Broghill, and had been brought up in a different way from his brothers, and encouraged to associate with a grander social set.[39] Yet the two shared an obligation to their father and his memory. If Broghill may be seen as the first earl of Cork's political heir, his elder brother became the social heir: the new patriarch, with responsibility for continuing and further strengthening the Boyle affinity, especially in Munster. This division of labour would become apparent only in the 1650s. For much of the decade after their father's death in 1643, Broghill and Cork were on different sides of the political divide. While Broghill decided to join Inchiquin and defect to parliament in the summer of 1644 (even raiding his brother's coffers at Lismore to provide funds for the Munster army), Cork remained a committed royalist. Cork was even prepared to return to Munster to use his influence to bring the Protestants back to the royalist camp. He travelled from Oxford to Bristol in August 1644, and although his departure was delayed for many months (for fear that his arrival 'might make Inchiquin the more avers & desperate'), he still professed his willingness to go over when summoned by Ormond in the beginning of 1645.[40] With the fall of Oxford, which marked the end of the first Civil War in 1646, Cork went to his estates in Yorkshire and began proceedings to compound for delinquency before leaving for the continent in January 1647.[41] In the later 1640s he moved from Holland to France, staying at Caen until 1650, when he returned to England to live privately under the commonwealth regime, eventually crossing back to Ireland in May 1651.[42] Cork's career could hardly

---

[39] Canny, *Upstart earl*, pp 94–5; for a full account of Cork's career see Barnard, 'Cork', passim.

[40] Cork to Ormond, 3 Aug. 1644 (Bodl., MS Carte 12, f. 12r); George Lord Digby to Ormond, 16 Dec. 1644 (ibid., MS Carte 13, f. 65v); Cork to Ormond, spring 1645 [misdated July 1644] (ibid., MS Carte 11, f. 669r–v); see also *Cal. S.P. Dom., 1644–5*, p. 452.

[41] *Boyle's correspondence*, i, 35; *H.M.C. Egmont*, i, 340; *Whitelocke Memoirs*, ii, 102.

[42] Cork to Percivalle, 20 Aug. 1647 (B.L., Add. MS 46931/B, f. 191r); Cork to Ormond, 2 Mar. 1649 (Bodl., MS Carte 24, f. 10r); William Thornton to 'Richard Richardson',

have been more different from that of Broghill, yet there remained some tentative contact between them, as in November 1646, when Broghill asked Sir Philip Percivalle 'to excuse me to Lord Cork . . . for not writing'.[43] On Cork's return to Ireland, however, the two brothers were immediately brought back into social contact, and Broghill made a point of accompanying Cork on his tour of the Munster estates, adding his own political authority to the social and legal claims to his brother. In 1652–3, Broghill was the prime mover in rescuing Cork's estates from sequestration, and from then on their relationship flourished, with Cork supporting Broghill in the parliamentary elections in 1654, 1656 and 1659, and during the 1656–7 sitting of parliament he attended Henry Cromwell in Dublin, apparently acting as his brother's agent. The months before the restoration saw Cork, now in London, reprise this political role, and he (with Francis Boyle) played a major part in encouraging his brother to accept the restoration in May 1660, and was present at the dinner party in August of that year when Broghill was personally reconciled with Charles II.[44]

Underlying this new political partnership was personal affection. The wild prophetic ramblings of Walter Gostelow, published (to the acute embarrassment of the Boyles) in 1655, give an interesting insight into the closeness of the Cork and Broghill households. In 1654 Gostelow had visited Cork's house at Youghal 'where that day were sate divers Persons of quality', and then described a coach-and-six which left for 'the Strand, where several Horsmatches were that day run', containing the countess of Cork and Lady Broghill, the countess's two daughters, and followed by the earl of Cork and Lord Broghill on horseback.[45] The accuracy of Gostelow's cameo is attested by a wealth of evidence from Cork's diaries, showing the close social connexion between the two families throughout the 1650s. Other instances can be seen in the financial and religious interests shared by the brothers, which once again show that Broghill's social relationship with Cork is difficult to disentangle from other aspects of his career. The ease with which Broghill and Cork came back into social, as well as political, collaboration after years of opposition and estrangement, testifies to the remarkable endurance of the bond between these two members of the Boyle family.

Lady Ranelagh was probably Broghill's closest friend within the family, despite being his senior by six years. Something of their intimacy can be seen in Lady Ranelagh's correspondence with the Scottish irenicist, John Dury, the German natural scientist, Samuel Hartlib, and other intellectual friends in

---

27 Dec. 1649, 14 Jan. 1650 (B.L., Althorp MS B6, unfol.); Cork's diary (Chatsworth, Lismore MS 29, unfol.), 28 May 1651.
[43] H.M.C. Egmont, i, 329.
[44] Barnard, 'Cork', p. 184.
[45] Gostelow, Charls Stuart and Oliver Cromwel United (20 Jan. 1655): (B.L., E. 1503(3)), pp 100–1; see also Barnard, 'Protestant interest', p. 218.

the 1650s, with whom she discussed a remedy for the stone which had helped Broghill (who, in turn, had heard of it from Richard Baxter),[46] and she proudly sent copies of Broghill's verses to her son, who had followed his uncle in studying at the Huguenot academy at Saumur.[47] As well as strong financial and religious connexions between brother and sister, they also shared an intellectual excitement at new schemes and inventions, which led Robert Wood to grumble that Hartlib's book on decimal coins was no longer in his hands, 'as she had transmitted it to her Brother my Lord Broghill, before I had an opportunity to request it from her'.[48] This open friendship belies the political differences between the two during the 1640s, when Broghill's leadership of the Irish Independents brought him into direct conflict with Lady Ranelagh's friends among the Presbyterians at Westminster, especially over such issues as the trustworthiness of the president of Munster, Lord Inchiquin. Lady Ranelagh's husband, Arthur Jones (who became Viscount Ranelagh on his father's death in 1643) lacked strong political convictions, came to be distrusted by all sides in the mid-1640s, and finally defected to parliament only very reluctantly in 1646, taking little part in politics thereafter. His wife was much more politically committed, urging her royalist friend, Sir Edward Hyde, to restart peace talks in March 1644,[49] and holding a political salon in London during the mid-1640s, where she associated with key Irish figures such as Sir John Clotworthy (who had married Viscount Ranelagh's sister), Sir Robert King and Sir Philip Percivalle. Unlike Broghill, all these men were staunch political Presbyterians, and prepared to work with Inchiquin and even Ormond.[50] The political divide between brother and sister was not permanent, however, as one incident demonstrates.

In the autumn of 1646, the English Independents suddenly changed their Irish policy, joining negotiations with Ormond, and leaving their Irish Independent allies stranded.[51] Broghill, fearing political isolation, made overtures to his rival, Lord Inchiquin, and the political Presbyterians, using Lady Ranelagh as a go-between. When the political wheel turned once more, Broghill abandoned attempts at reconciliation and again attacked Inchiquin. The president's reaction reveals Lady Ranelagh's importance in the earlier move. In January 1647 Inchiquin told Percivalle, sarcastically, that 'never man did perform a sister's undertaking in his behalf better than he [Broghill] has

---

[46] John Dury to Hartlib, 4 Sept. 1655 (S.U.L., Hartlib MS 4/3/123A); Hartlib's Ephemerides, 1657 (ibid., Hartlib MS 29/6/13A).
[47] Henry Oldenburg to Hartlib (ibid., Hartlib MS 39/3/5A).
[48] Wood to Hartlib, 8 Apr. 1657 (ibid., Hartlib MS 33/1/13A).
[49] Clarendon State Papers, ii, 166–8.
[50] Patrick Little, 'The marquess of Ormond and the English parliament, 1645–1647' in Toby Barnard and Jane Fenlon (eds), The dukes of Ormonde, 1610–1745 (Woodbridge, 2000), pp 85–6.
[51] For the full story, see above, ch. 2.

done, that is to say . . . the quite contrary way'.[52] In March, Inchiquin wrote to Lady Ranelagh herself, telling her of his disappointment,

> Believing that you could not likely be mistaken in your brother's intentions, and most confident that all the brothers in the world could not persuade you to write more than you credited, I was willing to flatter myself with an expectation that he would second his promises there with performances here, and therefore took occasion to rip up the jealousies that had arisen between us to the end that they might be removed, as I have formerly mentioned to you . . . The reason why I make this discourse, unusual concerning a brother to a sister who I know loves him and has no reason to regard me, is because I know the distance between us will come to your ears by other means, and then perhaps you may imagine that the malice I bear him might be of force to lessen the honour I owe to your ladyship, which really, Madam, I shall ever nourish.[53]

Inchiquin's testimony shows not only the respect that Lady Ranelagh was accorded by both sides, but the degree of influence which she was expected to wield over her brother. Broghill had used her good offices in the previous autumn, but by the spring of 1647 he had rejected her efforts. Even so, Inchiquin did not expect such political duplicity to damage the bond between brother and sister, rather fearing that Lady Ranelagh would be turned against him by her wily brother. In fact, Lady Ranelagh seems to have managed to keep on good terms with both, and was on hand to broker a similar compromise three years later.

In 1650 Lady Ranelagh was one of the few people who could expect to challenge Broghill and deflect him from a determination to act ruthlessly. In February of that year she wrote to her brother on behalf of their cousin, Sir Percy Smyth, who had sided with Inchiquin after the Cromwellian capture of the Munster towns, and now faced the death penalty for treachery.[54] The tone of Lady Ranelagh's letter is revealing. Rather than justifying Smyth's actions ('w[hi]ch I thinke he has scarce left it possible for any to doe wthout condemning themselves'), she begged Broghill 'to save his life . . . to shew you can doe good for Gods sake to one that can plead no merritt and from whom you have no greate reason to promise yourselfe gratitude', which was a primary 'Christian' virtue. Having appealed to Broghill's faith in a forgiving God and his concern to further his honour through generosity, she then turned to his duty to the Smyth family, to spare Sir Percy 'in Consideracon of his wife and children the first of whome is very fitt to be served and the latter are numerous and are like to be very distressed if they be left fatherless especially if they become soe this way'. Finally, having played the family card, she returned to

---

[52] *H.M.C. Egmont*, i, 356.
[53] Ibid., pp 374–5.
[54] Lady Ranelagh to Broghill, 9 Feb. 1650 (B.L., Add. MS 46932, ff 107r–v).

the religious factor, in this case, the fear of an unshriven death. 'I doubt he is not so prepared for death as to make an advantage of it to him and it were very severe to kill his body soule and ffamily at once.' Smyth's survival, and his family's re-incorporation within the Boyle clan, attests to Lady Ranelagh's ability to choose arguments that would most influence her brother, whether drawn from religion, honour or the importance of maintaining even rebellious family members.

Later in the 1650s, Lady Ranelagh, like the earl of Cork, became an important lieutenant for Broghill in his public role. During his absence in Scotland in June 1656, he even used his sister as intermediary with Oliver Cromwell, sending her to ask the protector for leave to come to England to secure his religious reforms north of the border. In a letter to Cromwell of 27 June, he reminded him of the result: 'By a fresh letter from my Sister Ranelagh I understand [she] mooved yo[u]r High[nes]s in my behalfe for yo[u]r [pass] for England for Three Months . . . [but] you thought my absence from hence [at this] time might Prove Disadvant[a]gious to y[ou]r service.'[55] Her role in this was helped by her own Presbyterian sympathies and her broad agreement with Broghill's support of the Cromwellian regime. Lady Ranelagh greeted news of the death of the protector with foreboding, as 'his loss wil be a growing affliction upon these nations'.[56] Broghill's continued reliance on Lady Ranelagh would show itself most strongly in the months before the restoration. The two families crossed to England together in February 1659,[57] and when Broghill returned hastily to Ireland on the collapse of the protectorate, he relied on Lady Ranelagh as well as Cork for intelligence from London. He wrote to her on 25 May 1659, announcing the reluctant capitulation of the Old Protestant officers to the newly-established commonwealth. This was not merely a private letter, as a copy was immediately passed on to Bulstrode Whitelocke, with instructions 'to make use of them as he should see occasion for the advantage of my Lord', an indication of Lady Ranelagh's continued activity as Broghill's political agent.[58] In October 1659 Lady Ranelagh's old friend, Sir Edward Hyde, told Ormond of her standing with men of influence in Ireland, indicating that she might be useful in the on-going project to win over Broghill.[59] In the early months of 1660 Lady Ranelagh, Cork, and their brother, Robert Boyle, met in London to discuss 'my brother Broghill's affairs', and her influence, like that of Cork, may have guided Broghill's actions as the restoration became an inevitability.[60]

---

[55] Broghill to Cromwell, 27 June 1656 (Bodl., MS Rawl. A. 39, pp 170–3). The MS is damaged, and the insertions in square brackets are the author's.

[56] *Thurloe S.P.*, vii, 396.

[57] Lady Ranelagh to Cork, 18 Feb. 1659 (Chatsworth, Lismore MS 30, no. 95).

[58] Broghill to Lady Ranelagh, 25 May 1659 (Longleat, Whitelocke papers, vol. xix, f. 129r); *Whitelocke diary*, 517.

[59] *Cal. Clar. S.P.* iv, 413.

[60] Chatsworth, Lady Burlington's Journal, unfol., entry for 28 Jan. 1660.

The relationship between Broghill and his sister was based on affection and a common enthusiasm for life and learning, and was often savoured by Lady Ranelagh's willingness to contradict or even oppose her younger brother. Broghill's relations with his older, grander brother, were more staid, more formal, and less spontaneous. Despite this, there were many similarities between Lady Ranelagh and the earl of Cork, not least in their political impact on Broghill. This political dimension is most obviously apparent in Cork and Lady Ranelagh's direct role in mitigating the effects of bitter factional conflict, whether reconciling Broghill to former allies or aiding his contacts with the royalist court in exile. But they also had an influence on Broghill's policies. Occasionally this influence was direct. For example, Cork's position as a former royalist demonstrated to Broghill the desperate need for reconciliation. Cork's own fear of decimation in 1656 certainly gave a personal edge to Broghill's hostility to the militia bill in parliament;[61] and his fate had long been recognised as a test-case for other Irish royalists. But there were knock-on effects also. Broghill's leniency to Scottish royalists may have been encouraged by his personal interest in Cork's fate, and Cork's English landholdings brought the other nation into focus as well. Lady Ranelagh may have had an influence on her brother's Scottish policies, not least because of her close relationship with Sir John Clotworthy and John Dury, both of whom encouraged Broghill to favour the Resolutioners in the Scottish Kirk. As Broghill himself stated, he saw such inclusive policies in Ireland and Scotland as a prelude for reform in England, at least in terms of religion. And, as I have argued earlier, his experiences in Ireland and Scotland can be linked with his later support for 'settlement' in all three nations. A broadly-based, civilian government would favour a family of such disparate political views as the Boyles, and it seems likely that his growing desire for a permanent political settlement was conditioned not just by his observations in the three nations, but also by his position within the closely-knit Boyle family.

III

The Boyle family was the most important personal influence over Broghill; and his relationship with them had close parallels with the sense of commitment which grew up between him and his wife's family, the Howards. Although the evidence is more patchy than for the Boyles, enough survives to show that the Howards had an impact on Broghill's political activities that was similar in kind, if of lesser intensity. The marriage, which took place in January 1641, provided Broghill with connexions across a wide spectrum of political opinion, including such leading opponents of Charles I as Lady Broghill's brother, the earl of Suffolk, her uncle, Lord Howard of Escrick, and

[61] See above, ch. 5.

her future brother-in-law, the earl of Northumberland (who already had connexions with Dungarvan through the Cliffords). Suffolk's own wife was the daughter of Henry Rich, earl of Holland, brother of the earl of Warwick, whose allegiances oscillated between king and parliament for much of the 1640s. Others were staunch royalists from the very beginning, including Lady Broghill's uncle, the earl of Berkshire, and her sister, Lady d'Aubigny, whose husband was the brother of the duke of Lennox, and a scion of the blood royal. The range of connexions established in 1641 would prove of great importance to Broghill over the next two decades.

Broghill's brother-in-law, the earl of Suffolk, was a prominent parliamentarian peer during the 1640s, and by the middle of the decade he was a leading member of the Presbyterian faction at Westminster. Like Lady Ranelagh, Suffolk's importance in the rival camp provided Broghill with an alternative contact at Westminster when relations soured between him and the English Independents in the autumn of 1646. In November 1646 Broghill hoped to use Suffolk to build bridges with the Presbyterians and to gain influence within the Irish committees, as he told Sir Philip Percivalle:

> the way I propound to myself is to get my Lord Suffolk, my Lord Willo[ugh]by and such other friends of theirs to meet at the Committee on Tuesday next as may be sure to carry the business . . . I pray, assure my Lord Suffolk that what he shall do in this, I will esteem it more done to my particular, by the same reason that I value my private less than the public.[62]

Broghill remained in touch with Suffolk in December 1646,[63] but, as with Lady Ranelagh, in the new year of 1647 Broghill had given up his attempt to make peace with the Presbyterians in England and Ireland, and instead resurrected his alliance with the Independents. By the summer of 1647 a political gulf had grown between Suffolk and Broghill. During the Presbyterian coup of July, Suffolk was one of the few peers to remain in parliament, and, as a result, was impeached for treason in September.[64] Even when it came to Irish affairs, Suffolk's sympathies now lay firmly with Broghill's enemies, including Inchiquin, Percivalle and William Jephson. After the impeachment, Percivalle retired to Suffolk's mansion at Audley End, and Jephson planned to join him there, to avoid the dangers of remaining in an Independent-dominated London.[65] Despite their earlier differences, during the 1650s relations between Broghill and Suffolk improved. The two shared similar religious viewpoints, and both were friends of Richard Baxter by 1655.[66] On 22 June 1655, Broghill

---

[62] H.M.C. Egmont, i, 329.
[63] Ibid., p. 340.
[64] Ibid., p. 441.
[65] Ibid., 462–3.
[66] See below, ch. 8.

asked Secretary Thurloe to hasten Suffolk's business before the lords commissioners, and in August 1655, as Broghill journeyed to Scotland, he stayed at Audley End. Suffolk's house seems to have become a favourite summer destination for the Broghill family: Broghill planned to 'stay four or five days' there on his return from Scotland in August 1656, and in August 1657 Lady Broghill was again a guest there.[67] These visits were particularly important after 1655, as Suffolk's family promised to provide Broghill with useful connexions with the Scottish peerage, through the Homes of Dunbar, the Stuarts of Lennox and other important families. On his return from the north in the autumn of 1656 Broghill, desperate to construct a parliamentary party in support of a civilian 'settlement' (and later kingship), also seems to have been keen to renew his contacts with key Presbyterians, including Suffolk, but also Warwick, Lady Ranelagh, and others in the Boyle network.

At the end of the 1650s, the Howards also proved important to Broghill for another reason – their connexions with the royalist court in exile. Suffolk and his brother, Thomas Howard, were both implicated in Sir George Booth's rebellion in 1659, and were strong supporters of a restoration (albeit one negotiated by the Presbyterians).[68] Other members of the family had been royalists from a much earlier date. Lady Broghill's sister, Lady d'Aubigny, was widowed at Edgehill, and later indicted for treason by parliament.[69] Yet in 1646 Broghill was solicitous in pursuing her bills of exchange, he dealt with her as a royalist agent in 1648–9, and even after her death in exile in 1650 he looked after the interests of her son, the earl of Lichfield.[70] Similarly, Broghill defended the former royalist, Viscount Grandison, who was brother of the earl of Suffolk's second wife, repeatedly asking Thurloe (in 1655) for the payment of his allowance, adding 'he is reddy to perish, and my lady Suffolke also, whos brother he is'.[71] This was despite earlier warnings of Grandison's involvement in royalist plots, and his undoubted importance as a royalist agent by the end of the 1650s.[72] Broghill's care for his royalist relatives in the Howard family was very similar to his efforts on the behalf of the second earl of Cork and other members of the Boyle family. The royalist Howards also provided Broghill with direct contacts with the court in exile in the later 1650s. Grandison's brother, Sir Edward Villiers, and another member of the extended family, Thomas Howard, son of the earl of Berkshire, were at the forefront of efforts to persuade Broghill to join Charles Stuart in 1659–60: their importance

[67] *Thurloe S.P.*, iii, 574, 727; v. 336; Broghill's accounts, 1657 (Petworth, Orrery Papers, MS 13192, unfol.).

[68] Bodl., MS Eng. Hist. e.309, p. 42.

[69] *Complete Peerage*; B.L., Add. MS 31116, pp 125, 152.

[70] H.M.C. *Egmont*, i, 340–1; *Cal. S.P. Dom. 1654*, p. 326; Broghill to Whitelocke, Apr. 1658 (Longleat, Whitelocke papers, vol. xviii, f. 125r).

[71] *Thurloe S.P.*, iii, 574, 727, 737.

[72] Ibid., i, 240; *Cal. Clar. S.P.*, iv, 90, 178, 659.

in this respect was eclipsed only by the activities of Francis Boyle and the earl of Cork in the months before the restoration.[73]

For Broghill, the Howards may have played second fiddle to the Boyles, politically and socially; but it is interesting to note the similarities between the two families, especially in their relationships with Broghill himself. There are strong parallels between Lady Ranelagh and the earl of Suffolk in the 1640s; between Lady d'Aubigny and Viscount Grandison on the one hand, and the second earl of Cork and the countess of Barrymore on the other in the 1650s; and between Francis Boyle, Sir Edward Villiers and Thomas Howard in 1659–60. Both families played a significant role in moulding Broghill's views, and in providing him with the political support necessary to carry them out. Most strikingly, his efforts to maintain social links with those with whom he disagreed would pay off in 1657, when he was able to construct a broadly-based party which encompassed those of many different political and religious backgrounds across all three nations, to deliver a parliamentary majority in favour of kingship. And the way in which family matters pervaded his political career, in some cases making the two almost indistinguishable, reinforces the idea that family obligations provide an important context for Broghill's political activities throughout the 1640s and 1650s.

[73] See above, ch. 6.

8

Finance

Although Broghill would later blame his father for providing him with a miserable inheritance, the first earl of Cork's land settlement was in reality a very generous one, especially for his younger sons.[1] The initial septpartite indenture of 1636, which allocated the Boyle estates among the five brothers, gave Broghill extensive lands in the north of County Cork and County Kerry, as well as all the Boyle possession in County Limerick, including the old Desmond castle of Askeaton.[2] The land allocation remained the same although the document itself was superseded when Broghill married Margaret Howard in 1641. A further deed, drawn up on 15 January 1641, granted Broghill's share of the inheritance to his brothers-in-law, Sir William Howard, Sir Robert Howard, Arthur Jones and Sir Arthur Loftus, on trust for Broghill's use.[3] A conveyance of the same lands was signed on 18 January 1641, and this document specified that Broghill was to gain immediate control of his wife's £5,000 (to be invested in English lands), the demesne of Broghill Castle and £500 per annum from the earl's estates until his death.[4] Lady Broghill's portion was soon afterwards invested in land at Marston Bigot in Somerset, and when the earl of Cork died in September 1643, the remainder of the Irish estate came into Broghill's possession. Thus, at the age of twenty-two, Broghill owned a large estate in Ireland, centred on Limerick, Kerry and north Cork, and lands in Somerset: not a bad start for a third son.

Yet the potential of Broghill's various estates could not be realised for many years to come. The 1641 Irish rebellion had reached Munster by early 1642; Cork's carefully apportioned estates were overrun, and his sons left with inheritances which were almost worthless in real terms.[5] Although perhaps overstating the case, Cork's complaint to the earl of Warwick of 25 February 1642 reflects the scale of the disaster: 'my revenue, besides my houses,

---

[1] Canny, *Upstart earl*, pp 114, 190–1 (note 144): citing remarks made by Broghill when settling his own estates in 1677.
[2] N.L.I., MS 2639, pp 129–45.
[3] Ibid., D.21,907–22,035, bundle 'years 1631, 1640(3)'.
[4] Ibid.
[5] For a similar case see Peter Roebuck, 'Landlord indebtedness in Ulster in the seventeenth and eighteenth centuries' in J. M Goldstrom and L. A. Clarkson (eds), *Irish population, economy and society: essays in honour of K. H. Connell* (Oxford, 1981), pp 147–51.

demeasnes, parkes and other royalties did yield me 50l a day rent, I doe vow unto your lordspp that I have not now 50d a week coming to me'.[6] Broghill's position was the same as his father's. Limerick was occupied by the Irish Confederates from 1642, and Protestant territory in Cork, confined to the vicinity of the coastal towns, did not include Broghill's estates to the north of the county. In November 1646 Broghill told Sir Philip Percivalle of his desperate need for money grants from England, 'my expenses being exceeding great and my purse very small'.[7] By 1649 the situation had not improved. Cromwell, when recommending Broghill for a reward in December 1649, told Speaker Lenthall that 'he having his whole fortune under the power of the enemy . . . I dare say his wants were scarce to be paralleled'.[8] In the same month, the Munster soldier, John Hodder, related Broghill's private complaints 'that he did not receive forty pounds from his estate since the wars'.[9] Even once the south-west of Ireland had been reconquered (a process completed by the end of 1652) the long arduous task of replanting, restocking, and retenanting the land would take many more years to complete.[10] Nor did Broghill's English estates provide much of an alternative source of income. Somerset was badly affected by the English Civil War; from 1644 Broghill was forced to use his estate at Marston Bigot as the collateral for debts; and by the mid-1650s the lands had become run-down, and his woods invaded by riotous locals and their livestock.[11] From 1641–2 until the mid-1650s, Broghill's estates in England and Ireland seem to have produced little, if any, income.

With his lands occupied, or in a state of ruin, for much of the 1640s and 1650s Broghill was forced to rely on alternative sources of subsistence. Foremost among these was his military pay. We have already seen (in chapter one) the importance of army commissions as a source of ready cash, and as collateral for loans, and that the possession of military rank often became the focus for bitter faction fighting in the early 1640s. As a fully commissioned captain of horse from June 1642, a colonel from the mid-1640s, and with the salaried position of master of the ordnance from 1648, Broghill should have received a number of concurrent, and fairly lucrative, wage packets, but there is no evidence that any of these were actually paid at the time. For example, in February 1648 Broghill was owed £2,000 in arrears, which parliament awarded him by ordinance from the excise.[12] Despite parliament's promises, the money was not paid, and Broghill was forced to mortgage the sum to a merchant for an immediate advance of £375 in cash – to the consternation of his creditors

---

[6] Cork to Warwick, 25 Feb. 1642 (B.L., Eg. MS 80, f. 32r).
[7] H.M.C. *Egmont*, i, 338.
[8] Abbott, *Writings and speeches*, ii, 177.
[9] H.M.C. *Egmont*, i, 491.
[10] For the second earl of Cork's experiences, see Barnard, 'Cork', passim.
[11] *Cal. S.P. Dom.*, 1654, pp 326, 337–8; *Cal. S.P. Dom.*, 1655, pp 131, 162; *Cal. S.P. Dom.*, 1655–6, p. 94.
[12] *C.J.*, v, 465.

who had expected to recoup their own money from his military arrears.[13] When Broghill joined Cromwell in 1649, his coffers were completely empty, and he was forced to get the general to intervene on his behalf to secure a mere £200 to allow Lady Broghill to join him in Ireland.[14]

From the end of 1649, Broghill, newly commissioned as colonel of a double horse regiment, might have expected regular pay under the efficient and well-funded Cromwellian establishment. But the surviving pay warrants suggest that things were not that straightforward. For example, after his appointment as lieutenant-general of the ordnance in early 1651, Broghill was paid only a fraction of his 'entertainment'. Edmund Ludlow, Broghill's main military rival at the time, recalled that his promotion was partly in order to give him 'some office of profit',[15] and the salary, of at least £1 per day,[16] would have made an important difference to Broghill's finances. We know that Broghill was paid as lieutenant-general in May and October 1651, February and October 1652, and April 1653, receiving on each occasion between £53 and £120.[17] But, added together, these sums amount to far less than his daily entitlement, and this raises questions about the financial impartiality of the parliamentary commissioners, who were penalising Broghill in other ways during this period. Later events suggest that Broghill had indeed been starved of income during the previous few years: there was a sudden payment of £263, apparently in arrears, in July 1653, and in the same month Broghill, clearly trying to recoup other arrears, wrote to James Standish requesting 'a Brief of what I have Received in all with the Times when; what is my full Pay what my Present, & what my Respyted Pay'.[18] Other fragments of evidence confirm that, for whatever reason, Broghill's cash crisis was as bad in 1653–4 as it had been in 1649, and in April 1653 and March 1654 he even borrowed small sums from his brother, the second earl of Cork, who was himself suffering financial difficulties.[19]

The foundation of the protectorate in December 1653 eased Broghill's financial, as well as his political, position. In May 1654, after Henry Cromwell's visit to Ireland, Broghill received another instalment of arrears from his lieutenant-general's pay, amounting to £329 – almost a year's back-pay[20] – and

---

[13] Case of Lucretia Plunkett, widow, 1 Mar. 1652 (Petworth, Orrery MS 13192, unfol.).

[14] Cromwell to Thomas Scot, 14 Nov. 1649 (Bodl., MS Tanner 56, f. 140r).

[15] *Ludlow memoirs*, i, 264.

[16] Calculated from accounts of Broghill's 'entertainment as lieutenant-general', Oct. 1656–Mar. 1660 (Petworth, Orrery MS 13192, unfol.). The pay of lieutenant-generals varied: in 1649 Cromwell was paid £4 *per diem*, while Michael Jones received only £2 *per diem* for the same rank: Abbott, *Writings and speeches*, ii, 87, 102n.

[17] P.R.O., S.P. 28/70, f. 289r; S.P. 28/71, f. 96r; S.P. 28/77, f. 162r; S.P. 28/81, f. 214r; S.P. 28/84, f. 73r; S.P. 28/88, f. 34r; S.P. 28/91, f. 286r.

[18] Ibid., S.P. 28/94, ff 50r, 80r, 81r.

[19] Second earl of Cork's diary (Chatsworth, Lismore MS 29, unfol.), entries for 24 Aug. 1654 (concerning money lent c.Mar.–Apr. 1653) and 13 Mar. 1654.

[20] Bodl., MS Rawl. A.208, p. 402.

for the rest of the year money came in every month, at the steady rate of £28 per month.[21] This new regularity probably continued through 1655 and 1656 (although records do not survive) and we know from Broghill's own accounts that he received his military pay, in regular instalments, from October 1656 until March 1660.[22] The near complete run of pay warrants and accounts relating to Broghill's salary as lieutenant-general make clear that his financial security was closely related to his political position. Whether by accident or design, payments through 1649–53 were irregular and incomplete, but with the establishment of the protectorate they became regular, and Broghill's immediate cash problems seem to have eased. The situation improved further in 1655, when Broghill was allocated £1,000 p.a. as president of the Scottish council (which was doubled in June 1656),[23] and from October 1656 he was able to reassign his lieutenant-general's salary to other causes, such as supporting his impoverished sister, Lady Ranelagh, or rewarding his political client, Henry Markham.[24]

Broghill's military salary may have improved from 1654, and with it his immediate cash-flow problems, but there were other, more deep-rooted problems, which continued to undermine his financial position. The most serious problem was debt. Broghill's indebtedness was caused by his financial embarrassment during the 1640s. With little or no landed income, and with only intermittent supplies from the government, Broghill was forced to raise money, for himself and for his troops, by other means. An early casualty was his Somerset estate. In December 1644, when he crossed to England to lobby for supplies to the Munster Protestants, Broghill borrowed £200 from Christopher Nicholson of London, with a ninety-nine year lease of part of the Marston Bigot estate as collateral if the money was not repaid in a year.[25] Broghill seems not to have met the deadline, but instead of conceding the lease, he entered a further bond with Nicholson for £600 (on a loan of £300) in January 1645.[26] By June 1647 he still owed Nicholson's heirs the £300 capital sum, but with a further £161 now due in interest and costs.[27] This was but the first example of how borrowing even small amounts could lead to an escalation of debt. Another of Broghill's debts, to his kinsman, William Tynt, became a long-term burden. Tynt lent Broghill £160 in 1647, on bond for payment the following month, and, although he received small amounts from Broghill's military pay and other sources, he was not fully repaid until January 1658 – over a decade later.[28]

---

[21] Ibid., pp 428, 432, 439, 450, 451.

[22] Broghill's 'entertainment', 1656–60 (Petworth, Orrery MS 13192, unfol.).

[23] *Thurloe S.P.*, iv, 526–7; vi, 472; *Cal. S.P. Dom.*, 1655, p. 290; Broghill to Cromwell, 27 June 1656 (Bodl., MS Rawl. A. 39, pp 170–3).

[24] Broghill's 'entertainment', 1656–60 (Petworth, Orrery MS 13192, unfol.).

[25] N.L.I., D.21,907–22,035, bundle 'years 1640, 1644, 1646'.

[26] P.R.O., L.C. 4/202, f. 298v.

[27] Note of debts, c.1652 (Petworth, Orrery MS 13192, unfol.).

[28] Receipt of 1657, bond of 1647, and Tynt's notes of money lent (ibid.).

The worst case of cumulative debt, and the clearest example of Broghill's inability to service his debts, involved a London silk merchant, Isaac Tully. In July 1641 Broghill, with Arthur Jones acting as surety, had bought silk worth £300 from Tully, on a bond to repay within the year.[29] In 1644 Broghill entered another bond, promising to repay the original sum, but in 1645 Tully won a case to recover £947 in damages and costs from both Broghill and Jones (now Viscount Ranelagh).[30] In 1647, Broghill and Ranelagh were busy fighting this case through Chancery, claiming that Tully had refused to release their defeazance, 'haveinge an intent & purpose if itt might bee to ruine yo[u]r Orators in their honoble estates'.[31] On 27 April 1649 the debt was converted to a loan, repayable at 8 per cent interest.[32] From then on Broghill, in the midst of his worst period of financial crisis, was desperately trying to scrape together funds to pay off £747 which remained due to Tully. Small payments followed until 1654, when agreement was finally reached with Tully's heirs to pay £335 in £15 instalments over a ten year period.[33]

The Tully case was a particular problem for Broghill because of the involvement of his brother-in-law, Viscount Ranelagh, who was jointly liable; nor was this the only instance of Broghill's financial problems threatening the Jones family. On 2 December 1641 Broghill borrowed £330 from Theophilus Biddulph, at 8 per cent interest.[34] In October 1646 Ranelagh again stood surety to Broghill in a bond to repay Biddulph's money, and as part of the transaction, Broghill was forced to sign an additional bond for £3,000, to 'defend save and keepe harmlesse' Ranelagh from any claims arising.[35] The debt was still unpaid in 1654, however, when the earl of Cork (who was also a surety) paid Broghill £300 in full settlement of his obligations 'because I had formerly protested never more to be bound for any body'.[36] Cork may have extricated himself, but Broghill (and Ranelagh) would be pursued by this debt for many years to come.[37] By the mid-1650s the financial obligations between Broghill and Ranelagh were thoroughly entwined. The Joneses faced their own financial crisis during the 1640s, and by 1648 Ranelagh had been landed with a bill for £1,100 which his father had borrowed from William Domville of Lincoln's Inn.[38] In July 1654 Broghill took the burden from Ranelagh's shoulders, and entered into a £1,200 bond in Domville's favour;[39] this was confirmed by

[29] P.R.O., C 3/435/59.
[30] Ibid.; N.L.I., D.21,907–22,035, bundle 'years 1654, 1656–7, 1658'.
[31] P.R.O., C 3/435/59.
[32] Account of repayments, c.1654 (Petworth, Orrery MS 13192, unfol.).
[33] Ibid.; N.L.I., D.21,907–22,035, bundle 'years 1654, 1656–7, 1658'.
[34] Note of debts, c.1652 (Petworth, Orrery MS 13192, unfol.).
[35] P.R.O., C 54/3359.
[36] Cork's diary (Chatsworth, Lismore MS 29, unfol.), 3 Apr. 1654.
[37] Note of Orrery's debts to Sir Theophilus Biddulph (Petworth, Orrery MS 13192, unfol.); Orrery still owed £224 to Biddulph in 1675.
[38] *Cal. S.P. Ire.*, 1647–60, p. 24.
[39] P.R.O., L.C. 4/204, fo. 11v.

indenture of defeazance, which stipulated that Broghill was to pay £612 by St Bartholomew's Day in the following month.[40] In his accounts for 1658, it is clear that the Domville defeazance had not yet been settled, and in mid-1659 Broghill was still faced with the £612 debt.[41] The cases of Tully, Biddulph and Domville demonstrate not only how debts escalated, but also how they drew in friends and relatives. If Ranelagh sank, the tentacles of debt would pull Broghill under as well. This was a pattern replicated within the Boyle family and the Old Protestant community in general.

If debt was the most serious long-term problem facing Broghill and his peers, the promise of the repayment of pre-1649 arrears was the most obvious solution. Parliament had already conceded that Broghill was owed considerable sums in 1648, but there is no evidence that any money was paid over. In January 1650, presumably at Cromwell's behest, Broghill was granted the custodiam of the estates of his old adversary, Viscount Muskerry, which were centred on Blarney Castle near the city of Cork, and he was given permission to extract an income of £1,000 per annum in lieu of income from his own estates, which were still under enemy control.[42] In June 1650, as news of Broghill's military successes in Munster reached Westminster, parliament resolved that he should be granted the same lands in fee simple, and that an act should be passed to that effect.[43] Such intentions did not easily translate into reality, however. Reintroduced in July 1651, the bill was delayed repeatedly until October, when it was referred to a committee.[44] There the bill rested, until it was incorporated into the bill for the plantation of Ireland in August 1652.[45] From now on the Muskerry lands, considered alongside a myriad of other claims by the adventurers and soldiers, faced an uncertain future.

Although a survey of suitable land had been ordered by parliament as early as April 1652, the report did not reach the parliamentary commissioners in Ireland until November.[46] After a further delay, a new survey had to be commissioned in September 1653, and this was found later to have underestimated the land allocation by at least 2,000 acres.[47] Not all of these delays can be attributed to incompetence: Broghill's unpopularity with the parliamentary commissioners also seems to have slowed proceedings in Ireland.

---

[40] Deed of 29 July 1654 (N.L.I., D.21,097–22,035).
[41] 'A note of such things sent to Broghill . . . 21 May 1658' (Petworth, Orrery MS 13292, unfol.) includes the defeazance papers; see also Sir James Shaen to Broghill, 14 June 1659 (ibid., MS 13221, unfol.).
[42] C.J., vi, 344.
[43] Ibid., p. 434.
[44] Ibid., pp 594, 605; ibid., vii, 6, 11, 15, 23, 49.
[45] Ibid., pp 161–2.
[46] Parliamentary commissioners to Algernon Sidney, 2 Nov. 1652 (Bodl., MS Firth c.5, f. 84r–v).
[47] C.J., vii, 316; Burton diary, ii, 179.

On 7 October 1652, for example, the commissioners allowed a counter-claim by Lady Muskerry, ordering that 'the Lord of Broghill do enjoy so much of the Lord of Muskerys Estate only as amounted to £1000 p annum & that the s[aid] Lady do receive the Rents & the Profits made out of the rest . . . in pursuance of the Articles made with his Lordship upon the late surrender of Ross Castle in Kerry . . . unless the s[ai]d Lady [*recte* Lord?] Broghill shall within 10 days after Notice of this order shew good Cause to the Contrary'.[48] The commissioners may have been following the letter of Broghill's grant for £1,000 p.a. from the estate, but by promoting the Muskerry claim they effectively prevented parliament from increasing his lands around Blarney, and this before the survey which would allow Broghill to take possession. It is certainly suspicious that the commissioners had suddenly become interested in protecting the Catholic Muskerry, and in upholding articles of war. This was a contrast to their attitude to Old Protestants who wished to compound under similar agreements during this period.

As well as facing obstruction by the parliamentary commissioners in Ireland, Broghill's land grant was threatened by the inactivity of the Rump Parliament in its last months. In a letter to Whitelocke of 20 December 1652 he outlined his situation and asked for

> assistance at the Comitee apoynted by Parlm[en]t to prepare an act for setling of 1000l. a yeere upon me & my heirs for ever where indeed It has bin stoped soe long as to bring me under one of the most sen[s]able sufferings that a gentleman or an honest man Can be subiected To, that is to have some friends who were Content to be bound for me troubled both In poynt of their liberties and their estates In passing this act (w[hi]ch has taken me off al other ways of Expecting payment from ye house for either my arreares or demands. And they are a very considerable some) unable to relieve them.[49]

Broghill's emphasis of not only his own financial difficulties, but also the outstanding obligations to his relatives (including an allusion to a specific case: that of Ranelagh) underlines the importance of the Blarney grant to his wider situation. Yet, despite this urgency, and the probable intervention of his friends in England, little progress was made in the following year. Barebones' Parliament passed the adventurers' bill in September 1653, but Broghill's case was not included. Instead, an order was made for a new survey and allotment for the £1,000 p.a. at Blarney, 'as a mark of the parliament's favour to him, for his eminent and faithful services to the commonwealth, and to satisfy his pay arrears up to 28 June 1650'.[50] The matter was thus once again referred to Broghill's enemies in Dublin, who apparently did nothing.

[48] B.L., Eg. MS 1,761, f. 39r.
[49] Broghill to Whitelocke, 20 Dec. 1652 (Longleat, Whitelocke papers, vol. xii, f. 188r).
[50] C.J., vii, 316.

The creation of the protectorate brought an improvement in Broghill's political position, as we have seen; but his finances would take rather longer to recover. In the summer of 1654 Broghill was forced to take drastic action to prevent his tottering financial edifice from collapsing altogether. In June and July, he made concerted efforts to settle his longer term debts – including the Domville defeazance and the Tully bonds – even on disadvantageous terms.[51] The process had been helped by the payment of a proportion of his salary arrears in May 1654, and the promise of regular payments in future, but this was not enough. On 27 June Broghill released more cash through the sale of 9,049 acres – the whole of the Blarney estate, worth £793 p.a. – to William Hawkins of London.[52] As yet the sale was provisional upon Broghill procuring an act of parliament for settling the fee simple on Hawkins and his heirs, but it seems that an unspecified amount of money changed hands in 1654, and it is tempting to speculate that the series of transactions completed by Broghill that summer were funded by the sale. In acting to sell land, recoup salary arrears and pay off his debts, Broghill seems to have been trying to draw a line under the financial chaos of 1649–54.

Broghill had survived, but his financial problems had not been solved. The 1654 rationalisation had given him more cash, but the short-lived 1654 parliament had not considered Broghill's lands at all, and so the remainder of his grant – and the perfecting of Hawkins' agreement – was still unattained; Broghill's appointment as president of Scotland brought a valuable additional salary, but his pre-1649 arrears were not yet satisfied. Through the spring of 1655 Broghill pursued further awards from the protector and the English council. In April he gained government support for a grant of £3,000 p.a. in Irish lands to settle his arrears once and for all.[53] In the same month, Broghill asked Secretary Thurloe to make sure that this latest grant was confirmed:

> This day seavennight I gave you the trouble of a business of myne concerninge my arreares beinge satisfied in money, accordinge as his highness and the councill were pleas'd to order it; the perfecting wherof you did promiss to favor me in . . . I have indeed som pryvate things of my owne which must suffer for want of this mony.[54]

Thurloe seems to have responded to this request: on 24 April the council ordered that two prominent courtiers, Sir Charles Wolseley and Colonel Philip Jones, were to consult with the solicitor-general and Broghill about the settlement of his land grant, and at the beginning of May the grant was passed

---

[51] Deeds of 21 June and 29 July 1654 (N.L.I., D. 21,097–22,035).

[52] N.L.I., D. 21,097–22,035, bundle 'years 1654, 1656–7, 1658'; cf. 14th rep. of the deputy keeper of the public records of Ireland (Dublin, 1882), p. 51.

[53] Cal. S.P. Dom., 1655, p. 107 (5 Apr. 1655).

[54] Thurloe S.P., iii, 396 (19 Apr. 1655).

as amended.[55] On 23 May the council ordered Serjeant Glynn to perfect the conveyance of land in satisfaction of £3,048 p.a. on Broghill's debenture for arrears of pay.[56] This order promised to increase Broghill's new lands by threefold.

Despite Broghill's efforts, and the apparently unambiguous orders of the English council, the promised £3,000 p.a. grant does not seem to have materialised, perhaps falling victim to the changing climate in England as Lambert and the major-generals became more influential. During Broghill's absence in Scotland, nothing more was done by the council. But there were still hopes that parliament would prove more amenable, and Broghill came to the 1656–7 session with his personal financial settlement, as well as the political settlement of the three nations, on his agenda. As we have seen, the connexion between politics and private finance was close.[57] The passage of Broghill's land bill coincided with the kingship debates, and its final reading, on 5 June 1657, caused the commons to divide on political lines, with Broghill's friends securing him an additional 2,000 acres only in the teeth of fierce opposition from Lambert and his allies.[58] The act to settle Broghill's lands, passed by the protector's consent on 26 June, allowed him a full £1,000 p.a. from Muskerry's lands, including Ballymaloe House and an extra 2,000 acres in Imokilly.[59]

The 1657 act was vital in easing Broghill's financial position, but it did not make him any richer in real terms. Under the articles of the 1654 agreement with William Hawkins, Broghill was immediately forced to alienate three-quarters of the estate, including Blarney Castle. And within a month of the act, he was using the remainder of the original grant to raise further cash sums. On 23 July 1657 Broghill sold the 1,800 acres in the barony of Muskerry included in the protector's grant to William Penn, for a consideration of £1,450, the bulk of which was paid the next day.[60] The sale of the Blarney estate, and also the doubling of his Scottish salary to £2,000 (ordered by Cromwell after the personal intervention of Lady Ranelagh in the summer of 1656) at last seems to have allowed Broghill to tackle his long-term debts.[61] William Tynt was paid off between July 1657 and January 1659; smaller debts to London merchants and agents were paid in July and August 1657; and the

---

[55] Cal. S.P. Dom., 1655, pp 139, 157.

[56] Ibid., p. 177.

[57] See above, ch. 5.

[58] C.J., vii, 517, 537; Burton diary, ii, 175–8.

[59] C.J., vii, 545–6, 577.

[60] N.L.I., D. 21,907–22,035, bundle 'years 1654, 1656–7, 1659'; see also P.R.O., C 54/3952/10; Broghill's accounts for 1657, entry for 24 July 1657 (Petworth, Orrery MS 13192, unfol.).

[61] Broghill to Cromwell, 27 June 1656 (Bodl., MS Rawl. A.39, pp 170–3); Thurloe S.P., vi, 472.

Domville debt was finally cleared in the same period.[62] Of the lands allocated by the act, only Ballymaloe and the Imokilly lands remained. But with his inherited estates returning to productivity, and a combined salary (as president of Scotland and lieutenant-general of the ordnance in Ireland) of over £2,365 p.a., by the autumn of 1657 Broghill had achieved a degree of financial security, for the first time in sixteen years.

Broghill's financial fortunes after 1649 fall into three distinct phases. Until the formation of the protectorate in late 1653, he was crippled by debts and obligations arising from the debts of others; his lands were ruined, and his pre-1649 arrears withheld from him by the incompetence and malice of politicians in England and Ireland. During this period, Broghill became dependent on small sums received in military salaries, a situation which made him all the more vulnerable to the parliamentary commissioners and others who opposed him politically. From 1654 to 1657, Broghill was forced to retrench his finances, selling land he had not fully acquired, settling debts on harsh terms, and constantly lobbying the English council for the settlement of his arrears. His dependence thus shifted from the commanders and commissioners in Dublin (who controlled military salaries) to the protectoral government (which paid his salary as president of Scotland, and promised generous land grants), at just the time that Broghill was affirming his political allegiance to the House of Cromwell. This reinforces the impression that Broghill's financial problems were influencing his political career, as became all too apparent during the debates over Broghill's land grant in parliament in 1657. After the closure of the 1656–7 session, Broghill entered the third stage of his financial 'career', in which he was able to sell land, clear most of his debts, and free himself from major money worries. Although less vulnerable financially, Broghill was still dependent on the regime – and particularly the administration of Henry Cromwell as lord deputy of Ireland from November 1657 – and with a vested interest in the survival of the protectorate.

Broghill's own financial position may have encouraged him to become a supporter of the Cromwellian regime, but this was not the only fiscal influence on him during the 1650s. For his financial commitments inevitably involved others, and thus created bonds of honour, which had to be fulfilled. In the early 1650s, Broghill had laboured hard to ensure the survival of the estates of his brother, the earl of Cork; and in the same period he was evidently anxious about the financial state of his sister, Lady Ranelagh, and her family. The ties of kinship and social interaction were reinforced by a web of financial obligation, with bonds and recognizances, trusteeships and mutual debts, enhancing the cohesion of the Boyle 'affinity'. Broghill's concern extended across the whole Boyle family, most of whom faced financial ruin at some point during the 1640s and 1650s. His brother-in-law, Sir Arthur Loftus, who had lost his

---

[62] Broghill's accounts for 1657 (Petworth, Orrery MS 13192, unfol.); Sir James Shaen to Broghill, 14 June 1659 (ibid., MS 13221, unfol.).

military salary in 1649, and was dependent on a small government salary and the promise of arrears, received help from Broghill later in the 1650s.[63] Another brother-in-law, the earl of Kildare, was imprisoned for debts between 1650 and 1655; on his death in 1657, Broghill and his brothers took control of his young heir's financial affairs, and acted as trustees for the estate.[64] Broghill's sister, the widowed countess of Barrymore, was a constant cause for concern for Cork and Broghill. In the 1650s, Cork took the Barrymores' finances in hand, ensuring that they received money promised in his father's will, and that the countess's daughters had respectable dowries. In 1657–8 Broghill joined his brother's efforts, in an attempt to settle the family's affairs, and to reach agreements with creditors.[65] Broghill's problems of unpaid arrears, spoiled land, and mounting debts were thus replicated throughout the Boyle family, and this made even more urgent his own desires for a settled government under the benign rule of the Cromwellian dynasty.

This imperative was made all the greater by the similarity of the Boyles' financial position to that of the Old Protestant community as a whole. In Munster, the tenants and clients of the Boyles had shared their ruin and now depended on their recovery. In the early 1650s, for example, Broghill's financial problems had been exacerbated by his need to pay substantial sums to his regiment and other troops in Munster, many of whom were Old Protestants with connexions with the Boyle family from before 1641.[66] These men relied on Broghill to secure their pre-1649 arrears; others in Munster waited for the Boyles to pay their local debts. Across Ireland, the unity of purpose of the Old Protestants – as seen in the lobbying which attended the Munster ordinance and the Irish union bill in 1654–5 – was undoubtedly increased by their shared concerns about financial matters. To take four examples: the Munster planter, Sir Hardress Waller, was dependent on irregular military pay in the early 1650s, and while awaiting his arrears to be settled in land, watched his debts increase;[67] the lord president of Connacht, Sir Charles Coote, was preoccupied

---

[63] Abbott, *Writings and speeches*, ii, 116n, 165; *Cal. Com. Comp.*, pp 2106–7; *Cal. S.P. Ire., 1647–60*, p. 797; for Broghill's intervention see his accounts for 1658 (Petworth, Orrery MS 13192, unfol.); William Fitzgerald to Broghill, 22 May 1658 (ibid., MS 13223(1), unfol.).

[64] *Cal. S.P. Dom., 1655*, pp 349, 380; Cork's diary (Chatsworth, Lismore MS 29, unfol.), 24–8 Sept. 1657; P.R.O.N.I., Leinster papers, D. 3078/14/14–20.

[65] See Cork's diary (Chatsworth, Lismore MS 29, unfol.), 31 Aug. and 15 Nov. 1651, 17 Feb. 1652, 28 June and 9 July 1653, 12 Jan., 28 May and 27 Aug. 1655, 12 Sept. 1657; Cork to countess of Barrymore, c.Sept. 1658 (ibid., Lismore MS 30, no. 23); Cork to earl of Barrymore, c.Oct. 1658 (ibid., no. 28); papers relating to earl of Barrymore, 1658 (Bodl., Rawl. A.61, ff. 380r–5v).

[66] Receipts dated 28 May, 1 and 9 June 1650, 24 July, 20 Aug., 2, 20 and 25 Oct., 16 Nov. 1652 (Petworth, Orrery MS 13192, unfol.); the total disbursed by Broghill in this period was at least £867.

[67] Waller's petition, 22 Mar. 1653 (Bodl., MS Tanner 53, f. 231r); *Thurloe S.P.*, vi, 773–4; *H.M.C. 7th Rep.*, p. 96.

by his concerns for the payment of arrears to himself and his extensive client group in Connaught and Ulster;[68] the Ulster settler, George Rawdon, was also active in trying to secure the pre-1649 arrears;[69] and the Leinster landowner, William Parsons, struggled to revive his family's finances, being heavily reliant on government pensions and the ability of his friends and neighbours to repay debts contracted many years before.[70] Four men from the four provinces of Ireland, and all in the same boat. Government action in allowing the payment of the pre-1649 arrears, in relieving debts, and releasing other financial pressures such as the heavy assessments and the restrictions on trade, would have an immediate impact on the whole of the Old Protestant community. The ubiquity of their complaints increased their sense of common purpose and their willingness to act as a coherent 'party' in the parliament of 1656; it also influenced their attitude towards union, with its intrinsic economic benefits, described in one account of the union debates of 1657 as 'the main of all'.[71] And Broghill's personal experience of financial crisis, inextricably linked to his concern for the survival of the Boyle family and of the Old Protestant community in general, underpinned his commitment to a new, civilian settlement under a Cromwellian monarchy.

---

[68] *Cal. S.P. Ire.*, 1647–60, p. 634.
[69] Ibid., pp 634, 658, 660; Edward Berwick (ed.), *The Rawdon papers* (1819), pp 179–80.
[70] Birr Castle, Rosse papers, A/12, ff 1r–2r, 8r–9r, 17r, 19r.
[71] *Burton diary*, i, 352.

9

Faith

Broghill's religious beliefs are as difficult to discern as his financial position. The absence of a personal archive, and the fact that most of his extant letters concern public business, make Broghill a slightly enigmatic figure in religious terms. Moreover, what survives does not seem to fit into the neat categories – Episcopalian, Presbyterian, Independent – so necessary for the databases of social historians. Further obstacles are created by the temptation to treat matters of faith with either cynicism or credulity, or to make anachronistic distinctions between the religious and political motives of seventeenth-century people, in an attempt to clarify an otherwise murky picture. Any attempt to unravel the strands of religious belief and secular motive, while remaining aware of the historical context, is fraught with problems. Yet the difficulty of the task is commensurate with its importance: as in the case of Oliver Cromwell, the political motives of Lord Broghill can only be fully understood when his religious context is taken into account.[1]

The key to understanding Broghill's later religious affiliations, as to so many of his other attributes, can be found in his upbringing as son of the godly first earl of Cork. The earl held strong Calvinist beliefs, which fitted with the conviction that his own rise to wealth and influence was providential (as reflected in his motto: 'God's providence is mine inheritance'); and, as we saw in chapter one, he was keen to cultivate similar attitudes in his children, although he was careful not to let them stray outside the theological confines of the Church of Ireland.[2] Twice-daily prayers, Sunday sermons, and long periods of religious reading and reflection formed the routine of the Boyle household in the 1630s, and the earl was on friendly terms with a range of ministers and clerics, from Stephen Jerome to Archbishop James Ussher.[3] The

---

[1] For Cromwell see J. C. Davis, 'Cromwell's religion' in John Morrill (ed.), *Oliver Cromwell and the English revolution* (1990), pp 181–208; J. C. Davis, *Oliver Cromwell* (2001), pp 112–37; Blair Worden, 'Oliver Cromwell and the sin of Achan' in Derek Beales and Geoffrey Best (eds), *History, society and the churches* (Cambridge, 1985), pp 125–45.

[2] See Canny, *Upstart earl*; also review of same by Toby Barnard in *E.H.R.*, c (1985), pp 405–7.

[3] Raymond Gillespie, *Devoted people: belief and religion in early modern Ireland* (Manchester, 1997), p. 12.

cycle of daily observance and religious contemplation was continued by Broghill and his siblings in later decades, and marked his political as well as social activities during the Cromwellian period.

As we have seen, Broghill's childhood experiences were reinforced by his continental education in the later 1630s, when his tutor, Isaac Marcombes, a French Huguenot, oversaw his studies in Geneva (in 1636–7) and at the Huguenot academy at Saumur (in 1638), studying under the Italian Calvinist, John Diodati, and the Scottish Huguenot, Mark Duncan.[4] The course of study at each place centred on religious instruction, and this seems to have made a deep impact on the young Broghill. Years later he related to Thomas Morrice his meetings with Diodati, who told him tales of Calvinist piety, and asserted that 'he was well affected to the government of the Church of England, and wished they of Geneva could come nearer to it'.[5] Broghill's evident approval of Diodati's comments suggests that he shared his father's own preferences for moderate Calvinism within the established church. Such views also had parallels with the liberal Calvinism taught at Saumur. At the academy, Broghill not only learned French and fencing with his aristocratic friends; he also came under the influence of Huguenot divines, lodging with Mark Duncan, and having 'the conveniency both of his, & Famous Mr du Plessis [Mornay] his lybrary'.[6] Another contact was the Huguenot divine, Francis Perraud, who wrote the famous account of demonic possession by the 'Divell of Mascon', and was 'well acquainted' with Broghill during his sojourn at Saumur.[7] Broghill continued to associate with Huguenots in later decades: he was still on good terms with his old tutor, Marcombes, in the 1640s; and the Huguenot minister, Peter du Moulin junior, was his friend in the 1650s.[8] Again, this was an affiliation he shared with his siblings. Robert Boyle had a great affection for Marcombes, who had been his own tutor in the early 1640s.[9] The second earl of Cork, who had also studied at Saumur, was du Moulin's principal patron, employing him as chaplain in Ireland and then (from 1656) as tutor to his sons at Oxford.[10] Lady Ranelagh, whose friends in the Great Tew circle were greatly influenced by Philippe du Plessis Mornay and the Dutch theologian,

[4] See above, ch. 1.

[5] Morrice, *Memoirs*, pp 3–5.

[6] Kinalmeaky to Cork, 28 May 1638 (B.L., Add. MS 19832, f. 45r).

[7] N. H. Keeble and G. F. Nuttall (eds), *Calendar of the correspondence of Richard Baxter* (2 vols, Oxford, 1991), i, 317; see Elisabeth Labrousse, 'Le Démon de Mâcon' in *Scienze, credenze occulte, livelli di cultura* (Florence, 1982), pp 249–75. I am grateful to Professor Michael Hunter for giving me a copy of this article.

[8] *Boyle's works*, i, p. xxxiii; *Baxter correspondence*, i, 317.

[9] *Boyle's works*, i, p. xxxiii.

[10] Second earl of Cork's diary (Chatsworth, Lismore MS 29, unfol.), entries for 15 Jan. 1651, 10 Sept. 1653, 24 Dec. 1654, 14–15 June 1656; Dungarvan to Sarah Digby, 8 June 1633 (ibid., Lismore MS 17, no. 146).

Hugo Grotius, duly sent her son, Richard Jones, to study at Saumur in the later 1650s.[11] Broghill's own sons would spend nearly a year at the Huguenot academy (lodging with Moise Amyrault's wife) in the early 1660s.[12] Like his brothers and sister, Broghill seems to have been impressed by the Huguenots and their ideas.

During the Irish wars of the 1640s and early 1650s, Broghill's religious experience became overlaid by political and military concerns. His chaplain in the early years of the war, Urban Vigors, was an Episcopalian of Calvinist leanings.[13] Broghill's imposition of strict Presbyterian practice at Youghal, and his own subscription of the covenant may reflect a hardening of his religious opinions, but they were also intended as a public statement of his allegiance to parliament.[14] Such moves may also have been prompted by Broghill's desire to show up his commander and rival, Lord Inchiquin, who declined the covenant, and was known to harbour Episcopalians, including a bishop and two deans, at Cork in 1644–5.[15] As the war continued, Broghill's distrust of Catholicism also seems to have increased, from the low levels of prejudice common to all Old Protestants before 1641, to a crescendo in the late 1640s. In August 1647, Broghill's charges against Inchiquin included not only collusion with Ormond, but also 'that publique Masse hath beene frequently said in Corke and Kinsale since his Lordship being made of the Province by the Parliament'.[16] Again, this may tell us as much about Broghill's skill as a propagandist as his views on Catholicism. But hatred of Catholicism almost certainly encouraged Broghill in his sometimes brutal treatment of the Irish and their clergy in the Cromwellian wars: for example, his decision to hang the Roman Catholic Bishop of Rosse in sight of the defenders of Carrigadrohid Castle in April 1650, seems to have been purely sectarian in motive.[17] Another incident, after his victory at Knocknaclashy in 1651, reveals Broghill's scorn of the superstitious Irish, and his loathing for the priests who had encouraged them to fight 'by sprinkling holy water on them, and by charmes . . . many of them were found quilted in the doublets of the dead'. As Broghill added: 'Had

[11] Hugh Trevor Roper, 'The Great Tew circle' in his Catholics, Anglicans and Puritans: seventeenth-century essays (1987), pp 190–3; Jones to Hartlib, 7 July 1657 (S.U.L., Hartlib MS 14/3/2A); Henry Oldenburg to Hartlib, 7 Jan. 1658 (ibid., Hartlib MS 39/3/5A); Jones to Hartlib, 21 Jan. 1658 (ibid., Hartlib MS 59/5/5A).

[12] Account of Lord Broghill's and Mr Boyle's grand tour, 1662–3 (Petworth, Orrery Papers, MS 13192, unfol.).

[13] Thomas Fitzpatrick, Waterford during the Civil War (1641–53) (Waterford, 1912), pp 124, 133.

[14] B.L., Add. MS 25287, f. 20r; certificate of committee for examinations, 24 Apr. 1645 (Bodl., MS Carte 14, f. 425r).

[15] Three severall letters of great importance (6 Dec. 1644), pp 5–7 (B.L., E.2196)).

[16] Articles . . . exhibited against the Lord Inchiquin (18 Aug. 1647), p. 3 (B.L., E. 402(19)).

[17] Several Proceedings in Parliament, no. 35 (23–30 May 1650), pp 503–4 (B.L., E.777(6)).

I been one of the charmed, I would have first tryed mine out on the Priest who gave it.'[18]

After the vivid contrasts of war, peace once again brought a degree of moderation to Broghill's religious attitudes. Something of the ambiguity of his private beliefs in the early 1650s can be gleaned from a comparison with his elder brother, the second earl of Cork. Despite his former royalism, Cork's religious views seem to have followed those of his father: he preferred a 'low-church' Episcopacy, with the Calvinist doctrines of the 1615 Articles, moulded by Archbishop Ussher.[19] Despite continuing government suspicions that 'I had the Common prayer in the house', Cork was free to employ as chaplains closet Episcopalians (including du Moulin), from whom he regularly received Holy Communion.[20] But Cork's religious tastes were not narrowly Episcopalian. His diary records that he also patronised Presbyterians, including Edward Worth and Joseph Eyres, and attended sermons by Independent ministers, such as James Wood and Claudius Gilbert (in Munster) and Samuel Winter (in Dublin).[21] This broad taste in theological issues was something Cork shared with Broghill. On the occasions when they were in the same place, the two families worshipped side by side.[22] Lady Broghill received Easter Communion (from an Episcopalian) at Cork's house on Easter Day, 1654; Cork 'prayed at Blarney' in company with Lady Broghill on a Sunday in the following July; and in October 1657 Broghill and Cork were both at Lismore when the Presbyterian, Joseph Eyres, preached a Sunday sermon.[23] There was a high degree of collaboration by the brothers on religious, as well as political and financial, matters. In 1655 Broghill and his ally, Vincent Gookin, used their influence in Whitehall to gain a pass for Thomas Hackett, one of Cork's Presbyterian friends, to go to Holland;[24] and in the same year, both Cork

---

[18] Broghill to [Cromwell?], c.1651 (P.R.O., S.P. 63/276, f. 174r); the incident was included in the manuscript version of Thomas Morrice's biography, but was omitted from the printed edition: see B.L., Sloane MS 4227, f. 56r–v; see also Pádraig Lenihan, *Confederate Catholics at war, 1641–49* (Cork, 2001), pp 202–3.

[19] For Ussher's influence over Old Protestant opinion in general see T. C. Barnard, *Cromwellian Ireland* (Oxford, 1975), pp 91–2; for the Calvinism of the Church of Ireland under Ussher see Alan Ford, 'The Church of Ireland, 1558–1634: a puritan church?' in Alan Ford, James McGuire and Kenneth Milne (eds), *As by law established: the Church of Ireland since the reformation* (Dublin, 1995), pp 52–68.

[20] Cork's diary (Chatsworth, Lismore MS 29, unfol.), passim, but see especially entries for 10 Sept. 1653, 16 July 1654, 10 Dec. 1654, 24 Dec. 1654, 31 Jan. 1656.

[21] Cork's diary (ibid.), 8 Oct. 1654, 15 Oct. 1654, 12 Nov. 1654, 22 Apr. 1655, 12 Aug. 1655, 31 Jan. 1656, 31 Jan. 1658. For more on these ministers and their views see Barnard, *Cromwellian Ireland*, pp 114–121.

[22] Walter Gostello, *Charls Stuart and Oliver Cromwell united* (20 Jan. 1655), p. 89 (B.L., E.1503(3)).

[23] Cork's diary (Chatsworth, Lismore MS 29, unfol.), 26 Mar. 1654, 9 July 1654, 18 Oct. 1657.

[24] *Cal. S.P. Dom., 1655*, p. 177; Cork's diary (Chatsworth, Lismore MS 29, unfol.), 19 Feb. 1654.

and Broghill were enthusiastic supporters of collections for the distressed Protestants of Savoy.[25] The two brothers may have had their differences on religious matters, with Cork seeming to prefer Episcopacy, while Broghill inclined towards Presbyterian forms; and these differences became more marked after 1660;[26] but in the 1650s they were united in a common concern for a settled, moderate, scripture-based Calvinist ministry (which encompassed Episcopalians, Presbyterians and Independents), as a safeguard against the threat of the Baptists and Quakers tolerated by Fleetwood's government.[27]

This desire for a broadly-based, orthodox ministry was also articulated by the two men who seem to have had most influence over Broghill's religious views in the 1650s: Archbishop Ussher and Richard Baxter of Kidderminster. Ussher's defence of Calvinism, and his great learning, made him acceptable to the parliamentarian cause despite his episcopal office.[28] Broghill's personal connexions with Ussher were another legacy of the first earl of Cork. Ussher supported Cork in his struggle against Wentworth over the St Patrick's Cathedral tomb in 1634, and his brand of Calvinist episcopacy fitted well with the earl's own views.[29] This link between Ussher and the Boyles continued after Cork's death, and in the 1650s the primate became involved in the intellectual circle centred on Samuel Hartlib, and patronised by Lady Ranelagh, Robert Boyle, the second earl of Cork, and Broghill himself.[30] There were also theological links between Ussher and the Boyles. For example, Broghill's sister, Mary Rich, recorded that her enthusiasm for stage plays had been quashed in the late 1640s 'by my Lord Primate of Irelandes Preaching';[31] Robert Boyle's study of Hebrew was encouraged by him;[32] and among the books sent to Broghill in England in 1658 was a copy of Ussher's 'Annals of the World'.[33] During his stay in London in 1654–5, Broghill renewed his acquaintance with

[25] Cork's diary (Chatsworth, Lismore MS 29, unfol.), 5 July 1655; Hartlib's Ephemerides, Apr.–Aug. 1655 (S.U.L., Hartlib MS 29/5/30b–31A). These collections were backed by their common friends, Samuel Hartlib and John Dury.

[26] In 1656 the Resolutioner, Robert Baillie, praised Broghill as 'by profession a Presbyterian': see Baillie letters, iii, 315; for the differences between Broghill and Cork after 1660 see Barnard, 'Cork', p. 176.

[27] Robert Boyle seems to have been rather more tolerant towards sectarians (if not Socinians): see Michael Hunter (ed.), Robert Boyle by himself and his friends (1994), p. lxxi; Michael Hunter, 'How Robert Boyle became a scientist' in History of Science, xxxiii (1995), pp 91–2.

[28] Barnard, Cromwellian Ireland, p. 91.

[29] Canny, Upstart earl, pp 27, 162–3, 203.

[30] Canny, Upstart earl, pp 142–3; T. C. Barnard, 'The Hartlib circle and the origins of the Dublin philosophical society' in I.H.S., xix (1974–5), p. 71.

[31] B.L., Add. MS 27357, f. 23v.

[32] Boyle's works, i. p. xlviii; Hunter, 'How Robert Boyle became a scientist', pp 72, 80; Hunter, Robert Boyle by himself and his friends, p. 27.

[33] Note of items sent to Broghill, 21 May 1658 (Petworth, Orrery MS 13192, unfol.): this was presumably Ussher's Annals of the Old Testament, published in 1650 and 1654.

Ussher, and when the 1654 parliament appointed a committee of divines to advise on religious matters, Broghill 'named the Primate of Ireland, Archbishop Ussher'.[34] Broghill's choice of Ussher was not coincidental. In the last years of his life, the primate had become increasingly involved in 'irenicism': efforts to find common ground between (in this case) Episcopalians and Presbyterians. In 1641, and again in 1648, Ussher had presented Charles I with his ideas for the 'Reduction of Episcopacy to the form of Presbytery', and in the early 1650s he continued to push similar ideas, with the final version of the *Reduction of Episcopacy* being published posthumously by his executor, Nicholas Bernard, in 1656.[35] Ussher's attempts to reconcile the different parties seem to have appealed to Broghill, whose own religious interests (and political concerns) were equally inclusive.

When Broghill failed to persuade Ussher to advise the 1654 parliament, he nominated instead a puritan divine, Richard Baxter.[36] This did not indicate a change in Broghill's sympathies, however, as Ussher and Baxter both subscribed to irenicist principles, although the latter wanted to extend the search for unity to include the Independents. In 1653 Baxter had reacted against the religious radicalism of Barebones' Parliament by founding the Worcester Association of ministers. Baxter's Association encouraged Independents in other counties to create their own, and efforts were made to spread the scheme to Ireland.[37] By 1654 Baxter was already well advanced in a related scheme to promote union between the Independent and Presbyterian churches against such threats as Unitarianism and Baptism. Encouraged by the work of John Dury on the continent, and Ussher's writings, Baxter established links with a number of prominent Presbyterians in London and the west country, and preached a series of irenicist sermons in the capital.[38] In the summer of 1654 Baxter became acquainted with Broghill, and the two grew very close. Baxter 'lodged at the Lord Broghill's' in Westminster during the following winter, and Broghill brought him to preach before Cromwell 'against the Divisions and Distractions of the Church'.[39] Broghill's approval of his earlier book, *The Saints Rest*, encouraged Baxter to publish 'some popular sermons more by me on that subject', which were dedicated to him.[40] It was as a result of this close connexion that Broghill nominated Baxter as Ussher's replace-

---

[34] Matthew Sylvester (ed.), *Reliquiae Baxterianae: or Mr Baxter's narrative of the most memorable passages of his life and times* (1696), pp 197, 206.

[35] Hugh Trevor-Roper, 'James Ussher, archbishop of Armagh' in his *Catholics, Anglicans and puritans* (1987), p. 151; Barnard, *Cromwellian Ireland*, pp 91–2; Sylvester, *Reliquiae Baxterianae*, p. 62.

[36] Sylvester, *Reliquiae Baxterianae*, p. 197; for Baxter see W. Lamont, *Richard Baxter and the millennium: Protestant imperialism and the English revolution* (1979).

[37] *Baxter correspondence*, i, 83, 94–5, 103.

[38] Ibid., pp 85–6, 127–8, 134, 151, 154–7, 161.

[39] Sylvester, *Reliquiae Baxterianae*, p. 205.

[40] *Baxter correspondence*, i, 189.

ment on the committee of divines in late 1654. Most important of all, Broghill was able to arrange a personal meeting between the two great irenicists, Baxter and Ussher. In previous years, the ageing Ussher had been unwilling to collaborate with Baxter, and had refused a proposal that 'wee should jointly subscribe what wee were agreed upon as our advice' on church unity.[41] But in early 1655, as Baxter recorded, everything changed: 'In this time of my abode at the Lord Broghill's, fell out all the Acquaintance I had with . . . Archbishop Usher . . . Sometimes he came to me, and oft I went to him.' These meetings proved very fruitful for the ambitious Baxter, for 'in this time I opened to Bishop Usher the motions of Concord which I had made with the Episcopal Divines'.[42]

Broghill's role as the catalyst to bring together Baxter and Ussher supports the idea that he too was eager to promote unity between the various churches. Broghill came from a background in the Church of Ireland where Episcopalianism and Calvinism fused; his experiences in Geneva, where men like Diodati spoke approvingly of the reconciliation of the churches, were reinforced by the irenicist theology of the Huguenot academy at Saumur. Du Plessis Mornay and Amyraut had pressed for union between the Protestant churches, and Amyrault praised John Dury's efforts in 'seeking the peace of the Evangelists' in the early 1650s.[43] Dury was well known to Ussher and Baxter, and also to Broghill, by 1655.[44] Amyrault's ideas were a strong influence on Baxter's own irenicist initiatives.[45] Baxter was also on good terms with Peter du Moulin junior (whose friends and patrons included the second earl of Cork and Lord Broghill), and later encouraged him to translate the book written by his father, a prominent Huguenot theologian, calling for greater unity between the Protestant churches.[46] In bringing together Ussher and Baxter, Broghill was adding his own contribution to a long tradition of irenicism within the Protestant churches of Britain and Europe. This was entirely consistent with what we know of his religious activities and affiliations in the years before and after the Irish wars, which approved a broadly based church, made up of all the more moderate, non-sectarian groups within the Protestant camp. The efforts of Broghill and Cork to encourage a range of Independent,

[41] Ibid., pp 93–4.

[42] Sylvester, *Reliquiae Baxterianae*, p. 206.

[43] A. R. and M. B. Hall (eds), *The correspondence of Henry Oldenburg* (13 vols, Madison, Wisc., and Milwaukee, 1965–86), i, 146–7.

[44] For Dury's acquaintance with Broghill see Dury to Hartlib, 13 May 1655 (S.U.L., Hartlib MS 4/3/97A–B); for his contacts with Baxter and Ussher see *Baxter correspondence*, i, 85–6, 93. Dury had been a close friend of Lady Ranelagh since 1644, and of Robert Boyle by 1647: see *Mr Dury's letter to ye Lady Ronaloe* (13 June 1645) (B.L., E. 288(14)); *Boyle's correspondence*, i, 56–7.

[45] *Baxter correspondence*, i, 113.

[46] Ibid., pp 317, 332; for Peter du Moulin senior, and his efforts to encourage James I to back Protestant policies, see his entry in the *D.N.B.*

Presbyterian and Episcopalian ministers in Munster in the early 1650s were but another manifestation of what was in itself a consistent, unified policy.

Irenicism was not just a practical attempt to promote unity between the orthodox Protestant churches; it was also a central pillar of the Calvinist theological system, which saw God's divine plan guiding men's affairs on earth. The union of the churches (seen as the gathering of the gentiles), along with the conversion of the Jews, was seen as part of the struggle against the Antichrist which preceded the Second Coming promised in the Book of Revelation.[47] Ussher, in particular, had focused his studies on the working of providence in the past, on the identification of the papacy with the Antichrist, and the dating (through his biblical chronology) of both creation (4004 BC) and the coming apocalypse (AD 1996).[48] On the continent, men like John Dury worked for the unification of the Calvinist and Lutheran churches, not as an end in itself, but as a prelude to a pan-Protestant alliance against the pope and his chief supporters, the emperor and the king of Spain. This belief in providence was not the same as the apocalyptic claims of the extreme religious sects including the Fifth Monarchists, so despised by Broghill and his friends, who saw the end of the world as imminent. Professor J. R. Jacob's assertion that Robert Boyle, Lady Ranelagh, and probably Broghill had a 'shared belief in an imminent apocalypse' has been successfully debunked by Malcolm Oster, who sees Boyle, at least, as part of the 'Protestant mainstream', which looked for signs of God's providence not as an imminent event but as part of a longer term divine plan.[49] After all, Ussher predicted the end of the world in the twentieth century, not the seventeenth.

Broghill's belief in divine providence may not have been apocalyptic, but it was still a crucial influence over his thoughts and actions. Just as the first earl of Cork had mused, after the fall of Strafford, on 'the uncertenty whereunto the greateste men are subiect',[50] so Broghill resorted to providential explanations of the fluctuating fortunes of himself and his political rivals. When reporting a victory over the Irish in 1651, Broghill acknowledged that 'there were in this signal mercy many sweete appearances of Providence towards us'.[51] On the death of Ireton later in the year, Broghill wrote 'If the poorest and most contemptible creature fall not without a providence,

---

[47] For the conversion of the Jews see R. H. Popkin, 'Hartlib, Dury and the Jews' in Mark Greengrass et al. (eds), *Samuel Hartlib and universal reformation: studies in intellectual communication* (Cambridge, 1994), pp 118–36.

[48] Trevor-Roper, 'James Ussher', pp 127–8, 132–3, 156–61.

[49] J. R. Jacob, 'Boyle's circle in the protectorate: revelation, politics and the millennium', *Journal of the History of Ideas*, xxxviii (1977), pp 131–40; Malcolm Oster, 'Millenarianism and the new science: the case of Robert Boyle' in Mark Greengrass et al. (eds), *Samuel Hartlib and universal reformation: studies in intellectual communication* (Cambridge, 1994), pp 137–48.

[50] Grosart, *Lismore papers* ser. 1, v, 165.

[51] Broghill to [Cromwell], c.1651 (P.R.O., S.P. 63/276, f. 175r).

doubtless those whom the Lord hath made instrumentall in his work, are not removed but to instruct us in a lesson'.[52] The desire to gain an insight into God's plans prompted Broghill to support the study of the Bible: the revealed word of God, where all the answers lay. Robert Boyle's unpublished *Essay on Scripture*, was written at Broghill's 'request' in the early 1650s; and his published version, *Some Considerations touching the Style of the Holy Scriptures* (written c.1652) was dedicated to him.[53] In these works, Boyle intended not only to refute the anti-scripturalism of some sectarians, but also to encourage gentlemen and statesmen to take the Bible seriously: for when '[I] see the addictedness of princes to the study of scripture . . . I shall expect to see the golden age elsewhere than in poets' dreams'.[54] Boyle's researches into the Bible had been prompted by Ussher, who 'engaged me in the study of the holy tongues', especially Hebrew.[55] Later in the 1650s Broghill was himself busy promoting this kind of biblical scholarship, and was behind a scheme to settle a salary of £200 on the professor of Hebrew at Edinburgh University.[56] Ussher's researches into the chronology of the world (which had great importance in understanding God's plans) had relied on such scholarship, and it is interesting to note that in 1658 Broghill sent for his own (annotated?) copy of the 'Annals' to consult while he was in London.[57] Correct scriptural texts and exact chronology were two of the three pillars (the other being accurate history) of Ussher's scheme to promote Protestant 'truth' as a weapon against popery.[58]

This heightened interest in the workings of providence, as traced in scripture, contrasted with a general scepticism towards the visions and prophesies common at the time. On 14 September 1652 Lady Ranelagh reported to Robert Boyle a number of reports of signs and wonders from across Europe, saying that they 'do hereby signify something; though I think he that would dare to affirm in particular what, might be as like to mistake as hit right; butt we have a sure word, that tells us, all this old frame of heaven and earth must pass, and a new one be set up in its place'.[59] In other words, the Book of Revelation was a more reliable guide to the will of God than the visions of private individuals. This was the assumption which underlay the reaction of the second earl of Cork and Lord Broghill to the mystical dreams of Walter

---

[52] *Mercurius Politicus*, no. 81 (18–25 Dec. 1651), p. 1301.
[53] *Boyle's works*, i, p. xlvii; ii, 247–322; Hunter, 'How Robert Boyle became a scientist', pp 72–4.
[54] *Boyle's works*, ii, 311.
[55] Ibid., i, p. xlviii; see Trevor-Roper, 'James Ussher', p. 134.
[56] Dickson to Sharp, 10 Nov. 1657 (N.L.S., Wodrow MSS Octavo xl, ff 20v–21r); Sharp to Edinburgh ministers, n.d. (ibid., f. 26r–v).
[57] Note of items sent to Broghill, 21 May 1658 (Petworth, Orrery MS 13192, unfol.).
[58] Trevor-Roper, 'James Ussher', pp 132–3.
[59] *Boyle's works*, vi, 534 (dated by mention of the death of Fenton Parsons, whose will was written on 4 Sept. and proved on 30 Sept. 1652: see Birr Castle, Rosse papers, A5/79).

Gostelow in Munster in 1654. At first Gostelow was given a patient hearing, and his call for the rebuilding of the church at Lismore (prompted by his meditation on scripture) had a strong impact on the earl of Cork. But when he publicly proclaimed such alarming predictions as the return of Charles Stuart to the throne and the exiled king's marriage to one of Cork's daughters, he was immediately condemned as 'Certainly Mad', and was soon imprisoned by Broghill until he agreed 'that I should not proclaim the King in the streets'.[60] In 1659, Broghill himself recorded strange apparitions seen in the Irish sky, but did not bother to interpret them.[61] Overall, it seems that visions and dreams made little impact on the Boyles; but other forms of revelation, especially those with a strong biblical basis, were taken very seriously. The approach of the last war against the Papal Antichrist had prompted the whole family to search their Bibles and to reconsider the chronologies produced by Ussher, as well as the irenicist schemes of John Dury and Richard Baxter.[62] It also seems to have encouraged them in their support for Oliver Cromwell. Like Gustavus Adolphus in the early 1630s, Oliver Cromwell was seen in providential terms, as the head of the pan-Protestant assault on Antichrist. For some, at least, there was no doubt that 'God hath a great work for him to do'.[63] Lady Ranelagh subscribed to this view, seeing him as God's agent to bring together the churches and defeat the papacy, thereby ushering in a new world order.[64] Her friend, Henry Oldenburg, echoed such sentiments when he told Robert Boyle of news that the English navy had defeated the Spanish: 'the continued success of the Protector is an evident sign that Heaven has some extraordinary task for him'.[65] Broghill had long feared Spanish support for a Stuart uprising in Ireland or Scotland, and the victory at Santa Cruz also caught his imagination, leading him to write verses in praise of Cromwell's 'resistless Genius'.[66] Interestingly, when Broghill's ally, William Jephson, left England as ambassador to Carl X Gustav in 1657, he had high hopes of persuading the Swedish king to join 'a general treaty betwixt al the Protestants'.[67] The extent to which Broghill shared this belief in Oliver Cromwell as a

---

[60] Gostelow, *Charls Stuart and Oliver Cromwel united*, pp 27, 33–40, 47, 50–3, 70–5, 82–90, 101, 125.

[61] Broghill to Cork, 11 Jan. 1659 (Chatsworth, Lismore MS 30, no. 63).

[62] See S. L. Adams, 'The Protestant cause: religious alliance with the west European Calvinist communities as a political issue in England, 1585–1630' (unpublished D.Phil. thesis, University of Oxford, 1973), pp 1–24.

[63] George Smith, *God's Unchangeableness* (15 Jan. 1655) (B.L., E. 824(4)), Sig. A2v; see above, ch. 5.

[64] Jacob, 'Boyle's circle in the Protectorate', p. 136.

[65] *Oldenburg correspondence*, i, 120.

[66] Dow, *Cromwellian Scotland*, pp 191–3; *Thurloe S.P.*, iv, 73, 160; ibid., vi, 774; Lynch, *Orrery*, p. 90; for Broghill's interest in continental affairs in the late 1650s see above, ch. 6.

[67] *Thurloe S.P.*, vi, 628–30.

Protestant hero is uncertain, but his adherence to irenicist ideals, and his interest in providence as revealed in the Bible, supports the notion that his allegiance to the protector was more than merely a matter of politics or personality.[68]

Whatever his providential hopes and fears, Broghill's adherence to Calvinism and desire for irenicism between the churches clearly found practical application in his political career. Such beliefs were closely connected with his conviction that only an inclusive, civilian 'settlement' of the three nations could bring stability and prosperity to the the the Cromwellian regime. As president of the Scottish council in 1655–6, Broghill had sought this by winning over the majority Resolutioner party, and persuading them to switch their political loyalty from the Stuarts to Cromwell. Broghill's opposition to the minority Protester faction was because they formed the greatest obstacle to a broad-based, moderate religious settlement, not least because divisions in the Kirk encouraged the growth of Baptist and Quaker influence in Scotland. Broghill's Scottish policy was made with an eye to the other two nations. As he told Cromwell in February 1656, 'heerby the presbiterians of England and Ireland, who are not inconsiderable, might probably be wonn unto your highnes'.[69] In Ireland, the political dangers of military rule had also been compounded by the growth of sectarianism, and there was a desperate need to promote unity between the Presbyterians and the Independents to encourage a stable, Calvinist, church settlement. This had long been a matter of concern for Irish Protestants,[70] and soon after his arrival in Ireland Henry Cromwell made a concerted effort to draw together the Presbyterian party and the moderate Independents. By February 1656 both Presbyterian and Independent ministers were being allowed government salaries.[71] Henry Cromwell also lent official support to informal ventures to bring ministers to Ireland. Efforts by Richard Baxter and his ally, Colonel John Bridges, to establish links between the English associations and the congregations in Dublin and elsewhere, were intended to address 'the extraordinary want of faithful and able Ministers' in Ireland.[72]

Broghill's concern at the impact of his Scottish policies on the 'presbiterians of England' is also significant. There were close parallels between the situation in Scotland and Ireland and that in England in the mid-1650s. Under the

---

[68] For the impact of providentialism on protectoral politics see Worden, 'Oliver Cromwell and the sin of Achan', passim.

[69] *Thurloe S.P.*, iv, 557.

[70] Gookin, *The author and case of transplanting the Irish into Connaught vindicated* (12 May 1655), p. 14 (B.L., E.838(7)); for Gookin see Patricia Coughlan, 'Counter-currents in colonial discourse: the political thought of Vincent and Daniel Gookin' in Jane Ohlmeyer (ed.), *Political thought in seventeenth century Ireland: kingdom or colony?* (Cambridge, 2000), pp 56–82.

[71] N.L.I., MS 758, ff 63r–4r.

[72] *Baxter correspondence*, i, 186.

commonwealth the religious sects had gained ground, while the Presbyterian church in particular faced official persecution. The attacks of Barebones' Parliament on tithes and lay patronage were a direct assault on the Presbyterians, who responded by seeking closer co-operation with the moderate Independents, who were themselves associating in response to the sectarian threat.[73] The protectorate had been welcomed by the Presbyterians as well as the Independents as a safeguard against the army, but subsequent attempts to introduce a conservative religious settlement in the 1654 parliament failed, and the rule of the major-generals and the ascendancy of Lambert and his friends at Whitehall signalled the growth of military power nationally and locally. Military influence over justice and religious practice, which had long caused tension in Ireland and Scotland, was once again part of the political situation in England. These broader similarities may have been brought home to Broghill by his extensive personal connexions with the Presbyterians in England, especially with the earls of Warwick and Suffolk.

A man of intense personal piety, Warwick had been the hub of a wide godly circle since the 1620s, and even as an old man in the 1650s he commanded enormous respect, counting Stephen Marshall, Edmund Calamy, Sir Nathaniel Barnardiston and the Bacon brothers among his many friends and allies.[74] In January 1657 the French Ambassador had described him as 'the chief of that sect [ie. the Presbyterians]'.[75] In the early 1650s Broghill was in contact with Warwick through his sisters, Mary Rich and Lady Ranelagh, and his brother, Robert Boyle, who were frequent visitors to the earl's houses in London and Essex.[76] In the mid-1650s Broghill and Warwick became firm friends, partly because of their shared respect for Archbishop Ussher and Richard Baxter.[77] Broghill's brother-in-law, the third earl of Suffolk, had gone into retirement under the commonwealth, but remained in close contact with Broghill and his wife throughout this period, and his religious views appear very similar to those of his brother-in-law. One example is particlularly telling. In 1655, when Baxter preached to Warwick and others in London, he 'sent the day before to secure room for the Lord Broghill and the Earl of Suffolk, with whom I was to go in the Coach'.[78] As with Warwick, Broghill's association with Suffolk shows that he moved easily within Presbyterian circles, especially when they coincided with the irenicist group centred on Richard Baxter.

---

[73] See, for example, Ann Hughes, *Godly reformation and its opponents in Warwickshire, 1640–62* (Dugdale society occasional papers), no. 35 (1993), pp 17–19.

[74] D.N.B.; Calamy, *A patterne for all* (2 June 1658) (B.L., E.947(1)).

[75] Bordeaux to Brienne, 23 Jan./1 Feb. 1657 (P.R.O., PRO 31/3/101, f. 44r).

[76] B.L., Add. MS 27357, ff 20r–25r; *Boyle's works*, i, p. xlv; vi. 46; *Boyle's corespondence*, i, 133, 136.

[77] For Warwick and Ussher see B.L., Add. MS 27257, f. 23v; Trevor-Roper, 'James Ussher', p. 148; Sylvester, *Reliquiae Baxterianae*, p. 205; *Baxter correspondence*, i, 162.

[78] *Baxter correspondence*, i, 162.

Broghill's connexions with Suffolk and Warwick may have given him access to other Presbyterians across England. The existence of a Presbyterian network of influence has been hinted at by Ann Hughes, among others.[79] Apart from the East Anglian group, there were well-established Presbyterian churches in the north of England, the west country, and of course, London. Broghill had direct or indirect links to all of these. From 1654 he was intimate with the prominent Wiltshire M.P., Thomas Grove, who was a powerful figure in western Presbyterian circles, and a dominant influence over religious affairs in the 1654 parliament.[80] Grove was a friend of Baxter, and may have introduced him to Broghill.[81] Other, indirect connexions between Broghill and the Presbyterian classes in other parts of the country included the rapport which existed between Sir John Clotworthy and Vincent Gookin and the London churches, and with other groups in the north of England.[82] The picture is incomplete, but it can be suggested that Broghill and his allies were in a good position to exploit the very strong Presbyterian undercurrents which persisted despite the policies of the commonwealth and the major-generals, and which broke the surface in the 1656 parliament. The large number of Presbyterian M.P.s returned in the 1656 elections was one of the factors which prompted the protector and his council to exclude over one hundred members, and even then, as Carol Egloff has shown, a strong body of 'moderate gentry', eager for political reform, remained in parliament.[83] These men formed an essential element in the kingship party in 1657, and the need to maintain their support in parliament was one of Broghill's main concerns throughout the 1650s.

Broghill's policy of harnessing the support of both Independents and Presbyterians against the army and the religious radicals was pragmatic; but it was also ideological. By the autumn of 1656 the irenicism of Broghill, Baxter, Ussher and their friends had become a political creed. Two examples demonstrate this transition. In November 1656 Dr Nicholas Bernard sent Secretary Thurloe copies of letters he had received from Dr John Gauden, the minister of Bocking in Essex (and future Bishop of Exeter), probably dating from September of that year. These showed Gauden's eagerness to promote 'a fraternall accord . . . [between] Not only Presbyterians and Independents . . . but even episcopall men', in the hope that 'sound doctrine, holy lifes, brotherly love, sanctity of dutys, might be restored and preserved to this reformed church'. Gauden connected this irenical plan with the political settlement of the three nations: 'Nor will any thing more oblige men to civill peace and

---

[79] Hughes, 'Godly reformation', passim.

[80] For Grove see History of Parliament, 1640–60 section, draft biography.

[81] Baxter correspondence, i, 189n.

[82] Thurloe S.P., vi, 19–21; for Clotworthy's relations with London see J. S. Curl, The Londonderry plantation (Sussex, 1986), pp 187, 372.

[83] Carol Egloff, 'Settlement and kingship: the army, the gentry and the offer of the crown to Oliver Cromwell' (unpublished Ph.D. thesis, Yale University, 1990), passim.

willing subjection than when they find themselves satisfied, and posterity like
to be blessed by soe great a blessing as is a well setled church, noe lesse than a
well ordered commonwealth.'[84] Gauden was not some backwoods theorist: he
had been chaplain to the earl of Warwick and retained strong connexion with
the Riches; he had been in contact with Broghill's irenicist ally, John Dury, in
the 1640s; and his marriage to the sister of Sir Francis Russell made him an
uncle of Henry Cromwell's wife, a connexion which both parties acknowledged
in the 1650s.[85] Nor was it a coincidence that Gauden wrote at this time to
Nicholas Bernard, who was the chaplain and apologist of Archbishop Ussher,
and editor of his irenicist text, the *Reduction of Episcopacy*, which had been
published in the same year.[86] The logical extension of Gauden's train of thought
was expressed independently in an exchange between Richard Baxter and his
relative, the Presbyterian M.P. for Herefordshire, Edward Harley. In September
1656 Harley urged Baxter to lend his weight to irenicist policies in the
forthcoming parliament, 'For', he added cryptically, 'I am sure that only *Fata
Ecclesiae* can auspiciat *Fata Imperii*'.[87] Baxter's reply was blunter: 'I looke not
for any setlement to purpose till we have agayne the ancient forme, of King
Lords & Commons.' Baxter continued by emphasising the need to reconcile
the Independents and the Episcopalians to the Presbyterians, and to take steps
to counter Presbyterian suspicions 'of the Protectors soundness in Religion,
& faithfullness to the ministry'.[88] Baxter, Harley and Gauden – a Puritan with
Independent sympathies, a Presbyterian and a future Episcopalian – were
all thinking along the same lines: the best hope for political settlement lay with
irenicism; and, conversely, the best hope for an irenical church settlement
lay with the re-establishment of a civil constitution under the royal House of
Cromwell.

Once again, Broghill's concurrence with such ideas cannot be proved. But
we have already seen Broghill's close affiliation with its main sponsors – Ussher,
Baxter and the earl of Warwick – and his subscription to their religious ideas,
which had resonances with the Calvinism of the Church of Ireland and the
Huguenot Church which had so impressed him before 1641. His commitment
to irenicist ideas can be seen in his religious policy in Scotland, which matched
the broad-based, inclusive settlement advocated by Henry Cromwell in
Ireland. These were reinforced by the providential implications of irenicism,

---

[84] *Thurloe S.P.*, v, 598; see also pp 598–601.
[85] Dury to Gauden, Dec. 1640/Jan. 1641 (S.U.L., Hartlib MS 6/4/159A); John and
Elizabeth Gauden to Henry Cromwell, 24 May 1658 (B.L., Lansdowne MS 823, f. 47r–v);
see History of Parliament, 1640–60 section, draft biography of Sir Francis Russell.
[86] *D.N.B.*; Barnard, *Cromwellian Ireland*, p. 92n; Trevor-Roper, 'James Ussher', p. 121;
Nicholas Bernard may have been the 'Dr Bernard' who received money for intelligence
reports from Secretary Thurloe in the summer of 1655: see P.R.O., S.P. 18/102, fos. 194r,
223r: receipts dated 19 May and 15 Aug. 1655.
[87] *Baxter correspondence*, i, 221–2.
[88] Ibid., 222, 224–5.

and the view – current in Boyle circles, but not explicitly articulated by Broghill – that Oliver Cromwell's rise to power was part of a divine plan of action.

Matters of faith, like family obligations and financial affairs, provide the essential context for Broghill's political career, whether looking at the turmoil of the 1640s or the brave new world of the 1650s. As we have seen in this and the previous two chapters, Broghill's growing desire for a civilian settlement with a Protestant (but non-sectarian) church and the old forms of government was motivated not by political expediency alone, but by an interlinking set of deeply-held convictions, rooted in his loyalty to his family and his belief in a providential deity. Broghill's private beliefs and public policies came together, to create an integrated world-view remarkably similar to that of his father, where prosperity and providence were compatible, where duty to family, to God and to the crown went hand-in-hand. Perhaps the scheme to offer the crown to Cromwell had its roots in the first earl of Cork's often asserted loyalty to the monarchy: the part of his father's plan which Broghill had been forced to reject in 1644 and again in 1649. Crowning Cromwell made political sense; it was also a matter of personal importance. And the amalgamation of the public and private spheres is the best way to explain Broghill's passionate support of kingship, and his sense of desolation after its failure.

Conclusion

In an aside during his detailed analysis of Irish politics in the months before the restoration of Charles II, Aidan Clarke passed judgement on the leading protagonist: 'Broghill's later claim to have written to the king late in February 1660 is difficult to reconcile with his recorded words and actions at the time, but it would not have been uncharacteristic for him to have thought it wiser to be prudent than consistent.'[1] Clarke's verdict exemplifies recent views of Broghill as 'Protestant Ireland's most subtle politician' and a student, if not a disciple, of Machiavelli.[2] In the upheavals of the 1640s and 1650s consistency, whether of policy or belief, had to be sacrificed in favour of political flexibility. A survivor like Broghill would surely value this above all else. Here was a man whose success was dependent on his cynical detachment from causes and loyalties: 'an "English" politician . . . [with] the intellectual contempt of a man who cared little for the principles and interests of the parties he was manipulating', according to Frances Dow.[3] In doubting Broghill's consistency, and even his sincerity, modern historians are not far removed from those in the seventeenth century who saw him as 'fickle and false', 'the Charlatan of Munster', whose vanity was matched only by his ambition.[4]

To an extent, the portrayal of Broghill as the consummate politician is accurate. In this study of his career at the height of his influence, we have come across numerous examples of his political skill. His feud with the lord president of Munster, Lord Inchiquin, during the 1640s was conducted ruthlessly, as he used insinuation and propaganda, as well as factional alignments in England, to destroy his rival's reputation at Westminster. He and his friends were equally cunning when it came to discrediting the lord lieutenant, the marquess of Ormond, in the same period. In 1649–50 Broghill cultivated Oliver Cromwell, manoeuvring himself into a position of influence in commonwealth Ireland, with military and political positions of authority. In 1652, when the Irish government froze after the death of the lord deputy, Henry

---

[1] Aidan Clarke, '1659 and the road to restoration' in Jane Ohlmeyer (ed.), *Ireland from independence to occupation, 1641–60* (Cambridge, 1995), p. 263.
[2] Barnard, 'Protestant interest', pp 219, 235.
[3] Dow, *Cromwellian Scotland*, p. 195.
[4] See Introduction; also ch. 6.

Ireton, Broghill seized the opportunity to extract concessions for himself and his family from the impotent parliamentary commissioners. In England in 1654, Broghill deftly interposed himself between the Irish Protestant lobbyists and Henry Cromwell, in effect monopolising access to the most sympathetic person around the new protector. In the parliament of 1654 he juggled apparently conflicting political and religious objectives, while retaining the confidence of the government. In Scotland in 1655–6 Broghill played the Protester factions off against each other, and was not afraid of taking on the regional might of the marquess of Argyll. He also conducted a rearguard action against General George Monck and those in the English council who opposed his reforms, and proved adept at presenting his arguments in ways that would appeal to, or alarm, Cromwell himself. In 1656–7, as in 1654–5, Broghill became an astute manager of parliaments, intervening at crucial points and knowing when to delegate to trusted friends and clients. It was largely through his skill in balancing competing interests that the Humble Petition and Advice was so strongly supported in the commons. Thereafter he tried all his old tricks, albeit without success, to persuade Cromwell to accept the triple crown. During the years of disillusion that followed, from 1657 through the collapse of the protectorate and the uncertainties of the restoration period, Broghill displayed another political skill – the ability to wait on events, and to turn them to his advantage. It was this 'prudence' that ensured his survival in 1660, and his continued influence in Ireland at least until 1672. Broghill's rise to power under Cromwell, his leadership between 1654 and 1657, and the damage limitation which marked his later career, all stand testimony to his abilities as a hard-nosed, prudent, politician. But there is more to his career than that.

Clarke's description of Broghill as a man who put prudence before consistency is not entirely accurate. Toby Barnard has hinted that the true picture is more complicated; for Broghill, although 'often excoriated for a pliancy tantamount to apostasy . . . exhibited great courage – political as well as physical – in expressing robust opinions'.[5] I would go still further. Throughout his years of influence, Broghill showed himself to be a man not only of principle but also of remarkable consistency. As this present study has tried to demonstrate, during the 1640s and 1650s Broghill developed a coherent programme. Although expanding in scope (and in particular, growing to include all three nations) there was very little change in his underlying aims, whether in 1647 or 1657. At the heart of this programme lay a desire for religious purity, based on a Calvinistic understanding of the cosmic struggle between God and Antichrist, and a belief in the workings of providence in the life of individuals and nations. This encouraged a hatred of Catholicism. Catholics were not just seditious or erroneous, they were the agents of evil. Any compromise with, for example, the Confederate Catholics, was out of the question, and those

---

[5] Barnard, 'Protestant interest', p. 233.

who supported such a compromise (such as Ormond, Inchiquin or, indeed, Charles I) were immediately suspected of duplicity and/or apostasy. In the Irish context, the solution was suppression, plantation and eventual conversion. In an international context, the Catholic powers in Europe had to be defeated, or at least contained, and Cromwellian hostility towards Spain was welcomed, just as the later Carolean alliance with France was hated. Despite this providentialism, and an at times almost hysterical fear of Catholicism, Broghill's world view was not apocalyptic, and had little sympathy with the more extreme sects, including Baptists and Quakers, who threatened social, as well as religious, order. Just as the Catholics bred sedition, so the sectaries, with their influence in the army and in the counsels of Oliver Cromwell, were a threat to be rooted out. Fear of both made the security of the Irish Protestant community all the more important, and this could only be done through suppressing Catholicism and reducing the influence of the army locally and nationally.

Broghill's desire to reintroduce civilian rule in Ireland and Scotland in the 1650s had a religious motive; but it was also fundamentally pragmatic: presenting the best chance for a civilian, moderate regime to survive. The need for such a stable settlement was repeatedly drawn to Broghill's attention during the 1650s, as he witnessed the effects of military and sectarian rule first in Ireland and then in Scotland. The upheavals of these years also heightened Broghill's sense of responsibility, towards his own extended family (which included English and Scottish as well as Irish members) and, by extension, to the Old Protestants in Ireland, and their counterparts in the other two nations. In order to safeguard the Protestant interest, a closer relationship with England was considered a necessity, whether as part of an 'English Empire' (as sought by the Boyle group of the 1620s and 1630s and the Irish Independents in the 1640s) or through incorporation into a formal union (the solution supported by the Old Protestants in the 1650s). For Broghill, this tightening of the bonds between the nations was central to his political programme, and informed his attitude towards the government of Scotland in the 1650s as much as it did his plans for Protestant Ireland. Union bills for both countries were promoted by Broghill and his allies through the Westminster parliaments of 1654 and 1656 (and, in the case of Ireland, in 1659 as well), and it can be argued that, by 1657, unionism lay at the very heart of Broghill's agenda for the whole of the British Isles, in the form of a unified kingdom. Kingship was the logical extension of union: promising equal treatment for Ireland and Scotland, and, under the right monarch, guaranteeing religious and social settlement across all three nations; a settlement based on civilian consensus, not military tyranny. Kingship also had providential overtones which in turn appealed to Broghill and his Calvinist beliefs, bringing us full circle. Broghill's programme may not be an attractive one to modern, liberal eyes; but it is difficult to deny its consistency.

The roots of Broghill's political programme can be found in a very specific setting: Protestant Ireland. This was home-grown radicalism, not imported from England between the covers of Edmund Spenser's *Faerie Queen*.[6] It originated instead in bitter experience, derived from the decades in which the first earl of Cork, Sir William Parsons, Sir Adam Loftus and their friends in the old 'Boyle group' had struggled to establish themselves as officials in the Dublin government and as landowners in the Irish provinces. Their policy was founded on reducing the powers of Irish lordships, on promoting plantation, on educating the heirs to ancient families as Protestants, on instilling civilised values in the mass of the Irish population, and on promoting closer links between England and Ireland. This was an attempt not at wholesale destruction but at harnessing what was worth preserving and removing what caused infection; above all, in the suppressing of Catholicism. Catholicism was dangerous to the state, and dangerous to the safety (and the souls) of the people.

These ideals of the 1620s and 1630s were brought into sharp focus by the events of 1641. During the decade of rebellion and warfare that followed, the mantle of the Boyle group was assumed by a radical faction within the Irish Protestant community, which can best be described as the 'Irish Independents'. This faction, which included Parsons and Loftus and others from the Boyle group, as well as Broghill, tried to exert influence in England to bring about a speedy (and bloody) end to the war, from which would follow confiscation, plantation, suppression of Catholicism, and many of the other demands of twenty years before. Broghill's own policy in Ireland (and in Scotland) in the mid-1650s was firmly based on this radical tradition, and he was particularly insistent on the need to reaffirm the relationship between England and Ireland. The 1640s had shown that the English were often very bad at supporting Protestant Ireland, which so easily became sidelined when domestic politics demanded. From 1654, therefore, Broghill and his allies pressed for a formal union along Scottish lines, and for Irish and Scottish influence to be exercised through the institutions of central government (principally, through parliament), rather than working through informal lobbying networks, which had proved so unreliable during the 1640s. In 1656, union bills were again promoted, before the bold attempt to resolve the issue of the three nations by creating a truly united kingdom under King Oliver. The rejection of the crown was followed, almost exactly two years later, by the collapse of the protectorate, and with it, the dissolution of the union. Broghill's role in fashioning the Cromwellian union was therefore the culmination of a tradition within Irish politics which stretched back thirty years.

The failure of the Cromwellian union marked the beginning of the end of Broghill's influence. In the years after 1657, Broghill's grand scheme began to unravel – a process completed in the new, duplicitous world of the restoration. The sense of lost opportunities was made all the more poignant by the parabolic trajectory of Broghill's rise and fall. This can be seen in various

---

[6] Cf. Nicholas Canny, *Making Ireland British, 1580–1650* (Oxford, 2001), p. 552.

aspects of his career. In the late 1630s and early 1640s he had been dependent on his family, and especially under the shadow of his domineering father. By the late 1640s, and through the 1650s until 1657, Broghill was himself the dominant individual within the Boyle clan, with the responsibility of protecting the political interests and landed estates of his brothers and sisters (and also those of his wife's family, the Howards). Yet in the three years before the restoration, Broghill became increasingly dependent on his extended family, who provided intelligence of events outside Ireland, and smoothed his path to reconciliation with Charles II and his elevation to the earldom of Orrery. During the 1660s and 1670s he was overshadowed by the second earl of Cork (and first earl of Burlington) and Viscount Shannon, both of whom moved far more easily within court circles than the tetchy Orrery. This pattern matches the increase and decrease in the breadth of Broghill's political horizons. In the early 1640s his attentions had been almost entirely focused on the war in Munster; by the late 1640s he had become involved in the politics of the whole of Ireland; and in the early 1650s he began to extend his influence in England. The middle of the decade saw Broghill emerge as a reforming president of the Scottish council, and a man of great influence in England and Ireland, capable of engineering the offer of the crown to Cromwell. After the crown had been rejected in 1657, Broghill's area of influence quickly began to contract. In his absence, Scotland came under the sole charge of George Monck; the failure of the protectorate removed Broghill as a major player in England; and in the year before the restoration his activities were focused almost exclusively on Ireland. After a brief period of influence on national policy from as lord justice in 1660–2, Orrery's sphere was reduced to Munster, and he lost even that provincial powerbase in 1672. As John Kerrigan has perceptively commented, by the 1670s the earl of Orrery was out of step with the political mainstream, clinging to 'an Englishness which was the more assertive and anxious for being Irish, and threatened by the power of France'. Indeed, as his death approached, and the English alliance with Catholic France grew stronger, Orrery was left with 'the sense that history was regressing to the condition of 1641'.[7]

Orrery's rapid decline into obscurity after 1660 was hastened by his failure to find a suitable patron. The lascivious Charles II could not inspire loyalty, the duke of Ormond had sold out long ago, the duke of Buckingham was a fair-weather friend. This lack of a guiding star was a serious blow to Orrery. As Lord Broghill, his most important political relationships had been with his father, the first earl of Cork, and his political master, Oliver Cromwell. The closeness of Broghill and Cork has been examined in detail in chapter one. In many ways Broghill's political programme, and his attitude towards Ireland, was an extension of the uncompromising reforms pushed by Cork and

[7] John Kerrigan, 'Orrery's Ireland and the British problem, 1641–1679' in D. J. Baker and Willie Maley (eds), *British identities and English Renaissance literature* (Cambridge, 2002), pp 213, 217.

the Boyle group in earlier decades. Underlying it all was a shared belief in providence, and in the rightness of the Protestant interest they were pro-moting. But what of Cromwell, the conqueror of Ireland, lord protector and (if Broghill had had his way) King Oliver I? There is little evidence of personal warmth between the two men. Cromwell treated Broghill with respect, not friendship. Broghill was undoubtedly close to Henry Cromwell and his brother Richard, but he treated their father not with affection, but with awe. In a peculiar way, this heightened sense of respect, this formal relationship, is reminiscent of the way in which Broghill treated his own father. There are other similarities between Broghill's attitudes to the two older men. Broghill's own hopes for Ireland were inherited from Cork via the Irish Independents; Cromwell's policies broadly agreed with the earlier plans, and promised to advance them further. This was true in 1649, when the long expected English reconquest was undertaken; something that Cork and then Broghill had been calling for since the very beginning of the rebellion of 1641. It was also true under the protectorate, when formal union became a real possibility, thus guaranteeing through statute the incorporation of Protestant Ireland within the 'English Empire' which had been a rallying cry for Cork and his friends since the 1620s.

In many ways, therefore, the Cromwellian union was the fulfilment of the Boyle group's ambitions for Ireland. This explains Broghill's loyalty to the protectorate; but what of his personal loyalty to the protector? Why did union turn into coronation as an objective? Once again, a comparison of Cromwell and Cork provides an insight. Cork had always emphasised the importance of loyalty to the crown. Alongside religion, it provided the foundation for the rest of his political career. In 1644, and again in 1649, Broghill had been forced to reject this loyalty to the Stuarts, considering it inimical to his greater loyalty to the Protestant interest and to God. The Stuarts had broken the close link between the crown and religion, and neither Charles I nor Charles II could thereafter command unequivocal loyalty from a man like Broghill. A new monarch – a godly monarch – could reconcile the two once again. And (apart from, perhaps, the first earl of Cork) no one could demonstrate such a startling rise from obscurity to predominance, such a self-evident sign of divine favour, as Oliver Cromwell.

Broghill's trust in Cromwell can perhaps best be seen in the Remonstrance – the original version of the Humble Petition and Advice – which Broghill may have drafted, and certainly supported, in the early weeks of 1657. The degree of trust to be placed in Oliver Cromwell is astonishing. Unlike the Instrument of Government of 1653, the ruler would not be bound to make decisions only with the consent of his council. Unlike the final version of the Humble Petition and Advice, parliament had no scope to limit his power, either. This was a return to monarchy without the shackles. The hard-fought concessions made by the Long Parliament against Charles I would be thrown away. What would emerge was a strong monarchy, with legal boundaries perhaps, but these were no greater than those experienced by Charles I before the Civil War. The monarchy would be similar, but the personality very different. This king would be brought to the throne by acclamation of Ireland and Scotland as well as England, to preside over a union parliament, over a united kingdom. This king would be the new King David, a man who would be worthy to exercise the divine right of kings over the three elect nations. The tragedy for Broghill was that in May 1657 the potential monarch saw the triple crown not as the just reward for the godly King David, but as the 'accursed thing' coveted by the sinful Achan.[8]

[8] See ch. 5, above.

Bibliography

PRIMARY SOURCES

Manuscripts

England

British Library

Add. MS 4820 (funerary papers).
Add. MS 19832 (Boyle papers).
Add. MS 25287 (Broghill's letterbook).
Add. MS 27357 (Lady Warwick's autobiography).
Add. MS 37047 (Long papers).
Add. MS 37344 (Whitelocke's annals).
Add. MS 43724 (Henry Cromwell's correspondence).
Add. MSS 46929–31 (Egmont papers).
Althorp MS B3 (septpartite indenture of Cork's estate, 1636).
Althorp MS B6 (letters of second earl of Cork).
Egerton MS 80 (Boyle papers).
Egerton MS 1762 (orders of state, 1651–7).
Egerton MS 1779 (orders of Irish commissioners, 1650–4).
Egerton MS 2519 (Disbrowe papers).
Harleian MS 6848 (Whitelocke papers).
Lansdowne MSS 821–3 (Henry Cromwell's correspondence).
Sloane MS 1008 (Borlase papers).
Sloane MS 4227 (Morrice's memoirs).

Public Record Office

C 3 (chancery depositions).
C 54 (close rolls).
C 219/44–5 (election indentures, 1654–6).
E 351/292–3 (army treasurer's accounts, 1639–40).
LC 4/202–4 (recognizances).
PRO 31/3/100–1 (Baschet's transcripts of French documents).

SO 1/3 (signet office, docquet books).
S.P. 16 (State papers, domestic).
S.P. 18 (State papers, commonwealth).
S.P. 21/16, 19–20 (committee of both kingdoms, letterbooks and order books).
S.P. 21/26 (Derby House committee, order books).
S.P. 28 (commonwealth exchequer papers).
S.P. 63 (State papers, Ireland).
S.P. 77 (State papers, Flanders).
S.P. 78 (State papers, France).

Bodleian Library, Oxford

MS Carte 3–30, 63, 67, 73, 74, 103, 214.
MS Clarendon 54, 57, 60–2, 71–2.
MS Eng. Hist.e.309.
MS Firth c.5.
MS Nalson 6.
MS Rawlinson A.27, 29, 32, 34, 39, 44, 51, 208.
MS Tanner 52–56.

Cambridge University Library

Add. MS 7094 (account of debts of second earl of Suffolk, 1640).
MS Ee.iii.25 (account of sale of Suffolk estates, 1641–6).

Cambridgeshire Record Office, Huntingdon

Cromwell-Bush Collection (MS 731).

Chatsworth House, Derbyshire (property of the duke of Devonshire and the trustees of the Chatsworth Settlement)

First earl of Cork's letterbooks I and II.
Lismore MSS 15–30 (including MS 29, second earl of Cork's diary, 1650–9).
Journal of Elizabeth, Lady Burlington, 1656–88.
Journal of the earl of Burlington, 1659–66.

Coventry City Archives

BA/H/Q/A79/302 (Robert Beake to Leonard Piddock, 28 Mar. 1657).

Cumbria Record Office, Carlisle

Leconfield MSS, D/Lec/107.

Dorset Record Office, Dorchester

D/SHC/3D/117 (unsorted box of Digby papers).
KG 1474 (Fitzgerald pedigree).

Hull Record Office (consulted at the History of Parliament, London)

Hull corporation letters 1635–62, L.628.

Longleat House, Wiltshire (property of the marquess of Bath; consulted on
   microfilm at the Institute of Historical Research, London)

Whitelocke papers, vols 11–12, 18–19.

Petworth House, Sussex (property of the earl of Egremont; consulted at the
   West Sussex Record Office)

MSS 13192, 13221–3 (Orrery papers).

Sheffield Central Library (consulted on microfilm at the Institute of
   Historical Research, London)

Strafford MS 18.

Sheffield University Library (consulted on CD-Rom)

Hartlib MSS.

Surrey History Centre, Woking

Loseley MS LM/1331/56

Worcester College, Oxford (consulted on microfilm at the Institute of
   Historical Research, London)

Clarke MSS 1/15–16, 3/2, 3/10–11

Ireland

National Archives of Ireland, Dublin

Ferguson MS 10.
Lodge's MSS 1.A.53.55.

National Library of Ireland, Dublin

MS 2639 (first earl of Cork's rentals, half-year to Mar. 1637).
MS 6897 (Cork's accounts, 1626–32).
MS 6899 (Cork's accounts, 1636–41).
MS 6900 (Cork's accounts, 1641–5).
D 21,907–22,035 (Orrery deeds).

Public Record Office of Northern Ireland, Belfast

D. 1759/1A/1 (minutes of the Antrim presbytery, 1654–8).
D. 207/15/3 (Foster-Massereene papers).
D. 3078/14 (Leinster papers).

Trinity College Library, Dublin

MS 844 (corresp. of Dr Henry Jones).

Birr Castle, Co. Offaly (property of the earl of Rosse; consulted on microfilm
   at Carroll Institute, London)

Rosse MS A/12 (Parsons accounts).
Rosse MS A5/79 (will of Fenton Parsons).

Scotland

National Library of Scotland, Edinburgh

Wodrow Folio MSS, vols. xxvi and xxx.
Wodrow Octavo MS xl.
MS 7032 (Yester papers).
Lockhart CH. A.1. (Lockhart charters).

National Archives of Scotland, Edinburgh

GD 26 (Leven and Melville papers).
GD 112 (Breadalbane papers).
GD 406 (Hamilton papers).

Edinburgh City Archives

SL 1/1/19 (Edinburgh council minutes, 1655–8).

Printed primary sources

Abbott, W. C., *The writings and speeches of Oliver Cromwell* (4 vols, Cambridge Mass., 1937–47).

Bell, Robert (ed.), *Memorials of the Civil War, comprising the correspondence of the Fairfax family* (2 vols, 1849).

Berwick, Edward (ed.), *The Rawdon papers* (1819).

Birch, Thomas (ed.), *A collection of the state papers of John Thurloe, Esq.* (7 vols, 1742).

Birch, Thomas (ed.), *Works of the Honourable Robert Boyle* (new ed., 6 vols, 1772).

Calendar of state papers, domestic series.

Calendar of state papers, Ireland.

Calendar of state papers, Venetian.

Caulfield, Richard (ed.), *The council book of the corporation of the city of Cork, 1609–43, 1690–1800* (Guildford, 1876).

Caulfield, Richard (ed.), *The council book of the corporation of Youghal* (Guildford, 1878).

Caulfield, Richard (ed.), *The council book of the corporation of Kinsale, 1652–1800* (Guildford, 1879).

Clarendon, Edward, earl of, *State papers collected by Edward, earl of Clarendon* (3 vols, Oxford, 1757).

Coate, Mary (ed.), *The letterbook of John Viscount Mordaunt, 1658–60* (1945).

A collection of the state letters of Rt. Hon. Roger Boyle, the first earl of Orrery (1742).

The correspondence of Sir Robert Kerr, 1st earl of Ancram and his son William, 3rd earl of Lothian (2 vols, Edinburgh, 1875).

Dunlop, Robert (ed.), *Ireland under the commonwealth* (2 vols, Manchester, 1913).

Firth, C. H. and Rait, R. S. (eds), *Acts and ordinances of the interregnum, 1642–1660* (3 vols, 1911).

Firth, C. H. (ed.), *The Clarke papers: selections from the papers of William Clarke* (4 vols, 1891–1901).

Firth, C. H. (ed.), *The memoirs of Edmund Ludlow* (2 vols, Oxford, 1894).

Firth, C. H. (ed.), *Scotland and the protectorate* (Edinburgh, 1899).

Fitzpatrick, Thomas (ed.), *Waterford during the Civil War (1641–53)* (Waterford, 1912).

Gardiner, S. R., *The constitutional documents of the puritan revolution, 1625–1660* (3rd ed., Oxford, 1906).

Gilbert, J. T. (ed.), *A contemporary history of affairs in Ireland from 1641–52* (3 vols, Dublin, 1880).

Gilbert, J. T. (ed.), *History of the Irish Confederation and the war in Ireland, 1641–3 . . .* (7 vols, Dublin, 1882–91).

Green, M. A. E., *Calendar of the proceedings of the committee for compounding, 1643–60* (5 vols, 1889–92).

Grosart, A. B. (ed.), *The Lismore papers, 1st series, viz. autobiographical notes and diaries of Sir Richard Boyle, 1st and great earl of Cork* (5 vols, 1886).

Grosart, A. B. (ed.), *The Lismore papers, 2nd series, viz. selections from the private and public correspondence of the 1st and great earl of Cork* (5 vols, 1887–8).

Hall, A. R. and M. B. (eds) *The correspondence of Henry Oldenburg* (13 vols, Madison, Wisc., and Milwaukee, 1965–86).

Historical Manuscripts Commission:

De Lisle MSS, vi (1966).
Egmont, i (1905).
House of Lords MSS n.s. iv (1908).
Leyborne-Popham (1899).
Pepys (1911).
Portland, i (1892).
5th report (1876).
7th report (1879).
10th report (1885).
Various collections, vi (1909).

14th report of deputy keeper of the public records of Ireland (Dublin, 1882).

Hogan, James (ed.), *Letters and papers relating to the Irish rebellion* (Dublin, 1936).

Hunter, Michael (ed.), *Robert Boyle by himself and his friends* (1994).

Hunter, Michael, Clericuzio, Antonio and Pincipe, Lawrence (eds), *The correspondence of Robert Boyle* (6 vols, 2001).

Jenks, Edward, 'Some correspondence of Thurloe and Meadowe' in *E.H.R.* vii (1892), pp 720–42.

Journals of the House of Commons (1803–13).

Journals of the House of Lords (1846).

Keeble, N. H. and Nuttall, G. F. (eds), *Calendar of the correspondence of Richard Baxter* (2 vols, Oxford, 1991).

Laing, David (ed.), *The letters and journals of Robert Baillie* (3 vols, Edinburgh, 1841–2).

Laing, David (ed.), *The diary of Alexander Brodie of Brodie* (Aberdeen, 1863).

Loftis, John (ed.), *The memoirs of Anne, Lady Halkett and Ann, Lady Fanshawe* (Oxford, 1979).

MacLysaght, Edward (ed.), 'Commonwealth state accounts, 1650–6' in *Analecta Hibernica*, xv (1944), pp 229–321.

Macray, W. D. (ed.), *Clarendon's history of the rebellion* (6 vols, Oxford, 1888).

MacTavish, D. C. (ed.), *Minutes of the synod of Argyll, 1652–1661* (Edinburgh, 1944).

Morrice, Thomas, *Memoirs of the . . . life and death of the right honourable Roger, earl of Orrery* [printed as the first part of *Orrery state papers* (1742)].

Nickolls, John (ed.), *Original letters and papers of state . . . among the political collections of . . . John Milton* (1743).

Ogilvie, J. D. (ed.), *Diary of Sir Archibald Johnston of Wariston, vol. iii, 1655–60* (Edinburgh, 1940).

Ogle, Octavius, Bliss, W.H., Macray, W. D. and Routledge, F. J. (eds), *Calendar of the Clarendon state papers preserved in the Bodleian Library* (5 vols, Oxford, 1869–1932).

The parliamentary or constitutional history of England (2nd ed., 24 vols, 1743).

Parry, E. A. (ed.), *Letters from Dorothy Osborne to Sir William Temple, 1652–4* (1903).

Pearsall Smith, Logan (ed.), *The life and letters of Sir Henry Wotton* (2 vols, Oxford, 1907).

Rushworth, John, *Historical collections of private passages of state* (7 vols, 1721)

Rutt, J. T. (ed.), *Diary of Thomas Burton, esq.* (4 vols, 1828).

Shaw, W. A., *Letters of denization and acts of naturalisation, 1603–1700* (Lymington, 1911).

Spalding, Ruth (ed.), *The diary of Bulstrode Whitelocke, 1605–75* (Oxford, 1990).

Stephen, William (ed.), *Register of the consultations of the ministers of Edinburgh . . . , vol i, 1652–7* (Edinburgh, 1921).

Stephen, William (ed.), *Register of the consultations of the ministers of Edinburgh . . . , vol. ii, 1657–60* (Edinburgh, 1930).

Sylvester, Matthew (ed.), *Reliquiae Baxterianae: or Mr Richard Baxter's narrative of the most memorable passages of his life and times* (1696).

Touchet, James, *The earl of Castlehaven's memoirs* (Dublin, 1815).

Warner, G. F. (ed.), *The Nicholas papers: correspondence of Sir Edward Nicholas, secretary of state* (4 vols, 1886–1920).

Whitelocke, Bulstrode, *Memorials of English affairs* (4 vols, Oxford, 1853).

[?Whitelocke, Bulstrode] *Monarchy asserted, to be the best, most ancient and legall form of government* (1660).

Wood, Marguerite (ed.), *Extracts from the records of the burgh of Edinburgh, 1655–65* (Edinburgh, 1940).

Thomason Tracts (by date)

Three several letters of great importance (6 Dec. 1644) (E. 21(6)).

Sir John Temple, *The Irish rebellion* (27 Apr. 1646) (E.508).

A letter from a person of quality residing in Kinsale (15 Sept. 1646) (E.354(6)).

The Irish papers, containing the Lord Digbies letter, and the Lord Inchiquins answer (1 Oct. 1646) (E.355(26)).

Adam Meredith, *Ormond's curtain drawn* (5 Oct. 1646) (E.513(14)).

A true and brief relation of the Lord Lisle's departure from his command in Ireland (30 Apr. 1647) (E. 385(13)).

William Prynne, *A full vindication and answer of the XI accused members* (15 July 1647) (E. 398(17)).

A letter from Lieutenant Colonel Knight in the province of Munster (22 July 1647) (E.399(23)).

A copy of a Remonstrance (24 July 1647) (E.399(33)).

Articles exhibited . . . against the Lord Inchiquin (18 Aug. 1647) (E.402(19)).

The cuckoo's-nest at Westminster; or the parlement between the two lady-birds, Quean Fairfax and Lady Cromwell (1648) (E.447(19)).

Articles of peace with the Irish rebels concluded by James, earle of Ormond (15 Feb. 1649) (E.555(21)).

Gookin, Vincent, *The great case of transplantation in Ireland discussed* (3 Jan. 1655) (E.234(6)).

Smith, George, *Gods unchangeableness* (15 Jan. 1655) (E.824(4)).

Gostello, Walter, *Charls Stuart and Oliver Cromwell united* (20 Jan. 1655) (E. 1503(3)).

Gookin, Vincent, *The author and case of transplanting the Irish into Connaught vindicated* (12 May 1655) (E.838(7)).

A narrative of the late parliament, so called (Feb. 1658) (E.935(5)).

Calamy, Edmund, *A patterne for all* (2 June 1658) (E.947(1)).

Mercurius Pragmaticus.

A Briefe Relation.

Several Proceedings in parliament.

Mercurius Politicus.

SECONDARY SOURCES

Books

Barnard, Toby C., *Cromwellian Ireland* (Oxford, 1975).

Barnard, Toby C., *A new anatomy of Ireland: the Irish Protestants, 1649–1770* (New Haven, 2003).

Bethell, Slingsby, *A narrative . . . of the late parliament* (9 June 1659).

Bottigheimer, Karl, *English money and Irish land: the 'adventurers' in the Cromwellian settlement of Ireland* (Oxford, 1971).

Boyle, Roger, *Parthenissa, a romance* (5 vols, 1655–6).

Boyle, Roger, *The Irish colours displayed* (London, 1662).

Boyle, Roger, *Answer of a person of quality* (Dublin, 1662).

Burke's peerage (1909 ed.)

Canny, Nicholas, *The upstart earl: a study of the social and mental world of Richard Boyle, 1st earl of Cork, 1566–1643* (Cambridge, 1982).

Canny, Nicholas, *Making Ireland British, 1580–1650* (Oxford, 2001).

Clarke, Aidan, *The Old English in Ireland* (Cornell, 1966).

Clarke, Aidan, *Prelude to restoration in Ireland: the end of the commonwealth, 1659–60* (Cambridge, 1999).

Cokayne, G. E., *The Complete Peerage* (new ed., 12 vols, 1910–59).

Connolly, S. J., *Religion, law and power: the making of Protestant Ireland, 1660–1760* (Oxford, 1992).

Coward, Barry, *The Cromwellian protectorate* (Manchester, 2002).

Crawford, Patricia, *Denzil Holles, 1598–1680: a study of his political career* (Royal Hist. Soc., 1979).

Curl, J. S., *The Londonderry plantation* (Sussex, 1986).

Davis, J. C., *Oliver Cromwell* (2001).

Dictionary of National Biography (66 vols, 1885–1901).

Dodd, A. H., *Studies in Stuart Wales* (Cardiff, 1971).

Donald, Peter, *An uncounselled king: Charles I and the Scottish troubles, 1637–41* (Cambridge, 1990).

Donaldson, Gordon, *Scotland: James V–VII* (Edinburgh, 1965).

Dow, Frances, *Cromwellian Scotland, 1651–1660* (Edinburgh, 1979).

Durston, Christopher, *Cromwell's major-generals: godly government during the English revolution* (Manchester, 2001).

Edwards, David, *The Ormond lordship in County Kilkenny, 1515–1642: the rise and fall of Butler feudal power* (Dublin, 2003).

Firth, C. H. and Davies, G., *The regimental history of Cromwell's army* (2 vols, Oxford, 1940).

Fraser, Antonia, *Cromwell, our chief of men* (1994 ed.)

Gardiner, S. R., *History of the commonwealth and protectorate, 1649–56* (4 vols, 1903).

Gentles, Ian, *The New Model Army in England, Ireland and Scotland, 1645–1653* (Oxford, 1992).

Gillespie, Raymond, *Devoted people: belief and religion in early modern Ireland* (Manchester, 1997).

Henning, B. D. (ed.), *The history of parliament: the House of Commons, 1660–90* (3 vols, 1983).

Hill, Christopher, *God's Englishman: Olver Cromwell and the English Revolution* (1971).

Hutton, Ronald, *The restoration: a political and religious history of England and Wales, 1658–1667* (Oxford, 1986).

Keeler, M. F., *The Long Parliament, 1640–1641: a biographical study of its members* (Philadelphia, 1954).

Kishlansky, M. A., *The rise of the New Model Army* (Cambridge, 1979).

Lamont, William, *Richard Baxter and the millennium: Protestant imperialism and the English revolution* (1979).

Lenihan, Pádraig, *Confederate Catholics at war, 1641–49* (Cork, 2001).

Lodge, John, *The peerage of Ireland* (4 vols, Dublin, 1754).

Lynch, Kathleen, *Roger Boyle, 1st earl of Orrery* (Knoxville, Tenn., 1965).

Mac Cuarta, Brian (ed.), *Ulster 1641: aspects of the rising* (Belfast, 1993).

Macinnes, Alan, *Clanship, commerce and the house of Stuart, 1603–1788* (East Linton, 1996).

Maguire, Nancy Klein, *Regicide and restoration: English tragicomedy, 1660–71* (Cambridge, 1992).

Moody, T. W., Martin, F. X. and Byrne, F. J. (eds), *A new history of Ireland*, iii: *Early modern Ireland, 1534–1691* (Oxford, 1976).

Morrice, Thomas, *Sermon preached at the funeral of Roger, earl of Orrery* (1681).

Ó Siochrú, Micheál, *Confederate Ireland, 1642–1649: a constitutional and political analysis* (Dublin, 1999).

Perceval-Maxwell, Michael, *The outbreak of the Irish rebellion of 1641* (Belfast, 1994).

Scott, Jonathan, *Algernon Sidney and the English republic, 1623–1677* (Cambridge, 1988).

Seymour, St John D., *The puritans in Ireland, 1647–1661* (Oxford, 1921).

Stevenson, David, *Revolution and counter-revolution in Scotland, 1644–51* (1977).

Stevenson, David, *Scottish covenanters and Irish confederates: Scottish-Irish relations in the mid-seventeenth century* (Belfast, 1981).

Stevenson, David, *Highland warrior: Alasdair MacColla and the civil wars* (Edinburgh, 1994).

Townshend, Dorothea, *The life and letters of the great earl of Cork* (1904).

Underdown, David, *Pride's Purge: politics in the puritan revolution* (Oxford, 1971).

Underdown, David, *Royalist conspiracy in England, 1649–1660* (1979).

Wedgwood, C. V., *Thomas Wentworth, 1st earl of Strafford, 1593–1641: a revaluation* (1961).

Wheeler, James Scott, *Cromwell in Ireland* (Dublin, 1999).

Woolrych, Austin, *Soldiers and statesmen: the general council of the army and its debates, 1647–8* (Oxford, 1987).

Woolrych, Austin, *Commonwealth to protectorate* (Oxford, 1982).

Worden, Blair, *The Rump Parliament* (Cambridge, 1974).

Worden, Blair, *Roundhead reputations: the English Civil Wars and the passions of posterity* (2001).

Articles

Adamson, John, 'The baronial context of the English Civil War' in *Transactions of the Royal Historical Society*, ser. 5, xl (1990), pp 93–120.

Adamson, John, 'Oliver Cromwell and the Long Parliament' in John Morrill (ed.), *Oliver Cromwell and the English revolution* (1990), pp 49–92.

Adamson, John, 'Strafford's ghost: the British context of Viscount Lisle's lieutenancy of Ireland' in Jane Ohlmeyer (ed.), *Ireland from independence to occupation, 1641–1660* (Cambridge, 1995), pp 128–59.

Adamson, John, 'The frighted junto: perceptions of Ireland, and the last attempts at settlement with Charles I' in Jason Peacey (ed.), *The regicides and the execution of Charles I* (2001), pp 36–70.

Armstrong, Robert, 'Ormond, the Confederate peace talks and Protestant royalism' in Micheál Ó Siochrú (ed.), *Kingdoms in crisis: Ireland in the 1640s* (Dublin, 2001), pp 122–40.

Barber, Sarah, 'Scotland and Ireland under the commonwealth' in Steven Ellis and Sarah Barber (eds), *Conquest and union: fashioning a British state, 1485–1725* (1995), pp 195–221.

Barnard, Toby C., 'Planters and policies in Cromwellian Ireland' in *Past and Present*, lxi (1973), pp 31–69.

Barnard, Toby C., 'Lord Broghill, Vincent Gookin and the Cork election of 1659' in *E.H.R.*, lxxxviii (1973), pp 352–65.

Barnard, Toby C., 'The Hartlib circle and the origins of the Dublin philosophical society' in *I.H.S.*, xix (1974–5), pp 56–71.

Barnard, Toby C., review of Canny's *Upstart earl*, in *E.H.R.*, c (1985), pp 405–7.

Barnard, Toby C., 'The political, material and mental culture of the Cork settlers, c.1650–1760' in P. O'Flanagan and C. G. Buttimer (eds), *Cork: history and society* (Dublin, 1993), pp 309–67.

Barnard, Toby C., 'The Protestant interest, 1641–1660' in Jane Ohlmeyer (ed.), *Ireland from independence to occupation, 1641–1660* (Cambridge, 1995), pp 218–40.

Barnard, Toby C., 'Conclusion. Settling and unsettling Ireland: the Cromwellian and Williamite revolutions' in Jane Ohlmeyer (ed.), *Ireland from independence to occupation, 1641–1660* (Cambridge, 1995), pp 265–91.

Barnard, Toby C., 'Land and the limits of loyalty: the second earl of Cork and first earl of Burlington (1612–98)' in Toby C. Barnard and Jane Clark (eds), *Lord Burlington: architecture, art and life* (1996), pp 167–99.

Barnard, Toby C., 'Introduction: the dukes of Ormonde' in Toby C. Barnard and Jane Fenlon (eds), *The dukes of Ormonde, 1610–1745* (Woodbridge, 2000), pp 1–53.

Brown, K. M., 'The Scottish aristocracy, anglicization and the court, 1603–38' in *H.J.*, xxxvi (1993), pp 543–76.

Buckroyd, Julia, 'Lord Broghill and the Scottish church, 1655–1656' in *Journal of Ecclesiastical History*, xxvii (1976), pp 359–68.

Casada, J. A. 'The Scottish representatives in Richard Cromwell's parliament' in *S.H.R.*, li (1972).

Choudhury, Mita, 'Orrery and the London stage: a loyalist's contribution to restoration allegorical drama' in *Studia Neophilologica*, lxii (1990), pp 43–59.

Clarke, Aidan, '1659 and the road to restoration' in Jane Ohlmeyer (ed.), *Ireland from independence to occupation, 1641–1660* (Cambridge, 1995), pp 241–64.

Coughlan, Patricia, 'Counter-currents in colonial discourse: the political thought of Vincent and Daniel Gookin' in Jane Ohlmeyer (ed.), *Political thought in seventeenth century Ireland: kingdom or colony?* (Cambridge, 2000), pp 56–82.

Cowan, E. J., 'Clanship, kinship and the Campbell acquisition of Islay' in *S.H.R.*, lviii (1979), pp 132–57.

Davis, J. C., 'Cromwell's religion' in John Morrill (ed.), *Oliver Cromwell and the English revolution* (1990), pp 181–208.

Dawson, Jane, 'The fifth earl of Argyle, Gaelic lordship and political power in sixteenth century Scotland' in *S.H.R.*, lxvii (1988), pp 228–31.

Durston, Christopher, 'The fall of Cromwell's major-generals' in *E.H.R.*, cxiii (1998), pp 18–37.

Edwards, David, 'The Butler revolt of 1569' in *I.H.S.*, xxviii (1993), pp 228–55.

Egloff, Carol S., 'Robert Beake: a letter concerning the Humble Petition and Advice, 28 March 1657' in *Historical Research*, lxviii (1995), pp 233–9.

Egloff, Carol S., 'The search for a Cromwellian settlement: exclusions from the second protectorate parliament' in *Parliamentary History*, xvii (1998), pp 178–97, 301–21.

Firth, C. H., 'Cromwell and the crown' in *E.H.R.*, xvii (1902), pp 429–42; xviii (1903), pp 52–80.

Ford, Alan, 'The Church of Ireland, 1558–1634: a puritan church?' in Alan Ford, James McGuire and Kenneth Milne (eds), *As by law established: the Church of Ireland since the Reformation* (Dublin, 1995), pp 52–68.

Gaunt, Peter, 'Law-making in the first protectorate parliament' in Colin Jones et al. (eds), *Politics and people in revolutionary England* (Oxford, 1986), pp 163–86.

Gaunt, Peter, 'Oliver Cromwell and his protectorate parliaments: co-operation, conflict and control' in Ivan Roots (ed.), *Into another mould: aspects of the interregnum* (2nd ed., Exeter, 1998), pp 70–100.

Gillespie, Raymond, 'The Irish economy at war, 1641–52' in Jane H. Ohlmeyer (ed.), *Ireland from independence to occupation, 1641–60* (Cambridge, 1995), pp 160–80.

Gillespie, Raymond, 'The religion of the first duke of Ormond' in Toby C. Barnard and Jane Fenlon (eds), *The dukes of Ormonde, 1610–1745* (Woodbridge, 2000), pp 101–14.

Goldwater, Ellen, 'The Scottish franchise: lobbying during the Cromwellian protectorate' in *H.J.*, xxi (1978), pp 27–42.

Harris, Amy, 'The funerary monuments of Richard Boyle, earl of Cork' in *Church Monuments*, xiii (1998), pp 70–86.

Hirst, Derek, 'The English republic and the meaning of Britain' in Brendan Bradshaw and John Morrill (eds), *The British problem, c.1534–1707: state formation in the Atlantic archipelago* (Cambridge, 1996), pp 192–219

Hirst, Derek, 'Concord and discord in Richard Cromwell's House of Commons' in *E.H.R.*, ciii (1988), pp 339–58.

Howell, Roger, jr, 'Cromwell and his parliaments: the Trevor-Roper thesis revisited' in R. C. Richardson (ed.), *Images of Oliver Cromwell* (Manchester, 1993), pp 124–35.

Hughes, Ann, *Godly reformation and its opponents in Warwickshire, 1640–62, (Dugdale society occasional papers)*, xxxv (1993).

Hunter, Michael, 'How Robert Boyle became a scientist' in *History of Science*, xxxiii (1995), pp 59–103.

Irwin, Liam, 'The suppression of the Irish presidency system' in *I.H.S.*, xxii (1980–1), pp 21–32.

Jacob, J. R., 'Boyle's circle in the protectorate: revelation, politics and the millennium' in *Journal of the History of Ideas*, xxxviii (1977), pp 131–40.

Kerrigan, John, 'Orrery's Ireland and the British problem, 1641–1679' in D. J. Baker and Willie Maley (eds), *British identities and English renaissance literature* (Cambridge, 2002), pp 197–225.

Kyle, C. R., 'Attendance, apathy and order? Parliamentary committees in early Stuart England' in C. R. Kyle and J. T. Peacey (eds), *Parliament at work: parliamentary committees, political power and public access in early modern England* (Woodbridge, 2002), pp 43–58.

Labrousse, Elisabeth, 'Le Démon de Mâcon' in *Scienze, credenze occulte, livelli di cultura* (Florence, 1982), pp 249–75.

Lindley, Keith, 'The impact of the 1641 rebellion upon England and Wales, 1641–5' in *I.H.S.*, xviii (1972), pp 143–76.

Little, Patrick, 'The earl of Cork and the fall of the earl of Strafford, 1638–41' in *H.J.*, xxxix (1996), pp 619–35.

Little, Patrick, 'Blood and friendship: the earl of Essex's protection of the earl of Clanricarde's interests, 1641–1646' in *E.H.R.*, cxii (1997), pp 927–41.

Little, Patrick, 'The marquess of Ormond and the English parliament, 1645–1647' in Toby Barnard and Jane Fenlon (eds), *The dukes of Ormonde, 1610–1745* (Woodbridge, 2000), pp 83–99.

Little, Patrick, 'The first unionists?: Irish Protestant attitudes to union with England, 1653–9' in *I.H.S.*, xxxii (2000), pp 44–58.

Little, Patrick, 'The English parliament and the Irish constitution, 1641–9' in Micheál Ó Siochrú (ed.), *Kingdoms in crisis: Ireland in the 1640s* (Dublin, 2001), pp 106–21.

Little, Patrick, 'The Irish "Independents" and Viscount Lisle's lieutenancy of Ireland' in *H.J.*, xliv (2001), pp 941–61.

Little, Patrick, 'Providence and posterity: a letter from Lord Mountnorris to his daughter, 1642' in *I.H.S.*, xxxii (2001), pp 556–66.

Little, Patrick, 'An Irish governor of Scotland: Lord Broghill, 1655–6' in Andrew MacKillop and Steven Murdoch (eds), *Military governors and imperial frontiers c.1600–1800: a study of Scotland and empires* (Leiden, 2003), pp 79–97.

Little, Patrick, 'The Geraldine ambitions of the first earl of Cork' in *I.H.S.*, xxxiii (2002), pp 151–68.

Little, Patrick, 'Irish representation in the protectorate parliaments' in *Parliamentary History* (forthcoming).

Lowe, John, 'Charles I and the Confederation of Kilkenny, 1643–9' in *I.H.S.*, xiv (1964), pp 1–19.

McGuire, James, 'Why was Ormond dismissed in 1669?' in *I.H.S.*, xviii (1972–3), pp 295–312.

Maguire, Nancy Klein, 'The rhymed heroic apology of Roger Boyle, earl of Orrery in N.K. Maguire *Regicide and restoration: English tragicomedy, 1660–71* (Cambridge, 1992).

Mahony, Michael, 'Presbyterianism in the City of London, 1645–7' in *H.J.*, xxii (1979), pp 93–114.

Murphy, J. A., 'The expulsion of the Irish from Cork in 1644' in *J.C.H.A.S.*, lxix (1964), pp 123–31.

Murphy, J. A., 'The politics of the Munster Protestants, 1641–9' in *J.C.H.A.S.*, lxxvi (1971), pp 1–20.

Noonan, Kathleen, '"The cruel pressure of an enraged, barbarous people": Irish and English identity in seventeenth century policy and propaganda' in *H.J.*, xli (1998), pp 151–77.

Oster, Malcolm, 'Millenarianism and the new science: the case of Robert Boyle' in Mark Greengrass et al. (eds), *Samuel Hartlib and universal reformation: studies in intellectual communication* (Cambridge, 1994), pp 137–48.

Pearl, Valerie, 'London's counter-revolution' in G. E. Aylmer (ed.), *The interregnum: the quest for settlement, 1646–1660* (1972), pp 29–56.

Perceval-Maxwell, Michael, 'Protestant faction, the impeachment of Strafford and the origins of the Irish Civil War' in *Canadian Journal of History*, xvii (1982), pp 235–55.

Perceval-Maxwell, Michael, 'Ireland and Scotland 1638–1648' in John Morrill (ed.), *The Scottish National Covenant in its British context, 1638–51* (Edinburgh, 1990), pp 193–211.

Pinckney, P. J., 'The Scottish representation in the Cromwellian parliament of 1656' in *S.H.R.*, lxvi (1967)

Popkin, R. H., 'Hartlib, Dury and the Jews' in Mark Greengrass et al. (eds), *Samuel Hartlib and universal reformation: studies in intellectual communication* (Cambridge, 1994), pp 118–36.

Porter, Eric, 'A cloak for knavery: kingship, the army, and the first protectorate parliament 1654–5' in *The Seventeenth Century*, xvii (2002), pp 187–205.

Ranger, T. O., 'Richard Boyle and the making of an Irish fortune, 1588–1614' in *I.H.S.*, x (1957), pp 257–97.

Roebuck, Peter, 'Landlord indebtedness in Ulster in the seventeenth and eighteenth centuries' in J. M. Goldstrom and L. A. Clarkson (eds), *Irish population, economy and society: essays in honour of the late K. H. Connell* (Oxford, 1981), pp 135–54.

Roots, Ivan, 'Lawmaking in the second protectorate parliament' in H. Hearder and H. R. Loyn (eds), *British government and administration* (Cardiff, 1974).

Scott, David, 'The "northern gentlemen", the parliamentary Independents, and Anglo-Scottish relations in the Long Parliament' in *H.J.*, xlii (1999), pp 347–75.

Shaw, F. J., 'Landownership in the Western Isles in the seventeenth century' in *S.H.R.*, lvi (1977), pp 34–45.

Simms, J. G. 'The restoration, 1660–85' in T. W. Moody, F. X. Martin and F. J. Byrne (eds) *A new history of Ireland, iii: Early modern Ireland, 1534–1691* (Oxford, 1976).

Smith, David, 'Oliver Cromwell, the first protectorate parliament and religious reform' in *Parliamentary History*, xix (2000), pp 38–48.

Sommerville, Johann, 'Oliver Cromwell and English political thought', in John Morrill (ed.), *Oliver Cromwell and the English revolution* (1990), pp 234–58.

Stevenson, David, 'Cromwell, Scotland and Ireland', in John Morrill (ed.), *Oliver Cromwell and the English revolution* (1990), pp 149–80.

Tait, Clodagh, 'Colonising memory: manipulations of death, burial and commemoration in the career of Richard Boyle, first earl of Cork (1566–1643)' in *Proceedings of the Royal Irish Academy*, ci (2001), sect. C, pp 107–34.

Trevor-Roper, Hugh, 'The Great Tew circle' in his *Catholics, Anglicans and puritans: seventeenth-century essays* (1987), pp 166–230.

Trevor-Roper, Hugh, 'James Ussher, archbishop of Armagh' in his *Catholics, Anglicans and puritans* (1987), pp 120–65.

Trevor-Roper, Hugh, 'Oliver Cromwell and his parliaments' in his *Religion, the reformation and social change* (3rd ed., 1984), pp 345–91.

Trevor-Roper, Hugh, 'The union of Britain in the seventeenth century' in his *Religion, the reformation and social change* (3rd ed., 1984), pp 445–67.

Trevor-Roper, Hugh, 'Scotland and the puritan revolution' in his *Religion, the reformation and social change* (3rd ed., 1984), pp 392–444.

Wilson, T. A., and Merli, F. J., 'Nayler's case and the dilemma of the protectorate' in *Univ. of Birmingham Hist. Jnl.*, x (1965), pp 44–59.

Worden, Blair, 'Oliver Cromwell and the sin of Achan' in Derek Beales and Geoffrey Best (eds), *History, society and the churches* (Cambridge, 1985), pp 125–45.

Theses and unpublished material

History of Parliament Trust, London, draft biographies, 1640–60 section.

Adams, S. L., 'The Protestant cause: religious alliance with the western European Calvinist communities as a political issue in England, 1585–1630' (D.Phil., Oxford University, 1973).

Adamson, John, 'The peerage in politics, 1645–49' (Ph.D., Cambridge University, 1986).

Armstrong, Robert, 'Protestant Ireland and the English parliament, 1641–1647' (Ph.D., Trinity College Dublin, 1995).

Egloff, Carol, 'Settlement and kingship: the army, the gentry and the offer of the crown to Oliver Cromwell' (Ph.D., Yale University, 1990).

Farr, David, 'The military and political career of John Lambert, 1619–57' (Ph.D., Cambridge University, 1996).

Jones, Sarah, 'The composition and activity of the protectorate parliaments' (Ph.D., Exeter University, 1988).

Kelly, William P., 'The early career of James Butler, twelfth earl and first duke of Ormonde (1610–43), 1610–88' (Ph.D., Cambridge University, 1995).

Little, Patrick, 'Family and faction: the Irish nobility and the English court, 1632–42' (M.Litt., Trinity College Dublin, 1992).

Little, Patrick, 'The political career of Roger Boyle, Lord Broghill, 1636–1660' (Ph.D., London University, 2000).

Pinckney, Paul J., 'A Cromwellian parliament: the elections and personnel of 1656' (Ph.D., Vanderbilt University, 1962).

Smith, L. M., 'Scotland and Cromwell. A study in early modern government' (D.Phil., Oxford University, 1979).

Note
The place of publication of all works cited is London, unless otherwise stated.

Index

Abbott, Daniel 129
Abbott, W. C. 2
Additional Petition and Advice (1657)
    132
Adventurers' acts (1642, 1653) 29, 33,
    71–2, 181, 215
Allen, William 77
Amyrault, Moise 223, 227
Annesley, Arthur, 1st earl of Anglesey 45,
    46n.75, 47n.80, 74, 75, 166, 185–6
Annesley, Sir Francis, 1st Lord
    Mountnorris and 2nd Viscount
    Valentia 15, 47n.80, 49, 185,
    195n.9
Appleby, Cumberland 29
Army 'interest' (1654–9) 78, 90, 121–3,
    126, 130, 133, 144, 153, 158,
    163–5, 165, 166, 168, 175
Art of War, Treatise on (1677) 180n.133,
    181
Ashe, John 147
Ashe, Simeon 133
Askeaton Castle, County Limerick 209
Aston, William 128, 132, 134, 135, 136,
    137, 139, 150, 151n.155,
    152n.164, 158
Audley End, Essex 24, 162, 206, 207
Axtell, Daniel 78, 78n.125

Bacon, Francis 127, 140, 151, 156, 232
Bacon, Nathaniel 127, 140, 151,
    152n.164, 156, 232
Baillie, Robert 86, 99, 100, 114, 225n.26
Ballymaloe House, County Cork 169, 199,
    217, 218
Bampfield, Thomas 143, 143n.109 and
    n.110, 144, 151, 156, 157, 158
Bandon, County Cork 25, 33, 61, 62, 67
Barnard, Toby 5, 6, 55, 89, 179, 181, 182,
    185, 237
Barnardiston, Sir Nathaniel 232
Barrington, Robert 158

Barrow, Robert 113
Barry, Alice, countess of Barrymore 13,
    196, 199, 208, 219
Barry, David, Viscount Buttevant and 1st
    earl of Barrymore 13, 15, 19, 21,
    27, 196, 197–8
Barry, John, colonel 50
Barry, Richard, 2nd earl of Barrymore
    166n.33
Barry family 14, 54, 194, 196
Battiere, James 19, 19n.45, 20
Baxter, Richard 80–1, 127, 146, 202, 206,
    226–7, 230–4
Baynes, Adam 126, 132, 141, 144, 148,
    158
Beake, Robert 127, 148, 151n.151
Bennett, Sir Henry, 1st Lord Arlington 2
Beresford, Tristram 128, 129n.28, 135n.58
Berkeley, George, 9th Lord Berkeley 183
Bernard, Nicholas 226, 233, 234, 234n.86
Berry, James 126, 147
Berwick, pacification of 21–2
Biddulph, Theophilus 213, 213n.37, 214
Bishop, George 65
Bisse, John 128, 129n.28, 135n.58, 140
Black Prince, The (c.1667) 181
Blackadder, Henry 170
Blair, Robert 97
Blake, Robert 60
Blarney Castle, County Cork 67, 162,
    214–15, 216, 217, 224
Blayney, Richard 128, 135n.58
Blount, Mountjoy, 1st earl of Newport
    177
Bodurda, Griffith 156, 158
Bond, Denis 137
Booth, Sir George 172, 173–4, 207
Bordeaux–Neufville, Antoine de 4, 232
Borlase, Sir John 26, 42, 44, 46
Borthwick, James 170
Bourke, Richard, 4th earl of Clanricarde
    195n.9

Bourke, Thomasina, baroness of
    Castleconnell 19
Bourke, Ulick, 5th earl and 1st marquess
    of Clanricarde 25, 40, 195n.9
Boyle, Alice *see* Barry, Alice
Boyle, Catherine, countess of Cork 196
Boyle, Dorothy *see* Loftus, Dorothy
Boyle, Elizabeth, Lady Dungarvan,
    countess of Cork and Burlington
    14, 62n.23, 66, 127, 194, 195, 198,
    201
Boyle, Elizabeth, Lady Kinalmeaky 22, 93,
    171, 195, 198
Boyle, Elizabeth, Lady Shannon 22, 172,
    172n.79, 195
Boyle, Francis, Viscount Shannon 11, 22,
    52, 172, 177, 179, 195, 197, 198,
    208, 240
Boyle, Joan *see* Fitzgerald, Joan
Boyle, Joshua 60
Boyle, Katherine *see* Digby, Katherine
Boyle, Lettice *see* Goring, Lettice
Boyle, Lewis, Viscount Kinalmeaky 18, 19,
    20, 21, 22, 24, 93, 195, 196, 197,
    198
Boyle, Margaret, Lady Broghill and
    countess of Orrery 22, 28, 62, 93,
    94, 162, 171, 188, 195, 201, 205,
    207, 209, 224
Boyle, Mary *see* Rich, Mary
Boyle, Michael, dean of Cloyne and
    archbishop of Dublin 37, 187
Boyle, Richard, 1st earl of Cork 1, 11–12,
    12–18, 60
  and 'Boyle group' 15–16, 41, 239
  and cessation of arms (1643) 30–1
  and English politics, 16, 54, 71–6
  family relationships 13, 14–15, 20–2,
    23–4, 193–200
  influence on Broghill 11, 13, 19–24,
    31–2, 43, 53–4, 70, 116, 182,
    186, 209–10, 221–2, 228, 235,
    240–1
  Irish, attitude to 14–18, 19
  and Irish rebellion (1641–3) 18, 24,
    25–7, 209–10
  loyalty to the crown 17–18, 235
  relations with the Butlers 16–17, 31–2
  relations with Inchiquin 26–9
  relations with Wentworth 12, 14, 17,
    21, 22–3, 228
  religious views of 12–13, 17, 18, 221–2,
    228
  wealth 12, 25

Boyle, Richard, Viscount Dungarvan, 2nd
    earl of Cork and 1st earl of
    Burlington 5, 11, 21, 29, 62n.23,
    172, 179, 184, 194, 195, 196n.15,
    197, 198, 199, 206, 240
  financial problems of 66–71, 211, 218,
    219
  influence over elections 77, 128, 201
  relations with Broghill 29–31, 33–4, 52,
    66–71, 77, 88, 123, 128, 135–6,
    139, 166n.32, 167, 174, 177–8,
    182, 198, 200–1, 204, 205, 207–8,
    213, 218, 224–5, 227
  relations with 1st earl of Cork 14, 17,
    18, 21, 24, 31–2, 194–5, 198–200,
    221–2
  religious views of 13, 222, 224–5,
    229–30
Boyle, Robert 11, 13, 59, 59n.3, 66, 97,
    177, 185, 195, 197, 198, 204,
    230
  religious views of 225, 225n.25, 228,
    229, 232
Boyle, Roger, Lord Broghill and 1st earl of
    Orrery
  and Bishops' Wars 21–2, 23
  Boyle family, relations with
    1st earl of Cork 11, 18, 19–24, 31–2,
      43, 53–4, 70, 116, 119, 185, 186,
      194, 195, 197, 200, 221–2, 225,
      228, 235, 240–1
    2nd earl of Cork 29–32, 66–71, 77,
      88, 89, 123, 128, 135–6, 142,
      166n.32, 167, 174, 177–8, 182,
      198, 200–1, 204, 205, 207–8, 211,
      213, 218–19, 224–5, 227, 229–30,
      240
    Francis Boyle 52, 172, 179, 198,
      240
    Katherine Jones 59, 167, 170, 177,
      198, 201–5, 213–14, 218
  and 'Boyle group' 31–2, 41, 43–4, 46–7,
    53–4, 87, 238–9
  and cessation of arms (1643) 30–1
  children of 28, 184–5, 196n.15, 223
  contemporary opinions of 1–2
  death and burial of 188
  defection to parliament (1644), 31–2,
    33–4
  duel fought by (1640), 22–3
  as earl of Orrery 179–89, 240
  early life 19
  and factions in Long Parliament 36,
    39–41, 42–50, 74

financial affairs 3, 59–60, 62, 63, 64, 70,
    73, 74, 146, 158–9, 162
  debts 210–11, 212–14
  income 211–12, 214–18
  inheritance 209–10
foreign connections of 20–1, 170–1,
    222–3
France, views on 180–2, 186–7
gout, attacks of 103, 125, 131, 132, 134,
    135, 136, 138, 140, 145, 162, 164,
    167, 179
historians' views of 4–7, 92–3, 96, 103,
    124–5, 180–1, 236–7
Howard family, relations with 93–4,
    205–8, 209, 240
Ireland
  and lieutenancy of 182
  as lord justice of 179, 182
  and parliamentary commissioners in
    64–72
  and presidency of Munster 1, 29, 43,
    63, 66, 178, 183, 185, 186
  and Protestant militia scheme in 5,
    15, 163, 165, 187
  service during rebellion and wars in
    24, 25, 27–8, 33–5, 64–5
  see also Ireland, Protestant interest in
and Irish 'Independents' (1640s) 41–55
literary works 180, 180n.133, 181,
    188–9
and lobbying in England (1654) 73–6
marriage of 23–4
and parliament
  first protectorate (1654–5) 79–89
  second protectorate (1656–8):
    allies and enemies in 125–30;
    disillusion with 153–5, 157–8,
    159–60, 161–3; Irish and Scottish
    affairs 130–9, 150; Kingship
    debates 3–4, 6, 132, 145–60;
    management of 130–2, 134, 135,
    137, 148, 150–2, 157, 237; Nayler
    case and militia bill 139–45
  third protectorate (1659): allies in
    165–6; failure to manage 167–8
and the protectorate, last days of
    (1657–9) 161–9
regiment of 62, 64–5, 128
relations with
  Annesley, Arthur 185–6
  Argyll, Marquess of 116–22, 237
  Baxter, Richard 80–1, 225–7, 230,
    234
  Charles II 51–3, 170, 170n.57, 174,

    176, 178, 179–82, 185–7, 188–9,
    201, 236, 240, 241
Cromwell, Henry 73, 75, 83, 113,
    121–3, 135–6, 139, 153–4, 155,
    163, 164, 165, 167, 169, 169n.52,
    218, 237
Cromwell, Oliver: 'defection' to
    (1649) 2–3, 11, 53, 59–60; alliance
    with (1649–54) 59–62, 63, 64, 65,
    66–7, 71, 88, 89, 210, 236; support
    for protectorate in parliament
    (1654–5) 81–3; offer of crown to
    (1657) 145–7, 153–8, 159–60, 161,
    235, 237, 239, 240–2;
    manipulation of 104, 143, 154–6;
    perceived providential role of
    155–6, 230–1, 235, 242
Cromwell, Richard 165, 167, 168n.50
Inchiquin, Lord 30–1, 33–55, 63,
    184–5, 200, 202–3, 223, 236, 238
Lambert, John 107, 119, 126, 130,
    132–4, 140, 141, 142, 144, 145,
    159, 162
Lisle, Viscount 20–1, 41–3, 46–7, 75
Monck, George 100–1, 103–4, 109,
    113–14, 114–16, 120–1, 166,
    166n.35, 237
Ormond, earl, marquess and duke of
    2, 31–2, 36–7, 40, 41–8, 51–3, 54,
    176, 182–4, 185, 186, 188, 236,
    238, 240
Ussher, James 80–1, 221, 225–6, 227,
    228, 229, 230
Whitelocke, Bulstrode 75, 127, 131,
    134, 138, 148 and see Whitelocke
religious views of 34, 38–9, 96, 99,
    221–35
  hatred of Catholicism 4, 54–5, 114,
    181–2, 184–5, 186–7, 223–4, 239
  and Huguenots 20, 222–3, 227
  influences on 13, 80–1, 203–4,
    221–5, 228, 235
  irenicism of 227–8, 231–5
  political dimension of 79–81, 96, 122,
    140, 143, 146, 150, 155–6, 160,
    165, 181–2, 186–7, 237–8
  providence and 228–31, 235
and the restoration 4, 161, 170–9
and the restored Rump 168–9,
    174–5
retirement (1648–9) 51–3, 59–60
retirement, threat of (1657–9) 162–3,
    164, 169
and Scotland

church policies in 96–109, 119–21,
176–7
presidency of 7, 89, 90–123, 131–2,
134, 155, 170, 182, 212, 216–18,
231, 237, 240
secular policies in 110–21
spy network of 170
unionist agenda of 7–8, 51, 79, 86–8,
89, 121–3, 130–1, 139, 139n.89,
145–6, 168, 169, 185, 205, 208,
219–20, 238–9, 242
Boyle, Sarah see Digby, Sarah
'Boyle group' 15–16, 31–2, 41, 43–4, 46–7,
53–4, 87, 238–9
Brandenburg, elector of 172
Brayne, William 117
Brett, John 129, 151n.155, 165
Bridges, John 127, 128, 147, 151, 153, 231
Broghill, Lord see Boyle, Roger
Broghill Castle, County Cork 209
Buckroyd, Julia 96, 103
Bulkeley, John 82
Burlamachi, Philip 19
Burnet, Gilbert 2
Burton, Thomas 124, 142, 148
Butler, Elizabeth, countess, marchioness
and duchess of Ormond 17
Butler, James, 12th earl, 1st marquess and
1st duke of Ormond
and English parliament (1645–8) 40,
44–5, 47–8, 50
and Irish wars 26, 27, 33, 36–7, 39, 59,
200, 202, 223
relations with Broghill 2, 31–2, 36–7,
41–8, 51–3, 54, 176, 182–4, 185,
186, 187, 188, 202, 238, 240
relations with 1st earl of Cork 17, 31, 41
and the restoration 171, 176, 177, 179,
202
Butler, Richard, Viscount Mountgarrett
27, 31
Butler, Thomas, Earl of Ossory 183
Butler, Walter, 11th earl of Ormond 16
Butler family 16, 54, 182, 183

Cadogan, William 78n.122
Calamy, Edmund 133, 232
Cambridge, Bene't College 11
Campbell, Archibald, 8th earl and 1st
marquess of Argyll 115–21, 122,
166, 237
Campbell, Archibald, Lord Lorne 115,
116, 117
Campbell, Sir Hew, of Cawdor 118

Campbell, John, of Glenorchy 120,
120n.191
Campbell, Sir Robert, of Glenorchy 117
Campbell clan 115, 116, 117, 118
Canny, Nicholas 12, 13, 193, 194
Capel, Arthur, 1st earl of Essex 179
Cappoquin, County Waterford, garrison of
28
Carew, Sir George 12
Carl X Gustav, king of Sweden 163, 230
Carleton, Dudley, Viscount Dorchester 15
Carrigadrohid Castle, County Cork 223
Cashel, County Tipperary 50
Castlelyons House, County Cork 13, 67,
199
Cavendish, Elizabeth, countess of
Devonshire 177
Cecil, William, 2nd earl of Salisbury 127,
195
Charles I, King 17, 21, 33, 149, 181, 188,
189, 205, 226, 238, 240
Charles II, King 3, 4, 6, 8, 52–3, 95, 99,
100, 108, 112, 117, 120, 132,
230–1
as king 179–89, 201, 240, 241
restoration of (1660) 161, 170, 172,
173, 174, 176–9, 207, 236, 240
Choudhury, Mita 180
Clanrannald, Captain of 118
Clarges, Thomas 138, 151n.155
Clarke, Aidan 4, 173, 175, 176, 178, 236,
237
Clarke, John 78n.125, 126
Cleypole, John 82, 83, 127, 142, 143
Clifford, Elizabeth see Boyle, Elizabeth,
countess of Cork and Burlington
Clifford, Henry, Lord 14
Clifford family 206
Clotworthy, Sir John 40, 49, 74, 74n.98,
89, 98, 99, 100, 108n.103, 202,
205, 232
Clotworthy, Mary, Lady 98, 98n.34, 99,
100, 202
Cochrane, William, 1st Lord Cochrane
127, 131, 140, 144, 151n.155
Cole, John 78n.122
'Commonwealthsmen' (1654–9) 81,
125–6, 163, 165, 167, 168
Constitutions, protectoral see Additional
Petition and Advice; Humble
Petition and Advice; Instrument of
Government; Remonstrance
Conway, Edward, 1st viscount 15
Conway, Edward, 2nd viscount 69, 89

Conway, Edward, 3rd viscount 142, 186
Cook, John 67
Cooper, Anthony Ashley, 1st earl of
    Shaftesbury 2
Cooper, Thomas 91, 101, 103, 113, 129,
    138, 151, 151n.155 and n.156, 170
Coote, Sir Charles senior 44
Coote, Sir Charles junior, 1st earl of
    Mountrath
  financial concerns of 219–20
  and protectorate 65, 71, 78, 78n.122,
    128, 129, 136, 165
  and restoration 175–6, 179, 182
Corbett, Miles 64
Cork, garrison of 25, 33, 38, 48, 60, 61, 62,
    63
Cork House, Dublin 198
Cotterell, Lieutenant-colonel 117
'Court party' or 'courtiers' (1654–9) 75–6,
    79, 82–3, 127, 129, 130, 139, 143,
    148, 151, 168
Courtenay, Francis 61
Courthope, Peter 128
Covenant, Solemn League and (1643) 36,
    38–9, 42, 96, 105
Cranston, William, 3rd Lord Cranston
    131
Cromwell, Henry, 100, 234
  as governor of Ireland (1655–7) 89–90,
    110, 113, 121, 134, 142, 231
  and Irish affairs (1654–5) 72, 78, 83, 87,
    211
  as lord deputy and lord lieutenant of
    Ireland (1657–9) 89, 162–3, 165,
    167, 173–4
  and parliament (1656–8) 126, 128, 129,
    132, 135, 137, 144, 147, 148, 150,
    151, 153, 156, 158
  relations with Broghill 73, 75, 83, 88,
    113, 121–3, 128–9, 135–6, 139,
    145, 153–4, 155, 163, 164, 165,
    167, 169, 169n.52, 189, 237, 241
Cromwell, Oliver
  decline and death (1658) 164, 165
  and 'defection' of Broghill in 1649 2–3,
    5, 6, 11, 53, 59–60
  as lord lieutenant of Ireland 1, 3, 53,
    59–62, 64, 65, 66, 138, 211,
    211n.16
  as lord protector (1653–8) 72, 78, 83,
    85, 86, 171, 226
    government of Scotland 91, 95, 97,
      99, 102n.64, 104, 105, 106, 109,
      110, 115, 116, 119, 120

offer of the crown to 3–4, 7, 8,
    81n.146, 109, 132, 145–60, 161,
    169, 235, 237, 239, 241–2
  succession question 144, 145
  relations with Broghill 62, 65, 71, 81,
    88, 104, 109, 145–6, 154, 204, 210,
    214, 230–1, 235, 237, 240–2
  religious views 79–81, 143, 155–6, 157,
    221, 238
Cromwell, Richard 165, 166, 166n.35,
    167–8, 168n.48 and n.50, 241
Croone, Henry 30
Cuffe, Joseph 65
Cunningham, William, 9th earl of
    Glencairn 94–5, 123
  rebellion of (1653–5) 91, 99, 112, 113,
    115, 132

Davies, John 47, 128, 129
Davies, Sir Paul 74, 75, 83, 85, 128, 129
Davis, Colin 6
Deane, Richard 119
Declaration of Indulgence (1672) 186
Devereux, Robert, 3rd earl of Essex 22, 39,
    40
Dickson, David 98, 100, 105, 106, 108
Dictionary of National Biography 4, 11, 92
Digby, George, Lord 37, 39
Digby, John, 1st earl of Bristol 22, 23, 196
Digby, John 197
Digby, Kildare, Lord Digby of Geashill
    198
Digby, Robert, Lord Digby of Geashill 15,
    196, 197
Digby, Sarah, Lady 66, 197
Digby family 14, 194, 198
Diodati, John 20, 222, 227
Disbrowe, John 79, 83, 126, 137, 141, 147,
    152, 159, 162, 163, 164, 164n.16,
    165n.29, 168
Disbrowe, Samuel 91, 101, 127, 130, 131,
    133, 136, 139, 141, 144, 151n.155,
    159
Dobbins, William 71, 72, 74
Domville, William 213–14, 216, 218
Doneraile House, County Cork 37
Douglas, Robert 97, 97n.29, 99, 100, 105,
    106, 108
Dover, secret treaty of (1670) 186
Dow, Frances 92, 96, 103, 112–13, 236
Downham, George 12
Downing, George 127, 130, 131, 135, 139,
    140, 141, 147, 158, 159, 170, 171,
    172

Drake, Francis 144
Drogheda, County Louth, sieges of (1642, 1649) 25, 60
Drummond, David 106
Duart Castle, Isle of Mull 117
Dublin, articles of (1647) 68, 70
Dublin, St Patrick's Cathedral in 196, 225
Dublin, Trinity College 19, 175
Duckenfield, John 165
du Moulin, Peter junior 222, 224, 227
du Moulin, Peter senior 227, 227n.46
Dunbar, battle of (1650) 95
Duncan, Mark 20, 222
Duncannon fort, County Wexford, siege of (1645) 34–5
Dungarvan, County Waterford, garrison of 16–17, 61
Dunstaffnage Castle, Argyllshire 115, 117
du Plessis Mornay, Philippe 20, 222, 227
Durston, Christopher 122
Dury, John 97, 98, 99, 105, 201, 205, 225n.25, 226, 227–8, 230, 234

Edinburgh, university of 229
Egan, Boethius, Catholic bishop of Rosse 223
Egloff, Carol 124–5, 233
Ellys, William, solicitor-general 216
English council (1650s)
  Irish committee of 68, 90, 107, 134, 137, 139, 162, 162n.3
  Scottish committee of 92, 106–9, 119, 130, 133, 162
Eyres, Joseph 224

Falkland, Henry Carey, Viscount 15, 19
Feilding, Elizabeth see Boyle, Elizabeth, Lady Kinalmeaky
Feilding, Mary, marchioness of Hamilton 93
Feilding, William, 1st earl of Denbigh 195
Feilding family 196
Fenton, Maurice 166
Fenton, Sir William 34, 61, 62, 69n.59, 73
Fiennes, Nathaniel 130, 133, 148, 151, 154, 168
Fiennes, William, 1st Viscount Saye and Sele 40
Firth, Sir Charles 5, 6
Fitzgerald, George, 16th earl of Kildare
  relations with the Boyles 14, 15, 17, 24, 66, 194, 196, 197–8, 199, 219
Fitzgerald, Joan, countess of Kildare 198, 199n.37

Fitzgerald, Wentworth, 17th earl of Kildare 185, 196, 199
Fitzgerald family 14, 17, 19, 54, 196
  of the Decies, County Waterford 16
  earls of Desmond 16
Fitzjames, Sir John 127, 150n.150, 152
Fitzwilliams, Oliver 40
Fleetwood, Charles
  as English councillor 107, 119, 120, 134, 139, 162, 162n.3
  as lord deputy of Ireland 69, 70, 76, 78, 83, 85, 86–7, 88, 89, 90, 113, 123, 225
  and parliament (1656–8) 126, 130, 133, 139, 158, 159
  and protectorate, last days of (1658–9) 163, 164, 164n.16, 165n.29, 168, 174
Foulke, Francis 60, 73, 166
Fowke, John 78n.122, 128, 151n.155

Galway city 65
Gardiner, S. R. 77, 78
Gauden, Dr John 233–4
Gaunt, Peter 6, 124–5
Geashill Castle, King's County 198
General, The (c.1664) 181
General Convention (at Dublin, 1660) 175–6, 178
Geneva, Switzerland 13, 20, 222, 227
Gethings, Richard 50
Gilbert, Claudius 224
Gillespie, Patrick 95, 97, 102, 103, 105, 119
'Gillespie's charter' 95, 97, 102, 102n.64, 104, 107, 108, 109
Glasgow, synod of 119
Gloucester, Irish 'donative' of 136–7
Glynn, John, lord chief justice 130, 141, 148, 152n.164, 153, 154, 217
Goddard, Guibon 79, 81
Godfrey, Lambert 156, 158
Goffe, William 164
Goodwin, John 158
Gookin, Vincent 72, 74, 75, 77, 78n.122, 83, 84, 88, 128, 135, 142, 144, 151, 166, 166n.33, 224, 232
Gordon, Sir Alexander of Gight 93
Gordon, Elizabeth see Home, Elizabeth
Goring, George Lord (senior) 195, 197
Goring, George Lord (junior) 174, 195, 197
Goring, Lettice, Lady Goring 195, 197
Goring family 196

Gostelow, Walter 201, 229–30
Graham, James, 1st marquess of Montrose 118n.178
Grenville, Sir Richard 63
Greven, Philip 193
Grotius, Hugo 223
Grove, Thomas 127, 151, 152, 158, 233
Gustavus Adolphus (King Gustav II Adolf of Sweden) 146, 230
Guthrie, James 95, 101, 102, 103, 104, 105, 107, 119, 133, 139

Hackett, Thomas 224
Halkett, Anne, Lady Halkett 94
Halkett, Sir James 94
Halsey, William 78, 128, 166
Hamilton, James, 1st Viscount Clandeboye 69
Hamilton, James, son of Viscount Clandeboye 196
Hampden, Richard 158
Harley, Edward 127, 234
Harrison, Frances 22–3, 171
Harrison, Sir Richard 22
Hartlib, Samuel 97, 201, 202, 225, 225n.26
Harvey, Francis 158
Hawkins, William 216, 217
Hay, John, 2nd earl of Tweeddale 130
Henrietta Maria, Queen 17–18, 21, 22, 171, 195
Henry V (c.1662) 181
Herbert, Philip, 4th earl of Pembroke 195
Hesilrige, Sir Arthur 125, 126, 163
Hewson, John 78n.125, 126, 128, 151, 151n.156
Highland, Samuel 138
Hill, Arthur 30, 78, 78n.122, 83, 84, 85
Hobart, Sir John 157, 158
Hodder, John 48, 210
Holles, Denzell 40, 49
Home, Elizabeth, countess of Dunbar 93
Home, George, 1st earl of Dunbar 93
Home family 94, 207
Howard, Anne 195n.14
Howard, Barbara, countess of Suffolk 207
Howard, Edward, Lord Howard of Escrick 24, 195, 195n.14, 205
Howard, Elizabeth, countess of Suffolk 93
Howard, Catherine see Stuart, Catherine
Howard, Charles 91, 95, 101, 127, 130, 131, 151, 151n.155, 152, 153n.171, 195n.14

Howard, Henry, son of 1st earl of Berkshire 171, 172
Howard, James, 3rd earl of Suffolk 24, 123, 162, 174, 195, 205, 206, 207, 208, 232–3
Howard, Margaret, see Boyle, Margaret
Howard, Sir Robert 209
Howard, Susanna, countess of Suffolk 206
Howard, Theophilus, 2nd earl of Suffolk 23
Howard, Thomas, 1st earl of Berkshire 22, 206, 207
Howard, Thomas, son of 1st earl of Berkshire 22, 171, 172, 207, 208
Howard, Thomas, brother of 3rd earl of Suffolk 171–2, 207
Howard, Sir William 209
Howard family 23–4, 93, 196, 205–8
Huguenot Church 234 see also Saumur
Humble Petition and Advice, The (1657) 1, 6, 123, 124, 130, 135, 139n.89, 148–53, 154, 156, 157, 158, 159, 160, 161, 163, 237, 241
Hutcheson, George 104n.77, 105
Hutchinson, Daniel 71, 74, 78n.122, 83, 84, 87n.189
Hyde, Sir Edward, 1st earl of Clarendon 4, 172, 173, 174, 176, 179, 183, 202, 204

Ingoldsby, (Sir) Henry 78n.123, 128, 129, 129n.28, 151n.155
Instrument of Government, The (1653) 76, 81–2, 123, 126, 129, 141, 153, 156, 241
Inveraray Castle, Argyllshire 115
Inverlochy, garrison of 117
Ireland
cessation of arms in (1643) 30–1, 33, 36, 38, 44, 54, 188
Confederate Catholics of 3, 27, 30, 33, 34, 36, 37, 39, 42, 44, 50–5, 113, 180, 182, 237
parliamentary commissioners in (1650–4 and 1659) 64, 68, 68n.55, 69, 70, 71, 72, 76, 78, 169, 214–15, 218
Protestant 'interest' in 5, 7, 12, 32, 54–5, 63, 65, 66, 71–2, 73–6, 77–8, 83–8, 88–90, 128–9, 137, 138, 142, 162, 164–5, 166, 169, 175–6, 178–9, 180, 181, 182–4, 186–8, 219–20, 223, 238, 241

Ireton, Henry 63, 64, 65, 66, 67, 68, 69, 228, 237
Irish colours displayed, The (1662) 186
Irish 'Independents' 41–50, 53–4, 184, 202, 238, 239, 241
Irish rebellion, The (1646) 43–4

Jacobs, J. R. 228
Jephson, William
  and Irish wars 26, 30, 30n.115, 40, 48, 49, 50, 206
  and parliament (1656–7) 128, 135, 136, 140, 144, 147, 153n.171, 157, 159
  and protectorate (1654–5) 77, 78n.122, 83, 84, 85, 89
  and Sweden, embassy to (1657–8) 163, 230
Jermyn, Henry, 1st Lord Jermyn 171
Jermyn, Richard 19
Jerome, Stephen 12, 221
Johnston, Archibald, of Wariston 101, 102, 104, 105, 119, 120, 132
Johnstone, James, 2nd earl of Hartfell 93, 94
Jones, Arthur, 2nd Viscount Ranelagh 98, 98n.34, 194, 196, 202
  financial affairs of 209, 213, 214, 215, 218
Jones, John 64, 72, 128
Jones, Katherine, Lady Ranelagh 13, 24, 66, 97, 165, 197, 198, 199
  relations with Broghill 59, 167, 169, 170, 177, 198, 201–5, 206, 207, 208, 212, 213–14, 217, 218, 232
  religious views of 222–3, 225, 228, 229, 232
Jones, Michael 3, 6, 52, 63, 83, 136, 211n.16
Jones, Philip 127, 129, 130, 133, 134, 147n.135, 148, 151, 152n.164, 154, 155, 159, 163, 164, 167n.41, 216
Jones, Richard, 3rd Viscount and 1st earl of Ranelagh 202, 223
Jones, Roger, 1st Viscount Ranelagh 15, 25, 29, 194
Jones, Theophilus 78n.122, 83, 84, 85, 128, 135n.58, 151n.155, 175
Jones family (Ranelagh) 14, 196, 198

Kelsey, Thomas 126, 130, 159
Kerr, William, 3rd earl of Lothian 94
Kerrigan, John 180, 181, 240

Killigrew, Elizabeth *see* Boyle, Elizabeth, Lady Shannon
Killigrew family 196
King, (Sir) John 128, 166
King, Ralph 78n.122, 128, 135n.58
King, Sir Robert 30, 30n.115, 71, 74, 78n.122, 83, 84, 85, 97, 128, 129, 163, 202
Kinsale, County Cork, garrison of 25, 33, 61, 62
Knocknaclashy, battle of (1651) 64, 223, 228
Knocknanuss, battle of (1647) 50

Lambert, John 69, 90, 232
  activity in Irish and Scottish committees 90n.198, 92, 107n.93, 109, 119, 130, 134, 139, 162n.3
  activity during parliament (1656–8) 126, 132–4, 136, 137, 139, 141, 142, 144, 152, 158, 159
  dismissal of (1657) 162
  later career 163, 168, 174, 175
  relations with Broghill 107, 119, 126, 130, 132–4, 140, 141, 142, 144, 145, 159, 162, 174, 217
Langton, John 33
Lawrence, Henry, President 107, 119, 126, 151
Leighs Priory, Essex 198
Lenthall, William, Speaker 49, 50, 60, 64, 137–8, 143, 154, 159, 210
Leslie, Alexander, Lord Balgonie 95n.21
Leslie, Alexander, 1st earl of Leven 95n.21
Levingston, Sir James, 1st earl of Newburgh 93, 94
Lilburne, Robert 91, 110, 115, 116
Limerick city, siege of (1650–1) 68
Lindsay, John, 17th earl of Crawford 98
Liscarroll, battle of (1642) 27, 198
Lisle, John 154, 156n.183
Lismore Castle, County Waterford 17, 19, 27, 28, 33–4, 35, 224
Livingstone, James, 1st earl of Callander 131
Lockhart, George 127, 130–1
Lockhart, John 118, 127, 130–1
Lockhart, (Sir) William 91, 101, 103, 118, 127, 127n.18, 133, 171, 173
Loftus, Sir Adam 15, 31, 41, 42, 44, 45, 46, 47, 48, 54, 239

Loftus, Sir Arthur 31, 32n.122, 39, 43, 44, 45, 47, 48, 49, 54, 194, 199
    finances of 66, 209, 218–19, 219n.63
Loftus, Dorothy, Lady 198, 199
Loftus, Dudley 168
Loftus, Edward, 1st Viscount Loftus of Ely 195n.9
Loftus family 14, 196, 198, 199
Lowther, Sir Gerard 75
Lucy, Sir Richard 127, 157, 158
Ludlow, Edmund 77, 81, 125
    comments on Broghill 1, 148, 167
    as general in Ireland (1659) 169, 174–5
    as parliamentary commissioner (1650–4) 63–4, 65, 66, 68, 72, 76, 77, 211
Lynch, Kathleen 2, 5, 92, 180

MacCarthy, Donough, 2nd Viscount Muskerry
    estates of 214, 215, 217 and see Blarney Castle
    and Irish wars 27, 29, 30, 31, 36, 54, 64, 65
MacCarthy, Eleanor, Lady Muskerry 215
MacColla, Alasdair 118n.178
MacDonald, Sir James of Sleat 118
MacDonald, Ronald of Tarsett 118
MacDonald clan 115
MacDowell, Sir James 158
MacLean, Daniel, tutor of Duart 117–18
MacLean clan 115
Maguire, Nancy Klein 180
Maitland, John, 2nd earl of Lauderdale 93
Major-generals, government of (1655–6) 122–3, 126, 139, 141–5, 217, 232
Mallow Castle, County Cork 61
Manton, Thomas 133
Marcombes, Isaac 19, 20, 222
Markham, Henry 127, 131, 135, 137, 140, 150n.150, 151, 166, 212
Marshall, Stephen 232
Marston Bigot House, Somerset 3, 51, 198, 209–10, 212
Mary, princess royal 171
Matthews, Joachim 152
Maynooth Castle, County Kildare 15, 198
Memoirs of . . . Roger, earl of Orrery (1742) 2, 4
Meredith, Adam 44
Meredith, Sir Robert 44, 46, 54, 78, 84
Meredith, William 77, 78, 78n.122, 83, 85, 151n.155
Middleton, John 91, 115

Monck, George
    in Ireland (1648–9) 52
    relations with Broghill 100–1, 103–4, 109, 113–14, 114–16, 120–1, 131, 166, 237
    religious beliefs 95, 101, 109, 114
    and the restoration 4, 173, 175, 177, 178
    in Scotland (1654–60) 91, 92, 95, 99, 100–4, 107, 109, 110–17, 120–3, 166, 240
Montagu, Edward, 2nd earl of Manchester 177, 178
Montgomery, Hugh, 3rd Viscount Montgomery of the Ards 69, 84n.165
Moore, Henry, 3rd Viscount Drogheda 66
Moore family 14, 194
Morgan, Anthony 77, 78n.124, 128, 134, 135, 136, 137, 148, 151, 151n.155, 158, 159
Morley, Herbert 82
Morrice, Thomas 2–6, 11, 23n.78, 53, 59, 168n.48 and n.49, 180, 188, 222, 224n.18
Mountagu, Edward 144, 151, 158, 172, 173
    relations with Broghill 75, 76n.107, 127, 147n.135, 148, 152n.164, 162, 163
Murray, Thomas 94

Nayler, James 131, 139–41, 142, 145, 150, 159
Neville, Mr 22
New Model Army 50
Newburgh, Thomas 78n.122, 128, 129
Nicholas, Sir Edward 52
Nicholson, Christopher 212

O'Brien, Murrough, 6th baron and 1st earl of Inchiquin 72n.82, 77, 203
    attacked as an 'Irishman' 49, 54
    and English factions 39–41, 42–50, 206
    relations with Broghill 30–1, 33–55, 63, 184–5, 200, 202–3, 223, 236, 238
    relations with Ormond 36–7
    service in Irish wars 26–8, 29, 30–1, 33–4, 36–7, 50, 59
O'Brien family 175, 184
Oldenburgh, Henry 230
O'Neill, Sir Daniel 172
O'Neill, Hugh, 3rd earl of Tyrone 11
Onslow, Sir Richard 154, 155, 158

Ormond's curtain drawn (1646) 44
Orrery, earl of *see* Boyle, Roger
Oster, Malcolm 228
O'Sullivan, Donnell, of Berehaven 19
Owen, Henry 128
Owen, Mr (spy) 170
Oxford, peace negotiations at (1643) 29

Packe, Sir Christopher 148, 152
Paget, William, 6th Lord Paget 98
Parliamentary factions (1654–9) *see* Army
  'interest'; 'Commonwealthsmen';
  'Court party'; Presbyterian
  'interest'
Parliaments
  Long Parliament (1640–53) 29, 34, 36,
    39, 45, 48, 71, 119, 136–7, 214,
    241
    committees of 34, 39, 40–1, 42–3, 45,
      46, 49, 50
    factional divisions in 36, 39–41,
      41–5, 47, 48–50, 202, 206
    see also Adventurers' acts; Irish
      'Independents'
  Nominated Assembly (Barebone's)
    (1653) 71, 215, 226, 232
  first protectorate (1654–5) 237
    constitutional debates 81–3
    elections to 77–8
    Irish affairs in 83–8
    religious debates 79–80, 226, 232
    Scottish affairs in 84–5, 86–7, 91,
      99
    union bills in 86–7, 136, 219, 238
  second protectorate (1656–8) 1, 7, 77,
    81, 95n.21, 109, 123, 161–2, 217,
    218, 237
    elections to 125–30, 233
    Irish and Scottish affairs in 124,
      130–9, 150, 158–9, 163
    kingship debates in 129, 132, 139,
      148–58, 217
    militia bill 7, 124, 130, 131, 139–40,
      141–5, 147, 155–6, 205
    Nayler's case 131, 139–41, 142, 145,
      150, 159
    Other House of 149–50, 162, 163
    second sitting of (1658) 163
    union bills in 87, 131, 134, 135–6,
      139, 145, 238, 239
  third protectorate (1659) 87
    elections to 165–7
    Irish and Scottish affairs in 166–7,
      168

  Irish union bill in 87, 168, 238
  Other House of 167–8
  restored Rump (1659–60) 168–9, 174
  Convention (1660) 177n.122, 178
  Cavalier (1661–79) 179, 183
  Irish (1661–6) 179, 181, 182, 183
  Scottish (various) 112, 119
Parsons, Fenton 229n.59
Parsons, Sir William 15, 26, 31, 41, 42, 44,
  45, 46, 47, 54, 239
Parsons, William 220
Parthenissa (1655–6) 180n.133
Peirce, Sir Henry 78n.123
Penn, William 217
Penruddock, John 122
Perceval-Maxwell, Michael 38
Percivalle, John 71, 74, 75
Percivalle, Sir Philip 26, 35, 39, 40, 43,
  45, 48, 49, 50, 201, 202, 206, 210
Percy, Algernon, 10th earl of
  Northumberland 23, 24, 35,
  35n.17, 40, 41–2, 43, 177n.122,
  195, 206
Perkins, William (financier) 19
Perkins, William (minister) 12
Perraud, Francis 222
Phaier, Robert 60, 61, 67, 77
Pickering, Sir Gilbert 126, 133, 164
Pierrepont, Henry, 1st marquess of
  Dorchester 177
Pierrepont, William 156, 158, 164
Pinckney, Paul 77, 78
Pinkie House, Musselburgh 107n.99
Popish Plot (1678) 181
Power, Richard 197
Presbyterian 'interest' (1654–9) 79–81,
  124, 127, 129–30, 139, 140, 142,
  144, 147–51, 156, 157, 158, 160,
  166n.36, 226, 231–2, 233–4
Presbyterian Knot (1660) 176
Preston, Richard, earl of Desmond 16,
  17
Puller, Isaac 158
Purefoy, William 78n.123
Pym, John 39

Ramsay, Andrew 127, 130, 151n.155
Rathfarnham Castle, County Dublin
  199
Rathmines, battle of (1649) 59, 60
Rawdon, George 220
Redman, Daniel 78n.124, 128
Remonstrance (1657) 132, 148–53, 160,
  241

Reynolds, Sir John 78n.124, 128, 134, 135, 136, 151n.155, 152, 152n.164, 156, 163
Rhodes, Sir Edward 91, 101, 127, 130, 131, 140
Rhodes, Godfrey 127, 130
Rich, Charles, 4th earl of Warwick 22, 174, 177, 194, 195, 197
Rich, Henry, 1st earl of Holland 24, 40, 120n.191, 195, 206
Rich, Mary, countess of Warwick 13, 22, 24, 194, 195, 195n.13, 197, 198, 225, 232
Rich, Robert, 2nd earl of Warwick 3, 6, 22, 40, 120n.191, 123, 127, 195, 206, 207, 209, 232–3, 234
Rich family 196
Robartes, John, 2nd Lord Robartes 183
Roberts, Sir William 157
Robinson, Luke 126, 136, 137, 144, 152
Rosamunde, Monsieur 19
Ross Castle, County Kerry 215
Rule, Robert 101, 133
Russell, Francis, 4th earl of Bedford 6, 19, 23
Russell, Sir Francis 158, 234

Sadleir, Thomas 78, 78n.125, 129, 165
St John, Oliver 40, 147n.135, 154, 164
St Leger, Sir William 26, 28, 54
St Leger family, 37, 184
St Patrick's Purgatory, County Donegal 16
Salmon, Edward 127
Salwey, Richard 77
Sankey, Jerome 78n.125, 126, 138, 139, 151n.156
Santa Cruz, battle of (1657) 230
Saumur, France, Huguenot academy of 13, 20, 202, 222, 223, 227
Savile, Anne, countess of Sussex 177
Savoy, Italy, Protestants of 225
Scot, Thomas senior 126
Scot, Thomas junior 78n.123
Scotland
    and Bishops' Wars (1639–40) 18, 21–2, 23, 197
    and Engagement (1647–8) 51
    and English parliament (1640s) 38, 40, 42, 46
    Kirk factions in 91, 95–109, 119–20, 121, 133–4, 166, 176–7, 205, 231
    protectoral council of 91–2, 94, 99, 100–3, 107–8, 110, 113, 117, 119, 127, 130, 134, 139, 175

Scrope, Adrian 91, 101
Sealed Knot, The 173
Seymour, William, 2nd earl and 1st marquess of Hertford 22
Shaen, Lady 199
Shapcott, Robert 158
Sharp, James 106, 109, 133, 134
Sherborne Castle, Dorset 22
Sidney, Algernon 20, 49
Sidney, Philip, Viscount Lisle 20–1, 41–3, 44, 46, 47, 48, 49, 74, 75
Sidney, Robert, 2nd earl of Leicester 21, 26, 29, 42, 44
Simpson, Matthias 133, 133n.52
Simpson, Sidrach 38–9
Skippon, Philip 141, 151
Smith, George (judge) 127, 130, 131, 140
Smith, George (theologian) 143n.109, 146n.127, 156n.183
Smithwick, Henry 60
Smyth, Sir Percy 35, 39, 60, 202–3
Somerset, Edward, earl of Glamorgan 37
Southwell, Thomas 65
Spenser, Edmund 239
Stafford, Sir Thomas 19
Stalbridge, Dorset 21, 22, 23, 196, 197
Standish, James 211
Stane, Dr William 144
Stanley, Thomas 166, 168n.50
Stapilton, Sir Philip 40, 49
Stone, Lawrence 193
Strafford, earl of see Wentworth
Strickland, Walter 126, 132, 133
Stuart, Catherine, Lady d'Aubigny 52, 93, 94, 198, 206, 207, 208
Stuart, Charles see Charles II
Stuart, Charles, 1st earl of Lichfield 94, 207
Stuart, George, Lord d'Aubigny 93, 206
Stuart, James, 4th duke of Lennox 93, 206
Stuart, James, duke of York 4
Stuart, Mary, duchess of Lennox 93
Stuarts of Lennox, family of 207
Swinton, John 91, 101, 102n.60, 130
Sydenham, William 126, 144, 148, 152, 153, 158, 159, 162, 165n.29
Synge, George, bishop of Cloyne 37

Talbot, Richard, 1st earl of Tyrconnell 184
Temple, Sir John 41, 43–4, 45, 46, 47, 48, 49, 50, 54, 78n.122, 83, 85
Thurloe, John

and Broghill's financial obligations 207, 216

and last years of protectorate (1657–9) 162, 163, 165, 166, 168

and parliament (1656–7) 127, 128, 130, 133, 134, 143, 148, 150n.150, 151, 152, 152n.164, 156, 158, 159, 233

and restoration 176, 177

and Scotland (1655–6) 100, 103, 104, 106, 109, 111, 113, 116, 116n.165, 118

Tighe, Richard 128, 129n.28, 135n.58, 140, 151n.155

Touchet, James, 3rd earl of Castlehaven 35, 36–7

Traill, James 128

Trevor, John 142, 142n.108, 144, 151, 156, 158

Trevor, Marcus 176

Trevor-Roper, Hugh 6, 7, 124–5

Tryphon (1668) 189

Tully, Isaac 213, 214, 216

Tynt, William 212, 217

Underdown, David 173

Ussher, James, archbishop of Armagh 12, 80, 81, 221, 224, 225–6, 227, 228, 229, 230, 232, 233

Vane, Sir Henry junior 40, 41, 125, 163

Venables, Robert 78n.124

Vernon, John 78

Vigors, Urban 13n.9, 223

Villiers, Sir Edward 172, 174, 176, 177, 207, 208

Villiers, George, 1st duke of Buckingham 17n.30

Villiers, George, 2nd duke of Buckingham 171, 183, 240

Villiers, John, 3rd Viscount Grandison 207, 208

Villiers, Mary *see* Stuart, Mary

Waller, Sir Hardress
  financial problems of 219
  and Irish wars (1640s) 26, 30, 45, 46n.75, 47, 50, 59
  and Protestant 'interest' (1650s) 78, 78n.122, 128, 129, 136, 165, 175

Waller, Thomas 166

Waller, Walter 128, 135n.58, 151n.155

Walley, John 33–4

Walsh, Sir Robert 170

Warden, William 65

Ware, Sir James 15

Wariston *see* Johnston, Archibald

Weaver, John 64, 126

Wemyss, Sir John 127

Wentworth, Sir Thomas, Viscount Wentworth and 1st earl of Strafford 12, 14, 17, 21, 22–3, 24, 194, 195n.9, 225, 228

West, Robert 158

Whalley, Edward 130, 137, 164

Wheeler, James Scott 5

Whetham, Nathaniel 91, 101, 133

White, Francis 141

Whitelocke, Bulstrode
  ambassador to Sweden 75, 75n.106
  collaboration with Broghill 68, 127, 129, 130, 131, 134, 137, 138, 139, 142, 142n.108, 143, 215
  comments on Broghill 1, 148, 150, 156
  and kingship debates 148, 150, 152, 152n.164, 154, 156
  and last days of protectorate (1657–9) 162, 168, 169, 204

Whitelocke, James 127

Wilkins, Dr John 167n.41

Willoughby, Francis, 1st Lord Willoughby of Parham 206

Windebanke, Thomas 20n.56

Winter, Samuel 224

Winthrop, Stephen 132

Wolseley, Sir Charles 164, 164n.16, 168, 216
  and first protectorate parliament (1654–5) 82, 83
  and second protectorate parliament (1656–8) 127, 129, 132, 133, 134, 147n.135, 148, 151, 152, 152n.164, 153, 156, 159, 163

Wolseley, Robert 127

Wood, James (Irish minister) 224

Wood, James (Scottish minister) 105, 106, 108

Wood, Robert 202

Worth, Edward 224

Wotton, Sir Henry 19

Youghal, County Cork
  college of 21, 62, 62n.23, 67, 69, 172
  garrison of 13, 25, 28, 33–4, 35, 38, 60–1, 62, 63, 223
  St Mary's church in 188